BASIC LEGAL
WRITING FOR
PARALEGALS

ASPEN COLLEGE SERIES

FOURTH EDITION

BASIC LEGAL WRITING FOR PARALEGALS

HOPE VINER SAMBORN

ANDREA B. YELIN

Wolters Kluwer
Law & Business

Published by Wolters Kluwer Law & Business in New York.

Wolters Kluwer Law & Business serves customers worldwide with CCH, Aspen Publishers, and Kluwer Law International products. (www.wolterskluwerlb.com)

To contact Customer Service, e-mail customer.service@wolterskluwer.com, call 1-800-234-1660, fax 1-800-901-9075, or mail correspondence to:

Wolters Kluwer Law & Business
Attn: Order Department
PO Box 990
Frederick, MD 21705

Printed in the United States of America.

1 2 3 4 5 6 7 8 9 0

ISBN 978-1-4548-0890-9

Library of Congress Cataloging-in-Publication Data

Samborn, Hope Viner.
  Basic legal writing for paralegals / Hope Viner Samborn, Andrea B. Yelin.— Fourth edition.
      pages cm.—(Aspen college series)
  Includes index.
  ISBN-13: 978-1-4548-0890-9
  ISBN-10: 1-4548-0890-X
  1. Legal composition. 2. Legal assistants—United States. I. Yelin, Andrea B. II. Title.

KF250.S236 2013
808.06′634—dc23

                                                                    2012039836

About Wolters Kluwer Law & Business

Wolters Kluwer Law & Business is a leading global provider of intelligent information and digital solutions for legal and business professionals in key specialty areas, and respected educational resources for professors and law students. Wolters Kluwer Law & Business connects legal and business professionals as well as those in the education market with timely, specialized authoritative content and information-enabled solutions to support success through productivity, accuracy and mobility.

Serving customers worldwide, Wolters Kluwer Law & Business products include those under the Aspen Publishers, CCH, Kluwer Law International, Loislaw, Best Case, ftwilliam.com and MediRegs family of products.

CCH products have been a trusted resource since 1913, and are highly regarded resources for legal, securities, antitrust and trade regulation, government contracting, banking, pension, payroll, employment and labor, and healthcare reimbursement and compliance professionals.

Aspen Publishers products provide essential information to attorneys, business professionals and law students. Written by preeminent authorities, the product line offers analytical and practical information in a range of specialty practice areas from securities law and intellectual property to mergers and acquisitions and pension/benefits. Aspen's trusted legal education resources provide professors and students with high-quality, up-to-date and effective resources for successful instruction and study in all areas of the law.

Kluwer Law International products provide the global business community with reliable international legal information in English. Legal practitioners, corporate counsel and business executives around the world rely on Kluwer Law journals, looseleafs, books, and electronic products for comprehensive information in many areas of international legal practice.

Loislaw is a comprehensive online legal research product providing legal content to law firm practitioners of various specializations. Loislaw provides attorneys with the ability to quickly and efficiently find the necessary legal information they need, when and where they need it, by facilitating access to primary law as well as state-specific law, records, forms and treatises.

Best Case Solutions is the leading bankruptcy software product to the bankruptcy industry. It provides software and workflow tools to flawlessly streamline petition preparation and the electronic filing process, while timely incorporating ever-changing court requirements.

ftwilliam.com offers employee benefits professionals the highest-quality plan documents (retirement, welfare and nonqualified) and government forms (5500/PBGC, 1099 and IRS) software at highly competitive prices.

MediRegs products provide integrated healthcare compliance content and software solutions for professionals in healthcare, higher education and life sciences, including professionals in accounting, law and consulting.

Wolters Kluwer Law & Business, a division of Wolters Kluwer, is headquartered in New York. Wolters Kluwer is a market-leading global information services company focused on professionals.

For Eve, Sarah, Benjamin, and
Randy with all of my love
—HVS

In memory of my Dad, Seymour Banchik,
who was one in a billion
—Andrea B. Yelin

SUMMARY
OF CONTENTS

CONTENTS

CHAPTER 8   QUESTIONS PRESENTED AND CONCLUSIONS OR BRIEF ANSWERS

CHAPTER 14   IN-HOUSE AND OBJECTIVE CLIENT DOCUMENTS

LIST OF ILLUSTRATIONS

Illustrations Included in Appendix C

PREFACE

The Role of the Paralegal in Legal Writing

Legal writing is one of the tasks paralegals must learn to perform efficiently and cost effectively for law firms and their clients. But to do so, paralegals must understand the legal system, research materials and legal writing techniques. Objective memos often must be drafted by paralegals to inform an attorney of the relevant law, both for and against a client's position, so that the attorney can best handle the matter. Paralegals also brief cases to expedite the research process, as well as write documents such as motions, briefs, complaints, and answers in litigation matters. Delegating the task of writing an objective memo to a paralegal is cost effective for an attorney and often saves a client money.

The Purpose and Structure of This Text

Basic Legal Writing for Paralegals guides the student and the practicing paralegal through the writing process in a step-by-step manner using the objective memo as a teaching tool. The text also introduces persuasive writing and instruments and documents drafted by legal assistants. In addition, the book contains information about grammar, editing, and writing processes as well as how to properly organize each portion of a document. The book is a valuable reference manual for any legal assistant who has to craft a document especially an objective memo.

Objective writing is explored in great detail. To master the art of objective writing, a paralegal must develop the ability to articulate legal concepts clearly, and to draft documents in a manner reflecting legal analysis. Learning to perform legal analysis and to organize a legal discussion is the basis of objective writing. Much time must be spent to refine and to master these skills. Only after a foundation has been built on objective writing skills can other forms of legal writing be learned.

The book begins with an overview of the legal system and then discusses case briefing. Understanding how our legal system operates and knowing how to read, brief, and analyze legal opinions are prerequisites to effective legal writing. You are provided with information about grammar and effective writing and editing techniques. Then, you are guided through the concept of the objective memo and its purpose. The next chapter discusses the question presented and the conclusion or brief answer. The facts and drafting the statement of the facts are explored in a separate chapter where you will learn to identify legally significant facts. The IRAC method is then introduced. IRAC, an acronym for Issue, Rule, Application, and Conclusion, is the format for the discussion portion of the memo. Building on the skills that you have acquired, you are then introduced to the task of synthesizing cases and authorities. Synthesis requires you to distill the general legal concept and then to create a statement of the law using more than one case or statute. These chapters are very detailed because you are also being taught legal reasoning and legal analysis. After you master these skills, other forms of legal writing are easier to master. The rest of the text discusses writing documents, persuasive writing, and letter writing, as well as citation.

Basic Legal Writing for Paralegals is designed to be both a handbook and a textbook, and therefore helps you develop your writing skills now and in the future. You will learn to convey the results of your research in written documents. You also will be shown how to articulate legal concepts, to convey information, to answer a question, or to craft a persuasive argument. These skills require attention to detail, keen analysis, and precision with language. Legal writing skills are developed through practice; often the best writing is done in revision.

You should view this book as a launching point in developing your legal writing skills. Refer to the guidelines and concepts in this book throughout your career as you hone your writing skills.

Hope Viner Samborn
Andrea B. Yelin

September 2012

ACKNOWLEDGMENTS

We would like to thank the special people who assisted us in creating this text and molding its contents.

We are also grateful for the help our students and colleagues provided us in shaping the exercises. Some students who deserve special thanks for their critiques and suggestions include Amy Berezinski, Nanette Boryc, Mara Castello, Patricia Cochran, Beverly Dombroski, Cheryl Morgan, Patricia Naqvi, Shay Robertson, Louise Tessitore, and Amy Widmer.

Thank you to Carolyn O'Sullivan, Betsy Kenny, Lisa Wehrle, Joan Horan, Katie Byrne Butcher, and John Lyman of Little, Brown and Company for their time, their counsel, and their expertise in putting together the first edition. We will always be indebted to Carolyn for getting us started on this project and *The Legal Research and Writing Handbook,* our first book. We are sorry she was unable to complete this project with us. And although Lisa did not work directly with this book, we appreciate how much her major contribution to *The Legal Research and Writing Handbook* helped to shape the words of this book.

Thank you also to Kaesmene Harrison Banks, Christie Rears, and Julie Nahil of Aspen Publishers, for their invaluable assistance in the production of prior editions of our writing book. Thank you to Sylvia Rebert for her assistance in the production of this edition. We also want to thank Aspen Publishers for continuing to work with us and publish our texts. Finally, a special thank you to Betsy Kenny for her excellent work in reviewing the text and her patience in coordinating all of the many details involved in producing this book.

Thanks to Julia Wentz, Patricia Scott, and Fred LeBaron at the Loyola University Chicago School of Law Library.

Thanks to Jean Hellman Ryan, Alice Perlin and Jennifer Brendel for the opportunity to teach in your wonderful programs.

Finally, thank you to both of our families. Randy, Eve, and Sarah, and the rest of my extended family, I will always be indebted to you for providing me with support, love, and the time to do this project.

Thanks to David, Rachel, and Henry, and to Andrea's parents, for all of your love and support.

Thanks to Thomson Reuters for their kind permission to reprint *Seymor v. Armstrong*, and also to LexisNexis for permission to reprint *Morganroth v. Whitall*, in Chapter 6.

We would also like to thank the reviewers listed below. Their careful review of the manuscript produced many valuable comments and suggestions. We greatly appreciate their efforts.

Laura Barnard	Lakeland Community College
Brenda L. Rice, J.D.	Johnson County Community College
Joy O'Donnell	Pima Community College
Eric Olson	Barry University
Holly L. Enterline	State Technical Institute at Memphis
Kay Y. Rute	Washburn University
Sy Littman	Platt College
Paul Klein	Duquesne University
Adelaide Lagnese	University of Maryland
Robin O. McNeely	McNeese State University

INTRODUCTION TO LEGAL RESEARCH

CHAPTER OVERVIEW

Before you begin to research and to write about a legal problem, you must understand your role as a paralegal. You are an important member of a team. To function effectively, you must know which legal system governs and how that system operates. This chapter first considers your role in researching a legal problem and communicating it to your supervising attorney. Next, it discusses the legal system. It focuses on the organization of the U.S. federal government, which is divided into three separate branches: the legislative, the executive, and the judicial. It also provides a general explanation of how state governments are structured. Finally, the role of major governmental bodies is explored.

A. INTRODUCTION TO LEGAL RESEARCH AND WRITING

1. The Role of the Paralegal in Legal Research and Writing

Legal research and legal writing are among the tasks paralegals can perform efficiently and cost-effectively for law firms and their clients. But to do so effectively, you must understand the legal system and a variety of legal concepts. You must be able to use all the research tools available to lawyers and their staffs. Paralegals retrieve information regarding the law as well as nonlegal information, such as financial information and test results.

▼ Why Do Paralegals Perform Research?

Often research is done to determine whether a client has a case. Other times, paralegals must research a particular issue raised after a case has been filed. Some research is done to support motions to be filed with courts. Research also may be done when a client is involved in a transaction and the attorney must determine the law and the steps to take in the transaction.

▼ What Tasks Do Paralegals Handle in the Research and Writing Process?

In practice, paralegals act as an arm of an attorney. The amount of research and the type of assignments paralegals perform vary throughout the country.

In some law offices, paralegals undertake all of the research in preparation for the filing of motions but attorneys draft the motions. In others, paralegals research and prepare rough drafts of motions. Once a research project is completed, you must communicate your research results effectively. To do this, you must understand the fundamentals of legal writing and be able to write detailed, clear, and thoughtful memoranda. Paralegals often are asked to prepare memoranda that summarize their research results. Some paralegals who work with judges prepare rough drafts of court decisions. This book is designed to help you complete each of these tasks.

When you are assigned a research problem, you are expected to work as a professional. You should complete the assignment in a timely fashion. More important, however, the written research results must be accurate, complete, and current. This book teaches you how to analyze, organize, and communicate the results of a research project.

ETHICS ALERT

Paralegals work under the supervision of attorneys, except in very limited, statutorily sanctioned situations. As a result, all research results and client memoranda should be submitted to an attorney before they are provided to a client. Work submitted to clients containing legal opinions should never be signed by a paralegal.

B. INTRODUCTION TO THE U.S. LEGAL SYSTEM

1. The Organization of the Legal System

The United States consists of a multi-tiered system of government. The **federal government** and the **state governments** are the top two tiers. See Illustration 1-1.

Several lower-tier governmental bodies, including **city, village, township**, and **county governments**, exercise authority over the citizens of the United States. For the most part, your research will concern either federal or state law. Therefore, this book focuses its discussion on the federal and state systems and how to find the law they generate. The knowledge of these systems, the types of laws they adopt, and how to find legal standards for these systems later can be applied to any research you undertake concerning other government bodies and their laws.

ILLUSTRATION 1-1.   U.S. and State Government Systems

*Most, but not all, state courts consist of three tiers.

▼ How Did the Federal and State Systems Originate?

Representatives of the states adopted a **constitution** for the United States that is the framework for the operation of this federal/state system of government. To that end, the U.S. Constitution creates three branches of government and defines their powers. You can think of the Constitution as an umbrella over all of the United States' governing bodies as it covers questions of not only federal government powers, but some state powers as well. The Constitution reserves for the states all the remaining powers not specifically designated to the federal government bodies. In addition, the Constitution establishes the rules for the relationship between the federal and state governments. The U.S. Constitution is the supreme law of the United States. For example, Congress, the legislative body of the federal government, cannot enact a law that is contrary to the U.S. Constitution. The state legislatures similarly are prevented from adopting laws that violate provisions of the U.S. Constitution.

2. Components of the Federal System and Governing Law

The federal government consists of three branches of government: the legislative, the executive, and the judicial. The U.S. Constitution created each branch and defines the relationship between them. The Constitution establishes a system in which each branch of government can monitor the activities of the other branches to prevent abuses. Each branch has the ability to alter actions of another branch. In this way, the Constitution provides **checks** and **balances** concerning the actions of each branch of government.

a. The Legislative Branch

The **legislative branch** of the federal government is called the **Congress.** It is comprised of two houses or chambers called the **Senate** and the **House of Representatives.** Both houses are comprised of individuals who are elected. The Congress creates laws called **statutes.** Some statutes are new rules of law. Other statutes supersede or adopt court-made law. Court-made law is referred to as **case law** or the **common law.** When Congress adopts common law as its own, the process is called **codification.** One pervasive example of this is patent law. Many laws were adopted based on court decisions concerning this area of the law. The statutes and the U.S. Constitution comprise one body of law called **enacted law.** The laws enacted by the federal government apply to all U.S. citizens and residents.

▼ How Is a Law Created?

Anyone can propose that Congress adopt a new law, and either chamber can introduce a law for consideration. When a proposed law is introduced, it is called a **bill.** Before the bill can become a law, both chambers must approve it. If both houses approve the same version of the bill, it is sent to the chief of the executive branch, our **president**. The president can sign or veto the bill or withhold action on it. If the president signs the bill, it becomes law. If the president does not act within ten days and the legislative session is still in progress, the bill becomes law. If the president vetoes the bill, Congress may override the veto by a two-thirds majority vote of each house.

If the president fails to act on the bill within the ten days and the legislature is out of session, the bill does not become law. This action is called a **pocket veto.**

b. The Executive Branch

The **executive branch** of the government, headed by the president, is the primary enforcer of the law. The president appoints the cabinet and oversees many federal agencies. The executive branch is responsible for the day-to-day management of the federal government. With the assistance of the vice president, the cabinet members, and the heads of federal agencies, the president helps to guide the day-to-day operations of the government. The president can issue executive orders to direct the operations of various agencies and the actions of the citizens of the United States. In addition, the president is the commander in chief of the armed forces and with the advice and consent of the Senate, he can enter into treaties. Most federal administrative agencies are under direct control of the executive branch. See Illustration 1-2.

As the country's top executive, the president has the authority to control many administrative agencies. However, some administrative agencies are independent. For example, the Department of Justice that includes the Office of the Attorney General is part of the executive branch. However, the Federal Trade Commission is an independent agency.

Administrative agencies enforce many of the laws of the United States. These agencies are responsible for the daily regulation of activities controlled by federal law. For a listing of some of the many administrative agencies, see Illustration 1-2.

Congress creates the agencies and delegates some of its own power to them because it alone is unable to handle the day-to-day enforcement of the overwhelming number of federal laws. Agencies, however, have the staff and often the technical expertise to deal with the daily enforcement of Congress's enacted laws. To do this, agencies often make rules that explain in detail how individuals should act to comply with congressional mandates. In some cases, agencies hold hearings to enforce the law. These agencies, therefore, function in quasi-judicial and quasi-legislative roles.

For example, Congress enacted the Consumer Product Safety Act and delegated its enforcement power to the U.S. Consumer Product Safety Commission. Congress charged the commission with the responsibility for the daily enforcement of that act. As part of the commission's

ILLUSTRATION 1-2. The Government of the United States

THE GOVERNMENT OF THE UNITED STATES

THE CONSTITUTION

LEGISLATIVE BRANCH

THE CONGRESS

SENATE   HOUSE

ARCHITECT OF THE CAPITOL
UNITED STATES BOTANIC GARDEN
GOVERNMENT ACCOUNTABILITY OFFICE
GOVERNMENT PRINTING OFFICE
LIBRARY OF CONGRESS
CONGRESSIONAL BUDGET OFFICE

EXECUTIVE BRANCH

THE PRESIDENT

THE VICE PRESIDENT

EXECUTIVE OFFICE OF THE PRESIDENT

WHITE HOUSE OFFICE
OFFICE OF THE VICE PRESIDENT
COUNCIL OF ECONOMIC ADVISERS
COUNCIL ON ENVIRONMENTAL QUALITY
NATIONAL SECURITY COUNCIL
OFFICE OF ADMINISTRATION

OFFICE OF MANAGEMENT AND BUDGET
OFFICE OF NATIONAL DRUG CONTROL POLICY
OFFICE OF POLICY DEVELOPMENT
OFFICE OF SCIENCE AND TECHNOLOGY POLICY
OFFICE OF THE UNITED STATES
TRADE REPRESENTATIVE

JUDICIAL BRANCH

THE SUPREME COURT OF THE
UNITED STATES

UNITED STATES COURTS OF APPEALS
UNITED STATES DISTRICT COURTS
TERRITORIAL COURTS
UNITED STATES COURT OF INTERNATIONAL TRADE
UNITED STATES COURT OF FEDERAL CLAIMS
UNITED STATES COURT OF APPEALS FOR THE
ARMED FORCES
UNITED STATES TAX COURT
UNITED STATES COURT OF APPEALS FOR VETERANS CLAIMS
ADMINISTRATIVE OFFICE OF THE
UNITED STATES COURTS
FEDERAL JUDICIAL CENTER
UNITED STATES SENTENCING COMMISSION

DEPARTMENT OF AGRICULTURE

DEPARTMENT OF COMMERCE

DEPARTMENT OF DEFENSE

DEPARTMENT OF EDUCATION

DEPARTMENT OF ENERGY

DEPARTMENT OF HEALTH AND HUMAN SERVICES

DEPARTMENT OF HOMELAND SECURITY

DEPARTMENT OF HOUSING AND URBAN DEVELOPMENT

DEPARTMENT OF THE INTERIOR

DEPARTMENT OF JUSTICE

DEPARTMENT OF LABOR

DEPARTMENT OF STATE

DEPARTMENT OF TRANSPORTATION

DEPARTMENT OF THE TREASURY

DEPARTMENT OF VETERANS AFFAIRS

INDEPENDENT ESTABLISHMENTS AND GOVERNMENT CORPORATIONS

AFRICAN DEVELOPMENT FOUNDATION
BROADCASTING BOARD OF GOVERNORS
CENTRAL INTELLIGENCE AGENCY
COMMODITY FUTURES TRADING COMMISSION
CONSUMER PRODUCT SAFETY COMMISSION
CORPORATION FOR NATIONAL AND COMMUNITY SERVICE
DEFENSE NUCLEAR FACILITIES SAFETY BOARD
ENVIRONMENTAL PROTECTION AGENCY
EQUAL EMPLOYMENT OPPORTUNITY COMMISSION
EXPORT-IMPORT BANK OF THE UNITED STATES
FARM CREDIT ADMINISTRATION
FEDERAL COMMUNICATIONS COMMISSION
FEDERAL DEPOSIT INSURANCE CORPORATION
FEDERAL ELECTION COMMISSION

FEDERAL HOUSING FINANCE BOARD
FEDERAL LABOR RELATIONS AUTHORITY
FEDERAL MARITIME COMMISSION
FEDERAL MEDIATION AND CONCILIATION SERVICE
FEDERAL MINE SAFETY AND HEALTH REVIEW COMMISSION
FEDERAL RESERVE SYSTEM
FEDERAL RETIREMENT THRIFT INVESTMENT BOARD
FEDERAL TRADE COMMISSION
GENERAL SERVICES ADMINISTRATION
INTER-AMERICAN FOUNDATION
MERIT SYSTEMS PROTECTION BOARD
NATIONAL AERONAUTICS AND SPACE ADMINISTRATION
NATIONAL ARCHIVES AND RECORDS ADMINISTRATION
NATIONAL CAPITAL PLANNING COMMISSION

NATIONAL CREDIT UNION ADMINISTRATION
NATIONAL FOUNDATION ON THE ARTS AND THE HUMANITIES
NATIONAL LABOR RELATIONS BOARD
NATIONAL MEDIATION BOARD
NATIONAL RAILROAD PASSENGER CORPORATION (AMTRAK)
NATIONAL SCIENCE FOUNDATION
NATIONAL TRANSPORTATION SAFETY BOARD
NUCLEAR REGULATORY COMMISSION
OCCUPATIONAL SAFETY AND HEALTH REVIEW COMMISSION
OFFICE OF THE DIRECTOR OF NATIONAL INTELLIGENCE
OFFICE OF GOVERNMENT ETHICS
OFFICE OF PERSONNEL MANAGEMENT
OFFICE OF SPECIAL COUNSEL
OVERSEAS PRIVATE INVESTMENT CORPORATION

PEACE CORPS
PENSION BENEFIT GUARANTY CORPORATION
POSTAL REGULATORY COMMISSION
NATIONAL RAILROAD RETIREMENT BOARD
SECURITIES AND EXCHANGE COMMISSION
SELECTIVE SERVICE SYSTEM
SMALL BUSINESS ADMINISTRATION
SOCIAL SECURITY ADMINISTRATION
TENNESSEE VALLEY AUTHORITY
TRADE AND DEVELOPMENT AGENCY
UNITED STATES AGENCY FOR INTERNATIONAL DEVELOPMENT
UNITED STATES COMMISSION ON CIVIL RIGHTS
UNITED STATES INTERNATIONAL TRADE COMMISSION
UNITED STATES POSTAL SERVICE

duties, it adopts rules or regulations. It also has administrative hearings, which often result in decisions.

In some cases, agencies use their **police powers** to enforce the law. For example, the U.S. Environmental Protection Agency will assist in prosecuting individuals or corporations that violate the Clean Air Act or other laws designed to protect the environment.

NET NOTE

Search for federal agencies and information at search.usa.gov/. Details about cabinet members, proclamations, executive orders, and issues facing the executive branch can be found at www.whitehouse.gov/. Another government source of information is usa.gov. Information on federal government agencies can be found at www.usa.gov/Agencies/Federal/All_Agencies/index.shtml.

---

c. The Judicial Branch

The third branch of government is the **judicial branch.** The federal judicial system includes three levels of courts that resolve disputes. See Illustration 1-3.

The entry-level court is the **trial court.** In that court, disputes are heard and decided by either a judge or a jury. The second level or intermediate level of courts is called **appellate courts.** These courts consider appeals of decisions of the trial court. The final level is the **U.S. Supreme Court.** Its decisions cannot be appealed to any court.

NET NOTE

The web site www.uscourts.gov provides links to all the U.S. appellate and district courts and U.S. bankruptcy courts, as well as the U.S. Supreme Court. Information is provided about judges, court personnel, locations, and court rules.

▼ Who Can Bring an Action in Federal Court?

A court can only consider a case if it has **jurisdiction** to hear it, that is, if the court is authorized to consider such cases. The federal court can consider all cases involving issues of federal law. In addition, it may hear cases involving disputes between parties of different states. Such cases are called **diversity cases.** Cases in which both the plaintiff, who is the

ILLUSTRATION 1-3.   Federal Judicial System

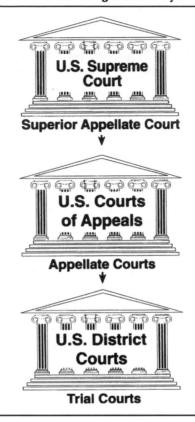

party bringing the lawsuit, and the defendant are citizens of different states are examples of diversity cases. Diversity cases often involve issues of state law.

ETHICS ALERT

If you are assisting an attorney in preparing a claim, be certain that the claim is made in a court that has jurisdiction over such a claim.

PRACTICE POINTER

State and federal courts can decide issues of state or federal law.

i. The Trial Courts

The **trial court** is the court that hears the facts concerning a dispute. It is generally the first place in which a party can seek a remedy in federal court. In that way, it is considered a court of **original jurisdiction.** However, this court also hears appeals from some administrative agencies and the federal bankruptcy courts. Some administrative agency decisions, however, are appealed directly to the appellate courts.

In the federal system, the trial courts are known as the **district courts.** These courts decide disputes when a party (which can be a person, corporation, or other entity) brings an action against another party. In such cases, the trial courts often are asked to interpret congressional enactments such as statutes, ordinances, charters, or executive branch-created laws, including agency rules or decisions. When a court interprets a statute or regulation, it is overseeing the actions of other government branches. Courts often consult a body of law called the common law before rendering any decisions. Common law is court-created law found in the judicial opinions or cases; it is not found in the statutes.

ii. The Appellate Courts

The federal trial courts' decisions can be appealed to one of the 13 **federal appellate courts** known as the **U.S. Courts of Appeals.** See Illustration 1-3. This second tier of federal courts is broken into numbered and named **circuits.** Eleven circuits are known as the First through Eleventh. The remaining circuits are the Federal Circuit and the District of Columbia Circuit. The circuits are geographic, except for the Federal Circuit. See Illustration 1-4. An online map is available at www.uscourts.gov/. These courts decide issues of law posed in appeals of trial court decisions located within its circuit. These courts do not consider new factual evidence. Witnesses are not brought before these courts. The Court of Appeals for the Federal Circuit has nationwide jurisdiction to hear appeals in specialized cases such as those arising from decisions of the Court of Federal Claims or the Court of International Trade. Decisions of the federal appellate courts can be appealed to the U.S. Supreme Court.

iii. The Supreme Court

The U.S. Supreme Court is the highest court in the United States. See Illustration 1-3. The U.S. Constitution establishes this court. Today nine justices, appointed by the president and confirmed by the U.S. Senate, sit on this tribunal. The U.S. Supreme Court has discretion to consider many issues. This discretion is called **certiorari.** If the court decides not to hear an issue, it denies certiorari. The effect is that the decision of the appellate court is final. If the U.S. Supreme Court

ILLUSTRATION 1-4. **Circuit Map of the U.S. Courts of Appeals**

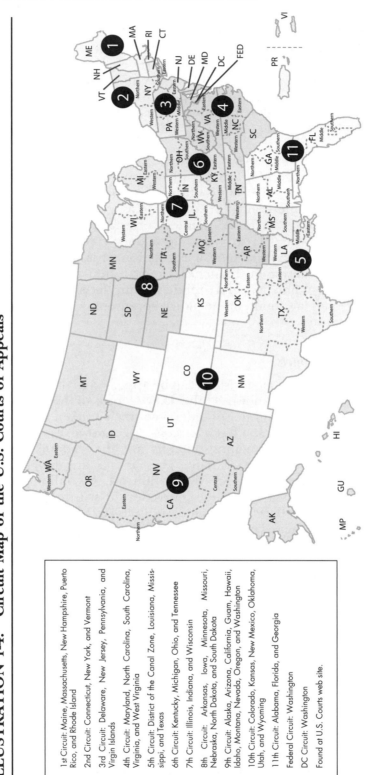

1st Circuit: Maine, Massachusetts, New Hampshire, Puerto Rico, and Rhode Island

2nd Circuit: Connecticut, New York, and Vermont

3rd Circuit: Delaware, New Jersey, Pennsylvania, and Virginia Islands

4th Circuit: Maryland, North Carolina, South Carolina, Virginia, and West Virginia

5th Circuit: District of the Canal Zone, Louisiana, Mississippi, and Texas

6th Circuit: Kentucky, Michigan, Ohio, and Tennessee

7th Circuit: Illinois, Indiana, and Wisconsin

8th Circuit: Arkansas, Iowa, Minnesota, Missouri, Nebraska, North Dakota, and South Dakota

9th Circuit: Alaska, Arizona, California, Guam, Hawaii, Idaho, Montana, Nevada, Oregon, and Washington

10th Circuit: Colorado, Kansas, New Mexico, Oklahoma, Utah, and Wyoming

11th Circuit: Alabama, Florida, and Georgia

Federal Circuit: Washington

DC Circuit: Washington

Found at U.S. Courts web site.

decides to hear an issue, it grants certiorari. It then will consider whether the appellate court's decision should stand. By law, the U.S. Supreme Court alone has the authority to hear appeals of a state court of last resort decision when a substantial federal constitutional issue is presented. The U.S. Supreme Court also may hear a dispute between two states. The Supreme Court also has original jurisdiction—that is the right—to directly take actions and proceedings in which ambassadors, other public ministers, consuls, or vice consuls of foreign states are parties. It also has original jurisdiction in all controversies between the United States and a state.

NET NOTE

The Federal Judicial Center provides information about the federal judiciary and its history. See www.fjc.gov.

---

3. Relationship Between Federal and State Governments

▼ Can a Federal Court Decide an Issue of State Law?

Yes. A federal court can decide an issue of state law if the state issue is presented with a related federal issue or if the state question is raised in a dispute between parties of different states in a case called a diversity action.

▼ What Effect Does a Federal Decision Have on State Law?

A federal court decision generally cannot change state law. It may persuade the state courts to review state law, but its decision usually does not force any change in the law. These decisions, therefore, are advisory for future litigants but must be followed by the parties directly involved in the case in which the decision was rendered. Because states are separate sovereigns, in almost all cases only the state governing bodies can change state law. One exception to this rule does exist. The U.S. Supreme Court can determine whether state law violates the U.S. Constitution. If such a violation is found, the decision of the U.S. Supreme Court could invalidate state law.

▼ Are Federal and State Agencies Part of One Governing Body?

No. The federal government is one sovereign or governing body and the state is a separate governing body or sovereign. That means that the state cannot control the federal government agencies or change federal law. In general, the federal government branches cannot control the state government or change state law. However, the U.S. Constitution, the umbrella, can limit actions of the state government. The Constitution prohibits the states from making any laws that are contrary to its provisions.

PRACTICE POINTER

Often attorneys choose to bring a case in a federal rather than state court or the other way around for tactical reasons. More often the reason for bringing an action in a particular court is based solely on the law that serves as the basis for the claim.

---

4. Organization of State Governments

Most state governments are organized in a manner similar to that of the federal government. State governments are governed by constitutions. That constitution defines the organization of the state's government and the relationship between the branches of government. The states have legislative, executive, and judicial branches.

The legislative branches operate in a manner similar to that of Congress and often feature two chambers. Some legislatures enact enabling laws that create administrative agencies and provide such agencies with the responsibility for the daily enforcement of state laws. The chief executive in each state is a governor.

Each state has a judicial system. However, not all state systems mirror the federal government's three-tier court system. Each state establishes which courts can hear different disputes. Some states have a three-tier system similar to that of the federal judicial branch. In some states, the intermediate appellate court is eliminated. The following systems do not include an intermediate appellate court: Delaware, District of Columbia, Maine, Montana, Nevada, New Hampshire, Rhode Island, South Dakota, Vermont, West Virginia, and Wyoming. The creation of such a court in Nevada is being studied.

PRACTICE POINTER

The Supreme Court may not be the highest court in a state. This is the case in New York.

NET NOTE

For more information about the state trial courts, see the National Center for State Courts web site, www.ncsc.org. Information about court structures and links to the court are provided.

▼ What Are the Duties of the State Courts?

In most state court systems, trial courts determine the facts and legal issues of a case. A trial court might include a family, a municipal, or a small claims court. The jurisdiction of these courts is generally limited, sometimes according to the amount of money in dispute.

The next level generally is an appellate level court. However, as noted above, some states do not have this level. As in the federal court system, this court usually does not hear new facts or evidence. Instead, it decides whether the lower court erred in deciding substantive law or procedural issues. Finally, most states have another appellate level court, similar to the U.S. Supreme Court, which is the final arbiter of disputes. In some states, there are two such courts—one for criminal cases and the other for civil cases. Texas and Oklahoma are two states that have such courts.

PRACTICE POINTER

An appellate court may hear facts and evidence if it is the court of original jurisdiction. That is the court charged with first hearing the case.

▼ Can State Courts Decide Issues of Federal Law?

Yes, state courts can decide issues of federal law. Although a state court decision concerning federal law does not change the federal law, it may persuade federal governing bodies to change federal law. The state court decision's impact is limited to the case in which the federal issue was presented, and therefore only parties involved in that case are bound or required to follow that ruling.

The federal government controls all issues of federal law. The state governments exercise authority over all issues of state law. These areas are not always well defined. In some areas, both the state and federal governments exercise authority. For example, both the state and federal governments control how industries dispose of their wastes. Do not be discouraged if you have difficulty separating state and federal issues in some cases. Many times courts struggle with these issues.

CHAPTER SUMMARY

In this chapter, you learned about the branches of the U.S. government and their functions, as well as the general structure of the state governments. The United States has three branches of government: the legislative, the executive, and the judicial. All of these branches were created by the U.S. Constitution, which guides their activities. In addition, administrative agencies enforce the laws created by the legislature.

The legislature, which consists of the House of Representatives and the Senate, creates laws called statutes.

The executive branch enforces the laws of the United States, and the judicial branch resolves disputes and interprets the laws.

The judicial branch is comprised of a three-tier court system. The highest court is the U.S. Supreme Court; the middle courts are the U.S. Courts of Appeals; the trial or lowest courts are the U.S. District Courts. All three branches of government create law.

KEY TERMS

administrative agencies
appellate courts
balances
bill
case law
certiorari
checks
circuits
city government
codification
common law
Congress
constitution
county government
district courts
diversity cases
enacted law
executive branch

federal appellate court
federal government
House of Representatives
judicial branch
jurisdiction
legislative branch
original jurisdiction
pocket veto
police powers
president
Senate
state governments
statutes
township government
trial court
U.S. Courts of Appeals
U.S. Supreme Court
village government

EXERCISES

1. Draw a diagram of your state government.
2. How many houses does your legislature have? What are the names of each chamber?
3. Diagram your state court system. Is there an intermediate court?
4. Draw a flow chart of the federal bill process.
5. Draw a flow chart of the state bill process for your state.
6. Who is the chief executive?

7. Go to the National Center for State Courts web site and review the structure of your state court.

8. What are the monetary requirements for filing an action in the trial court in your state?

9. Go to *usa.gov* and click around the site to find links to the Congressional Budget Office and the Domestic Policy Council.

10. What are the branches of the U.S. government and what are the responsibilities of each branch?

11. What are Congress-created laws called?

12. What is the body of law created by the courts called?

13. Name the judges on your high court. Where did you find this information?

14. Find your state's web site. Note it.

15. Find a web site for your state courts. Note it.

16. Find a web site for your state legislature. Note it.

LEGAL AUTHORITIES AND HOW TO USE THEM

CHAPTER OVERVIEW

In researching legal issues, you must have goals and understand the value of the legal authorities you find. This chapter explains the concept of legal authority and the determination of governing law. It discusses the value of various authorities and how authorities interrelate with each other. You will learn which authorities should determine the outcome of a case and which authorities merely provide persuasive support for a case. You will learn how to determine which authorities to use in documents you write.

A. DETERMINATION OF GOVERNING LAW

To determine what law controls your case, you must first determine the jurisdiction. Next, you must identify the current law that applies to your case by examining the hierarchy of authorities. Looking at relevant precedent and dicta completes your strategy for determining the governing law.

1. Jurisdiction

Jurisdiction is a complex concept that has several different definitions. It is the authority of a government body to exercise control over a conflict. In the broadest sense, jurisdiction is the right of a state or of the federal government to apply its laws to a dispute. It also is the right of a court to interpret and apply the law to a particular case. When a court or a governing body has jurisdiction over a case or situation, it has the authority to control the case or outcome of the situation.

▼ What Factors Determine Which Jurisdiction Governs Your Case?

A variety of factors affect which jurisdiction governs a claim in a particular case, including where the dispute arose, the parties involved in the case, and the nature of the dispute. Sometimes making this determination is a complex task. Ask the assigning attorney to assist you in making this determination. Various statutes, procedural rules, and cases also can assist you in understanding which court has jurisdiction. For example, federal court jurisdiction is specified by federal law.

2. Precedent

You already have learned that the courts generate decisions of cases that become law. The basic rule of law decided by the court is the **holding.** If the court is presented with more than one issue, the decision includes more than one holding. The holding also is called the **precedent.**

Theoretically, the lower courts must follow decisions or precedents of the higher courts in their jurisdiction. This theory is called **stare decisis.** The idea behind it is that parties should be able to rely on what the courts have done in the past. Doing so allows parties to predict how a court is likely to rule in their cases.

The doctrine of stare decisis makes your job as a researcher important. You must determine what the courts have decided in the past to assist the attorneys in predicting what the court is likely to do, or likely to be persuaded to do, in your case. Sometimes a court will not follow precedent. Even though stare decisis and precedent are the controlling doctrines, courts decide cases based on the facts before them and the changes in society. This allows the law, through the holdings, to evolve and to meet contemporary needs. It is these holdings that you must consider after reviewing the theories of hierarchy of authorities.

3. Hierarchy of Authorities

Once you have determined the jurisdiction, you then must identify the current law that applies to the case. To determine what law applies to your case, you must determine the **hierarchy of authorities.** This is a system in which legal authorities such as court decisions, statutes, administrative rules and decisions, and constitutions are ranked according to the effect they have in controlling the law of a governing body. You can think of this in part as a chain of command. For example, U.S. Supreme Court cases outrank federal appeals and trial courts concerning issues of federal law. Determining the hierarchy of authorities can be simple or complex depending in large part on the system of government and structure of the courts, the law applicable to the dispute, and the underlying claim. Other factors that play a role in determining whether one authority outranks another is the currency of an authority and competing laws within a jurisdiction.

a. Currency

You must first determine which authority is most current. Suppose you find that the law governing your case is a federal law and the case involves a question of federal constitutional law. At first glance the highest legal authority would appear to be the U.S. Constitution because it is the supreme law of the United States and because the legal issue in question is constitutional in nature. However, if the U.S. Supreme Court has interpreted the Constitution on the issue presented in your case, its decision is more current and would therefore be the highest legal authority.

In another case that does not involve a constitutional issue, a federal statute might be the highest authority. This would depend on whether a court had interpreted the statute. If a federal court had interpreted the statute's language and that language affected the issue involved in your case, you would need to determine whether the court decision or the statute is more recent. The most current authority is the highest authority.

EXAMPLE OF THE HIERARCHY QUESTION BETWEEN A STATUTE AND A CASE

Your case involves a legal issue that was addressed in a statute that was enacted on December 1, 2011. All the court cases you have found that may have a bearing on this legal issue involved in this case were decided before December 1, 2011. Therefore, the statute—the most current authority—is the highest authority concerning this issue. For another example, see Illustration 2-1.

ILLUSTRATION 2-1.   Example of Ranking Authorities

The problem presented is whether the U.S. constitutional provision that requires due process applies to aliens held under the USA Patriot Act.

> Applicable law:
>
> U.S. Constitution
>
> The USA Patriot Act (2001)
>
> Supreme Court case 2012 determining that the Due Process Clause of the U.S. Constitution is not applicable to persons held under the USA Patriot Act

Rank of authorities and reason for the ranking:

1. Supreme Court case 2012 interpreting the Constitution and the USA Patriot Act would be first. It is the most current authority.
2. The next authority is likely to be the USA Patriot Act if it directly addresses this point. It is the second most current authority.

b. Levels of Court

Next, you must consider the level of each authority, that is, where the court or government body ranks in order of its authority. The trial courts, appellate courts, and U.S. Supreme Court do not carry the same weight. For example, a decision of the highest court, the U.S. Supreme Court, would be at the top of the hierarchy of authorities of federal court decisions. Its decisions would trump those of other federal courts.

Except for the U.S. Supreme Court, all the federal courts are within defined groups called **circuits.** Within each circuit are a group of district courts and one circuit court of appeals. The key to the relationship between the federal courts is that the district courts, which are the entry-level courts, must follow decisions of the U.S. Circuit Court of Appeals within its circuit. A district court does not have to follow decisions of appellate courts that are outside of its circuit. For a review of the circuit divisions, review Chapter 1. However, the decisions of appellate courts outside of a circuit often are used to persuade an appellate court to make a certain decision if it has not addressed that issue earlier. Such a decision is **persuasive authority** discussed later in this chapter.

PRACTICE POINTER

For each jurisdiction in which you often undertake research, create a chart that lists the primary and secondary authorities to consider.

Two examples of how such a hierarchical ranking would work in practice follow.

EXAMPLES OF HIERARCHY BETWEEN COURTS

The U.S. District Court for the Northern District of Illinois, which is in Chicago, falls in the Seventh Circuit. See Illustration 1-4. If the federal district court in Illinois was asked to determine whether federal law permitted a union to charge a fee to nonmembers for activities that benefit nonmembers, it would be bound to follow any U.S. Seventh Circuit Court of Appeals decision concerning this issue. This is because this appellate court is a higher court than the district court within the Seventh Circuit. If the U.S. Sixth Circuit Court of Appeals in Cincinnati handed down a decision on this issue that conflicted with the Seventh Circuit Court of Appeals, the District Court for the Northern District of Illinois, a trial court, would be bound to follow the decision of the Seventh Circuit Court of Appeals, a court that is above it in rank and status, not the Sixth Circuit Court of Appeals, as the Illinois court is within the Seventh Circuit. The Seventh Circuit decision would be considered **mandatory binding authority** for the Illinois court. But the Illinois district court would not have to follow decisions of the U.S. Sixth Circuit Court of Appeals in Cincinnati concerning the above issue because it is not part of the Sixth Circuit. The Sixth Circuit opinion would be primary persuasive authority.

Similarly, the U.S. District Court for the Northern District of Ohio, based in Cleveland, falls within the Sixth Circuit. See Illustration 1-4. That district court must follow decisions of the Sixth Circuit appellate court, not those of the Seventh Circuit Court of Appeals in Chicago, because decisions of the Sixth Circuit Court would be mandatory binding authority for the Ohio court. Decisions of the Seventh Circuit would be primary persuasive authorities for the Ohio court.

c. Conflicting Decisions Between Circuits

Each circuit is independent of the other circuits. Therefore, their decisions may conflict. Each appellate court can make its decision independent of any decisions concerning the same issue rendered by other appellate courts. If two appellate courts have conflicting decisions concerning the same issue, how can you, as a researcher, decide what law governs? You must determine what circuit court authority is **mandatory authority** for your case. If the question is a particularly significant federal issue, check if the U.S. Supreme Court has decided the issue or is about to render a decision concerning such an issue. If so, a decision of the Supreme Court—the highest level of court—will be at the top of the hierarchy of authority.

Often, however, one appellate court may be guided in its decision by the decision of another appellate court. For example, if the Seventh Circuit had not rendered an opinion in the union fee case, but the Sixth Circuit had issued a decision concerning that matter, the Illinois district court facing a decision in a union fee case or even the Seventh Circuit Court of Appeals may be guided by the Sixth Circuit opinion. That decision rendered by a court outside of the Seventh Circuit would be persuasive authority rather than mandatory or binding authority. That is because the two courts would not be bound to follow the Sixth Circuit's decision.

d. State and Federal Decisions Concerning an Issue

What happens if the issue in your case involves both state and federal decisions? How do you make sense of the hierarchy of authorities in such cases? The key is to determine which court has jurisdiction or the right to hear the case. The court systems of the state and federal governments operate in tandem. As explained above, the federal courts may decide issues of both federal or state law. For example, a federal diversity case may involve a negligence issue—a state law issue.

Next, you must determine whether federal or state law applies. If you find this difficult, ask the assigning attorney. The federal courts must look to decisions of the highest court of the state to make a determination of state law. The federal court decision, however, does not bind later state court decisions.

State courts also may decide issues of either federal or state law. The state court decisions concerning federal law are merely persuasive authority, however, because federal courts are not required to follow these decisions. For instance, a plaintiff may bring an age discrimination case based on both the state and federal age discrimination in employment statutes. State courts will look to federal courts for guidance in deciding issues of federal law. However, they are not bound to follow those decisions. Similarly, a state court may decide a federal age discrimination issue, but the federal courts can disregard that decision when facing the same question.

e. Conflicts in Federal and State Authority

Although the federal and state governments are independent governments, they sometimes regulate some of the same areas, such as environmental pollution. In some cases, the federal government by congressional action will control an area extensively, and a state will attempt to monitor the same area. Who controls varies. Often, a determination of which of the **conflicting authorities** governs is decided by reviewing the Constitution. Other times, federal or state law might specify which law governs.

The federal courts sometimes are asked to decide who controls. The courts may look to the Constitution for guidance or may consider who has pervasively regulated an area. For example, if a case involves a section of the U.S. Constitution, the U.S. Supreme Court is the final authority. In other cases, it depends on the area being regulated.

f. State Court Decisions

Each group of state courts is a separate court system. State courts of one state are not required to follow decisions made by courts of other states. Often, however, state courts consider other states' court decisions for guidance in how to decide a case. Decisions of one state's courts are merely advisory or persuasive decisions for another state's courts, not decisions that control the law of the first state.

4. Dicta

Often a court addresses an issue that is not directly presented by the parties. In such cases, a court states what it would do if it was presented directly with the issue. When the court makes such statements, they are called **dicta.** Dicta do not have the same force and effect as holdings. They are not authoritative, and lower courts are not bound to follow such statements.

You might use dicta when no court has ever been asked directly to decide the issue addressed. The dicta explain how the court would decide the issue if it was directly presented to the court. Because of this, the dicta might help you to predict how a court might decide an issue. Dicta also can be used to persuade a court to decide an issue in a certain manner. Although dicta may be helpful, finding dicta is not the goal of your research.

B. GOAL OF YOUR RESEARCH

Your task is to find primary authority "on point" or "on all fours" with your case, in other words, cases that are similar in fact and in legal issue to your case and whose holdings address an issue presented in your case.

1. Primary Authority

Primary authority is law generated by a government body. Cases decided by any court are primary authority. Legislative enactments such as constitutions, statutes, ordinances, or charters are primary authorities. See Illustration 2-2. Administrative agency rules and decisions are primary authorities.

These authorities often are published chronologically. However, statutes are arranged by subject. Some sources of primary authorities will be more appropriate for your research than others. In some cases, primary authority is mandatory or binding authority because a government body must follow that authority when it makes future decisions. The words *mandatory* and *binding* are interchangeable.

ILLUSTRATION 2-2. Authorities and Finding Tools

Primary Authorities	Secondary Authorities	Finding Tools
Court decisions	Encyclopedias	Digests
Statutes	*American Law Reports*	Citators
Agency rules and regulations	Periodicals and law reviews	Updaters
Constitutions	Dictionaries	Annotated statutes
Charters	Thesauri	
Ordinances	Model codes	
Adopted pattern jury instructions	Unadopted uniform laws	
Court rules	Treatises	
State-adopted model code provisions	Restatement of the Law	
State-adopted uniform laws		

▼ How Do You Determine Whether a Case Is Mandatory or Binding?

To determine whether a case is mandatory or binding, you must consider the rank of the authorities. Follow the steps below.

1. Determine the jurisdiction that applies to your case. Then, look to the hierarchy of the courts within that jurisdiction.
2. Note what court decided the case you are reviewing.
3. Determine whether this is a court within the jurisdiction that applies to your case.
4. If the court is within the appropriate jurisdiction, you must determine the level of that court within the court system. Is it a trial court or an appellate court? Is it the highest court of the system? States often have rules that specify the effect of a court decision on other courts within the same system. In general, the lower courts in a system must follow the decisions of the highest court in the system. The rules concerning which courts must follow the decisions of the intermediate-tier courts vary by jurisdiction. Consult the rules for that jurisdiction.

An authority is mandatory only if it controls or shapes the law of a particular jurisdiction, for example, an opinion from a state appellate court or an applicable state statute.

An authority is persuasive when it is made by a court outside of a particular jurisdiction. For example, decisions of one state court are not binding on courts of other states. Decisions of the Arizona Supreme Court are mandatory or binding on the lower courts in Arizona, but these decisions are merely persuasive primary authority in Michigan.

A decision is also persuasive rather than mandatory if it is made by a court whose decisions according to the law do not bind other courts. For example, decisions of the federal trial courts do not have to be followed by other federal courts.

Persuasive authority can be invaluable in persuading a court. This is especially true in decisions concerning statutory interpretation that involve statutes that are identical. For example, Kansas and Ohio adopted the same comparative negligence statute at different times. Kansas courts faced challenges concerning the statutory language. The decisions were highly persuasive authority when Ohio courts faced similar challenges years later, particularly since it was likely that the Ohio legislators were aware of the Kansas interpretations when they adopted the Ohio statute.

PRACTICE POINTER

Use persuasive authority if you do not have primary authority on point. For statutory disputes, determine whether legislators would have been aware of the persuasive authority when the statute was adopted.

---

2. Secondary Authority

Another type of authority is **secondary authority.** Such authority is not generated by government bodies. Instead, secondary authority includes commentary of attorneys or other experts. Secondary authority is persuasive only, and it is never binding or mandatory. In general, an attorney would not base an argument to a court on a secondary authority.

Secondary sources are helpful in understanding an issue of law, in determining other issues, and in finding primary authorities. Sometimes secondary authorities help to interpret primary authority for you and the court. Secondary sources include treatises, Restatements of the Law, dictionaries, encyclopedias, legal periodicals, *American Law Reports*, books, and thesauri. See Illustration 2-2. Often these sources direct you to cases, statutes, and other primary authorities.

Some secondary authorities are more persuasive than others. Many Restatements and treatises are authoritative and can be noted in court documents and legal reports called memoranda addressed to attorneys. However, most secondary authorities should not be noted in these reports.

One type of secondary authority that is often confused with primary authorities is uniform codes. Many uniform codes exist throughout the country. These are suggested laws, often devised by experts. If a state adopts the uniform code in total or in part, its adopted statute is primary authority, but the recommended or uniform code remains as secondary authority. This, however, is often very persuasive secondary authority.

PRACTICE POINTER

If you have a primary authority on point, do not cite a secondary authority to make the same point.

PRACTICE POINTER

Secondary authorities are rarely cited in court documents. However, some secondary authorities carry significant persuasive weight, for example, commentaries to uniform laws.

---

3. Finding Tools

To find primary and secondary resources, often you need to consult **finding tools**, such as digests and citators. See Illustration 2-2. These finding tools are neither primary nor secondary authority. They should never be noted or cited in memoranda or court documents. Among the finding tools are **digests**, which are books containing case abstracts arranged according to publisher-assigned topics rather than in chronological order. **Annotated statutes** also include case abstracts written by the publishers. **Citators**, such as *Shepard's*®, provide you with listings of cases and some secondary authorities.

PRACTICE POINTER

Attorneys do not look favorably on paralegals who cite finding tools as authority.

---

4. Hybrid Sources of Authority

Hybrid sources of authority contain primary authorities, secondary authorities, regulations, cases, and finding tools. Hybrid sources of authority include loose-leaf services, form books, and proof of facts. These resources can be useful in finding multiple authorities. However, be certain that you distinguish the primary and secondary authorities and finding tools, and that in most cases you cite only the primary authorities.

5. Nonlegal Sources

You often must consult nonlegal sources, such as newspapers or corporate information statements. These sources are not authoritative. Never use nonlegal sources to determine the law that governs a case. However, they can assist you in your work. Sometimes it is necessary to cite these sources as relevant **factual authority** in a motion or a brief. These sources often provide insight into the purpose behind a court decision or the enactment of a law.

C. USE OF AUTHORITY OR SOURCES IN YOUR LEGAL WRITING

1. Essential Sources to Cite

Primary authority is the key type of authority you should use in any form of legal writing such as a legal memorandum (discussed in detail later in this book). As explained earlier, primary authority is the highest authority in the chain of command. In particular, you should use primary, binding authority for the jurisdiction in which your action will be filed or is pending. Primary, binding authority that is tailored to your case—that is, one that is similar in fact and legal issues to your case—is best. However, do not ignore primary, binding authority that does not support your client's case. If you have not found any primary, binding authority that matches your case facts or legal issues, then consider primary, persuasive authority that matches your case facts or legal issues. For example, if you are working on a case in the federal district court in Florida and you cannot find a U.S. Supreme Court or an Eleventh Circuit appellate court decision on point, you can use a case from the federal Second Circuit Court of Appeals if it has considered a similar case. If, however, you are writing a legal memorandum for an attorney, you should mention all primary, persuasive authorities, both for and against a particular case if you cannot find any primary, binding authorities. An attorney needs to know the cases that support his or her client's position as well as those that oppose it.

2. Valuable Sources to Cite

Primary, persuasive authorities are valuable sources to cite if you do not have primary, binding authority that is similar in fact and law to your case. However, some secondary authorities such as Restatements of Law or treatises are very persuasive and can be cited when you lack primary authority on point. When you cite these secondary authorities, you need to be careful to note, however, that you did not have any primary authority on point.

3. Sources Never to Cite

Do not cite digests, the annotations in secondary authorities, or the case abstracts listed in the annotated statutes. Citing these nonauthorities can result in serious consequences, including ethical violations. Nonlegal sources such as newspapers should not be cited to support a legal issue. Only cite these sources to support factual statements.

Checklist

1. Review all of your sources of authority.
2. Divide the sources into primary and secondary authorities and finding tools.
3. Make a list of all of the primary authorities.
4. Separate primary authorities that are applicable to the jurisdiction that applies in the case you are handling.
5. Make a ranking of those primary authorities—determine which are binding and which are merely persuasive. To rank these authorities, determine which authority is highest in the chain of command as explained in the hierarchy of authority section of this chapter. Consider which authority is most current and which authority is precedential in value rather than merely dicta.
6. Determine whether these binding authorities match your facts or legal issues.
7. Determine whether the primary persuasive authorities match your facts or legal issues.
8. Make a ranking of the secondary authorities and determine whether these match your facts or legal issues.
9. Start your analysis and written summary with the primary, binding authorities that match your facts and legal issues.
10. Next incorporate primary, persuasive authorities that match your facts and legal issues. However, you should use these authorities only if the primary, binding authority does not match your facts or legal issues in total.
11. Finally, consider incorporating secondary authorities into your writing if none of the primary authorities address your facts or legal issues.
12. Never cite a secondary authority when you have a primary binding authority on point.
13. Never cite a newspaper article or a finding tool to support a legal issue. Nonlegal sources such as newspapers should be cited only to support a factual issue.

IN-CLASS EXERCISE

FACTS

You are a paralegal in the state in which you live. You have been assigned to research whether an individual can bring an action in state court against a car dealer and the car manufacturer of a car that has been trouble-ridden since the individual purchased it eight months ago.

RESEARCH RESULTS

You have found a statute that explains lemon law actions in your state, two cases in your state that interpret the statute, a federal case that explains the lemon law's application in your state, a case from another state that explains the lemon law, an encyclopedia explanation of the statute, a periodical article in a bar journal about lemon law actions in your state, and a newspaper article that explains how to bring a lemon law action and what actions are barred.

DISCUSSION QUESTIONS FOR THE CLASS

a. What type of authority is the lemon law statute in your state?
b. What type of authority are the two cases from your state?
c. What type of authority is the case from another state?
d. What type of authority is the federal case?
e. What type of authority is the encyclopedia reference to the statute?
f. What type of authority is the periodical article?
g. What type of authority is the newspaper article?
h. Which, if any, authorities might be binding or mandatory authorities?
i. Which authorities might be noted in a memorandum to a court?

Determine whether the authorities are primary mandatory, primary persuasive, or secondary authorities, and rank authorities according to which authorities the students would use first, second, third, and so on, if at all.

CHAPTER SUMMARY

In this chapter, you learned that determining governing law involves examining jurisdiction and the hierarchy of authorities. You also learned how precedent and dicta influence governing law. As a researcher, your goal is to find cases that are similar to yours in fact and legal issue and whose holdings address an issue presented in your case. In reaching this goal, you first seek primary authorities because these authorities carry more weight with the courts than secondary authorities. Primary authorities include court decisions, statutes, court rules, constitutions, and administrative rules and regulations.

Some primary authorities are binding. If an authority is binding, a court must follow that authority. Other authorities are merely persuasive. Such authorities provide guidance to the courts and often are followed by the decision-making tribunal.

As you are researching, you often will refer to secondary authorities. Secondary authorities provide you with information to understand primary authorities. Generally, secondary authorities are commentaries prepared by experts in a particular field. These authorities often include citations to primary authorities. Secondary authorities are persuasive only. Therefore, you would rely on a primary authority rather than a secondary authority. Secondary authorities include encyclopedias, treatises, and legal periodicals.

Finding tools are designed to assist you in your research, but they are not considered authorities. These tools provide you with citations to primary and secondary authorities. Finding tools include annotated statutes, digests, and citators.

Finally, you learned how to incorporate these authorities into your legal writing. You learned that primary, binding authority is the best authority to use to support a legal proposition. Primary, persuasive and some secondary authority also may be cited. Finding tools and nonlegal sources should not be used to support a legal theory.

KEY TERMS

annotated statutes
binding authority
circuits
citators
conflicting authorities
dicta
digests
factual authority
finding tools
hierarchy of authorities

holding
hybrid sources of authority
jurisdiction
mandatory authority
persuasive authority
precedent
primary authority
secondary authority
stare decisis

EXERCISES

COURT SYSTEMS

Exercises

1. What is the highest court of your state? Where can you find this information on the Internet? Give a web site.
2. Within your state's court system, what type of authority are decisions made by the highest court named in question 1?
   a. primary binding
   b. primary persuasive
   c. secondary binding
   d. secondary persuasive
3. What is the name of the trial court of your state?
4. Are the trial court's decisions binding on the highest court of the state?
5. What is the highest court of the federal system of government?

6. Within the federal system of government, what type of authority are decisions made by the highest court named in question 5?
   a. primary binding
   b. primary persuasive
   c. secondary binding
   d. secondary persuasive
7. What is the name of the trial court of the federal government?
8. Are decisions of any federal trial court binding on any federal appellate court?
9. Are all federal appellate court decisions binding on every federal trial court? Why or why not?
10. Can state courts decide issues of federal law?
11. Can federal courts decide issues of state law?
12. What is primary authority?
13. What is binding or mandatory authority?
14. When would you use primary authority?

Research Strategy

15. Can the Arizona Legislature adopt a law that contradicts the U.S. Constitution?
16. Must the U.S. Circuit Court of Appeals for the Ninth Circuit follow a decision of the U.S. Supreme Court concerning a federal issue?
17. Must an Arkansas trial court follow a decision of the U.S. Supreme Court concerning an issue of federal law?
18. You are a paralegal assigned to research the components necessary to create a valid will in your state. List in order the types of authorities you would consult and why. Next, rank the authorities according to whether they are primary mandatory, primary persuasive, or secondary.
19. You are a paralegal who has just researched what constitutes a breach of contract in a case involving the delivery of dairy products in Wisconsin. Rank the following authorities and list whether each is a primary binding, primary persuasive, or secondary authority.
    a. a Wisconsin Supreme Court case involving a breach of contract dispute
    b. a Wisconsin statute that defines breach of contract
    c. a Wisconsin statute that defines the term *delivery* in a contract
    d. a Wisconsin trial court case involving a breach of contract dispute
    e. an Illinois Supreme Court case involving a breach of contract dispute
    f. a Uniform Commercial Code section concerning breach of contract. (The Wisconsin statute is derived in part from this section but does not adopt it in total.)
20. You are researching the question of whether a company that employs 50 individuals is an employer under the federal law regulating age discrimination in employment. Your case is pending in the federal district court in Toledo, Ohio. You learn that the definitions in the age discrimination statute were derived from those already in the sex discrimination statute.

Rank the following authorities and list whether each is a primary binding, primary persuasive, or secondary authority:

a. the federal age discrimination in employment statute that defines the term *employer*

b. the federal sex discrimination in employment statute that defines the term *employer*

c. a U.S. Supreme Court case that interprets the definition of *employer* contained in the federal age discrimination in employment statute

d. a U.S. Supreme Court case that interprets the definition of *employer* contained in the federal sex discrimination in employment statute

e. a decision of the Northern District Court of Ohio, Western Division, concerning the definition of *employer* under the federal age discrimination in employment statute

f. a law review article in the *University of Toledo Law Review* concerning the definition of *employer* contained in the federal age discrimination in employment statute

g. a section of an employment law treatise that explains the definition of *employer* under the federal age discrimination in employment statute

h. an Ohio Supreme Court case that explains the definition of *employer* under the federal age discrimination in employment statute

i. Which authorities would you use in a legal memorandum you are writing for an attorney and why?

21. You are asked to research the validity of a New York statute that bars high school students from wearing t-shirts bearing antigovernment slogans. Your case is pending in the state court of New York. Rank the following authorities and list whether each is a primary binding, primary persuasive, or secondary authority:

a. the New York statute in question

b. the U.S. Constitution's First Amendment regarding free speech

c. a U.S. Supreme Court case that prohibits states from banning the wearing of symbols by high school students because such a ban violates the U.S. Constitution

d. a case decided by the highest court in New York that holds that the statute is invalid

e. a California case involving an identical statute adopted in California that holds that the statute is valid

f. an encyclopedia entry that states that such bans are invalid

g. a newspaper article in *The National Law Journal* that predicts that the U.S. Supreme Court will invalidate the New York statute

h. Which authorities would you use in a legal memorandum you are writing for an attorney and why?

GETTING READY TO WRITE

CHAPTER OVERVIEW

Writing involves planning—the more planning, the more effective the written document. Legal writing has three components: prewriting (which includes researching and planning your written document), drafting, and revising. This chapter explains how to draft documents and how to revise your work so that it is written clearly and concisely. This chapter provides step-by-step techniques to use when preparing to write. You must systematically prepare to write by determining the purpose, audience, and organization of the document. Also, you must carefully revise your work product to tailor it precisely to the assignment, the client, and the facts. The focus of this chapter is the fundamentals of good writing. Specific tips are provided to improve your drafts.

A. WRITING GOALS AND HOW TO ACHIEVE THEM

The keys to writing well are **clarity** and **organization.** Your readers must understand what you are trying to convey to them. Whether you are writing a letter or a memorandum, your communication must be clear so that it can be understood. Often several proper formats, used at different times, will make your writing easier to read and understand.

▼ How Do You Plan Your Communication and Revise It?

You must think about what you want to say. Outline the communication. Next, write it using correct grammar and spelling, and most important, rewrite it several times. As you rewrite your letters and memos, you will always find that you can eliminate unnecessary words and legalese. Use simple words even though you know more elaborate ones. Doing so makes your writing inviting rather than pompous.

B. THE WRITING PROCESS

Follow a method or format when preparing to write to make the actual drafting process easier. Focus on the mechanics and components of the writing process rather than the finished product. The method that follows is a checklist to ensure thoroughness and to give you confidence in your newly acquired skills. The fundamental components of process writing are assessing the document's purpose and intended audience, drafting a detailed outline before writing, revising your findings into the categories of purpose and audience, and outlining and revising your work.

1. Preparing to Write: Purpose and Audience

▼ How Do You Complete the Research Process and Make the Transition to Writing?

Remember that what we plan as we prepare to write is as important as the final product. The more time you can put into the process, the better is the product. Spend at least 50 percent of the time budgeted for writing in the **prewriting stage.** However, time management is crucial with any assignment because time is money and knowing when to stop researching and when to begin writing is important. Therefore, when the project is assigned ask how much time you should spend on the project. What is the budget? A good clue as to when you have completed your research is when you do not retrieve any new information; the same sources keep appearing. Ask your law librarian or another paralegal to briefly review your research strategy and ask if there are any other avenues that he or she would have taken.

Take detailed notes and make careful citations to references for each source. Also, keep a complete list of all sources consulted, whether a statute, case, regulation, periodical article, or other source. Your list of sources consulted helps later on, when you may have to expand your research. You can then check the list to see if you already reviewed a source and to see if it was pertinent.

Shepardize or KeyCite any primary authority that you use in your memo to ensure that the authority, whether it is a case, statute, or regulation, is still good or valid law. Never start to write using a source of authority without Shepardizing or KeyCiting it first.

NET NOTE

llrx.com/columns/grammar10.htm has tips on word selection in legal writing.

---

a. Purpose

▼ What Is the Purpose of the Document?

When you sit down to write, begin by asking yourself: What is the **purpose** of the document that I am preparing? Because a legal document has a variety of goals (to inform, persuade, or advise), you must determine the document's intent before writing. The purpose determines the posture and the format of your work product. If the document is to inform the attorney as to all available law on a particular issue, it is neutral in tone and takes the form of an objective memo. If your goal is to convince another party that your position is correct, then the document may be in the form of a memo for the assigning attorney, a memo for the court, a trial or an appellate brief, and the tone will be persuasive. Sometimes a persuasive document takes the form of a letter that requests an individual or entity to act in a certain way. Examples of persuasive letters are demand letters requesting payment owed, or eviction letters demanding that a tenant vacate the premises. Sometimes you must convey an attorney's advice to a client. The document may then be in the form of a letter giving counsel, written as simply as possible, to be signed by the supervising attorney. Simplicity is best for a client who may not have a legal education. The purpose of the document determines its format and the rhetorical stance: objective, persuasive, or instructive.

NET NOTE

topics.law.cornell.edu/wex/legal_writing provides a brief overview of the types of legal writing.

---

b. Audience

▼ To Whom Are You Speaking?

As you prepare to write, determine carefully who the **audience**, or reader, is. Is the reader the assigning attorney? This is often the case when the project is the preparation of an office memo. The memo should be easy for the intended reader to understand; you should insert headings, if necessary, to guide the reader. If the document is intended for a court, then the reader will be a judge and opposing counsel, and your tone will be formal yet persuasive. The assertions or points that you want to prove should be clear and straightforward. The document should always be prepared using language that the reader can comprehend; this is also required when drafting client letters and demand letters.

PRACTICE POINTER

Ask the assigning attorney questions after you have reviewed the assignment, but before you begin to write, make sure that the purpose and audience are agreed upon.

---

2. Drafting a Detailed Outline

▼ How Do You Organize Your Ideas?

The next stage is to prepare an **outline** of whatever document you are writing. If it is an office memo, outline the issues and subissues of points that you want to articulate. Make sure that the outline flows logically. See if there are any gaps by reviewing your outline carefully. Organization is crucial to effective legal writing to ensure completeness. Having a complete outline also helps when you have to put your project down for a considerable period of time, or when you must work on more than one matter at a time and want to easily pick up where you left off.

Organize your research findings according to where they are pertinent in your outline. It is best to let your issues or assertions determine where the research should be placed rather than letting the sources determine the placement in the document. Never use your sources as your outline; rely on the issues.

3. Revision: The Final Part of the Process

PRACTICE POINTER

When revising, consult a dictionary to ensure that all of the words are properly spelled and used. Check a thesaurus to vary your terms.

Rewriting is a continuous part of the writing process and a vital final step. Reread the material after you have reviewed your word choices and eliminated unnecessary words. Rewriting may seem like a tedious waste of time, but it is one of the most important steps in preparing a well-written document.

Review all the steps you have taken in the prewriting stage. Ask yourself: Is the purpose of the document being prepared according to the assignment, and is it meeting the client's needs? Does the document clearly fulfill its goal of either informing, persuading, or advising? Do the language and format reflect the purpose?

Examine your intended audience. What language is appropriate for the intended reader? What level of sophistication is required? Ask yourself about voice (how it will sound), diction (word choice), and rhetoric (the way you use speech).

Review your outline. Check to see if the outline is well organized, logical, and flows smoothly. At this point, reexamine the issues or assertions that you want to include and make sure that the points are clearly discernible. Insert the appropriate research findings in the relevant place in the outline, as well as the necessary facts and the conclusions that you want to draw. Now you are ready to write. After you write the first draft, revise and pay attention to these details.

PRACTICE POINTER

Review documents in files to see the firm's writing style.

4. Example of Process Writing Techniques

Ms. Partner calls you into her office and asks you to prepare a client letter to Mrs. Jones advising her as to a course of action that she can take to rectify the problem of her mislabeled fur coat. The facts of the problem are as follows: Mrs. Jones bought a fur coat from John J. Furriers. The coat was labeled 100 percent raccoon. One day Mrs. Jones was smoking a cigarette and a hot ash fell on the coat while she was wearing it. The ash melted a hole in the coat. Mrs. Jones knew that fur burns, but acrylic melts.

First, what is the purpose of the document? The document's goal is to advise Mrs. Jones as to a course of action against the seller, John J. Furriers. The partner specified the document's form, a letter.

Next, you must examine your audience. Who is your reader? Is Mrs. Jones an attorney? Probably not. You can ask the attorney making the assignment for some background information about the client. This will help you tailor a document to the reader's precise needs. Mrs. Jones is a stock analyst. She is a sophisticated individual but she does not possess a legal education. The language used in the letter must be understandable to Mrs. Jones. The voice—how the letter sounds—should be instructive and advisory without being condescending. The diction, or word choice, should be simple; avoid legalese.

Now outline the points that you want to address in the letter. Begin by restating the facts as you know them. List the points.

1. The fur coat was mislabeled.
2. The seller misrepresented his product.
3. If the misrepresentation was intentional, there is the possibility of fraud.
4. Mrs. Jones would like to obtain a full refund for the coat that she purchased.
5. If a refund is not given in seven days, court action will proceed.

Insert your research findings, in general language, in the appropriate spot in the outline. In a client letter of this nature there is no need to cite to authority. Use the facts to draft a letter for the attorney to advise Mrs. Jones as to how she should proceed with the matter. Remember that an attorney must always review and sign any letter that you prepare that gives legal advice. Only an attorney may sign such a letter.

Revise all your prewriting steps by checking your purpose, audience, and outline once again. Now you are ready to write.

PRACTICE POINTER

Prewriting preparation is time well spent. Thoroughness and accuracy are so important, and attorneys have little patience for anything besides perfection. Careful note taking, outlining, and citing will provide not only an excellent start to a writing project but ample material if you are called on to discuss a project prior to its completion.

CHECKLIST

1. When you receive the problem
   a. Clarify the legal issues being researched.
   b. Determine the relevant jurisdiction.
   c. Determine the area of the law.
   d. Gather all the facts.
   e. Draft a statement of the issue or question that you are researching.
2. Introductory research
   a. Educate yourself in the area of the law.
   b. Consult a legal encyclopedia for a general overview to find major cases on point.
   c. Learn the relevant vocabulary.
   d. Note the major cases.
   e. Make an outline of the issues and subissues in your problem.
3. Process writing
   a. Purpose: Determine the purpose of the document. The document's goal is either to inform, to persuade, or to advise. Select the appropriate rhetorical stance and determine the format (office memo, court memo, brief, or letter).
   b. Audience: Find out who the reader or readers will be. Determine the language that is most comprehensible to the particular reader. Select an appropriate voice for the purpose, format, and reader. Note your diction.
   c. Outline: Outline the issues, assertions, or points that you want to include. Organize research findings according to the outline. Place facts in the appropriate spot and state conclusion.
   d. Revise: Review the purpose and the audience of the intended document and check your outline for appropriateness. Revise your outline to reflect any new knowledge, legal or factual. Reread the outline to ensure that it is complete and flows logically.

NET NOTE

A list of resources for legal writers is at www.ualr.edu/cmbarger/resources.htm.

CHAPTER SUMMARY

This chapter led you through the writing process. This will ensure thoroughness when planning and starting a writing project. Before writing, determine the purpose of your assignment. This will guide your writing. Also, determine the audience for your work. This will determine the style of your writing.

Carefully outline the document before writing and then revise the document by preparing an outline of the material that you prepared, an after-the-fact outline. Review the after-the-fact outline to make sure that it is logically organized and includes all points that the issues require to be addressed.

The time that you spend in the prewriting stage ensures a better work product that is produced more efficiently than one created by lunging into the writing process. Think about what you want to say, outline it, and write it using good grammar and correct spelling. Then rewrite and edit your work. Prewriting takes planning, but with the methodology outlined in this chapter you will be equipped to write.

KEY TERMS

audience   prewriting stage
clarity   purpose
organization   rewriting
outline

EXERCISES

PREPARING TO WRITE

1. Why would you use a process method for legal writing?
2. Why would you outline before you write as well as create an outline of your finished document?
3. Why is it important to determine the audience and purpose before writing?

PROCESS-WRITING EXERCISE

4. Read the following fact pattern and answer the questions.

Facts

John Clark comes to your firm with a question regarding the tax status of his residence. He has just been ordained as a United Methodist minister and will be receiving a housing allowance from First United Methodist Church, where he will be an assistant pastor. He wants to know if this housing allowance can be excluded from income on his tax return even though the residence is his own.

a. How would you phrase this issue if you were researching this problem?
b. What would be your research strategy?
c. Construct an outline of this problem.

5. The assignment partner requests that you draft a letter of your findings to Rev. Clark. List, in detail, the purpose, audience, and resulting outline of the letter.

6. How would the purpose, audience, and outline change if the assignment partner requests a memo concerning your research findings? Once again, how would the purpose, audience, and outline change if you are requested to prepare a court brief?

IN-CLASS EXERCISES

1. For this exercise, use a paper that you have already written.
   a. Examine the paper. What is the purpose and the audience?
   b. Extract an outline from the paper. Outline the ideas explained in the paper.
   c. Revise your outline to clarify your ideas.
2. Write a letter to a neighbor discussing the highlights of the past season.
   a. What is the audience and, consequently, the tone?
   b. Rewrite the letter to a government official. In the rewritten letter, express dissatisfaction with a service that is supposed to be provided by the local government and was not provided adequately during the past season. For example, in the letter to your neighbor, you write about the great snowfall during the winter. In the rewritten letter to a government official, you also write about the great snowfall, but also include how the locality failed to plow sufficiently. What is the purpose and audience of the letter to the government official?

CLEAR WRITING AND EDITING

CHAPTER OVERVIEW

The key to effective writing is clarity. Preparing a first draft of a document can be quite an undertaking, but that is only a start. You have not completed your project until you have carefully edited and revised your drafts at least once. This chapter provides you with guidance in editing and revising your documents and preparing them for clients, courts, and attorneys.

A. PURPOSE OF EDITING

Editing and revising are essential if you want to have well-drafted and organized documents. A well-drafted document is one in which your readers understand what you are trying to convey. Be clear and make it easy to read. Few documents are written well after one draft. Good writing entails rewriting. Each time you review your document and revise it, you improve its content and make it more understandable. **Editing** allows you to review your word choices, your grammar, your spelling, and your outline and organization of each sentence and paragraph, as well as the outline and organization of the entire document. It enables you to determine whether the document you wrote is clear and will be understood by your audience. Editing also provides you with the opportunity to enhance your work with additional thoughts and clarify your document by eliminating unnecessary words, ideas, and legalese.

B. PROCESS OF EDITING

The process of editing starts with a first draft and often ends after many more drafts. After you complete your first draft, you must proofread and edit your work. Consider each word you select. Review your overall outline and organization. Then review the outline and organization of each sentence and paragraph.

When you review your draft, you should read it as if you were reading it for the first time. Pretend that you are a stranger to the project and that you don't know anything about it. Ensure that it is understandable. If you have time, put the first draft aside for a day or two and then review it again. It will give you a fresh perspective.

Next, consider whether each part follows the next. The work should flow in a logical order. Consider whether the organization of the document or of any paragraphs or sentences should be revised. Question the structure and organization of each sentence and paragraph. Change passive voice sentences to active voice. For more discussion of passive and action voice, review this chapter, Section C-2, Voice.

Read your writing aloud. Do you notice anything is missing? Sometimes when you read your work aloud, you find that it is missing something needed to get you from point A to point B in the discussion. Add any such missing elements.

Note whether your writing contains transitions and easily flows from one section to the next. If it doesn't, revise it. Add transitional words, phrases, or sentences where necessary. **Transitions** help move readers from one sentence to the next and from one paragraph to the next.

Next, think about whether you can eliminate unnecessary words, a process called tightening or editing. Focus on your words. Change elaborate or unfamiliar words to simpler words—often those you used in grade school. Doing so makes your writing inviting rather than pompous. Make certain that your words provide the reader with a visual image of what you mean. Ensure that your words accurately convey your ideas. For additional information about word choice, see this chapter's Section C-1, Diction.

Review your grammar. Ensure that your punctuation is correct and that the elements of each sentence and paragraph are correct. Check your citation for errors, as well.

C. SPECIFIC ITEMS TO REVIEW WHILE EDITING

1. Diction

▼ What Is Diction?

Diction means choice of words when writing. Selecting the appropriate words to express your idea precisely is a skill that is developed over time. When you are revising a document, read it over to make sure that the words you selected convey your ideas precisely. Sometimes you must use a dictionary or thesaurus to assist you in selecting the best word.

Select concrete words that allow the readers to visualize what you are saying. Read the following example:

> He harmed one of his body parts in the device at issue in the case.

It is better to say:

> His arm was severed when the threshing machine stalled and he fell forward in front of the machine.

The second example is clearer because the reader knows what happened and to which body part it happened: The arm was severed. The second sentence also conveys that the device was a threshing machine and that it stalled, throwing the man forward.

▼ What Are Concrete Verbs?

Use **concrete verbs** that exactly describe the action taken. Read the following examples:

> The parties entered into an agreement on July 8, 2012.
> There was an agreement entered into on July 8, 2012.
> The parties agreed to the terms on July 8, 2012.

The last example is the best because it is the simplest and uses the word *agreed* as a verb rather than as a noun. It is the easiest sentence of the three to understand and to visualize.

The first two examples turn the verb *agree* into a noun, a process called **nominalization.** The following illustrates a second example:

> The parties entered into an agreement on November 15, 2012, to make a change in the purchase price of the original contract from $1,500 to $2,000.

It is better to say:

> The parties agreed to increase the original contract purchase price from $1,500 to $2,000.

In the second sentence, *entered into an agreement* becomes *agreed* and *to make a change* becomes *increase*. These changes eliminate the use of verbs as nouns.

Another example is as follows:

> The plaintiff made a statement to police that the defendant ran a red light before the crash.

It is better to say:

> The plaintiff told police that the defendant ran the red light before the crash.

or

> The plaintiff stated to police that the defendant ran the red light before the crash.

Select simpler words and make sentences short. Review the following example.

> Prior to 9/11, airport security was incomplete.

It is better to say:

> Before 9/11, airport security was lax.

Before is a simpler word than *prior to* and *lax* is more descriptive than *incomplete*.

Review these statements and determine which is clearer.

> The state driver's license bureau now requires a social security card as **verification** of a person's identity.

or

> The state driver's license bureau now requires a social security card as **proof** of a person's identity.

The second sentence is clearer. The use of the simple word *proof* rather than the pompous word *verification* makes the sentence easier to understand.

▼ How Do You Avoid Legalese or Legal Speak?

Avoid **legalese** or **legal speak.** What does this mean? Use plain English that your nonattorney clients would use. Consider your audience. Clear writing avoids using unnecessary legal words. For example, do not use the word *scienter* for *intent.* At the end of an affidavit, you often see the phrase *Further affiant sayeth not,* which means that the person signing the affidavit has nothing further to say. Because that should be clear without the legalistic phrase, skip the phrase and others like it that add nothing to your writing.

2. Voice

Voice is the tone of your document. In professional writing, the document's tone is formal. Selecting language that is not colloquial and avoiding slang are ways to ensure that the tone of the document is correct for the law firm or corporate legal department environment. Avoid anything that personalizes the contents. Never use the first person. Conjunctions like *can't* are more casual than *cannot.* When revising, be sensitive to the tone of your document; it should have the requisite formal voice.

▼ What Is the Difference Between Active Voice and Passive Voice?

Active voice is when the subject of the sentence is doing the action of the verb. Active voice emphasizes the actor. Active voice is the preferred voice because it is clearer, more concise, and more lively than passive voice.

Active voice: Ben hit a home run.
Sarah danced the tango.

Passive voice is when the subject of the sentence is being acted on. Although passive voice has its uses, it is generally wordier and not as strong as active voice.

Passive voice: The home run was hit by Ben.
The tango was danced by Sarah.

Often the word *by* is used in a passive voice sentence. When you see the word *by,* consider rewriting the sentence.

Passive example: Their initial quote for heat stamping equipment was rejected by Abbey.

Rewritten example: Abbey rejected their initial quote for heat stamping equipment.

The second example is clearer and more concise.

Passive voice, however, is sometimes acceptable. In some cases, the person or thing performing the action is unknown. For example:

Taxes were not deducted from her paychecks.
Jenna received health and life insurance benefits.

In other cases, the actor does not need to be mentioned because he or she is less important than the action. If you believe it advantageous to change the emphasis of the sentence from the person doing the action to the action, use passive voice. For example, if your client is the defendant in a proceeding and you do not want to emphasize her action, you would write a sentence in passive voice, as follows:

The action stems from a contract dispute in which goods were rejected by the defendant.

This sentence in active voice would emphasize the defendant, as follows:

The defendant rejected the goods, resulting in a contract dispute.

3. Paragraphs

A **paragraph** is a collection of statements that focus on the same general subject. Effective paragraphs have a unified purpose, a thesis or topic sentence, and transitions between sentences.

The **topic sentence** is generally the first sentence of a paragraph; it tells the reader the subject of the paragraph. This sentence also indicates that a new topic will be discussed. In legal writing, this sentence often introduces the issue or subissues that will be discussed within the paragraph.

You should use transitions to guide your reader from one paragraph to the next. Transitions tell the reader that the ideas follow from each other and are related. A transitional sentence ties two paragraphs together. Think of this sentence as a bridge. Whenever you start your new paragraph, think about how you will relate it to the previous paragraph.

4. Sentences

A **sentence** is a statement that conveys a single idea. It generally should be written in active voice and must include a subject and predicate. To avoid confusing your reader, do not place the subject too far from the verb. The focus of your sentence should be the idea you wish to convey. Do not make your readers work too hard to understand your sentence.

Be direct and to the point. Keep your sentences short, generally not more than 25 words. As with any rule, you may break this rule about sentence length, but be careful not to make your sentences too complex.

One common mistake in writing sentences is to use **a sentence fragment** or incomplete sentence.

Incomplete sentence: The extent of the employer's control and supervision over the worker.

Complete sentence: The court will consider the extent of the employer's control and supervision over the worker.

The first example is a sentence fragment. It is incomplete and is missing a verb. The second sentence is a complete thought. It contains both a subject and a verb.

Another common mistake in drafting a sentence is when two sentences are combined without punctuation or by using a comma only. That is a **run-on sentence**.

Incorrect: The attorneys waited outside, the court was about to make its decision.

Correct: The attorneys waited outside. The court was about to make its decision.

Incorrect: There were ten findings of fact in the opinion, they all favored the plaintiff.

Correct: There were ten findings of fact in the opinion. All favored the plaintiff.

5. Other Key Rules

Do not start your paragraph or sentence with a citation. Instead, start with the rule summarizing the cited authority.

Use quotations sparingly. Most often, you can paraphrase what a court decision or other authority states. Your words will convey the concept more clearly to the reader. Direct quotations that are used to convey an idea often are cluttered with unnecessary words or do not effectively explain a concept in the context of your use of the quotation. An added bonus for you when you paraphrase a court decision or other authority is that you are forced to analyze the language of the authority. This ensures that you understand the concepts presented.

Review the following paragraph. Note that unnecessary words are located in parentheses.

The plaintiff (made a statement) that in his (own) opinion, during (the course of) (a period of) a year, the defendant (completely) destroyed the furniture the plaintiff hired the defendant to restore.

The defendant failed to warn the plaintiff (in advance) that he couldn't restore the piece (properly) and that the price of the work originally estimated (roughly) at $600 would now cost her $2200.

None of the words in parentheses add anything to the reader's understanding of the sentences or paragraph. The phrase *made a statement* should be shortened to *stated.* When you read your paragraphs, review each word and determine whether it adds to the sentence. If not, delete it.

CHECKLIST

1. Does the material make sense?
2. Do the words accurately convey what happened?
3. Would another word more accurately convey your intended meaning?
4. Can the reader visualize what occurred?
5. Is it logical?
6. Should the organization of the piece be changed?
7. Does one paragraph flow into the other?
8. Does one sentence follow from the next?
9. Should the paragraphs be rearranged?
10. Should the organization of any sentence be changed?
11. Are there any gaps in the sentence?
12. Review your voice.
13. Is the voice consistent?
14. Is the voice the intended voice?
15. Review each word to ensure that it conveys what you intend to say.
16. Can and should you eliminate passive voice?
17. Be certain the verbs are concrete.
18. Check for nominalizations.
19. Are there any punctuation errors?
20. Are any words misspelled?
21. Are there any typographical errors?
22. Are there any citation errors?
23. Eliminate any legalese.

CHAPTER SUMMARY

This chapter led you through the editing process generally and then more specifically. It outlined essential items to check during your editing process.

Choose your words carefully. Select concrete verbs and avoid legalese. Most often, use active voice in which the subject of the sentence is doing the action of the verb.

Make sure your paragraphs focus on a single subject or aspect of a subject and use topic and transition sentences. Use full sentences that are direct and convey the idea you intend.

Use quotations sparingly to effectively convey your messages.

KEY TERMS

active voice	passive voice
concrete verbs	run-on sentence
diction	sentence
editing	sentence fragment
legal speak	topic sentence
legalese	transitions
nominalization	voice
paragraph	

EXERCISES

Eliminate the unnecessary words from the following statements:

1. At the time when the parties entered into the agreement of purchase and sale it is important to note that neither of them had knowledge of contents of the dresser drawer. Because of the fact that previous to the contract the seller did not own the dresser and the seller's mother had not had many valuable pieces of jewelry despite having a large income, the seller had made the assumption that the dresser did not contain anything. Due to the fact that the seller had made a statement to the buyer of the fact that his mother did not own any jewelry in the buyer's thinking, he had no purpose to make any further investigation or inspection of the drawers as he might otherwise have considered making. For these reasons, there was no provision in the contract for an upward modification in the payment to be made by the buyer to the seller in the event that the dresser drawer later proved to be filled with jewels.

2. The police report said that Mr. Harris had a blood alcohol level of 1.7 based on an on-site blood alcohol test and states further that there were swerve marks on the street. The report also stated that there were no brake marks and that the driver was cited by the officer for drunk driving.

3. The personnel manager did all of the hiring and firing of the restaurant and golf course and the part-time accountant manages all bookkeeping and tax work for the restaurant and golf course.

4. Candy Graham who did not have an employment contract was, despite her freedom to set her own hours and work from her own home, also an employee.

5. Which is the best sentence? Why?
   a. A modification to the contract occurred on January 28, 2012.
   b. There was a modification of the contract January 28, 2012.
   c. Harry and Morgan modified their contract on January 28, 2012.

TIGHTENING

6. At approximately 7:30 P.M. on May 4, 2012, the plaintiff, Lidia Gregory, was weeding the front garden at her home at 2088 Vista Drive in Phoenix. She

was about five feet from the street. The children also were playing in the front yard which was near the street.

7. Based on a blood alcohol test done at the scene of the accident, it was determined that Ronnie Walden was intoxicated.

8. The day the accident occurred it was very clear and had not rained to make the road slick.

9. The issue is whether or not it is a nuisance.

10. The U.S. Supreme Court has nine fine justices Ruth Bader Ginsburg is one of the most talented.

11. Deciding thousands of cases. The U.S. district courts are among the busiest courts.

SCREENING FOR LEGALESE—SAY IT IN ENGLISH, PLEASE

12. In the aforementioned case, the funeral home was not found to be a nuisance because the court held that the funeral home in question was "reasonably located on the outskirts of the city."

13. Now comes the plaintiff, by and through her attorney, causes this complaint to be filed with the court.

14. Further affiant sayest not.

15. The party of the first part claims that the party of the second part said that he wanted to cause her to go out of business.

ACTIVE AND PASSIVE EXERCISES

16. Two businesses are owned by Ned and Wally Maine and they are being sued in federal court by two former workers for sex discrimination.

17. Cammy Ashton's office supplies and office were provided by Whole In One.

18. The funeral home was controlled by William Halsey and owned jointly by Halsey and Ivy Courier.

WRITING BASICS

CHAPTER OVERVIEW

This chapter reinforces grammar concepts and focuses on problem areas. It provides concrete examples of grammatically correct and incorrect sentences and explains the difference. Because it cannot address all points of grammar that students need to know, it suggests other grammar resources for your consideration.

A. PUNCTUATION

The punctuation of a sentence, especially the placement of a comma, can change the meaning of that sentence. Therefore, you must carefully place each punctuation mark. The following provides you with some basic rules for checking your punctuation placement.

1. Commas

Commas tell a reader to pause. Use commas to separate a series of items. For example:

Wally ran to the school, the store, the baseball field, and then home.

Commas also are used to set apart parenthetical phrases. In such a situation, commas should be used in pairs.

The defendant, George K. Dwyer, filed an answer to the complaint.

The name *George K. Dwyer* is parenthetical because the meaning of the sentence would not be changed if the name was omitted. In contrast, read the following examples:

Judges who take bribes should be indicted.

Judges, who take bribes, should be indicted.

In these examples, the phrase *who take bribes* is not parenthetical. If it was omitted, the sentence would say, "judges should be indicted." The phrase *who take bribes* must be part of the sentence to convey the correct meaning. Therefore, it is not parenthetical, and the commas should be omitted.

Place commas around unnecessary words or phrases. For example, a client has one child, William, and wants to name him as the executor of her estate. In a document to name him as executor, you could use either of the following sentences and the meaning would not be altered.

I name my son, William, as the executor of my estate.

I name my son as the executor of my estate.

Do not place commas around words or phrases that are necessary in order to understand a sentence.

In the next example, your client has two sons, William and Randall. She wants William to be the executor of the estate. The document should read as follows:

I name my son William as the executor of my estate.

The following sentence would be incorrect:

I name my son, William, as the executor of my estate.

2. Special Comma Rules

Commas separate a year from the date.

The plaintiff and the defendant agreed to the settlement on November 15, 2011.

Commas also set off the date from a specific reference to a day of the week.

The judge decided the summary judgment motion on Monday, November 7, 2011.

Commas separate a proper name from a title that follows it.

The plaintiff sued RAM Enterprises and Samuel Harris, company president.

Commas and periods should always appear inside quotation marks. This rule is often mistakenly broken.

"But I wasn't in Toledo on the night of the murder," the defendant protested. "I was in Scottsdale with my elderly mother."

3. Semicolons

Semicolons are similar to commas because they tell a reader to pause and they break apart thoughts. Semicolons are used to separate two independent sentences.

Two sentences: The paralegal's responsibilities are broad. They include summarization of depositions.
One sentence: The paralegal's responsibilities are broad; they include summarization of depositions.

Semicolons separate clauses of a compound sentence when an adverbial conjunction joins the two.

The defendants presented a good case; however, they lost.

Semicolons are used to separate phrases in a list.

The committee members were Robert Harris, vice president of Harris Enterprises; Edna Williams, owner of Walworth Products; Barbara Halley, an attorney; and Benjamin Marcus, an accountant.

4. Colons

Colons are marks of introduction: what follow are explanations, conclusions, amplifications, lists or series, or quotations. A colon is always preceded by a main clause, one that can stand alone as a sentence. A main clause may or may not follow a colon.

> Help was on the way: Someone had called the police.
>
> Sandra had two assignments: a five-page paper and a book report.
>
> The mayor stepped to the podium: "I regretfully must submit my resignation."

Colons should appear only at the end of a main clause. They should never directly follow a verb or a preposition.

Incorrect: The hours of the museum are: 10:00 A.M. to 6:00 P.M.

Correct: The hours of the museum are 10:00 A.M. to 6:00 P.M.

Incorrect: Marc loved many sports, such as: soccer, tennis, and softball.

Correct: Marc loved many sports, such as soccer, tennis, and softball.

As with any punctuation mark, use colons only when they best serve your writing purpose. Do not overuse them.

5. Parentheses

Parentheses tell the reader that the idea is an afterthought or is outside the main idea of a sentence.

> The tort involved a banana peel (the classic culprit) and a crowded grocery store.

Use parentheses infrequently because they tend to break the flow of the sentence.

6. Double Quotation Marks

These marks enclose direct quotations.

> The judge said, "The trial date will not be continued."

Note that the first word of the quotation should be capitalized if it is a complete sentence.

7. Single Quotation Marks

These marks are used to define a quotation within a quotation.

> The client told the lawyer, "My boss said, 'You cannot be a good accountant and be a good mother,' and then he fired me."

If you end a quotation with quoted words, you place a single quotation mark and follow it with a double quotation mark.

> The witness testified, "The robber said, 'Give me all your money.'"

8. Apostrophes

An apostrophe replaces letters that are omitted in contractions.

> He's the defendant.

He's replaces *he is.* It also is used with an *s* to indicate the possessive case.

> The defendant's car struck the plaintiff.

When a noun ends in an *s,* the possessive case is indicated with only an apostrophe.

> The attorneys' clerks researched the applicable law.

To indicate a possessive for one item that two people share, use the apostrophe next to the name of the last person mentioned.

> Ben and Sarah's motion is sound.

However, use an apostrophe after each name if the item is not shared. If Ben has a motion and Sarah also has a motion, the sentence should read as follows:

> Ben's and Sarah's motions are sound.

A common mistake is for a writer to use *it's* when writing about possession. *It's,* however, is a contraction for *it is.*

Finally, **apostrophes** are used to indicate plurals for numbers or letters.

> The attorney told the defendant to watch his p's and q's in the courtroom.

B. MODIFIERS

Modifiers provide a description about a subject, a verb, or an object in your sentence. If you misplace a modifier, you might confuse your reader or convey an incorrect message. A modifier should be placed in proximity to the subject, verb, or object it modifies.

Incorrect: Deadlocked for more than two days, the judge asked the jury to continue to deliberate.

Correct: The jury had been deadlocked for two days. Nonetheless, the judge asked the jury to continue to deliberate.

In the first example, the phrase *deadlocked for more than two days* incorrectly modifies the judge rather than the jury. This is a dangling modifier.

C. PARALLEL CONSTRUCTION

Parallel construction is when you make each of the phrases within your sentence follow the same grammatical pattern or number. A plural subject must have a plural verb. A singular subject must have a singular verb. You also must use parallel tenses when you are listing a series of activities. A parallel grammatical pattern makes your writing balanced.

Incorrect: The paralegal association set the following goals: recruitment of new members, educating the community, and improvement of paralegal work conditions.

Correct: The paralegal association set the following goals: recruitment of new members, education of the community, and improvement of paralegal work conditions.

In the correct example, the words *recruitment, education,* and *improvement* are parallel.

D. SUBJECT AND VERB AGREEMENT

Subject and verb agreement, so essential to proper sentence construction, causes great confusion for many writers. The following are sample situations in which errors are most often made. You must use plural pronouns and verbs when the subjects are plural.

Incorrect: Software Developments Inc. sent Cheryl Faith, a company sales representative, and Nicholas Tallis, their plant manager, to Bailey's plant.

Correct: Software Developments Inc. sent Cheryl Faith, a company sales representative, and Nicholas Tallis, its plant manager, to Bailey's plant.

The second example is correct because *Software Developments Inc.* is a singular subject; therefore, the pronoun before *plant manager* should be the singular possessive *its* rather than *their*.

Incorrect: To assert the attorney-client privilege, the claimant must show that the statements were made in confidence and was made to an attorney for the purpose of obtaining legal advice.

Correct: To assert the attorney-client privilege, the claimant must show that the statements were made in confidence and were made to an attorney for the purpose of obtaining legal advice.

The second example is correct because the verbs must be plural when they have a plural noun. In this example, the word *statements* should have a plural verb.

If you have a singular subject, then each of the descriptive pronouns in the sentence should be singular.

Incorrect: To receive this protection in the corporate setting, an individual must show that they were a decision-making employee.

Correct: To receive this protection in the corporate setting, an individual must show that he or she was a decision-making employee.

Collective nouns such as *jury, court, committee,* and *group* often pose a problem for writers. They take a singular verb because they are considered one unit. For example, *jury* is considered one unit; it refers to the group, not to individual jurors.

Incorrect: The jury were to eat lunch at noon.

Correct: The jury was to eat lunch at noon.

Compound subjects also cause confusion. Subjects joined by the word *and* usually use a plural verb, regardless of whether any or all of the individual subject are singular.

Incorrect: The attorney and the paralegal was available for the client.

Correct: The attorney and the paralegal were available for the client.

When a compound subject is preceded by *each* or *every*, the verb is usually singular.

Incorrect: Each attorney and paralegal in the room have access to the library.

Correct: Each attorney and paralegal in the room has access to the library.

When a compound subject is joined by *or* or *nor*, it takes a singular verb if each subject is singular. It takes a plural verb if each subject is plural. If one subject is singular and the other is plural, the verb follows the closest subject.

Subjects singular: An apple or an orange is my favorite snack.

Subjects plural: Apples or oranges are my favorite snacks.

Subjects singular and plural: Neither the mother nor the children were happy.

To avoid awkwardness, place the plural noun closest to the verb so that the verb is plural.

Awkward: Neither the dogs nor the cat was anywhere in sight.

Revised: Neither the cat nor the dogs were anywhere in sight.

Indefinite pronouns may also throw up roadblocks for writers. Indefinite pronouns are those that do not refer to a specific person or thing. Some common indefinite pronouns are

all	nobody
any	none
anyone	nothing
each	one
either	some
everyone	something

Most indefinite pronouns refer to singular subjects and therefore take a singular verb.

Incorrect: Everyone are free to go. Each of the stores were open on Sunday.

Correct: Everyone is free to go. Each of the stores was open on Sunday.

Some indefinite pronouns (all, any, none, some) may take either a singular or plural verb depending on the meaning of the word to which they refer.

Singular: All of the library was quiet. (The library was quiet.)

Plural: All of the paralegals were researching the case. (The paralegals were researching the case.)

E. RUN-ON SENTENCES

A **run-on sentence** is one in which two separate sentences are connected by using a comma or are sentences without punctuation. Be careful not to use commas to divide run-on sentences. The first example below should be two separate sentences.

Incorrect: Tildy's role is merely advisory, although she might be asked to supply facts about the spill, her opinion probably would not form the basis of any final decision.

Correct: Tildy's role is merely advisory. Although she might be asked to supply facts about the spill, her opinion probably would not form the basis of any final decision.

In the second example, the two sentences are correctly separated with a period. You also could use a semicolon to fix the sentence. For some run-on sentences, you could divide the sentences with a comma and a conjunction such as *and*. In the above example, that solution would not cure the problem because the second sentence is too long.

F. SENTENCE FRAGMENTS

A **sentence fragment** is a piece of a sentence. It is an incomplete statement as it lacks either a subject or a verb.

Incorrect: The judge presiding over the case.

Correct: The judge was presiding over the case.

Check to see if a sentence has a verb and a subject. If one is missing, add it.

Incorrect: A case on point.

Correct: The attorney cited a case on point.

G. THAT AND WHICH

Whether to use that or which depends on whether the clause that follows is essential to convey the meaning of the senses. If the clause cannot be omitted, use *that*. If the clause can be omitted and the sentence meaning will not change, then use *which*. As stated earlier, a clause that can be omitted or that contains superfluous information is set off with commas. A clause that is essential should not be surrounded by commas.

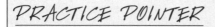

PRACTICE POINTER

Consult these books for additional guidance:

The Elements of Style by William Strunk, Jr., and E.B. White

The Careful Writer: A Modern Guide to English Usage by Theodore Bernstein

NET NOTE

Strunk and White is available online at www.bartleby.com.

CHAPTER SUMMARY

This chapter reviewed basic grammar rules concerning punctuation, modifiers, parallel construction, and subject-verb agreement. It emphasized the importance correct grammar plays in legal writing by demonstrating how errors like incorrect punctuation, misplaced modifiers, and faulty subject-verb agreement can affect meaning.

KEY TERMS

apostrophes   modifiers
collective nouns   parallel construction
colons   parentheses
commas   run-on sentences
compound subjects   semicolons
indefinite pronouns   sentence fragments

EXERCISES

Edit the following sentences. Name the grammar mistake in each sentence (e.g., misplaced modifier, faulty parallelism, and so forth). Then correct the error by rewriting the sentence.

1. At a time when many law firms and corporations are eliminating jobs for the purpose of elimination from the budget excess expenditures, paralegals may become more of an asset.

2. Because of the fact that paralegals' time is charged at lower rates, paralegals may be employed by law firms and corporations to perform tasks previously performed by lawyers.

3. With specificity, paralegals may be asked to perform legal research of case and statutory materials in the event that a client requests an answer to a problem of a legal nature and is concerned about saving money.

4. In the situation where a paralegal is well trained, that paralegal can be asked by an attorney to perform legal research for the purpose of determining a response to the client's question.

5. With regard to ethical considerations, paralegals can perform legal research under the supervision of an attorney.

6. Subsequent to the research, however, the attorney must be the person who renders the legal opinions that need to be made, the reason being that a paralegal cannot provide legal advice.

7. It is important to note that some states are considering allowing paralegals to practice independently.

8. Try this schedule; shower, eat breakfast, drive to the train, go to work, and come home.

9. There are only one hour and thirty-five minutes left to voir dire, the judge stated.

10. Among the defendants was Craig Fisher, David Michaels, and Mitchell White.

11. The prosecutor will attempt to within the course of the trial persuade you that the defendant committed the crime.

12. The foreman, as well as half of the jury, were late for the afternoon court session.

13. Every one of the councilmen we have named to the commission want to serve.

14. The heart of a trial are the witnesses.

15. None of the players were willing to sign contracts.

16. The substance of Walter Mondale's speeches is more similar to Jimmy Carter.

17. The house was vacated by the tenants.

18. The judge said to the jurors, "please refrain from discussing the case."

19. Four of the five jurors were men (These were Steer, Halsey, Grodsky, and Molitor.).

20. In her testimony, the witness said she remembered that the defendant asked her "Do you have an aspirin"?

21. These modems are shared with the other subscribers, so the more people on the connection the slower.

22. Working at a law firm from 8:30 A.M. to 5 P.M. handling high-level paralegal work may seem ideal, especially if you rarely work weekends.

23. The National Association of Paralegals said 12 percent of the law firms responded to their survey.

24. Mrs. Newman, at first thought her son, Patrick, was dead because of the amount of blood and broken bones that surrounded the car.

25. The extent of the employer's control and supervision over the worker, including directions on scheduling and performance of work.

26. In the line up the man which was wearing a red shirt committed the crime.

27. The judge based her decision on the case which had a similar set of facts.

28. The juror in green.

29. The judges's clerks draft opinions.

30. Law clerks Robert and Karen each wrote a motion. Robert and Karen's motions were excellent.

CASE BRIEFING AND ANALYSIS

CHAPTER OVERVIEW

This chapter teaches you a skill called case briefing. It introduces you to each of the components of a case brief: the issue, the holding, the facts, the rationale or reasoning, and the disposition. This chapter also teaches you how to use cases to perform legal analysis. It also introduces you to the concept of dicta. You will learn what to include in each section of the brief and how to skillfully draft the brief.

Case briefing is a skill that you must master to effectively record your research results and analyze a case. Often attorneys will ask you to summarize a case in the form of a case brief. The key to a good brief is that it must be usable. You must be able to return to the brief months after you have prepared it and still be able to quickly understand the facts, the issues, the holdings, and the reasoning of the court.

A good case brief can be done in a variety of ways. Always ask an attorney if he or she has a preference. If not, you should consider the method discussed in this chapter.

A. PURPOSE OF A CASE BRIEF

The goal in writing a **case brief** is to summarize a court decision. A well-drafted brief saves you time because you do not have to reread the original decision to understand its significance. You are able to review the brief to obtain any necessary information. The next goal in briefing a case is to put the components of a decision in a uniform format. This is why we have specified eight set categories for a brief: citation, procedural facts, issues, holding, facts, rationale, dicta, and disposition. The rationale contains the basis for the judge's opinion. The judge relies on the relevant legal rule to support her holding. The legal rule is the test, principle, or standard set down in prior opinions. However, many attorneys use their own uniform format, and sometimes that format will depend on why you are briefing a case.

Sometimes you must brief cases in response to a particular legal issue that you are researching. Sometimes you must brief cases just to summarize decisions.

Remember that a brief is a case summary in a uniform format with established categories of information. The set categories make it easier to compare and contrast decisions. Also, this enables you to see how a case supports a client's problem.

B. DIAGRAM OF A DECISION

Before you begin to write your brief, read the case thoroughly several times. See Illustration 6-1. Consider the questions the court was asked to decide. Determine the parties in the action and what each party is seeking. Sometimes this is complicated, and it helps to draw a diagram of the parties. For example, when the parties are involved in a three-way dispute such as a cross-claim, it might take some time to determine what each party is seeking. Make a column for each party in which you list an issue raised and a remedy sought. After you have read the case, you are ready to write the case brief.

Write the brief in your own words and paraphrase rather than quote a court's statements unless the statements are well phrased, concise,

ILLUSTRATION 6-1.   Sample Case, *Seymour v. Armstrong*

Westlaw.

64 P. 612
62 Kan. 720
(Cite as: 64 P. 612)   ①

Supreme Court of Kansas.

SEYMOUR   ②
v.
ARMSTRONG et al.

April 6, 1901   ③

Syllabus by the Court.

1. A contract may originate in an advertisement or offer addressed to the public generally, and, if the offer be accepted by any one in good faith, without qualifications or conditions, it will be sufficient to convert the offer into a binding obligation.   ④

2. If the acceptor affixes conditions to his acceptance not comprehended in the proposal, there can be no agreement without the assent of the proposer to such conditions.

3. If persons carrying on a trade or business give to words and phrases a technical or peculiar meaning, they will be presumed to have contracted with reference to such meaning or usage, unless the contrary appears.

4. Where a term employed in a written contract has a meaning different from the ordinary meaning when used in connection with a trade or business, evidence is admissible to show such meaning, and the sense in which it was used by the parties.

Error from court of appeals, Northern department, Eastern division.

Action by T. F. Seymour against Armstrong & Kassebaum. Judgment for defendants was affirmed by the court of appeals (61 Pac. 675), and plaintiff brings error. Affirmed.

West Headnotes

⑤ Contracts ☞18
95k18 Most Cited Cases

A contract may originate in an advertisement or offer addressed to the public generally, and, if the offer be accepted by any one in good faith, without qualifications or conditions, it will be sufficient to convert the offer into a binding obligation.

Contracts ☞23
95k23 Most Cited Cases

Where the acceptor affixes conditions to his acceptance not

comprehended in the proposal, there can be no agreement without the assent of the proposer to such conditions.

Contracts ☞175(1)
95k175(1) Most Cited Cases

Where persons carrying on a trade or business give to words and phrases a technical or peculiar meaning, they will be presumed to have contracted with reference to such meaning or usage, unless the contrary appears.

Evidence ☞456
157k456 Most Cited Cases

Where a term employed in a written contract has a meaning different from the ordinary meaning when used in connection with a trade or business, evidence is admissible to show such meaning, and the sense in which it was used by the parties.
*612 J. A. Rosen and David Martin, for plaintiff in error.

Isenhart & Alexander, for defendants in error.

JOHNSTON, J.   ⑥

This was an action to recover damages for the breach of an ⑦ alleged contract. On February 15, 1896, Armstrong & Kassebaum, commission merchants of Topeka, inserted an advertisement in a weekly newspaper, which, among other things, contained the following proposition: "We will pay 10 1/2 c., net Topeka, for all fresh eggs shipped us to arrive here by February 22. Acceptance of our bid with number of cases stated to be sent by February 20th." On February 20, ⑧ 1896, T. F. Seymour, a rival commission merchant of Topeka, sent the following note to Armstrong & Kassebaum

1. Citation
2. Case name
3. Date of decision
4. Syllabus by court
5. West key Numbers and Headnotes
(written by West editors and not
part of the opinion)
6. Judge's name authoring the opinion
7. Opinion
8. Facts

business of Armstrong & Kassebaum, sealed up, and then pushed a short distance over to their business house. They

Continues

ILLUSTRATION 6-1.   Continued

Westlaw.

64 P. 612
62 Kan. 720
(Cite as: 64 P. 612)

refused to receive the eggs, and Seymour shipped them to Philadelphia, where they were sold for $391.83 less than they would have brought at the price named in Seymour's note of acceptance. For this amount the present action was brought, and the plaintiff is entitled to recover if the defendants' offer on eggs was unconditionally accepted. At **(9)** the trial a verdict was returned in favor of the defendants, and the result of the general finding is that the pretended acceptance of Seymour was not unconditional, and that no contract was, in fact, made between him and the defendants.

(11A) Did the negotiations between the parties result in a contract? A contract may originate in an advertisement addressed to the public generally, and, if the proposal be accepted by any one in good faith, without qualifications or conditions, the contract is complete. The fact that there was no limit as to **(10)** number or quantity of eggs in the offer did not prevent an acceptance. The number or quantity was left to the determination of the acceptor, and an unconditional acceptance naming any reasonable number or quantity is sufficient to convert the offer into a binding obligation. It is **(12A)** essential, however, that the minds of the contracting parties should come to the point of agreement,-- that the offer and acceptance should coincide; and, if they do not correspond in every material respect, there is no acceptance or completed contract. In our view, the so-called "acceptance" of the plaintiff is not absolute and unconditional. It affixed conditions not comprehended in the proposal, and there could be no agreement without the assent of the proposer to such conditions. It is true, the plaintiff agreed to furnish **(10)** eggs at 10 1/2 cents per dozen, but his acceptance required the defendant to pay 15 cents each for the cases in which the eggs were packed, or to return the cases, or new ones in place of them. It appears from the record that according to the usages of the business the cases go with the eggs, as was done in this case.

One of the grounds of complaint is that the court erred in **(11B)** admitting testimony as to the sense in which the word "net" was used in the negotiations between the parties, and in submitting to the jury the question of whether the offer of the defendants was accepted. The plaintiff is hardly in a position to question the propriety of receiving evidence as to the meaning of the word "net," used in the offer and acceptance. *613 He was the first to open an inquiry, and to bring out testimony as to what was meant by the term when used in connection with a sale of eggs. Aside from that consideration, the term appears to have a meaning in connection with the business different from the ordinary meaning, and in such case evidence of the meaning given by usage of the trade or business is admissible. If persons **(12B)** carrying on a particular trade or business give to words or phrases a technical or peculiar meaning, they will be

presumed to contract with reference to the usage, unless the contrary appears. There was abundant evidence to show that the use of the word "net," according to the usage of the business, includes the cases of eggs like the one in question. The witnesses stated that it means a price clear to the purchaser without commissions, cartage, or any charge for the cases. The finding of the jury, in effect, is that it was understood and agreed that the cases went with and were included in the price quoted for the eggs, and the acceptance, therefore, did not correspond with the offer, nor complete the contract. We think that under the circumstances parol testimony of the sense in which the terms were used, and as to what the parties intended by them, was properly received, and that the court properly charged the jury as to the elements entering into a contract. Cosper v. Nesbit, 45 Kan. 457, 25 Pac. 866. Others of the instructions are criticised, but we find nothing substantial in any of the objections made nor in any of the grounds assigned for reversal. The judgment of the court of appeals and the district court will be affirmed.

All the justices concurring **(13)**   **12A+B**

64 P. 612, 62 Kan. 720

END OF DOCUMENT

> **9. Procedure**
> **10. Rationale or reasoning**
> **11A. Issue 1**
> **11B. Issue 2**
> **12A. Holding 1**
> **12B. Holding 2**
> **13. Disposition**

Reprinted with permission of Thomson Reuters/West.

and understandable. Paraphrasing helps you analyze a case and allows you to understand the brief quickly when you return to it later. Also, paraphrasing cases helps when you are writing about an opinion in a memo. The memo will read more smoothly if you use your own voice when you import the information from case brief rather than using quoted language from the opinion.

C. ANATOMY OF A CASE BRIEF

Because a brief is a summary of a decision in a uniform format, there are set categories. You should label the remaining sections of the brief: citation, procedural history or procedure, issue, holding, rationale (which includes the legal rule or standard), dicta (if it exists in the case), and disposition.

1. Citation

The case brief starts with a **case citation**, which allows you to find the case at a later date. First, note the name of the case, which is generally found at the top of the page. Then add the case citation or docket number of the case. See Illustration 6-2. Be sure to include the date of the decision and the name of the deciding court. Next, you might want to make a note concerning whether the decision is primary binding or primary persuasive authority. (For more information about binding and persuasive authority, see Chapter 2.) Follow either *Bluebook* or *ALWD* rules for case citation format.

NET NOTE

Important tips for briefing cases are at http://cjed.com/brief.htm.

PRACTICE POINTER

Obtain all of the citation information when you are using the reporter or have accessed the case online. Once you record all of the citation information in the brief, you will not have to revisit the decision later to get the cite information.

ILLUSTRATION 6-2.   Sample Case, *King v. Miller*

KING v. MILLER
1000 E.R. 108 (Karen Ct. App. 1998)

Evelyn King, an insurance agent who worked for the defendant, Miller Company, filed a lawsuit claiming that the defendant discriminated against her on the basis of her sex in violation of Title VII, 42 U.S.C. §2000e et seq. Upon a motion for summary judgment, the district court granted the motion in favor of Miller. The district court found that King was not an employee of the defendant. She did not work in a manner consistent with an employee. The court said that King was an independent contractor. As an independent contractor, her discrimination claim was outside the protection of the federal law. King appealed the trial court's decision.

In 2009, King was hired by Miller to work as an "employee agent." As such, she was paid a salary. Income taxes and Social Security were withheld by Miller. She was promoted to "independent contract agent." King could not remain an employee agent for more than one year. When she was promoted she had to sign an agreement that stated that she was an independent contractor.

As an independent contract agent, King earned a commission on her sales and some bonuses. She did not receive any paid holidays, sick days, or vacation days. She paid for her own health, life, and disability insurance.

Miller, however, provided office space, furniture, file cabinets, rate books, forms, shared secretarial services, stamps, computers, and Miller's stationery. King purchased her own personalized stationery, pens, and business cards. Miller paid King's tuition for required special insurance seminars, provided lunch at such programs, and rented the space for the sessions.

King had wanted to work for Miller because Miller had a good reputation. Before coming to Miller's office, King worked for three other insurance companies. King was a single, 30-year-old mother of two children. Before her experience in the insurance industry, she worked as a sales clerk at a local boutique.

While working as an independent contract agent for Miller, King could not sell insurance for any other company. She also could only sell insurance in the county designated by the company manager. She had to work at the Miller office three and one-half days a week and every third Saturday, attend two hour-long meetings each week, and retrieve mail every day.

King was responsible for finding her own customers and deciding which products to offer. She could set the hours she worked and she worked without direct supervision. Miller did not regularly review her work. King was fired in 2010, and a man was hired to take her place.

ILLUSTRATION 6-2.   Continued

The district court found that based upon these facts, King was an independent contractor, not an employee. The court focused on the economic realities test. One of the factors it considered as part of its test for determining whether King was an employee or an independent contractor was Miller's right to control King. *Spirides v. Reinhardt*, 613 F.2d 826, 831 (D.C. Cir. 1979), is the leading case regarding the question of whether an individual is an employee, or an independent contractor, under the federal discrimination laws. The *Spirides* court adopted an 11-part test. These factors are:

> 1) the kind of occupation, whether the work is usually done under the direction of a supervisor or without a supervisor; 2) the skill required; 3) whether the "employer" provides the equipment used and the workplace; 4) how long the individual has worked; 5) how the individual is paid, whether by assignment, piece, or time; 6) how the work relationship is to be terminated, i.e., was notice required; 7) whether vacation is provided; 8) whether retirement benefits are provided; 9) whether the employer deducts social security and income tax payments; 10) whether the work is an integral part of the employer's business; and 11) the intention of the parties.

Id.

The Karen district court focused on five of those factors: 1) the extent of Miller's control and supervision of King concerning scheduling and performance of work; 2) the kind of occupation and the nature of the skill required; 3) the division of the costs of the operation, equipment, supplies, and fees; 4) the method and form of payment and benefits; 5) length of job commitment. Central to its decision was the lack of control Miller exercised over King. The court found that King had a great deal of freedom to select her hours, her clients, and the insurance products she sold.

King must prove that an employment relationship existed between herself and Miller in order to maintain a Title VII action against Miller. Independent contractors are not protected by Title VII. *Spirides*, 613 F.2d at 831. Title VII defines employee "as an individual employed by an employer." 42 U.S.C §2000E(f). "In determining whether the relationship is one of employee-employer, courts look to the 'economic realities' of the relationship and the degree of control the employer exercises over the alleged employee." See *Unger v. Consolidated Foods Corp.*, 657 F.2d 909, 915-916 n.8 (7th Cir. 1981).

On appeal, King contends that the district court placed too much weight on the "control factor" and the fact the Miller did not supervise King's work and did not dictate King's hours, products or customers. Based upon this emphasis, King argues that the district court's decision was erroneous.

However, this court finds that the district court correctly considered other facts such as that King was paid on commission, did not receive

ILLUSTRATION 6-2.   Continued

benefits, and provided many of her own supplies, including stationery and business cards.

Although this court was not asked to determine whether the district court should have considered all of the facts that were relevant to each of the 11 factors stated in the *Spirides'* economic realities test, this court finds that the district court should have done so.

Although we think that the district court should have focused its analysis on all 11 factors, we do not think that its decision is clearly erroneous; therefore, we affirm the decision of the district court in granting summary judgment for the defendant, Miller.

2. Procedural History

This section of the case brief should be labeled **procedural history** or simply procedure. These facts explain the status of the case. You will summarize how this case traveled through the court system to reach this point. See Illustration 6-3. In this section, you note the action of the prior courts. For example, if the decision concerns an appeal to a federal appellate court, note that. Also, state whether the court reversed or affirmed the lower court's decision and whether the case was remanded.

PRACTICE POINTER

Always validate any case that you brief by using *Shepard's* or KeyCite. Note the date validated at the top of the brief so that you know to update if necessary.

ILLUSTRATION 6-3.   Sample Case Brief, *King v. Miller*

KING v. MILLER
1000 E.R. 108 (Karen Ct. App. 2011)

PROCEDURAL HISTORY
    The case was on appeal from the District Court's grant of summary judgment for the defendant Miller.

ISSUE
    Is King, a worker subject to only minimal company control and who was paid commissions rather than a salary and benefits, an employee

ILLUSTRATION 6-3.   **Continued**

protected by Title VII or an independent contractor who is outside the protection of the federal law?

HOLDING

King, a worker subject to only minimal company control and who was paid commissions rather than a salary and benefits, was an independent contractor rather than an employee protected by Title VII.

FACTS

King first worked for Miller as an employee agent. During that time, she received a salary and the company withheld income tax and social security payments. King later was promoted to independent contract agent.

As an independent contract agent, King earned a commission and bonuses but did not receive a salary. She signed an agreement that stated that she was an independent contractor. As a contract agent, she did not receive paid holidays, sick days, or vacation days, and she paid for her own health, life, and disability insurance. King supplied her own personalized stationery, business cards, and pens. She found her own customers, decided which products to sell, and set her own hours.

For its contract agents, Miller supplied office space, furniture, file cabinets, forms, shared secretarial services, stamps, computers, and stationery. Miller also paid for required insurance seminars. Miller required that contract agents, such as King, attend weekly meetings, work in the office three and one-half days per week and every third Saturday, check their mail and retrieve messages daily, and sell only Miller insurance. Miller also restricted King's sales area. Miller did not regularly review King's work.

REASONING

In order to determine whether an individual is an employee or an independent contractor, the employment relationship between the parties needs to be evaluated based upon the economic realities and circumstances of the relationship. The court considered the control exercised by the "employer" over the worker; the method of payment; who paid for the individual's benefits, such as life and health insurance; and who paid for the operation. In this case, the court found that King was an independent contractor because she was paid on commission, she paid for her own benefits, she supplied her own supplies, and she controlled her work. The court found that she set her own hours, selected the product she sold, and generated her own clients. Based upon these facts, the appellate court found that King should be considered an independent contractor rather than an employee.

ILLUSTRATION 6-3.   Continued

DICTA
   The 11-part test set by the *Spirides* court should be applied to determine whether an individual is an employee or an independent contractor.

DISPOSITION
   The Court of Appeals affirmed the district court's judgment in granting summary judgment for the defendant.

PRACTICE POINTER

Obtain all of the citation information when you are using the reporter or accessing the case online. Record all of the citation information in the brief, including the precise pages where you obtained the information, the pin cites. Write the cites in *Bluebook* or *ALWD* format. Later, when writing, you will not have to revisit the decision to get the cite information.

3. Issues

Next, list the **issue** or issues presented in the case. See Illustration 6-3. Although determining the issues in a case is a difficult process at first, it does get easier with practice.

   The issues are the questions the parties asked the court to decide. In most cases, multiple issues are presented. To determine the issues, you must understand the legal rules that govern a particular case. If you are briefing a case and you have not been assigned an issue to research, list all the issues presented in the case. If you have been given a research assignment, you need only brief the issues that are relevant to your research, listing each one separately.

▼ How Do You Determine the Legal Issue or Issues Presented When Examining a Client's Problem?

To understand this process, assume you have been asked to research whether your firm's client, Whole In One, will be subject to the federal antidiscrimination laws. Whole In One is a seasonal restaurant and golf course in Glenview, Illinois. Two women, Victoria Radiant and Karen Walker, brought suit against Whole In One for sex discrimination. Their claims are based on a federal antidiscrimination statute commonly known as Title VII. You have been asked to research whether Whole In One is an employer and whether the women are employees under the definitions included in the federal law. During your research, you find the case of *King v. Miller*. Review Illustration 6-2.

To determine the issue, read the case. Ask yourself, "What did the parties ask the court to determine?" Sometimes the court will note the issue directly in its opinion. Other times, you must search through the opinion to determine the issue. After you have read the *King* case, you should note that it involves a question of sex discrimination. However, your research is limited to the issues that concern the definitions of *employer* and *employee*. Therefore, the case brief should focus on issues that relate to your research problem.

Once you have read the *King* case, you will find that it addresses the question of whether an individual is an employee protected by Title VII. Now you are ready to draft the issue.

▼ How Do You Draft a Statement of the Issue or Issues?

For the *King* case, you might start with this brief issue:

> Is King an employee protected by Title VII or an independent contractor who is outside the protection of the federal law?

Now that the issue is presented in question format, you could leave the issue section here. However, the issue would be more meaningful for your research if you included more information about the legal issue the court focused on in making its determination. In its discussion, the *King* court focused on the amount of control that an employer must exercise before an individual is viewed as an employee rather than an independent contractor. You could incorporate the court's focus on control into the issue as follows:

> Is King, a worker subject to only minimal company control, an employee protected by Title VII, or an independent contractor who is outside the protection of the federal law?

You also should include relevant facts in your issue statement. Again, this will make the issue more meaningful for your research. In this case, for example, you might add some facts about the company's method of payment and its lack of provisions for benefits:

> Is King, a worker subject to only minimal company control who was paid commissions rather than salary and benefits, an employee protected by Title VII or an independent contractor who is outside the protection of the federal law?

The final issue statement is the best because it incorporates the relevant facts that affect a court's decision concerning this issue and the **rule of law** that will be applied.

You might wonder why the issue did not focus on the appellate court's consideration of the district court's action in granting the motion for summary judgment in favor of the defendant. Students often phrase such an issue as follows:

> Did the district court err in granting summary judgment in favor of the defendant?

However, this issue focuses too heavily on the procedural question posed in the *King* case and does not include the applicable law or any of the legally significant facts. Your issue should concern the legal, not the procedural, questions a court was asked to decide. As you learned above, the *King* case involved a motion for summary judgment.

To find the substantive legal issue, determine the legal question the parties asked the court to answer in the motion for summary judgment. In the *King* case, the parties asked the court to determine whether, as a matter of law, King was an independent contractor rather than an employee. This is the central legal issue. By focusing on this substantive issue rather than the procedural issue, your brief will be more useful to you in your research of the *Whole In One* case.

Some of you might wonder why you do not focus on the question of discrimination in your issue section. Remember the issue you were asked to answer with your research. You were asked to deal with the issues of the definitions of *employee* and *employer*. You should tailor your brief to address only these issues.

4. Holding

The next section should be your **holding.** Essentially a holding is the court's answer to the issue or question presented. However, it is not a yes, no, or maybe answer to the issue. The holding should be a full sentence that responds directly to the issue posed and that incorporates both the legal standards and the most significant legal facts on which the answer is based. A holding differs from a legal rule in that a legal rule is the standard, test, or principle that the court uses in its rationale, or reasoning, to explain its holding. The holding addresses the specific question before the court.

▼ How Do You Draft a Holding?

The process for drafting the holding is similar to the process for writing your issue statement. First, your holding should be a statement that answers the issue. Assume you selected the first issue statement considered in this discussion:

> Is King an employee protected by Title VII or an independent contractor who is outside the protection of the federal law?

You might consider answering it as follows:

> King is an independent contractor rather than an employee and therefore is outside the protection of Title VII.

While this statement is simple and direct, similar to the first issue statement, it does not contain any relevant facts or incorporate any legal standards. This holding should be rewritten, incorporating the elements or legal standards that would be considered. Such a change would make the holding more meaningful in the context of this research.

The rewritten issue, for which we will draft a holding, could read:

> Is King, a worker subject to only minimal company control, an independent contractor or is she an employee protected by Title VII?

Again, you might want to include additional facts the court considered in determining that King was an independent contractor. For the holding, rewrite the final issue statement drafted above in the form of a statement.

> King, a worker subject to only minimal company control who was paid commissions rather than salary and benefits, was an independent contractor rather than an employee protected by Title VII.

The key to drafting a clear issue statement, holding, or any other component of the brief, is rewriting and editing. You must make your holding broad enough so that it could be useful for various research projects involving different fact patterns. However, a clear holding incorporates facts from the case at hand that make it unique and that limit the holding so that you can understand the facts that form the basis for the court's decision. These facts are the **legally significant facts.** Also, try to make the statement of the holding narrow enough so that it reflects the unique legal issue in the case. Refine your statements and assess whether they are helpful in your research summary.

Also, be careful to incorporate the facts and the underlying law into your holding statement, as you did in your issue statement. A holding such as

> The district court did not err in granting summary judgment in favor of the defendant.

is not valuable for your research. It does not explain why the court found that the district court's decision was correct.

5. Facts

The next section of the brief should be the **facts.** Be certain to include the names of the parties, a notation concerning whether the party is a plaintiff, a defendant, an appellant, or appellee, and some details about the party, such as whether it is a corporation or an individual. State the relevant rather than procedural facts in this section. Also, explain why a party sought legal assistance.

▼ What Are the Relevant Facts?

Relevant facts are those facts that may have an effect on the legal issues decided in a particular action. To write this section, you must clearly understand the issues decided by the court. Decide which facts the court relied on to make its decision. Those are the facts that you should include in this section. The facts should be presented in a paragraph form rather than in a list or in bullet points. Also, mention any facts that will assist you in understanding the relationship between the parties and the nature of the dispute.

In the *King* case, the court relied on facts that explained the relationship between King and the Miller Co. For example, the court considered that King earned commissions and bonuses rather than a salary. That fact should be listed. Before you write your facts statement in paragraph format, make a rough outline of all the facts that the court considered in making its decision. Sometimes a chronological timeline helps when organizing the facts. For the *King* case, your outline might look like this:

> King first worked as an "employee" agent
>> As an employee agent, King was paid salary, and the company withheld taxes
>
> King later was designated an "independent contract" agent, earned commission and bonuses but no salary
> King signed an agreement that she was an independent contractor
> Did not receive paid holidays, sick days, or vacation
> Paid for her own health, life, and disability insurance
> Miller supplied office space, furniture, file cabinets, forms, shared secretarial services, stamps, computers, and Miller stationery
> Miller paid for insurance seminars and lunches at the seminars
> Miller required that King attend weekly meetings, work in the office three and one-half days per week and every third Saturday, check her mail and retrieve messages daily, and sell only
> Miller insurance
> Miller restricted King's sales area
> Miller did not regularly review King's work
> King supplied her own personalized stationery, business cards, pens
> King found her own customers, decided which products to sell, and set her own hours

The court listed additional facts, such as:

> King had wanted to work for Miller because Miller had a good reputation
> Before coming to Miller's office, King worked for three other insurance companies

King was a single, 30-year-old mother of two children
Before her experience in the insurance industry, she worked as a
   sales clerk at a local boutique

Note that for its decision the court did not consider any of the facts contained in the outline under additional facts. Therefore, they are not relevant, or legally significant, facts and should not be included in your brief. After you have made your outline and determined which facts are relevant, you should draft your facts statement in a paragraph format. A list is not as helpful as a paragraph when you want to review the brief at a later date.

▼ How Do You Organize Your Facts Statements?

Your facts statement could be written in chronological order, in topical order, or using a combination of the two methods. Chronological order often works best when the case involves facts that need to be placed in order according to when they occurred. For example, in a personal injury action that results from a car accident, a chronological set of facts is best. Start with the first fact that occurred and work forward.

A chronological organization for the facts in the *King* case would read as follows:

> In 2009, King started to work for Miller. King first worked for Miller as an employee agent. During that time, she received a salary and the company withheld income tax and social security payments. King later was promoted to contract agent. King was fired in 2010, and a man was hired to take her place.

A topical organization is the best choice for facts that have no temporal relationship. Instead, these facts are grouped by topic or legal claim. In this case, the topic is the legal question of whether King was an independent contractor. Therefore, you would group together all the facts that relate to this question.

> As an independent contract agent, King earned a commission and bonuses but did not receive a salary. She signed an agreement that stated that she was an independent contractor. As a contract agent, she did not receive paid holidays, sick days, or vacation days, and she paid for her own health, life, and disability insurance. King supplied her own personalized stationery, business cards, and pens. She found her own customers, decided which products to sell, and set her own hours.
>
> For its independent contract agents, Miller supplied office space, furniture, file cabinets, forms, shared secretarial services, stamps, computers, and Miller stationery. Miller also paid for required insurance seminars. Miller required that contract agents, such as

King, attend weekly meetings, work in the office three and one-half days per week and every third Saturday, check their mail and retrieve messages daily, and sell only Miller insurance. Miller also restricted King's sales area. Miller did not regularly review King's work.

In the *King* case, a combination of a chronological and topical organization works best. The *King* brief facts statement might read as follows:

> King first worked for Miller as an employee agent. During that time she received a salary and the company withheld income tax and social security payments. King later was promoted to independent contract agent.

> As an independent contract agent, King earned a commission and bonuses but did not receive a salary. She signed an agreement that stated that she was an independent contractor. As a contract agent, she did not receive paid holidays, sick days, or vacation days, and she paid for her own health, life, and disability insurance. King supplied her own personalized stationery, business cards, and pens. She found her own customers, decided which products to sell, and set her own hours.

> For its contract agents, Miller supplied office space, furniture, file cabinets, forms, shared secretarial services, stamps, computers, and Miller stationery. Miller also paid for required insurance seminars. Miller required that contract agents, such as King, attend weekly meetings, work in the office three and one-half days per week and every third Saturday, check their mail and retrieve messages daily, and sell only Miller insurance. Miller also restricted King's sales area. Miller did not regularly review King's work.

The above facts statement begins with a chronological organization. It explains the beginning of the relationship between King and Miller. Next, it states all the facts that pertain to King's benefits and her control of her work. The next paragraph explains what Miller provided for the independent contract agents and what Miller required of them. Following this facts section, you should include a reasoning or rationale section in a brief.

6. Reasoning

In the **reasoning** or **rationale** section, you should explain the court's thought process and relevant cases or statutes, then apply the law to the facts of the case you are briefing. Essentially, you will explain the law the court relied on in making a decision and why the court reached its decision. The court will base its opinion on the relevant legal rule. The legal rule is the principle, test, or standard. Sometimes the court uses more than one rule. For example, the *King* court reviewed the definition of *employee* contained in Title VII and past case precedent, such as *Spirides v. Reinhardt*, 613 F.2d 826, 831 (D.C. Cir. 1979), and *Unger v. Consolidated Foods Corp.*, 657 F.2d 909, 915-916 n.8 (7th Cir. 1981), to determine that independent contractors are not protected by Title VII. Both of these cases are from different jurisdictions. The *Spirides* case is primary binding authority only in the District of Columbia Circuit and *Unger* is primary binding authority only within the Seventh Circuit. However, both are persuasive authorities in other circuits. Explain in this section whether the court relied on binding or persuasive authority.

You also must review a decision for any tests a court considered in making its decision. In *King*, the court considered the economic realities test. Finally, note how the court applied the law to the facts of the particular case.

For the *King* case, you might include the following reasoning section in your brief:

> To determine whether an individual is an employee or an independent contractor, the employment relationship between the parties needs to be evaluated based on the economic realities and circumstances of the relationship. The court reviewed several of the factors set forth by the District of Columbia Circuit Court in *Spirides v. Reinhardt*, 613 F.2d 826, 831 (D.C. Cir. 1979), a persuasive authority, and the economic realities of the situation as defined by the Seventh Circuit court in *Unger v. Consolidated Foods Corp.*, 657 F.2d 909, 915-916 n.8 (7th Cir. 1981), another persuasive decision. Based upon these factors, the King court considered the control exercised by the "employer" over the worker; the method of payment; who paid for the individual's benefits, such as life and health insurance; and who paid for the operation. In this case, the court found that King was an independent contractor because she was paid on commission, she paid for her own benefits, she provided her own supplies, and she controlled her work. The court found that she set her own hours, selected the products she sold, and generated her own clients. Based on these facts, the appellate court found that King should be considered an independent contractor rather than an employee.

Or you could prepare the reasoning section without any reference to the underlying, or embedded, case law.

> To determine whether an individual is an employee or an independent contractor, the employment relationship between the parties needs to be evaluated based on the economic realities and circumstances of the relationship. The *King* court considered the control exercised by the "employer" over the worker; the method of payment; who paid for the individual's benefits, such

as life and health insurance; and who paid for the operation. In this case, the court found that King was an independent contractor because she was paid on commission, she paid for her own benefits, she provided her own supplies, and she controlled her work. The court found that she set her own hours, selected the products she sold, and generated her own clients. Based on these facts, the appellate court found that King should be considered an independent contractor rather than an employee.

In the reasoning section, you should include an application of the law to the facts of the case and a mini-conclusion that summarizes the court's decision. In the above example, the following section is the application of the court's reasoning to the facts of the case.

In this case, the court found that King was an independent contractor because she was paid on commission, she paid for her own benefits, she provided her own supplies, and she controlled her work. The court found that she set her own hours, selected the products she sold, and generated her own clients.

This also provides insight into the legally significant facts, so that when you examine your problem, you will look at parallel facts to determine if the client was an employee.

In the above example, the following statement is the mini-conclusion:

Based on these facts, the appellate court found that King should be considered an independent contractor rather than an employee.

In some cases, you will find that a court bases its decision on reasons other than statutes or past cases. For example, a court might consider whether its decision would be fair under the circumstances. This type of analysis is called the court's consideration of policy, which sometimes is a question of what would benefit society, such as equal rights in an educational setting. Incorporate this policy into your reasoning section whenever it is useful for your research. After the reasoning or rationale, discuss any dicta contained in the court's decision.

7. Dicta

If a court makes a statement concerning a question that it was not asked to answer, this statement is called **dicta.** Although dicta does not have any binding effect, it is often useful to predict how a court might decide a particular issue in the future. Therefore, you want to include any dicta that might affect your case.

In the *King* case, the court stated that it was not asked to decide whether the district court should have considered all 11 factors before it rendered its decision. However, the court stated that the district court should have based its decision on all 11 factors. This statement by the court was dicta. It is helpful for your research problem because it states the factors that this circuit court might consider in determining whether an individual is an independent contractor rather than an employee.

The dicta section for the *King* case might read as follows:

> The 11-part test set by the *Spirides* court should be applied to determine whether an individual is an employee or an independent contractor.

8. Disposition

The final section of your brief is the **disposition.** The disposition of a case is essentially the procedural result of the court's decision. For example, in the *King* case, the court found that the district court's decision to grant summary judgment for the defendant was correct. Therefore, the disposition section would state:

> The court of appeals affirmed the district court's judgment in granting summary judgment for the defendant.

Finally, remember to rewrite your brief, but do not spend too much time rewriting it. Use your own words rather than many quotes from the court opinions. Paraphrasing in your own words helps you analyze the case and better understand it when you review your brief in the future. Also, paraphrasing allows you to import the information from the brief into a document that you draft later. You may even cut and paste portions of a well-drafted brief into a memo. See Illustration 6-4 for an overview of the case briefing process.

PRACTICE POINTER

Reread your brief as if you were unfamiliar with the case. If you cannot understand what happened, rewrite your brief.

NET NOTE

A basic overview of how to brief a case is found at www.lib.jjay.cuny.edu/research/brief.html.

ILLUSTRATION 6-4. Case Briefing Process

IN-CLASS EXERCISE

Sometimes learning to brief can seem like an abstract exercise. The following exercise is designed to hone your brief drafting skills. It is best for students to read the illustrations for this exercise before class. Read the abridged *Molitor* case found in Illustration 6-5. Then read the case brief in Illustration 6-6. After reading the case and the brief, go back to the case and try to find where the issue, facts, holding, and reasoning were obtained. This will give you insight into the information that must be pulled from a case to write a brief.

ILLUSTRATION 6-5.   *Molitor v. Chicago Title & Trust Co.*

MOLITOR v. CHICAGO TITLE & TRUST CO.
325 Ill. App. 124, 59 N.E.2d 695 (1945)

SCANLAN, Justice.

Robert H. Molitor, plaintiff, sued Chicago Title & Trust Company, a corporation, for breach of an employment contract, and also sued Justin M. Dall for damages resulting from the breach of the said contract because of his want of authority, if the evidence should show a want of authority. A jury returned a verdict finding the issues in favor of plaintiff and against Chicago Title & Trust Company and assessing plaintiff's damages at $15,480, and also a verdict finding the issues in favor of defendant Dall. The trial court reserved rulings on motions of defendants for directed verdicts and after verdicts sustained a motion of Chicago Title & Trust Company for judgment in its favor notwithstanding the verdict against it. Plaintiff appeals from that judgment. Judgment was entered upon the verdict in favor of defendant Dall after plaintiff's motion for a new trial had been denied. Plaintiff has not appealed from that judgment. Some days after the entry of the judgment against Chicago Title & Trust Company it entered a motion for a new trial and the trial court entered an order granting the motion, but providing that "this ruling shall not become effective unless and until the order granting the motion for judgment notwithstanding the verdict shall hereafter be reversed, vacated or set aside in the manner provided by law." Plaintiff also appeals from that judgment. . . .

. . . The complaint alleges that Chicago Title & Trust Company, on or about March 20, 1936, "desiring to continue the service of plaintiff permanently, promised and agreed that in consideration of the plaintiff giving up his residence in the State of New York, and giving up and forgoing all his other engagements and professional connections as aforesaid by moving his family to Cook County, State of Illinois, and thereafter devoting all his time exclusively to the service of the Company, that it would give plaintiff steady, continuous and permanent employment as an examiner of titles; that is to say, for

ILLUSTRATION 6-5. Continued

and during the period of his natural life, or so long as said Company required the services of an examiner of titles and plaintiff was willing and able to do such work." Said defendant, in its answer, denies the aforesaid allegations. We may assume from the briefs filed by both parties that the trial court based his ruling upon the assumption that there was no evidence offered by plaintiff that tended to prove an enforceable agreement that plaintiff was to have permanent employment. . . .

. . . Observing these rules we find the following evidence: The Chicago Title & Trust Company is engaged, inter alia, in the business of insuring titles to and interests in real estate in Cook County and elsewhere. It employs a large number of men known as title examiners, who are especially trained and experienced in the law of real property and the validity of real estate titles. It depends upon the ability and integrity of these title examiners to discover defects, it there be any, in real estate titles. In the selection of title examiners it exercises great caution, and applicants for such position go through a long probationary period before they are given "continuous employment." In 1920 plaintiff applied for a position as title examiner and was employed on probation. He had theretofore been engaged in the practice of law in South Dakota. After a number of years of service as a probationer, he was made a regular examiner at a salary of $85 per week. In August, 1927, he quit the services of the defendant company and moved, with his family, to New York to take employment in the office of a former client, the new position paying him twice the salary he was getting as a title examiner. Because of the economic depression, he lost the New York position on February 1, 1933, and he then started to practice his profession in New York—having been admitted to the bar in New York—and by June, 1934, he was commencing to build up a paying practice. About that time one of the departments of defendant company, that was managed by Mr. Dall, was swamped with thousands of HOLC orders for title insurance, and speedy service was demanded. Mr. Dall, in letters and telegrams to plaintiff, asked him to reenter the employ of defendant company. Dall stated that the company was very busy with rush orders from the HOLC but that there was no profit in the business and that the work would probably last about six months. Plaintiff told Mr. Dall that since 1933 conditions had changed for the better for him and his family and that they now had an income; that from time to time he was getting law business which paid substantial fees; that his wife had a music class in New York from which she derived a substantial income every month and that he might have trouble inducing her to give up her work unless plaintiff would have better prospects in Chicago than in New York. Further correspondence followed, and plaintiff finally accepted the offer of employment with the understanding that when the HOLC work gave out that Mr. Dall might be free to dispense with his services. In view of the temporary character of the agreement plaintiff decided not to move his family to Chicago. He

ILLUSTRATION 6-5. Continued

came to Chicago on July 23, 1934, and told Mr. Dall, in a conference, that he desired to preserve his business connections in New York and to have his wife retain her music classes there, and that it would be necessary for him to be absent from his work with the defendant company when matters came up in New York that required his presence there. Mr. Dall agreed to this arrangement. Immediately following this conference plaintiff went to work for defendant company and for three or four months thereafter the title examiners were obliged to work four hours overtime every day, all day Saturdays, and some Sundays. Plaintiff spent five days in New York in the following September to attend to a legal matter in which he had been appointed referee. He was also absent from his work during the month of June, 1935, when he was conducting legal business for clients in New York and Philadelphia, and was absent again, upon like work, between December 14, 1935, and February 17, 1936. All of the absences were with the knowledge and consent of Mr. Dall. The HOLC work was tapering off in 1935, and it ended on June 12, 1936. About this time Mr. Dall was preparing for an anticipated improvement in the regular business of defendant company and he became dissatisfied with the arrangement that allowed plaintiff to be absent from his work on trips to New York, and in a conference with plaintiff it was agreed that the trips to New York caused undesirable breaks in plaintiff's work and a new arrangement as to plaintiff's employment was made. The following is plaintiff's evidence as to the agreement: Dall stated to him that the HOLC work would soon be played out but that they were looking for a big boom in regular real estate business, and he asked plaintiff to abandon his New York connections and move his family to Chicago so that he could give the company his continuous service from then on. Plaintiff replied that he would not give up his New York connections so long as there was any uncertainty about his employment in Chicago being continuous. Mr. Dall stated that two of the examiners had died, that there was now a place for plaintiff and that he could depend on the position being permanent. Plaintiff asked him what he meant by that, to which Dall replied, "You can consider yourself employed from now on—the custom here is to retain examiners as long as we can. We have men that have been here all their lives, and there is no reason why you couldn't have a job here the rest of your life." Plaintiff replied that if he could rely on that promise he would buy a house in Chicago and move his family here, that his wife had a big music class in New York and that she would refuse to move unless he had a permanent position in Chicago, to which Mr. Dall replied, "You can rely on it being permanent." Plaintiff then accepted the position and told Mr. Dall that he would abandon his New York connections, buy a house here, and move his family to Chicago. His salary was fixed at $70 per week. Plaintiff thereupon continued in his work with defendant company and began preparations for carrying out his part of the agreement. He abandoned all his business in New York and his wife abandoned her music classes. He bought

ILLUSTRATION 6-5.   Continued

a home at 7219 Vernon Avenue and the family moved to Chicago. The defendant company loaned plaintiff $200 to enable him to move. Plaintiff thereafter continued in the employ of defendant company under the arrangements made with Mr. Dall until March 15, 1938, when he was discharged by defendant company upon the ground that business had fallen off to such an extent that the company could not afford to hold plaintiff any longer. There was evidence tending to show that defendant company about two years prior to plaintiff's discharge employed thirteen new title examiners whose salaries averaged less than $40 per week, and that only one of the thirteen was discharged at the time of plaintiff's discharge.

In passing upon plaintiff's instant contention we must assume that defendant company promised plaintiff "permanent employment" and that plaintiff accepted employment because of that promise, and the question is, What did the parties intend by "permanent employment"?. . . .

. . . In *Riefkin v. E.I. Du Pont De Nemours & Co.*, 53 App. D.C. 311, 290 F. 286, the plaintiff was induced to resign from a position with the United States government on a promise of permanent employment. After about two and one-half years of service he was discharged without cause although he had rendered satisfactory service to the defendant. In its opinion the Court of Appeals of the District of Columbia stated (290 F. at page 289):

"The circumstances surrounding the making of this contract largely control the interpretation to be given the words 'permanent employment' as used therein, for it must be assumed that the parties, knowing those circumstances, contracted with reference to them. The plaintiff held a position with the United States government, and the defendant agreed that, if he would resign from that position and take charge of the purchase of coal for the defendant, he would be given 'permanent employment in that capacity so long as he rendered satisfactory services and was loyal to its interests.' Relying upon this agreement, plaintiff did resign and perform his part of the contract. May it be said that it was within the contemplation of either party that 'permanent employment,' as used in the contract, meant that the plaintiff, the day following his resignation from his position with the government and the assumption of his new duties, could have been summarily discharged without any liability on the part of the defendant? Such a result could not have been contemplated by either party. The more reasonable view is that the parties contemplated that, so long as the defendant continued in a business requiring the purchase of coal and the plaintiff performed loyal and satisfactory service, he would continue to be employed in the capacity specified in the contract." . . .

. . . "The rule is that a contract for lifetime employment will be given effect, according to its terms, if the intention of the parties to make such an agreement is clear, even though the only consideration for it, so far as the employer is concerned, is the promise of the employee to render the service called for the contract."

ILLUSTRATION 6-5.   Continued

But the defendant contends (a): "There was no evidence that Dall had authority to enter into the alleged contract to employ plaintiff for life or that defendant company ratified the alleged contract;" and (b) "There was no evidence that defendant company acted in bad faith in discharging plaintiff." All of these contentions involve disputed questions of fact and therefore they cannot be considered in determining the instant contention of plaintiff. After a careful consideration of the question before us we have reached the conclusion that the trial court erred in entering judgment for the defendant company not withstanding the verdict for plaintiff . . .

The judgment order of the Superior Court of Cook County entered May 13, 1943, entering judgment in favor of the defendant Chicago Title & Trust Company non obstante veredicto is reversed. The judgment order of the Superior Court of Cook County entered June 3, 1943, setting aside the verdict of the jury and granting the defendant Chicago Title & Trust Company a new trial is affirmed. The cause is remanded for a new trial.

SULLIVAN, P.J., and FRIEND, J., concur.

ILLUSTRATION 6-6.   Case Brief for *Molitor v. Chicago Title & Trust Co.*

MOLITOR v. CHICAGO TITLE & TRUST CO.
325 Ill. App. 124, 59 N.E.2d 695 (1945)

PROCEDURE

Plaintiff, Molitor, appeals judgment in favor of the defendant, Chicago Title, notwithstanding the verdict and judgment granting a new trial.

ISSUE

Was there a breach of an oral contract for permanent employment when the plaintiff moved to Chicago in consideration of the defendant's promise to employ him, and when the defendant promised to employ the plaintiff for as long as he was willing and able to do the work?

HOLDING

A contract for lifetime employment is in effect if the intention of the parties is clear even if the only consideration for the contract is the promise of the employee to render the service called for by the contract.

ILLUSTRATION 6-6. Continued

FACTS

The plaintiff, Robert Molitor, was employed by Chicago Title & Trust as a probationary examiner for seven years before leaving and moving his family to New York to work for a former client. After losing that job, he began to practice law in New York. In June 1934, Mr. Dall of CT&T contacted the plaintiff and asked him to reenter CT&T's company temporarily. The plaintiff and Mr. Dall arranged for the plaintiff to work for a period for CT&T while retaining his law practice. He was absent from his work for CT&T to attend to his practice on several occasions with the knowledge of Mr. Dall. In June 1936, Mr. Dall offered the plaintiff a new agreement, asking him to leave his law practice and move his family to Chicago for permanent employment with CT&T. The plaintiff replied that if he could rely on that promise of permanent employment, he would buy a house in Chicago and move his family there. Mr. Dall replied that the position was permanent. Then the plaintiff severed his New York connections and moved his family. On March 15, 1938, Mr. Dall discharged him.

REASONING

To decide what was meant by "permanent employment," the situation, and the relationship of the parties, and the common understanding of the meaning of the words used must be considered. The surrounding circumstances in the making of a contract must also be considered to ascertain what the parties intended by "permanent employment."

DISPOSITION

Reversed in part and remanded.

After reading *Molitor* and its brief, read the *Heuvelman* decision found in Illustration 6-7. Although it is also decided by the Illinois Appellate Court and deals with the issue of permanent employment, it was decided 14 years after *Molitor*. Read the brief following the decision found in Illustration 6-8. You will notice that *Heuvelman* cites *Molitor;* this is an example of how legal precedent is used and why we perform case law research. Now compare the briefs for the two cases. Since both sets of briefs are drafted with the same categories (citation, procedure, issue, facts, holding, rationale, and disposition), you can compare and contrast cases easily and quickly. Compare the issues and you will see that they are similar. Now compare the facts and the holdings and you will notice that they differ.

ILLUSTRATION 6-7.   *Heuvelman v. Triplett Elec. Instrument Co.*

HEUVELMAN v. TRIPLETT ELEC. INSTRUMENT CO.
23 Ill. App. 2d 231, 161 N.E.2d 875 (1959)

SCHWARTZ, Justice.

The trial court sustained both defendant's motion for a summary judgment and its motion to strike the amended complaint, and thereupon dismissed the suit with prejudice. From these orders plaintiff has appealed. The principal issue involved turns on an alleged oral agreement for permanent employment.

The amended complaint consists of three counts. Count 1 seeks a declaratory judgment finding that plaintiff and defendant entered into a contract for the permanent employment of plaintiff as a sales representative for the sale of electrical and radio equipment; that the contract was breached; and that plaintiff suffered damages in the sum of $250,000. . . .

. . . The pertinent facts extracted from these documents follow. From 1925 to January 1933 plaintiff was employed by an agency which served as defendant's sales representative in the Midwest. In January 1933 defendant hired plaintiff as its sole sales representative for the territory previously covered by the agency. The agreement specified no definite time of employment. In April 1933 defendant desired to secure the services of another sales representative, Jerome T. Keeney, employed by competitor of defendant, and defendant brought plaintiff and Keeney together for the purpose of having them become associated as joint representatives for the sale of defendant's products. At that meeting, as plaintiff alleges, defendant agreed that plaintiff's employment would continue as long as defendant manufactured and sold electrical equipment and as long as plaintiff acted as sales representative in that field. Plaintiff charges that it was on the basis of that agreement that he consented to enter into a partnership with Keeney. Instead of a partnership, however, a corporation was formed, the Instrument Sales Corporation, in which plaintiff and Keeney owned stock.

The business association between plaintiff and Keeney continued until 1940, when Keeney left plaintiff to join the Simpson Electric Company, a competitor of defendant. At that time Simpson also made plaintiff an offer. Plaintiff orally discussed with defendant the matter of his leaving and, as stated by plaintiff but denied by defendant, Triplett, president of defendant company, told plaintiff as they walked down State Street in Chicago, that their arrangement was a permanent one. It continued until October 1955, when defendant notified plaintiff that it terminated the relationship effective November 30, 1955.

We will first consider the motion for summary judgment as it applies to Count I. Oral contracts for "permanent employment" (meaning that as long as defendant was engaged in the prescribed work and as long as plaintiff was able to do his work satisfactorily, defendant would

ILLUSTRATION 6-7.   Continued

employ him) have been sustained, provided such contracts are supported by a consideration other than the obligation of services to be performed on the one hand and wages to be paid on the other. *Molitor v. Chicago Title & Trust Co.*, 1845, 325 Ill. App. 124, 132-133, 59 N.E.2d 695-698; *Carnig v. Carr*, 1897, 167 Mass. 544, 46 N.E 117, 35 L.R.A. 512; *Riefkin v. E. I. Du Pont, etc., & Co.*, 1923, 53 App. D.C. 311, 290 F. 286; *Eggers v. Armour & Co.*, 8 Cir., 1942, 129 F.2d 729; *Roxana Petroleum Co. of Oklahoma v. Rice.*, 1924, 109 Okl. 161, 235 P. 502. In the *Molitor* case the consideration was the giving up by the employee of a profitable law practice in New York in order to move to Chicago in reliance on a promise of permanent employment. The *Molitor* case was supported and approved, but distinguished, in *Goodman v. Motor Products Corp.*, 1950, 9 Ill. App. 2d 57,77 132 N.E.2d 356, 366. In *Carnig v. Carr*, supra, the plaintiff gave up a going and competitive venture to go with his employer. In *Riefkin v. E. I. Du Pont, etc., a & Co.*, supra, the employee gave up his position in government, a position of security and prestige. The case of *Roxana Petroleum Co. v. Rice*, supra, concerned a firm's giving up its whole law practice in order to represent a single client. Where there is no particular detriment to the employee, the act of terminating other employment is not a sufficient consideration to make the new contract binding. *Edwards v. Kentucky Utilities Co.*, 1941, 286 Ky. 341, 150 S.W.2d 916, 135 A.L.R. 642.

In the instant case the time of the first alleged conversation on which permanent employment is based is April 1933. At that time plaintiff was already employed by defendant and the formation of a partnership with Keeney, terminable at will, so far as appears from anything in the record, cannot be considered a detriment but an advantage, Keeney being a man of considerable experience and competence, as was plaintiff in this business. The alleged renewal of the offer in 1940, when plaintiff was being solicited to join Simpson, is presented in such a vague, indefinite way that it is impossible to consider it as an obligation. Plaintiff says Simpson offered him a 25% interest in a new business venture. It does not appear whether this was a gift or a capital contribution. It is not sufficient consideration for a contract of permanent employment to forgo another employment opportunity. *Lewis v. Minnesota Mutual Life Insurance Co.*, 1949, 240 Iowa 1249, 37 N.W.2d 316; *Skagerberg v. Blandin Paper Co.*, 1936, 197 Minn. 291, 266 N.W. 872.

It is our further conclusion that . . . , no contract for permanent employment was made, nor was any adequate consideration to support one shown. Such contracts extending for a long duration and resting entirely on parole should have for their basis definite and certain mutual promises. The words and the manner of their utterance should not be of that informal character which expresses only long continuing good will and hopes for eternal association. . . .

ILLUSTRATION 6-7. Continued

. . . The order insofar as it sustains the motion to strike Count I and enters summary judgment thereon is affirmed. The order insofar as it sustains the motion to strike Counts II and III and enters summary judgment thereon is reversed and the cause is remanded with directions to vacate the summary judgment and overrule the motion to strike Counts II and III, and for such further proceedings as are not inconsistent with the views herein expressed.

Affirmed in part and reversed in part, and cause remanded for further proceedings.

DEMPSEY, P.J., and McCORMICK, J., concur.

ILLUSTRATION 6-8. Case Brief for *Heuvelman v. Triplett Elec. Instrument Co.*

HEUVELMAN *v.* TRIPLETT ELEC. INSTRUMENT CO.
23 Ill. App. 2d 231, 161 N.E.2d 875 (1959)

PROCEDURE
   The plaintiff appeals summary judgment for the defendant, dismissing his suit for breach of oral contract for permanent employment.

ISSUE
   Whether there an oral contract for permanent employment between plaintiff and defendant?

HOLDING
   No oral contract for permanent employment was made, nor was adequate consideration to support one shown by the employee forsaking another offer. . . . Instead the employer verbally extended a gesture of goodwill.

FACTS
   The plaintiff was hired by the defendant as a sales representative in January 1933. The agreement specified no definite time of employment. The defendant hired another sales representative in April 1933 to work with the plaintiff. Plaintiff consented to enter into a sales partnership with the new representative on the basis of defendant's promise of permanent employment. A competitor offered plaintiff a job in 1940, which he refused after discussing it with defendant. After the other sales representative resigned, plaintiff received an offer from another employer and mentioned it to Triplett, his current employer. Plaintiff claims the defendant told him, orally, that the employment

ILLUSTRATION 6-8.   Continued

arrangement was permanent as they walked together down State Street. The defendant denies the claim. In October 1955, the defendant terminated plaintiff's employment as of November 30, 1955.

REASONING

The act of terminating other employment is not sufficient consideration to make a new contract binding if there is no detriment to the employee. Oral contracts for permanent employment are valid as long as they are supported by a consideration other than the obligation of services to be performed on the one hand and wages to be paid on the other. Where there is no particular detriment to the employee, the act of terminating other employment is not a sufficient consideration to make the new contract binding. When plaintiff was being solicited to join the competitor, the renewal with Triplett Electrical was presented in a vague and indefinite way and cannot be considered as an obligation. Contracts extending for long duration resting entirely on oral statements, parole, should have basis on definite and mutual promises. Words should not be of informal character expressing goodwill and hope for eternal association.

DISPOSITION

Affirmed Count I granting defendant summary judgment on claim of breach of contract, reversed in part, and remanded.

D. CASE ANALYSIS

Comparing and contrasting decisions to assess the outcome of an issue posed by a factual scenario is called **case analysis.** Case analysis is particularly important when you want to evaluate a client's situation and get an idea of how the law will determine the outcome. We look to prior cases to anticipate how a court will rule on the issue we are researching. You must determine if the question before the court, the issue, is the same as or different than the question the client's problem raises. You must examine the facts of the case and the facts of the client's problem to ascertain the similarities and differences. Sometimes only one component of the decision addresses one part of a client's problem. Last, you must use the relevant cases from the appropriate jurisdiction.

1. Sample Single Case Analysis

Read the following abridged case and then read the fact pattern from the client's situation.

ILLUSTRATION 6-9.   Shila Morganroth, Plaintiff-Appellant v. Susan Whitall and The Evening News Association, Inc.

SHILA MORGANROTH, PLAINTIFF-APPELLANT v. SUSAN WHITALL AND THE EVENING NEWS ASSOCIATION, INC., A CORPORATION, DEFENDANTS-APPELLEES

Docket No. 91215

COURT OF APPEALS OF MICHIGAN

161 Mich. App. 785; 411 N.W.2d 859; 1987 Mich. App. LEXIS 2608; 14

Media L. Rep. 1411

April 14, 1987, Submitted

July 21, 1987, Decided

"Truth is a torch that gleams through the fog without dispelling it."
—Claude Helvetius, *De l'Esprit.*

In this heated dispute, the trial court granted summary disposition in favor of defendants on plaintiff's claims of libel and invasion of privacy by false light. Plaintiff now appeals and we affirm.

Plaintiff alleges that she was libeled and cast in a false light by an article written by defendant Whitall which appeared in the Sunday supplement of the *Detroit News* on November 11, 1984. The article was entitled "Hot Locks: Let Shila burn you a new 'do." The article was accompanied by two photographs, one depicting plaintiff performing her craft on a customer identified as "Barbara X" and the second showing Barbara X and her dog, identified as "Harry X," following completion of the hairdressing. Central to the article was the fact that plaintiff used a blowtorch in her hairdressing endeavors. According to the article, plaintiff's blowtorch technique was dubbed "Shi-lit" and was copyrighted.[1] The article also described two dogs, Harry and Snowball, the latter belonging to plaintiff, noting that the canines have had their respective coats colored at least in part. The article also indicated that the blowtorch technique had been applied to both dogs. Additionally, the article described plaintiff's somewhat unusual style of dress, including a silver holster for her blowtorch and a barrette in her hair fashioned out of a $100 bill. Much of the article devoted itself to plaintiff's comments concerning her hairdressing and the trend of what, at least in the past, had been deemed unusual in the area of hair styles . . .

Plaintiff's rather brief complaint alleges that the article, when read as a whole, is false, misleading and constitutes libel. More specifically, the complaint alleges that the article used the terms "blowtorch lady," "blowtorch technique" and the statement that plaintiff "is dressed for blowtorching duty in a slashed-to-there white jumpsuit" without any factual basis and as the result of defendants' intentional conduct to distort and sensationalize the facts obtained in the interview. The complaint further alleges that the article falsely portrayed plaintiff as an

ILLUSTRATION 6-9.   Continued

animal hairdresser, again as part of a deliberate action by defendants to distort and sensationalize the facts. In her brief on appeal, plaintiff also takes exception to her being cast as an animal hairdresser and claims as inaccurate the portrayal in the article that she does "mutt Mohawks for dogs" and the reference to "two canines who have been blowtorched."

Defendants brought their motion for summary disposition pursuant to both MCR 2.116(C)(8), failure to state a claim, and MCR 2.116(C)(10), no genuine issue of material fact . . .

A motion for summary disposition under MCR 2.116(C)(10) tests the factual support for a claim. *Stenke v Masland Development Co, Inc,* 152 Mich App 562; 394 NW2d 418 (1986). In ruling on this motion, the trial court must consider not only the pleadings, but also depositions, affidavits, admissions, and other documentary evidence, MCR 2.116(G)(5), and must give the benefit of any reasonable doubt to the nonmoving party, being liberal in finding a genuine issue of material fact. *Rizzo v Kretschmer,* 389 Mich 363; 207 NW2d 316 (1973). Summary disposition is appropriate under this subrule only if the court is satisfied that it is impossible for the nonmoving party's claim to be supported at trial because of a deficiency which cannot be overcome. *Hetes v Schefman & Miller Law Office,* 152 Mich App 117; 393 NW2d 577 (1986) . . . If the nonmoving party fails to establish that a material fact is at issue, the motion is properly granted. *Stenke, supra.* As noted by defendants and admitted by plaintiff at the motion hearing, plaintiff has failed to file any response to defendants' motion and has come forward with no evidence to support a finding that a genuine issue of material fact exists.

The elements of defamation were stated by this Court in *Sawabini v Desenberg,* 143 Mich App 373, 379; 372 NW2d 559 (1985):

> The elements of a cause of action for defamation are: "(a) a false and defamatory statement concerning plaintiff; (b) an unprivileged publication to a third party; (c) fault amounting at least to negligence on the part of the publisher; and (d) either actionability of the statement irrespective of special harm (defamation per se) or the existence of special harm caused by the publication (defamation *per quod*)." *Postill v Booth Newspapers, Inc,* 118 Mich App 608, 618; 315 NW2d 511 (1982), lv den 417 Mich 1050 (1983), citing Restatement Torts, 2d, β 558; *Curtis v Evening News Association,* 135 Mich App 101, 103; 352 NW2d 355 (1984); *Ledl v Quik Pik Food Stores, Inc,* 133 Mich App 583; 349 NW2d 529 (1984).

See also *Rouch v Enquirer & News of Battle Creek,* 427 Mich 157, 173-174; 398 NW2d 245 (1986).

ILLUSTRATION 6-9. **Continued**

The *Sawabini* Court further commented on the appropriateness of dismissing a defamation claim by summary disposition:

> The court may determine, as a matter of law, whether the words in question, alleged by plaintiff to be defamatory, are capable of defamatory meaning. See, *e.g., Ledsinger v Burmeister,* 114 Mich App 12, 21; 318 NW2d 558 (1982). Where the words are, as a matter of law, not capable of carrying a defamatory meaning, summary judgment under GCR 1963, 117.2(1) is appropriate. See *Lins v Evening News Association,* 129 Mich App 419, 422; 342 NW2d 573 (1983).
>
> "A communication is defamatory if it tends so to harm the reputation of another as to lower him in the estimation of the community or to deter third persons from associating or dealing with him. *Nuyen v Slater,* 372 Mich 654, 662, fn; 127 NW2d 369 (1964); *Ledsinger v Burmeister,* 114 Mich App 12, 21; 318 NW2d 558 (1982)." *Swenson-Davis v Martel,* 135 Mich App 632, 635-636; 354 NWd 288 (1984), *lv den* 419 Mich 946 (1984). In assessing whether language is defamatory, the circumstances should be considered. *Ledsinger v Burmeister, supra.* [143 Mich App 379-380.]

In determining whether an article is libelous, it is necessary to read the article as a whole and fairly and reasonably construe it in determining whether a portion of the article is libelous in character. *Sanders v Evening News Ass'n,* 313 Mich 334, 340; 21 NW2d 152 (1946); *Croton v Gillis,* 104 Mich App 104, 108; 304 NW2d 820 (1981).

Reading the article as a whole, we believe that it is substantially true; therefore plaintiff's complaint lacks an essential element of her defamation claim, namely falsity. In looking at plaintiff's specific allegations of falsity, for the most part we find no falsehood. Considering as a group the various references to plaintiff's using a "blowtorch" in hairstyling, we note that *The Random House College Dictionary, Revised Edition* (1984), defines "blowtorch" as follows:

> [A] small portable apparatus that gives an extremely hot gasoline flame intensified by air under pressure, used esp. in metalworking.

In looking at the photographic exhibits filed by defendants, we believe that the instrument used by plaintiff in her profession can accurately be described as a blowtorch.[2] Accordingly, while the use of the term "blowtorch" as an adjective in connection with references to plaintiff or her hairdressing technique may have been colorful, it was not necessarily inaccurate and certainly not libelous. As for the reference that plaintiff was "dressed for blowtorching duty in a slashed-to-there white jumpsuit," we have examined the photographic exhibits submitted by defendant at the motion hearing and we conclude that reasonable

ILLUSTRATION 6-9.   Continued

minds could not differ in reaching the conclusion that plaintiff did, in fact, wear a jumpsuit "slashed-to-there."

> We acknowledge that *The Random House Dictionary's* definition did not list hairdressing as an example. However, we are not persuaded that the dictionary's editors intended their examples to be exclusive. See also "blowtorch," *Webster's New World Dictionary, 2d College Edition* (1976).

Finally, while having disposed of the allegedly libelous claims contained in the complaint, we briefly turn to the additional allegations of false statement listed in plaintiff's brief on appeal. In her brief, plaintiff claims that defendants inaccurately described her as being a hairdresser for dogs, giving dogs a Mohawk cut, and using a blowtorch on the dogs. While it appears that plaintiff did do hairdressing on dogs, it is not necessarily certain at this point that she did, in fact, use the blowtorch on the dogs. However, as noted above, plaintiff filed no response to the motion for summary disposition in the trial court and, thus, presented no affidavits or other evidentiary showings that the statements in the article were false. Thus, there has been no showing by plaintiff that the statements relating to the dogs were false.

Moreover, inasmuch as it appears undisputed that plaintiff at least dyed the fur of the dogs, which would constitute hairdressing of dogs, we are not persuaded that the article, when read as a whole, becomes libelous because of an inaccurate reference to using the blowtorch on the dogs. This is particularly true since, by plaintiff's conduct, she asserts that blowtorching is a safe practice when performed on humans. Therefore, it would appear that, from plaintiff's perspective, blowtorching would also be safe on dogs, even if she did not engage in such a practice. Furthermore, her claim that she was libeled by labeling her as both a dog hairdresser and a human hairdresser is unsupported in light of the tinting of the dogs' hair. Since the undisputed factual showing indicates that plaintiff did blowtorch her human clientele and style her pooch's fur, we will not split hairs at this point to conclude that the statement that she used her blowtorch on dogs, even if inaccurate, is libelous.

For the above-stated reasons, we conclude that, when reviewing the article and accompanying photographs as a whole, the article was not libelous.

On appeal, plaintiff also argues that the article invaded her privacy by casting her in a false light. . . .

See Restatement Torts, 2d, β 652 E, comment a. Furthermore, comment b to β 652 E, p 395, explains that:

> "The interest protected by this section is the interest of the individual in not being made to appear before the public in an objectionable false light or false position, or in other words, otherwise than as he is. In many

ILLUSTRATION 6-9. Continued

cases to which the rule stated here applies, the publicity given to the plaintiff is defamatory, so that he would have an action for libel or slander. . . . In such a case the action for invasion of privacy will afford an alternative or additional remedy, and the plaintiff can proceed upon either theory, or both, although he can have but one recovery for a single instance of publicity.

"It is not, however, necessary to the action for invasion of privacy that the plaintiff be defamed. It is enough that he is given unreasonable and highly objectionable publicity that attributes to him characteristics, conduct or beliefs that are false, and so is placed before the public in a false position. When this is the case and the matter attributed to the plaintiff is not defamatory, the rule here stated affords a different remedy, not available in an action for defamation."

As indicated in the above discussion under the theory of defamation, with the exception of certain references to hairdressing dogs, none of the conduct attributed to plaintiff in the article was false. Therefore, it could not place plaintiff in a false light. With reference to the assertions concerning her hairdressing of dogs, we do not believe that a rational trier of fact could conclude that, even if inaccurate, those references are unreasonable or put plaintiff in a position of receiving highly objectionable publicity. The article did not indicate that plaintiff harmed, injured or inflicted pain upon the dogs. Rather, at most, the article inaccurately stated that plaintiff used techniques on the dogs, such as blowtorching, which she also used on humans. While the article may have overstated the techniques that she uses on dogs, inasmuch as she advocates those techniques for use on humans, we cannot conclude that plaintiff would believe it highly objectionable that those techniques also be performed on dogs. Similarly, she cannot have been placed in false light as being both the hairdresser of dogs and humans inasmuch as the tinting of the canines' fur would constitute hairdressing. Thus, it would not be placing plaintiff in a false light to indicate that she served both dog and man. Accordingly, we believe that summary disposition was also properly granted on the false light claim.

In summary, although the manner in which the present article was written may have singed plaintiff's desire for obtaining favorable coverage of her unique hairdressing methods, we cannot subscribe to the view that it was libelous. We believe that the trial court aptly summarized this case when it stated that "this Court is of the Opinion that the Plaintiff sought publicity and got it." Indeed, it would appear that the root of plaintiff's dissatisfaction with defendants' article is that the publicity plaintiff received was not exactly the publicity she had in mind. While the publicity may have been inflammatory from plaintiff's vantage point, we do not believe it was libelous. At most, defendants treated the article more lightheartedly than plaintiff either anticipated or hoped. While this may give plaintiff cause to cancel

ILLUSTRATION 6-9. Continued

her subscription to the *Detroit News,* it does not give her cause to complain in court.

Affirmed. Costs to defendants.

CLIENT'S FACTUAL SCENARIO

The partner asked you to apply the Morganroth case to the client's facts. Mrs. Smith came to your firm because of her concern with an article published in the local newspaper, *The Star News. The Star News* reported that Mrs. Smith is a professional pancake flipper and cheerleader for she dresses in a cheerleader's outfit and performs cheers when she delivers the platters of pancakes. Mrs. Smith claims that she was libeled by the article because the depiction is untrue. Mrs. Smith asserted that she is a business owner and a professional chef. Mrs. Smith hoped that the article would provide a restaurant review highlighting the culinary integrity of her cuisine. Additionally, the article had a picture of Mrs. Smith in a cheerleader's skirt and a letter sweater. Also, there was a picture of Mrs. Smith jumping in the air after she delivered a platter of pancakes to a table. Mrs. Smith claims that she is merely energetic and enthusiastic. Mrs. Smith also claims that the outfit fits in with the restaurant's theme as it is called "Collegiate Cakes." Mrs. Smith claims that the article is libelous when because portraying her as a cheerleader is inaccurate.

The first task is to brief the case focusing solely on the issue that Mrs. Smith raised. Mrs. Smith's sole issue is whether the newspaper article portraying her as a cheeleader was libelous. The case also analyzes the issue of false light but since this is not relevant for our analysis it will not be included in the brief.

Reprinted with the permission of LexisNexis.

ILLUSTRATION 6-10. Brief of *Morganroth v. Whitall*

MORGANROTH V. WHITALL,
411 N.W.2d 859 (Mich. Ct. App. 1987).

PROCEDURE

Plaintiff, Shila Morganroth appeals the trial court's decision granting summary disposition to the defendants on the libel claim.

ISSUE

Whether the plaintiff was libeled in an article, written by Whitall a reporter for *The Evening News,* entitled: "Hot Locks: Let Shila burn you a new do" indicated that the plaintiff used a blowtorch to style hair, that she also styled dogs' hair and that she wore a jumpsuit "slashed-to-there" that when read as a whole, can be fairly and reasonably construed as true.

ILLUSTRATION 6-10. Continued

HOLDING

The article was not libelous because as a whole it was true as the instrument the plaintiff used to style hair could be considered similar to a blowtorch, she did color dogs' hair and her jumpsuit, as shown in photos, was revealing.

FACTS

The plaintiff, Ms. Morganroth, was a hairdresser. The article about Ms. Morganroth and her hair styling techniques was in the Sunday supplement of the *Detroit News* on November 11, 1984. The article stated that Ms. Morganroth used a blowtorch to style hair and that she styled the hair of both humans and dogs. Additionally, the article stated that Ms. Morganroth dressed in an unusual manner and wore a holster to hold her blow torch. The article also had pictures of Ms. Morganroth in a jumpsuit with a deep slash in the front. The plaintiff alleged that the defendant 's article was libelous as it did not contain any factual basis when it used the terms "blowtorch lady," "blowtorch technique," and "is dressed for blowtorching duty in a slashed-to-there white jumpsuit."

REASONING

The court determined that the motion for summary disposition should be affirmed because the plaintiff did not file a response indicating that there was a genuine issue of material fact. The court examined the rule of defamation. The court noted that the first element, of defamation, requires that for a statement to be defamatory, it must be false. The court also noted that the words may be examined to determine if they alone have defamatory meaning. The article must be read as a whole to evaluate its meaning to see whether it is libelous completely or whether a part of it is. The court stated that the article, when read in totality, was substantially true. The court construed the dictionary definition of "blowtorch" and determined that the photgraphs of the plaintiff showed that the instrument she used matched the dictionary definition of "blowtorch." Also the photographs showed the plaintiff wearing a revealing jumpsuit. Consequently, because the article as a whole was true, it was not libelous.

DISPOSITION

Affirmed.

Process for Case Analysis: The second task is to look at the parallels between the case and the client's situation.

Both the case and the client's facts concern a person alleging that she was libeled by a newspaper article. In both instances the articles were substantially true. In our facts, Mrs. Smith does dress in a cheerleading skirt and letter sweater when waiting on tables. Mrs. Smith also

ILLUSTRATION 6-10. Continued

does jump in the air at the restaurant. Although jumping in the air may not be a "cheer," it is pretty similar to cheerleading.

The court, in Morganroth, stated that if the article read as a whole is false and misleading then it constitutes libel. Here, Mrs. Smith actually dresses in a cheerleading skirt and letter sweater when she waits on tables. The article in *The Star News* depicted Mrs. Smith, both in text and in photos, as she actually dressed at work and therefore it is substantially true. Because the article in *The Star News* is substantially true, it lacks an essential element of the claim for defamation. Defamation requires the statement concerning the plaintiff to be false. Therefore, based on Morganroth, the article in *The Star News* is most probably not libelous.

2. Sample Analysis Using Two Cases

Compare the briefs in Illustrations 6-6 and 6-8. The holding for *Molitor* is:

> A contract for lifetime employment is in effect if the intention of the parties is clear even if the only consideration for the contract is the promise of the employee to render the service called for by the contract.

The holding for *Heuvelman* is:

> No oral contract for permanent employment was made, nor was adequate consideration to support one shown by the employee forsaking another offer, instead the employer verbally extended a gesture of goodwill.

Note the differences in the holdings. *Molitor* states that the only consideration required to support the permanent employment contract is for the employee to perform the services required by the contract. *Heuvelman* states that a contract for permanent employment requires additional consideration beyond forgoing another employment opportunity. *Molitor* is from 1945 and *Heuvelman* is from 1959.

Now let's examine the following fact pattern:

> Howard Smith contacted Mary Dole, the senior partner of Dole, Dole & Dole regarding the situation described below.
>
> Howard Smith is a well-regarded college administrator. For the past ten years he has been vice president for development at State University, located in Springtown, Illinois. He gained a national reputation for successful fundraising. He also held the faculty rank of full professor with tenure.
>
> In the spring of 2012, Prestige University of Urban, Illinois, a private university 200 miles north of Springtown, was looking for a new vice president for development. Smith was encouraged by a

friend at Prestige to apply for the position. Smith submitted an application to Mark Clark, Prestige's president.

Clark knew of Smith's fine reputation, and immediately scheduled interviews with Prestige's search committee. The interviews went extremely well, and at the end of the day Clark offered the job to Smith.

Smith responded, "Well, I'm very flattered. But frankly, it would have to be a major deal. I'd be giving up a happy situation and a very secure position with tenure and all."

Clark replied, "I think we can make you even happier. We will offer you $200,000 a year to start, plus a new car. And I look forward to having you at Prestige University for the rest of your life."

Smith responded, "The money is great, but I am concerned about the job security and moving 200 miles."

Clark replied, "Like I said, I look forward to your presence at Prestige for the rest of your life."

Smith immediately accepted the position at Prestige. No written document was signed. The men did shake hands immediately after Clark stated his acceptance.

Smith soon resigned his position at State, moved to Urban, purchased a home for $500,000, and started his new position as Vice President for Development at Prestige University. However, within five months, Smith and Clark had several disagreements over fundraising strategies. When the disagreements continued, Clark fired Smith, less than ten months after the agreement was reached.

Smith wants to file suit against Prestige University for the breach of an oral contract for permanent employment. Please assess whether a valid oral contract for permanent employment existed between Smith and Prestige University or whether the contract was terminable at will.

Examine the *Molitor* brief and the *Heuvelman* brief, particularly the holdings and the reasoning, as applied to the Smith problem set out above. Look for parallels and distinctions from the cases when compared to the Smith fact scenario. *Molitor* holds that the only consideration required to support an oral contract for permanent employment is for the employee to perform the services required by the contract. In our problem, it seemed that Smith and Clark had disagreements over how Smith was performing his job. The facts did not contain a specific job description for the Vice President for Development at Prestige. However, because of the battles between Smith and Clark over fundraising strategies, it seems that Smith was not performing his job as expected by Clark. Therefore, since Smith did not perform the services implied by their agreement, Smith did not render adequate consideration to support the permanent employment contract.

However, *Heuvelman* holds that a contract for permanent employment requires additional consideration beyond forgoing another employment opportunity. Aside from relinquishing his position at State, Smith purchased a home for $500,000 and moved 200 miles. Additional consideration, aside from forgoing another employment opportunity, exists to support a contract for permanent employment between Smith and Prestige University.

Notice how the facts are examined in our client's situation and applied to the holdings from the cases. We also try to parallel the courts' reasoning by inserting our facts into the tests that the courts used. These are essential parts of legal analysis. Also, compare and contrast the decisions. Briefing cases on a single page, in uniform categories, helps us compare and contrast decisions easily. Look carefully at the facts that the judge uses to apply the law to the issue raised in the case—this provides crucial insight into legally significant facts.

PRACTICE POINTER

When evaluating which case or cases to use, remember that cases from the appropriate jurisdiction are essential for binding precedent. Also, newer cases are stronger than older cases. Cases from higher courts are stronger than those from lower courts.

CHAPTER SUMMARY

A case brief has several components, including a citation, the procedural history, an issue, a holding, the relevant facts, the reasoning, and the case disposition. These briefs are designed to assist you and sometimes an attorney in understanding a case.

The brief's procedural facts statement should explain briefly how a case came before a court.

The issue statement presents the questions posed by the parties. The holding is the rule of law established by the court. The facts statement should include any relevant facts that affected the court's decision in the case. The reasoning explains how the court developed the rule of law and how it relates to the facts of the case. The disposition is the procedural result of the case.

Dicta often is included in a court decision. It is a statement made by a court concerning an issue other than one the court was asked to decide.

This chapter also provides you with your first exposure to legal analysis. You learned the step-by-step process of drafting a case brief as well as how to compare cases with one another and a legal problem.

KEY TERMS

case analysis	issue
case brief	legally significant fact
case citation	procedural history
dicta	rationale
disposition	reasoning
facts	relevant facts
holding	rule of law

EXERCISES

IN-CLASS
Issues

1. Review the following issues prepared for a case brief of the *King* case. List any problems you find. Which issue of the following five is best, and why?

Issue 1. Was the district court's decision that King was an independent contractor rather than an employee of the Miller Co. erroneous?

Issue 2. Whether King was an employee of Miller or an independent contractor for these reasons:

a. The control factor, in which agents are restricted in the selling of insurance as to whom or where. Agents also have mandatory requirements for working at designated times and dates. In addition, they are expected to attend weekly meetings and engage in daily office tasks.

b. The economic factor, in which agents are not allowed to sell products for anyone but Miller and that agents are "integral" to Miller's business.

c. As with employees, services, supplies, and education expenses are provided. Compensation is made in the form of commissions.

d. Work hours are based on flexibility for prime selling.

e. Performance evaluations and documents of rules of conduct are customary requirements of an employer-employee relationship.

Issue 3. Whether, in finding the plaintiff was not an employee under the Title VII definition, the trial court erred by:

f. failing to properly evaluate the nature of insurance sales;

g. failing to evaluate and weigh the integral economic relationship between the defendant and the plaintiff; and

h. failing to discuss other evidence regarding the "control" criterion used to judge eligibility.

Issue 4. Whether the district court was clearly erroneous in determining that an insurance agent is an independent contractor rather than an employee when the individual is paid commissions and bonuses rather than a salary and her work is not supervised by the company.

Issue 5. Does an employer have to exercise control over a worker before that individual is considered an employee under Title VII?

Holdings

2. Review the holdings below that were drafted for a brief in the *King* case, list any problems you see with each, and note which is the best.

> Holding 1. The court of appeals affirmed the lower court's decision that King is an independent contractor rather than an employee of the Miller Co.
> Holding 2. Because the trial court did understand the law and its factual findings are not clearly erroneous, its decision is affirmed.
> Holding 3. The district court's underlying factual findings are not clearly erroneous; therefore, the decision of the district court was affirmed.
> Holding 4. Yes. An employer must exercise control over a worker before that individual is considered an employee under Title VII.

HOMEWORK

Briefing

3. Brief *Kalal v. Goldblatt Bros.*, 368 N.E.2d 671 (Ill. App. Ct. 1977).
4. Brief the following case:

KREIGER v. KREIGER

No. 371
SUPREME COURT OF THE UNITED STATES
334 U.S. 555; 68 S. Ct. 1221; 92 L. Ed. 1572; 1948 U.S. LEXIS 2085
February 2-3, 1948, Argued
June 7, 1948, Decided

COUNSEL: James G. Purdy argued the cause for petitioner. With him on the brief was Abraham J. Nydick.

Charles Rothenberg argued the cause and filed a brief for respondent.

JUDGES: Vinson, Black, Reed, Frankfurter, Douglas, Murphy, Jackson, Rutledge, Burton

OPINION BY: DOUGLAS

OPINION: Opinion of the Court by MR. JUSTICE DOUGLAS, announced by MR. JUSTICE REED.

This is a companion case to *Estin v. Estin*, ante, p. 541, also here on certiorari to the Court of Appeals of New York.

The parties were married in New York in 1933 and lived there together until their separation in 1935. In 1940 respondent obtained a decree of separation in New York on grounds of abandonment. Petitioner appeared in the action; and respondent was awarded $60 a week alimony for the support of herself and their only child, whose custody she was given.

Petitioner thereafter went to Nevada where he continues to reside. He instituted divorce proceedings in that state in the fall of 1944. Constructive service was made on respondent who made no appearance in the Nevada proceedings. While they were pending, respondent obtained an order in New York purporting to enjoin petitioner from seeking a divorce and from remarrying. Petitioner was neither served with process in New York nor entered an appearance in the latter proceeding. The Nevada court, with knowledge of the injunction and the New York judgment for alimony, awarded petitioner an absolute divorce on grounds of three consecutive years of separation without cohabitation. The judgment made no provision for alimony. It did provide that petitioner was to support, maintain, and educate the child, whose custody it purported to grant him, and as to which jurisdiction was reserved. Petitioner thereafter tendered $50 a month for the support of the child but ceased making payments under the New York decree.

Respondent thereupon brought suit on the New York judgment in a federal district court in Nevada. Without waiting the outcome of that litigation she obtained a judgment in New York for the amount of the arrears, petitioner appearing and unsuccessfully pleading his Nevada divorce as a defense. The judgment was affirmed by the Appellate Division, two judges dissenting. 271 N.Y. App. Div. 872, 66 N.Y.S.2d 798. The Court of Appeals affirmed without opinion, 297 N.Y. 530, 74 N.E.2d 468, but stated in its remittitur that its action was based upon *Estin v. Estin*, 296 N.Y. 308, 73 N.E.2d 113. Respondent does not attack the bona fides of petitioner's Nevada domicile.

For the reasons stated in *Estin v. Estin*, ante, p. 541, we hold that Nevada had no power to adjudicate respondent's rights in the New York judgment and thus New York was not required to bow to that provision of the Nevada decree. It is therefore unnecessary to pass upon New York's attempt to enjoin petitioner from securing a divorce or to reach the question whether the New York judgment was entitled to full faith and credit in the Nevada proceedings. No issue as to the custody of the child was raised either in the court below or in this Court. The judgment is

Affirmed.

MR. JUSTICE FRANKFURTER dissents for the reasons stated in his dissenting opinion in *Estin v. Estin*, ante, p. 549.

MR. JUSTICE JACKSON dissents for the reasons set forth in his opinion in *Estin v. Estin*, ante, p. 553.

---

5. Brief *Talford v. Columbia Med. Ctr. at Lancaster Sub., L.P.*, 198 S.W.3d 462 (Tex. App. 2006).
6. Brief *DeMercado v. McClung*, 55 Cal. Rptr. 3d 889 (Ct. App. 2007).

Analysis Exercises
7. Review *Seymour v. Armstrong* in Illustration 6-1. An attorney asked you to apply the holdings of *Seymour* to the following fact pattern.

Mrs. Johnson, the owner of Frocks, Etc., ordered 50 dresses at the price of $35 per dress to be delivered in one week. Mrs. Johnson ordered the dresses from ABC Dress Company and sent a contract stating that she requests 50 dresses at $35 per dress, totaling $1750 payable upon receipt of the dresses. Mrs. Johnson assumes that when ABC ships the dresses this indicates that they are assenting to the contract by their action. However, ABC sends an invoice with the dresses for $1750 plus shipping of $106. The attorney wants to know, in light of the holding in *Seymour,* if ABC is imposing a new condition in the contract, with no agreement existing between ABC and Frocks, Etc.?

8. Reread *Seymour v. Armstrong* in Illustration 6-1. Now find and read *Steele v. Harrison,* 522 P.2d 957 (Kan. 1976).
   a. Was there a meeting of the minds in the contract in *Steele?*
   b. Was there a meeting of the minds in the contract in *Seymour?*
   c. How is *Steele* similar to *Seymour?*
   d. How does *Steele* differ factually from *Seymour?*
   e. Does *Steele* apply the holding from *Seymour?*
9. Read *Farone v. Bag'n'Baggage, Ltd.,* 165 S.W.3d 795 (Tex. App. 2005). How is *Farone* factually similar to the Smith/Prestige University fact pattern in section D of this chapter? Which facts differ?

THE LEGAL MEMORANDUM

CHAPTER OVERVIEW

This chapter introduces you to the legal memorandum. You learn about your audience and how to write objectively. You are introduced to the components of the memorandum, such as the issues, conclusion or brief answer, facts, and discussion sections. The chapter concludes with a brief overview of the process of writing a memorandum.

A. THE LEGAL MEMORANDUM

▼ What Is an Objective Legal Memorandum and Why Is It Written?

An **office memorandum,** often called a memo, explains in an objective rather than a persuasive or argumentative manner the current state of the law regarding an issue. It clarifies how that law applies to a client's transaction or legal dilemma. A memo should explain the current law—both favorable and unfavorable—and any legal theories pertaining to the issues.

The balanced approach of a legal memo helps an attorney see the strengths and weaknesses of a transaction or dispute. Only when an attorney can see all sides of an issue can the attorney determine how best to represent a client. Sometimes your research will determine whether the client has a case or not. If in writing a memo you advocate a single position or attempt to persuade an attorney, the attorney cannot make an informed decision about a dispute or transaction. This can be a very costly error in terms of money, time, client loyalty, and court favor.

A memo also assists an attorney in predicting how a court might decide a particular issue. A memo could be drafted to address an issue raised as a case progresses in court. As a paralegal, you might research whether the law provides for the dismissal of an action; your research and memorandum might form the basis for such a motion to dismiss or for subsequent court documents or motions. You might also write a memo to assist an attorney in drafting an appellate brief, a document used to appeal a trial court's decision.

ETHICS ALERT

Never send to a client a research memo that you write without an attorney's review and approval.

B. AUDIENCE

▼ Who Reads a Memorandum?

You will usually research a legal question to determine whether a client has a claim or should proceed with a case. Following your research, you generally prepare a memo for an attorney. Your memo also might be sent to the client. Your primary audience, then, is the attorney, and the secondary audience is the client.

Often memoranda are saved in **memo banks** accessible to all firm or corporation attorneys and paralegals, so other attorneys and paralegals might review your memo.

C. COMPONENTS OF A MEMORANDUM

▼ What Is Included in a Memorandum?

A memorandum can have a variety of components arranged in different orders. The components and their order often vary from attorney to attorney. Ask the assigning attorney if your firm or corporation has a particular style. Request a sample memo so that you can review the style he or she prefers, or go to the memo bank to review a sample. The format discussed in this chapter is one commonly accepted style. See the sample memo in Illustration 7-1. Additional sample memos may be found in Appendix B.

ILLUSTRATION 7-1.   Sample Memorandum

MEMORANDUM

To: Benjamin Joyce
From: William Randall
Date: January 28, 2012
Re: *Harris v. Sack and Shop*

QUESTION PRESENTED
    Is Sack and Shop, a grocery store, liable for injuries sustained by Harris, a store patron who slipped on a banana peel that had been left on the grocery store floor for two days?

BRIEF ANSWER
    Probably yes. Sack and Shop, a grocery store, probably will be liable based on negligence for injuries sustained by Harris, a store patron who slipped on a banana peel that had been left on the grocery store floor for two days.

FACTS
    Our client, Sack and Shop Grocery Store, is being sued for negligence by Rebecca Harris.
    Harris went to the store to purchase groceries on July 8, 2011. While she was in the produce section, she slipped on a banana that a grocery store employee left on the floor. The employee had dropped it on the floor two days earlier and had failed to clean it up after a patron asked him to do so.
    Harris sustained a broken arm and head injuries as a result of the slip and fall.

DISCUSSION
    The issue presented in this case is whether Sack and Shop Grocery Store was negligent when Rebecca Harris slipped in the store's produce section. A grocer will be found negligent if a store employee breached

ILLUSTRATION 7-1. Continued

the store's duty of reasonable care to its patrons and, as a result of that breach, the patron was injured. *Ward v. K Mart Corp.*, 554 N.E.2d. 223 (Ill. 1990). In *Ward*, the grocery store employee failed to clean up a banana peel for two days and that peel caused a patron to be injured. Similarly in our case Sack and Shop failed to remove the banana peel for two days. Therefore, Sack and Shop is likely to be found liable for the injuries Harris sustained.

The first element to consider is whether Sack and Shop owed a duty of reasonable care to Harris. A grocery store owes a duty of care to any patron. *Ward*, 554 N.E.2d at 226. Harris was a customer in the store. Therefore, Sack and Shop owed her a duty of care.

The next question to consider is whether Sack and Shop breached its duty of reasonable care to Harris. A store will be found to have breached its duty of reasonable care to a patron if a store employee fails to properly and regularly clean the floor of the store. *Olinger v. Great Atl. & Pac. Tea Co.*, 173 N.E.2d 443 (Ill. 1961). In *Olinger*, the store was found liable because a store employee failed to clean the floor for one day and a patron slipped on a substance on the floor. 173 N.E.2d at 447. No one had told any store employee about the slippery substance. *Id.* at 447. Nonetheless, the Illinois Supreme Court found the store liable, saying that the store employees had sufficient time to notice the substance if they had used ordinary care. *Id.* In our case, Sack and Shop's employee had two days to clean the floor before Harris fell. In addition, a customer had placed the store employee on notice of the banana. Therefore, Sack and Shop breached its duty of care to Harris.

The plaintiff, however, still must establish proximate cause—that is, that the injury resulted as a natural consequence of Sack and Shop's breach of its duty. A store owner's failure to clear debris from a store floor, resulting in injury to a patron who slipped on the floor, was found to be the proximate cause of the patron's injuries. *Id.* at 449. In this case, Sack and Shop's failure to clean the peel from the floor was a breach of its duty of care to Harris. This breach resulted in injury to Harris. Sack and Shop's breach will be found to be the proximate cause of Harris's injuries.

The final element that must be established is that the plaintiff, Harris, suffered injuries. Harris sustained a broken arm and head injuries as a result of the slip and fall. Therefore, she will be able to show that she was injured.

CONCLUSION

Sack and Shop owed Harris a duty of reasonable care. The store is likely to be found to have breached that duty of reasonable care because an employee failed to remove a banana peel from the grocery store floor during the preceding two days. The injuries Harris sustained were directly caused by a slip on a banana peel. Therefore, Sack and Shop is likely to be found liable to Harris.

1. Heading

In Illustrations 7-1 and 7-2 the first part of the memo is the heading. A sample heading also is shown in Illustration 7-3. The first notation in the heading of either illustration is the word "MEMORANDUM," placed in all capital letters at the top of the page. The next notations in Illustrations 7-1, 7-2, and 7-3 tell the reader who the memorandum is written to and from, the date, and the subject. The regarding line, indicated by the "Re:," varies depending on the firm's style. For example, some insurance clients ask that you include claim numbers in the regarding line. Some attorneys prefer court case numbers, and still others prefer clients' billing numbers and file numbers.

ILLUSTRATION 7-2.   Sample Memorandum: McMillan Battery Action

---

MEMORANDUM

To: William Houck
From: Ivy Courier
Date: November 7, 2011
Re: McMillan Battery Action

QUESTION PRESENTED
 Did an actionable battery occur when Mann intentionally struck McMillan with a bucket, without McMillan's consent, causing McMillan to suffer physical and monetary injuries?

CONCLUSION
 Mann's intentional striking of McMillan with a bucket and sand was an actionable battery.

FACTS
 Our client, Mary McMillan, a 36-year-old bank teller, wants to bring an action for battery against Carol Mann, a 36-year-old mother, who threw a metal bucket filled with sand at McMillan at a local park. While McMillan sat on a park bench, she teased Mann's seven-year-old son. Mann did not like this teasing and threw a bucket filled with sand at Mary. Sand landed in McMillan's eyes while she was wearing soft contact lenses. As a result, McMillan's contacts had to be replaced. The bucket also cut McMillan's eye and cheek. She had stitches in both places. McMillan asked Mann to pay for her doctor bills and for the new contacts. Mann refused and added, "I'm not sorry. I meant to hurt you."

DISCUSSION
 The issue presented is whether Mann's intentional touching of McMillan with a bucket rather than her person is an actionable battery. A battery is the intentional touching of another without consent, which causes

ILLUSTRATION 7-2. Continued

injury. *Anderson v. St. Francis-St. George Hosp., Inc.,* 77 Ohio St. 3d 82, 671 N.E.2d 225 (1996). A touching can occur when an object rather than an individual's body contacts the other party. *Leichtman v. WLW Jacoc Communications, Inc.,* 92 Ohio App. 3d 232, 634 N.E.2d 697 (1994); *Smith v. John Deere Co.,* 83 Ohio App. 3d 398, 614 N.E.2d 1148 (1993). In this case, Mann intentionally struck McMillan with a bucket without McMillan's consent and that touching resulted in injuries. Therefore, a battery occurred.

The threshold issue is whether a touching occurred when the bucket struck McMillan. A contact between a nonconsenting party and object rather than the actor's body can be a battery. *Leichtman v. WLW Jacoc Communications, Inc.,* 92 Ohio App. 3d 232, 634 N.E.2d 697 (1994); *Smith v. John Deere Co.,* 83 Ohio App. 3d at 398, 614 N.E.2d at 1148. In *Leichtman,* one person blew cigar smoke at another person, resulting in injuries. The court found that the cigar smoke was an extension of the person and that a contact between the smoke and the nonconsenting person met the requirement of a touching for civil battery. In this case, Mann threw the bucket at McMillan, and the bucket contacted her face. Following the reasoning in the *Leichtman* case, the bucket would be an extension of Mann's body, and the contact between McMillan and the bucket would be considered a touching under the theory of civil battery.

Next, the question to consider is whether under the statute Mann intended to touch McMillan when she struck her with the bucket. A person intends his or her conduct when he or she undertakes an action with a knowing mind. *Smith v. John Deere Co.,* 83 Ohio App. 3d 398, 614 N.E.2d 1148 (1993). In *Smith,* a police officer handcuffed the plaintiff. The court found that the officer must have intended his actions because you could not accidentally handcuff a person. *Smith,* 83 Ohio App. 3d at 399, 614 N.E.2d at 1149. In McMillan's case, Mann aimed the bucket at McMillan purposefully trying to strike her; Mann later told McMillan that she deliberately threw the bucket at her. McMillan probably will be able to establish that Mann had the statutory intent.

The next factor to consider is whether McMillan consented to the contact. If a person consents to the touching, a battery has not occurred. *Love v. Port Clinton,* 37 Ohio St. 3d 98, 524 N.E.2d 166 (1988). In our case, McMillan did not consent to Mann's throwing of the bucket at her face. Therefore, McMillan did not consent to any contact. Finally, the question is whether McMillan suffered physical injuries. A battery occurs only if a plaintiff sustains physical injuries as a result of the touching. *Anderson v. St. Francis-St. George Hosp., Inc.,* 77 Ohio St. 3d 82, 671 N.E.2d 225 (1996). McMillan sustained cuts on her face and the sand flying out of the bucket into her eyes. McMillan will be able to show that she sustained physical injuries as a result of the contact with the bucket.

ILLUSTRATION 7-3.   Sample Memorandum Heading

MEMORANDUM

To: Sarah E. Lillian
From: Kelsey Barrington
Date: July 8, 2012
Re: Negligence Action between Sack and Shop Grocery Store and
     Rebecca Harris

2. Questions Presented or Issues

The next portion of the memo seen in Illustrations 7-1 and 7-2 consists of the questions presented section, sometimes called the issues section.

The terms **issues** or **questions presented** are synonymous. For our purposes, we will use the terms *question presented* or *questions presented*. The questions presented are the specific legal questions an attorney has asked you to research. The question presented is phrased in the form of a question concerning the legal issue posed, and it includes a reference to the applicable law and some legally significant facts. See Illustration 7-4. The legal issue in Illustration 7-4 is whether the grocery store owner was negligent and whether he owed a duty to the patron. The legally significant facts are that the patron slipped on a banana peel that had been on the grocery store floor for two days. (A detailed explanation of how to draft the questions presented is provided in Chapter 8.) Note the facts included in the questions presented section of Illustration 7-2. These facts are the legally significant facts. They are interwoven with the standard of law applicable to this case.

ILLUSTRATION 7-4.   Question Presented

Is a grocery store owner liable for injuries sustained by a store patron who slipped on a banana peel that had been on the grocery store floor for two days?

3. Conclusion or Brief Answer

You should follow the questions presented section with a brief answer or a conclusion. Brief answers and conclusions differ in format, although their purposes are similar. A brief answer is a short statement that directly answers the question or questions presented. See Illustration 7-5. A conclusion is similar, but it is usually longer. In Illustration 7-2, you will find an example of a conclusion. If there were two issues presented, you would include two conclusions. Both would be placed in the same order as the issues that they answer.

ILLUSTRATION 7-5. Brief Answer

Probably yes. A grocery store owner probably will be liable based upon negligence for injuries sustained by a store patron who slipped on a banana peel that had been on the grocery store floor for two days.

▼ What Is the Difference Between a Conclusion and a Brief Answer?

Some attorneys prefer a brief answer immediately following the question or questions presented and a formal conclusion at the end of the memo. The brief answer should be presented in the same order as the questions they answer.

For other attorneys, a conclusion without a brief answer is sufficient. A conclusion is an in-depth answer to the question presented. There is no set length for a conclusion; it should be a succinct statement that summarizes the substance of the memo. See Illustration 7-6. As you can see in Illustration 7-6, the conclusion is more in-depth than the brief answer. However, note that both the conclusion and the brief answer include references to the legally significant facts: the failure to remove the banana peel from the grocery store floor. In the conclusion, you provide your opinion concerning the case. However, a paralegal should refrain from telling an attorney how to proceed. For example, do not say "I think that we will lose this case, so we should settle it." Instead, say "This case is not likely to be won." Allow the attorney to determine whether the case should be settled. (Drafting conclusions and brief answers is explained in detail in Chapter 8.)

ILLUSTRATION 7-6. Conclusion

A grocery store owner owes a patron a duty of reasonable care. The store owner is likely to be found to have breached that duty of reasonable care because he failed to remove a banana peel from the grocery store floor during the preceding two days. The injuries the patron sustained were directly caused by a slip on a banana peel. Therefore, the grocery store owner is likely to be found liable to the patron.

ETHICS ALERT

Refrain from providing a legal opinion. Your memorandum may be given to a client and may be construed as providing legal advice.

4. Facts

Following the conclusion or brief answer, you should include a facts statement that explains the status of the case and all the facts that might have a bearing on the outcome of a client's case. These facts are called legally significant facts. You should include facts that cast your client's dispute or transaction in a good light and those that shade it in a negative light. See Illustration 7-7. The presentation of facts should be balanced rather than slanted.

ILLUSTRATION 7-7.   Facts Statement

Our client, Sack and Shop Grocery Store, is being sued for negligence by Rebecca Harris.

Harris went to the store to purchase groceries on July 8, 2012. While she was in the produce section, she slipped on a banana peel that had been left on the floor by a grocery store employee. The employee had dropped it on the floor two days earlier and had failed to clean it up after a patron asked him to do so. Harris sustained a broken arm and head injuries as a result of the slip and fall.

5. Discussion

Following the facts, you will include your discussion in which you will explain the current state of the applicable law, analyze the law, and apply the law to the legally significant facts noted in the facts statement. Any problems posed in the client's case and counterarguments should be presented here. This should not be an exhaustive review of the history of the law but should be focused analysis of the current state of the law. The law should be applied to each of the legally significant facts. Note if the law is primary binding or merely persuasive authority. Use only highly persuasive secondary authorities if primary authorities are not available.

Finally, following the discussion, you should include a conclusion if a brief answer rather than a conclusion has been used earlier. Review the discussion sections in Illustrations 7-1 and 7-2.

PRACTICE POINTER

Review memos prepared previously for the attorney who assigned the memorandum. Follow that format or ask the assigning attorney what format he or she prefers.

D. STEPS IN DRAFTING A MEMORANDUM

▼ What Steps Should You Take in Drafting a Memo?

1. An attorney will assign a research problem to you. Discuss the problem thoroughly with the attorney. Be certain to ask the attorney questions to clarify the legal issues and the facts of a dispute or transaction. Ask for guidance concerning possible topics to research and resources to consult.

2. Immediately following your meeting, draft a preliminary statement of the legal issues and the relevant facts.

3. Begin your research. To develop an understanding of the issues and the general legal rules applicable to your problem, and to provide you with some search terms, read secondary authorities such as encyclopedias. During your research, you often will discover other issues that may be relevant, and you will find additional facts that are important. If you are uncertain whether to pursue these additional issues, ask the attorney who assigned the case whether the issues are relevant.

4. If you have additional questions about the facts of a case, ask the attorney or the client for additional facts to assist you in determining what authorities are relevant to your research.

5. Find primary binding authorities. If you are unable to find those, locate persuasive primary or secondary authorities.

6. After you find relevant authorities, validate the authorities and review the citators for more current, valuable authorities. If necessary, review these additional authorities.

7. Prepare case briefs of the relevant cases. (See Chapter 6 for a detailed discussion of case briefing.)

8. After you have completed your research, rewrite the questions presented.

9. Rewrite the facts and then draft the brief answers or conclusions (or both).

10. Next, outline the discussion section. (See Chapter 12 for a discussion of outlining and organizing the memorandum.) While you are preparing your outline, you should synthesize the legal authorities. (This process is explained in Chapter 11.) You should formulate your discussion and paragraphs in a special format called IRAC, which is an abbreviation for the formula Issue, Rule, Application, and Conclusion. (This format is discussed thoroughly in Chapter 10.) You can now begin to write your memorandum.

CHECKLIST

1. Discuss the case with the attorney
   a. Discuss the legal issues presented
   b. Discuss the known facts
   c. Determine whether additional facts should be investigated

      d. Determine what law governs

      e. Check the memo bank to determine firm's style and to learn whether the issue has been researched previously

2. Draft a preliminary statement of the facts
3. Draft a preliminary statement of the legal issues or questions presented
4. Research the legal issue or issues

      a. If you find additional relevant issues, discuss them with the attorney

      b. Determine whether additional facts should be considered in light of the new issues; ask the attorney or client about additional facts

      c. Research the new issues, if necessary

5. Rewrite the issues or questions presented after your research has allowed you to focus them better
6. Draft a brief answer or a conclusion (or both)
7. Rewrite the facts statement of the memo
8. Draft an outline of the discussion section of the memo; organize the discussion
9. Draft the discussion section
10. Reevaluate the facts and rewrite the facts statement to include only legally significant facts
11. Rewrite the conclusion

1. Memo Drafting Tips

You should be careful to guide your reader through each section of your memo and from issue to issue. To do this, introduce the legal issues in the facts section and again in the discussion section. Also, use headings and transitions to guide your reader into the new sections. Your memo should be clearly written, accurate, concise, and thorough. Use everyday language rather than legalese. Write the memo as if the reader is unfamiliar with the law, but do not be condescending.

Your memo should not trace the legal history of the law. Instead, it should be a statement of the current state of the law.

When you approach a legal rule, start with the rule rather than the citation for the authority. Doing so makes your discussion stronger.

Be certain that your discussion supports your conclusions. Incorporate the relevant facts into your discussion.

CHAPTER SUMMARY

The legal memorandum is composed of issues, conclusions and brief answers, facts, and a discussion section. These are written for attorneys and clients. Memoranda are designed to assist them in determining the current state of the law regarding a legal issue and how that law applies to the facts presented in a particular case.

In the next few chapters, you will learn about each one of the components of a memorandum, the questions presented, the facts, the conclusions, the brief answers, and the discussion.

KEY TERMS

brief answer	issues
conclusion	legally significant facts
discussion	memo banks
facts statement	office memorandum
heading	questions presented

EXERCISES

TRUE OR FALSE

1. A memorandum should be persuasive in its style.
2. A memorandum should present only facts that are favorable to your client's position.
3. A memorandum should inform the attorney and the client about the favorable authorities and known facts as well as the authorities and facts that pose problems for a client's case.
4. Your memorandum will never be read by a client.
5. You should include descriptive words in the facts section. Slant the facts in favor of your client's position.
6. What are the components of a memorandum?

CHAPTER 8

QUESTIONS PRESENTED AND CONCLUSIONS OR BRIEF ANSWERS

CHAPTER OVERVIEW

Chapter 7 introduced you to the legal memorandum and its components. This chapter explains the reasons for drafting questions presented, issues, brief answers, and conclusions, and teaches you how to draft these items.

A. QUESTIONS PRESENTED OR ISSUES

The questions presented or issues are the problems you must research to answer the attorney's or client's questions. These questions provide a preview to the reader about the applicable legal standards and the relevant facts. They are always posed in the form of a question.

▼ Who Reads the Questions Presented Statement?

The questions presented statement often is the first portion of a memorandum an attorney reviews. Many attorneys focus on these questions and the conclusions or brief answers. Some attorneys read these questions and answers without reading the entire memorandum. Therefore, your questions presented statement must be easy to understand and allow the reader to quickly grasp the legal questions that the memo will address.

1. First Draft

The first draft of the questions presented should be done following the receipt of the initial research assignment from the attorney. Draft a simple statement that explains the questions you were asked to research. For example, suppose an attorney provides you with the following facts:

> While driving a car Ronnie Randall struck Janice Kahn's son at 5:00 P.M. on August 29, 2011. It was bright and clear. No skid marks appeared on the dry street following the accident.
>
> Janice Kahn was working in her garden about five feet from the accident scene at the time of the accident. Her son was playing a game in the street before Randall's car struck him. Kahn saw the car strike her son. When she first looked up from her garden, she thought her 11-year-old son, Bill, was dead. He was covered with blood and had several broken bones. However, Kahn's son was conscious after the accident.
>
> Immediately after the accident, Randall, who had a blood alcohol level of .11, was cited for drunk driving and driving with a suspended driver's license. Police had charged him with drunk driving and had suspended his license two weeks earlier after the car he was driving struck another child at the same spot. Randall has a drinking history.
>
> Following the accident, several witnesses said Randall was upset and wobbled as he walked. One witness said that Randall intentionally turned the steering wheel to hit Kahn's son. Kahn stated that Randall often swerved down her street to get her attention.
>
> Rhonda Albert, Kahn's neighbor, said she heard Randall say he would get even with Kahn after Kahn broke off a ten-year relationship with him. During Kahn and Randall's ten-year relationship, Randall was close to Kahn's son. He took him to ball games, including one in April, and attended the son's baseball games. Randall knew that Kahn's son was the most important person in her life.

Since the accident, Janice Kahn vomits daily and suffers from anxiety and headaches. Dr. Susan Faigen, Kahn's internist, states that the vomiting, anxiety, and headaches are the result of the accident.

The attorney wants you to research whether Janice Kahn has a claim against Ronnie Randall for intentional infliction of emotional distress. Your first draft of the question presented might be:

> Does Janice Kahn have a valid claim for intentional infliction of emotional distress against Ronnie Randall?

This statement is devoid of legally significant facts.

▼ What Are Legally Significant Facts?

These are facts that will have an impact on a jury's or judge's decisions concerning Kahn's claim. This question presented is too vague. To make your question more understandable in the context of Kahn's case, you must incorporate legally significant facts.

Legally Significant Facts

Kahn saw Randall strike her 11 year-old son
Randall struck the boy with his car
Kahn now suffers from anxiety, headaches, and vomiting

You might rewrite the question presented with the fact that Kahn saw Randall strike her 11-year-old son with his car. That fact is legally significant. The rewrite might read as follows:

> Does Janice Kahn have a valid claim for intentional infliction of emotional distress against Ronnie Randall when Kahn **saw** Randall strike her 11-year-old child with his car?

By incorporating some legally significant facts, you have drafted a question presented that places the issue in perspective for the reader and that clearly identifies the parties in the action. This question presented allows the reader to understand the legal issue in the context of the factual circumstances surrounding the claim.

2. Research the Issue and Revise It

Now you are ready to research the issue. After you complete your research, you determine what law applies to a claim for intentional infliction of emotional distress. Once you determine the legal standard, you rewrite the question presented to incorporate that standard and only the legally significant facts. Your rewrite should frame the questions presented around the applicable legal standard and should present the applicable legal standard in the context of the facts that will affect the determination of a claim.

In the case of Janice Kahn, you learn from a decision of the highest court in your state that intentional infliction of emotional distress is "an act done by a person which is extreme and outrageous, done with intent to cause another to suffer severe emotional distress, and which results in distress and emotional injury to another. The emotional injury must manifest itself with a physical problem." If you rewrite the question presented above to incorporate the legal standard and legally significant facts, it might read as follows:

> Does Janice Kahn have a valid claim for intentional infliction of emotional distress against Ronnie Randall after Kahn saw Randall turn his car to strike Kahn's 11-year-old child in front of her, causing her to suffer daily from anxiety, headaches, and vomiting?

This question presented incorporates legally significant facts and provides these facts in the context of the legal standard. Randall's intention is one of the legal factors or elements in determining whether Kahn has a claim for intentional infliction of emotional distress. The question presented notes the legally significant fact that Randall turned his car to strike the child. The fact that Kahn now suffers daily from anxiety, headaches, and vomiting also is legally significant and relates to the legal standard because it may show that Kahn suffers from severe emotional distress. Although you should mention legally significant facts and the legal standard, keep the issue short enough for the reader to understand.

When you have multiple questions presented, the conclusion section should answer the questions in the same order as they were presented.

IN-CLASS EXERCISE

Review the question presented in Illustration 8-1. Determine what legal issue is presented. Then find the legally significant facts that are included in the question presented.

ILLUSTRATION 8-1.   Question Presented

Is the grocery store owner liable for injuries sustained by a store patron who slipped on a banana peel that had been on the grocery store floor for two days?

3. Specificity and Precision

The facts should be specific, and your characterization of the parties and the issues should be precise. For example, consider a case that concerns whether an individual, Walker, is an independent contractor or an employee of the Whole In One, a small company. Walker did not work for any other companies. She paid her own taxes quarterly rather than through payroll deductions. She worked with limited company supervision. Title VII of a federal law applies. You could pose the question presented as follows:

> Under Title VII, was Walker an employee when she worked exclusively for Whole In One, paid her own taxes quarterly rather than through deductions, and worked with limited company supervision?

The facts in this case are specific: Walker paid her taxes quarterly rather than through payroll deductions. However, the question presented is not precise because it does not characterize the legal issue presented completely. The legal issue is whether Walker is an independent contractor rather than an employee. Therefore, the question presented could be refined as follows:

> Under Title VII, was Walker an independent contractor rather than an employee when she worked exclusively for Whole In One, did she pay her own taxes quarterly rather than through deductions, and did she work with limited company supervision?

You must only ask a question in the question presented, not provide an answer. You will answer the question presented in the brief answer or conclusion section.

If you have more than one issue or question presented, place each question in a logical order and make that order consistent throughout the memo. The first question presented, then, should be answered first in the conclusion or brief answer statement and should be the first issue addressed in the discussion.

B. BRIEF ANSWERS AND CONCLUSIONS

1. Brief Answers

Brief answers are the quick answers to the question or questions presented. A brief answer is a short statement. Some attorneys prefer a brief answer that is later accompanied by a formal conclusion at the end of the memorandum. The brief answer allows an attorney to read a memo in a hurry and determine the legal issues. See Illustration 8-2.

ILLUSTRATION 8-2.   Question Presented and Brief Answer

Question Presented: Does Janice Kahn have a valid claim for intentional infliction of emotional distress against Ronnie Randall after Kahn saw Randall turn his car to strike Kahn's 11-year-old child in front of her, causing her to suffer daily from anxiety, headaches, and vomiting?

ILLUSTRATION 8-2.   Continued

Brief Answer: Yes. Kahn can bring a successful action for intentional infliction of emotional distress against Ronnie Randall because she saw Randall turn his car to strike her 11-year-old son, causing her to suffer severe anxiety, headaches, and vomiting daily.

The brief answer should include a brief statement of the applicable law and some relevant facts. A brief answer for the question presented above in Illustration 8-1 could be presented as follows in Illustration 8-3.

ILLUSTRATION 8-3.   Brief Answer

Probably yes. A grocery store owner probably will be liable based upon negligence for injuries sustained by a store patron who slipped on a banana peel that had been on the grocery store floor for two days.

In the memorandum, it would appear as follows:

Question Presented: Is the grocery store owner liable for injuries sustained by a store patron who slipped on a banana peel that had been on the grocery store floor for two days?

Brief Answer: Probably yes. A grocery store owner probably will be liable based upon negligence for injuries sustained by a store patron who slipped on a banana peel that had been on the grocery store floor for two days.

The legal standard applicable to this case, negligence, is mentioned along with legally significant facts.

2. Conclusions

A conclusion also is an answer to the question presented and a summary of the discussion section. For some attorneys, a conclusion without a brief answer is sufficient. However, other attorneys prefer both a brief answer and a conclusion.

▼ How Is a Conclusion Different from a Brief Answer?

A conclusion does not have a set length, but it is generally longer than a brief answer. It, however, is not a detailed or in-depth discussion of the legal issue presented in the case. It is a succinct summary of the substance of the memo. The conclusion should include legally significant facts and the applicable legal standard. In the conclusion, you must answer the question presented and provide your best prediction concerning the outcome of the case. It is acceptable to use terms such as *likely* or *probably* when you think that the outcome of an action is uncertain.

3. Drafting Conclusions

Before you draft your conclusion, review the questions presented and your preliminary facts statement. (A detailed explanation of the facts statement is presented in Chapter 9.)

Next, write the conclusion as an answer to the question presented and incorporate some of the relevant facts contained in the facts section of the memo. Refine the conclusion so that the reader understands the legal standard and the applicable facts. Conclusions often work well when drafted in an IRAC formula: Issue, Rule, Application, and Conclusion. (For a thorough discussion of the IRAC formula, see Chapter 10.)

For the facts and the question presented in the Kahn case, the following conclusion might be prepared:

> The central question is whether Janice Kahn has a valid claim for intentional infliction of emotional distress against Ronnie Randall. To successfully prove a claim for intentional infliction of emotional distress, Kahn must show that the act that caused the distress was extreme and outrageous and done with intent. In the case, Kahn saw Randall turn his car and strike her 11-year-old child, Bill. Seeing this accident caused Kahn to suffer from anxiety, headaches, and vomiting daily. Several witnesses can testify that Randall said he intended to harm Kahn, and Kahn states that Randall turned the car to strike her son. Two factors, however, might show that Randall lacked intent: the statement that he made to the police that he did not intend to hit the child and the fact that his blood alcohol level was .11, possibly preventing him from formulating the needed intent. Kahn probably has a claim for intentional emotional distress.

This conclusion provides a summary of the writer's prediction of the outcome of the case after the legal standards are applied to the legally significant facts:

> Janice Kahn probably has a valid claim for intentional infliction of emotional distress against Ronnie Randall.

Facts such as that Kahn saw Randall turn the car to strike her son and that witnesses can testify concerning what Randall said he intended to do are relevant to the question of whether the act was extreme and outrageous. The legal standard provides that the act must be extreme and outrageous before an individual can be liable for intentional infliction of emotional distress. In addition, the extreme and outrageous act must be done with intent. Randall's intent also is discussed in the conclusion.

Many students include an authority, such as a statute or case, in the conclusion. Most often, however, your analysis of a claim requires that you synthesize a number of authorities to determine the applicable law. It would be misleading, therefore, to include only one authority in your conclusion. You might include an authority if it is the sole authority governing a claim.

When two or more questions presented are noted in the memorandum, a conclusion or a brief answer and then a conclusion for each question should be noted in the same order as the question presented. See Illustration 8-4.

ILLUSTRATION 8-4.   Questions Presented and Conclusion

QUESTIONS PRESENTED

1. Does Janice Kahn have a valid claim for intentional infliction of emotional distress against Ronnie Randall after Kahn saw Randall turn his car to strike Kahn's 11-year-old child in front of her, causing her to suffer from anxiety, headaches, and vomiting?

2. Does Janice Kahn's 11-year-old child, Bill, have a claim against Randall for battery after Randall turned his car to strike Bill, and did strike him, breaking Bill's bones?

CONCLUSIONS

1. The central question is whether Janice Kahn has a valid claim for intentional infliction of emotional distress against Ronnie Randall. To successfully prove a claim for intentional infliction of emotional distress, Kahn must show that the act that caused the distress was extreme and outrageous and done with intent. In the case, Kahn saw Randall turn his car and strike her 11-year-old child. Seeing this accident caused Kahn to suffer daily from anxiety, headaches, and vomiting. Several witnesses can testify that Randall said that he intended to harm Kahn, and Kahn states that Randall turned the car to strike her son. Two factors, however, might show that Randall lacked intent: the statement that he made to the police that he did not intend to hit the child and the fact that his blood alcohol level was .11, possibly preventing him from formulating the needed intent. Kahn probably has a claim for intentional emotional distress.

2. Bill Kahn is likely to make a successful claim for battery against Randall. A battery is the intentional touching of another without consent, which causes injury. A touching can occur when an object rather than an individual's body contacts the other party. In this case, Randall struck Bill Kahn with his car without Bill Kahn's consent and that touching resulted in injuries. Intent may be an issue because Randall said he did not intend to hit the child and his blood alcohol level was .11, possibly preventing him from formulating the needed intent. However, the fact that he turned the wheel to strike Bill Kahn is likely to show intent.

PRACTICE POINTER

When you have multiple questions presented, the conclusion section should answer the questions in the same order as they were presented.

IN-CLASS EXERCISE

Read the questions presented in Illustration 8-4.

1. Discuss the issues and conclusions.
2. After reviewing the questions presented, what legal standards do you think will determine the applicable law?
3. Does the conclusion answer the questions presented? Are the legal standards discussed? What, if any, standards are noted?

CHAPTER SUMMARY

In this chapter, you learned how to draft questions presented, issues, brief answers, and conclusions. Questions presented or issues should incorporate legally significant facts and the rule of law. Legally significant facts are facts that will affect a decision concerning an issue of law.

Legally significant facts and the current rule of law also should be included in the conclusions in the conclusions or brief answers that answer the questions presented or issues.

Some attorneys prefer both a brief answer and a conclusion, while others require only a conclusion.

The process of writing the questions presented, issues, brief answers, and conclusions requires that you rewrite these components of a memorandum several times. The questions presented or issues should be drafted before you perform your research. The conclusions or brief answers also should be rewritten in light of the facts presented in a case.

In the next chapter, you learn how to draft facts statements for your memoranda.

KEY TERMS

brief answers
conclusion
issues
legally significant facts

precise
questions presented
specific

EXERCISES

SHORT ANSWER

1. What is a brief answer?
2. How does a brief answer differ from a conclusion?
3. Is an issue or question presented written as a statement or a question?
4. If you have four questions presented, how many conclusions or brief answers should you have?
5. What is the purpose of a question presented?
6. What is the purpose of a conclusion?

QUESTIONS PRESENTED

Draft questions presented for memos in the following cases.

7. You work as a paralegal for the country prosecutor's office in Houcktown County. One of the assistant prosecutors asks you to research whether Bonnie Bill has committed aggravated burglary under the Houcktown Rev. Code §2911. The attorney has provided you with the following facts:

Merriweather Halsey and Bonnie Bill were at the Masonic Temple for a fundraiser to fight AIDS. During the fundraiser Bill told a drunken Halsey that she intended to steal the $8,000 fundraiser proceeds from the Masonic Temple after the fundraiser and that she intended to steal a pearl necklace from Alice McKinley.

Bill, who had helped organize the fundraiser, watched as the chairperson of the fundraiser opened the safe and placed the money in it. She memorized the combination and decided that she would use it later to steal the money.

After the fundraiser, Bill walked home to get a credit card and a crowbar to open the door if she needed it. Bill went to the Masonic Temple after the fundraiser, wearing a disguise, showed the guard her invitation, and told him that she lost her mother's diamond brooch inside. Although the guard did not remember her, he allowed her to go into the temple. She wandered around the building for about an hour with the brooch inside her purse.

When the guard decided to eat his supper and call home, Bill went to the safe. She opened it and pulled out all the money, except for $1,000.

Bill told the guard she found the brooch and then left. She went to Alice McKinley's home, entered the house through an open ground-floor window, took the pearl necklace she had seen Alice wearing earlier, and then left.

The relevant statute is as follows:

§2911 Aggravated Burglary

(A) A person is guilty of aggravated burglary when the person, by force or deception, trespasses in any house, building, outbuilding, watercraft, aircraft, railroad car, truck, trailer, tent vehicle or shelter with the purpose of committing a theft; and

(1) inflicts or attempts or threatens to inflict physical harm to another; or

(2) the person has a deadly weapon, which is any instrument, device, or thing capable of inflicting death or designed or specially adapted for use as a weapon; or

(3) the person has a dangerous ordnance such as any automatic or sawed off firearm, zip gun or ballistic knife, explosive or incendiary device; or

(4) the structure is the permanent or temporary dwelling of a person.

8. An assistant county prosecutor wants you to research whether Merriweather Halsey committed aggravated burglary based on the following facts:

Merriweather Halsey considered borrowing money from a friend who worked at the local bulb factory. She wandered into the factory around 4:00 A.M., after an AIDS fundraiser. The guard had stepped away from the door for a break. Halsey headed toward her friend's workstation, but she stumbled into an open office where the petty cash was kept. She fell over a secretary's desk. Her leg caught the desk and pulled open a drawer that contained $500. She thought about taking the money, but she passed out before she took it. She woke up at about 6:00 A.M., when a secretary found her and summoned the security guard.

Halsey then fell onto the security guard, causing him to crash his head into a planter. The guard cut his head and later required six stitches. Halsey thought the security guard was a robber, so she grabbed a letter opener from a nearby desk and told the security guard to back off. The security guard took the letter opener. Halsey's mind was still fuzzy from the alcohol, but she decided to pull a squirt gun out of her pocket to scare the robber.

Draft a question presented for this problem based on the aggravated burglary statute noted in Question 7 above.

CONCLUSIONS

9. Draft a conclusion for the problem discussed in Question 7.
10. Draft a conclusion for the problem discussed in Question 8.
11. Review the following facts. Make a list of the legally significant facts. Then prepare an issue statement and a conclusion for this problem.

Your client, Hospitality Resorts International, Inc., which does business in your state, is defending an action against James Panhandle, a 70-year-old doctor from Akron, Ohio, who slipped and fell at a London hotel bearing the name Hospitality Resorts of London on January 28, 2012. Panhandle, a semi-retired general practice physician, smashed his head on some wet marble flooring next to the pool. A sign saying "slippery when wet" was set up next to the pool, but Panhandle didn't see the sign. He sustained severe and permanent injuries and was unable to practice medicine for two years.

Panhandle often stayed at the Hospitality Resorts. The resorts were known for cleanliness and hospitality. The staff was friendly and always helpful. The advertising for the resorts claimed that it was the "cleanest in the world. We stay on top of our hotels." Most advertisements stated that the hotels were independently owned and operated. Some ads, such as the one that appeared in the *Doctor's Weekly*, which Panhandle read, did not state that independent owners owned the London hotel. That ad boasted about the resort, "We care about you. We take care of you. We take care of your home—our resort."

Hospitality Resorts was a trade name. The company that licensed the name Hospitality Resorts to other hotels was called Hospitality Resorts International, Inc. (HRII), your client. Hospitality Resorts licensed its trade name to Fred and Ethel Carrigan of London, England, for use in a hotel there. The Carrigans called the hotel Hospitality Resorts of London. As part of the license agreement, Hospitality Resorts provided training to the staff. The Carrigans hired and fired the staff. HRII had no authority to hire and fire staff.

Panhandle did not know anything about the training or the connection between the London hotel and HRII.

HRII provided operations manuals and suggested procedures and menus. Personnel from HRII regularly traveled to London to advise the hotel employees about their jobs. HRII had no ownership interest in the London hotel. HRII was not authorized to act on behalf of the hotel nor was the hotel authorized to act on behalf of HRII.

The license agreement between HRII and Hospitality Resort of London only provided for HRII to provide its name Hospitality Resort to the London hotel as well as some manuals and technical assistance. It did not authorize the London hotel to act as its agent and HRII was not an agent of the London hotel. HRII did include the Hospitality Resort of London in its list of Hospitality Resorts. That list appeared in many ads as well as in a brochure.

Plaintiff filed suit against the Hospitality Resort in London and Hospitality Resorts, and Hospitality Resorts International, Inc., alleging that HRII is in an agency relationship or apparent or ostensible agency relationship with the London Hospitality Resort. Thus, plaintiff claims that HRII and the London hotel are both responsible for his injuries. This suit was filed in the United States District Court for your area. All the rules of that court and the Federal Rules of Civil Procedures apply.

> Does our client have a good defense to the plaintiff's claim that it was in an agency relationship with the London hotel?
>
> Assume that the highest court in your state has held that a hotel owner can be liable based upon the theory of apparent agency. Under that theory, if a business allows another to hold itself out as its representative or the individual or entity holds itself as acting on behalf of the business, the business may be liable for the acts of the individual or entity. Also assume that a decision of the federal appellate court in your area follows your high court's decision.

12. Review this question presented and this conclusion. What legally significant facts are included in the question presented? What legally significant facts are included in the conclusion?

Question Presented

Did an actionable battery occur when Mann intentionally struck McMillan with a bucket, without McMillian's consent, causing McMillian to suffer physical and monetary injuries?

Conclusion

Mann's intentional striking of McMillan with a bucket and sand was an actionable battery.

13. You are a paralegal with the firm of Probing and Will. You must research whether Sarah Wakefield can renounce Adam Antwernts' will and collect a portion of the estate in your state.

Your firm's client is Sarah Wakefield. She was married to Adam Antwernt. Antwernt died on June 6, 2012, in your state following a long illness. Wakefield was Antwernt's second wife. She had been married to him for more than 20 years and lived in their home in the Highlands of your state. Antwernt purchased the home with his first wife, Carry MacOver. MacOver died in 1989. When Antwernt married Wakefield he never changed the deed for the home to include Wakefield. Wakefield kept her maiden name. Antwernt adopted a son with MacOver in 1982. The son, who is now 30 years old, is Grayson Antwernt.

Antwernt drafted his will in May of 2003. He and his wife were getting along fine. However, he excluded her from his will. He did not leave her any property. Instead, he left all of his property to Grayson. Antwernt's will was admitted to probate on July 8, 2012.

Wakefield wants to know whether Antwernt's will is valid and whether he can divest her of the marital property or whether she can renounce the will and collect a portion of the estate.

Grayson is out of town and his attorney told Wakefield that she will get her share of the estate once Grayson returns. He is scheduled to return on August 14, 2012.

Please prepare an issue statement for this problem.

14. Nate Late, a business owner, has two partners in the operation of Loose Cannon Manufacturing in Anytown in your state. He owns 33 1/3 parts of a $3 million company. Late is ill but is not dying. He is grooming a 26-year-old boy, Ivan T. All, to run the business. He tells his family he likes the boy and that he wants to teach him the business. The business owner, Nate Late, dies. The most current will leaves the estate of Late to his wife, Shirley Late, and his only son, Lou Sier. All tells Mrs. Late that Late intended to give All Late's one-third interest in the company and that Late told this to All in front of a banker on the day of his death in

front of a banker. The conversation took place during a meeting and the agreement was never put into writing. Before this meeting, on the day of Late's death other employees of Loose Cannon heard Late say that he intended for All "to get" the business. Family members knew that Late intended for All to run the business and for All to get something if the business was sold. None of the family believed that Late intended to give the business to this newcomer. Late's shares of stock were never given to All. The shares were in the safe deposit box shared by Late and his wife of 24 years.

Rob R. Baron also claims that Late promised to give him the shares in the future. Baron admits that Late did not physically give him the shares before he died, but Baron insists that Late said "I shall give you my shares in two years."

Mrs. Late said that Mr. Late planned to give her the shares. He told her this when he opened the joint safety deposit box and gave her the key.

You work for a firm which has been retained by Mrs. Late. She would like to know if All can prove that Mr. Late gave All Mr. Late's interest in the company.

Draft an issue statement for the Late case.

CONCLUSION—DRAFTING EXERCISES

15. Assume that the statute in your state provides that Wakefield, the spouse, can renounce the will within six months of its admission to probate and that she would be entitled by statute to one-third of the estate and Grayson would be entitled to the remainder of the estate. Prepare a conclusion for the Wakefield problem.
16. Assume that the highest court in your state has held that a hotel owner can be liable in a case similar to the one outlined in Exercise 11. The liability is based upon the theory of apparent agency. Also assume that a decision of the federal appellate court in your area follows the opinion of the state's high court. Draft a conclusion for the problem outlined in Exercise 11.
17. Assume that the following statements are the law of the land concerning a gift. Draft a conclusion for the problem outlined in Exercise 14.

A gift is a voluntary transfer of property from one person to another without any compensation or consideration. To be a valid gift, it must actually be made or executed. A gratuitous promise to make a gift in the future is not binding.

A living gift is called a *gift inter vivos.*

There are three requirements for such a gift: donative intent, acceptance of the gifts, and delivery.

Clark v. Davis, Clark told Davis, a friend, that after he got his life together, he would give Davis his coin collection. Until that time, Clark planned to use the collection and show it and maybe sell some of it. Court said that a donor must have a present mental capacity and intent to give away his property. Court held that there was no present intention to make a gift of the collection to Davis. Therefore, a gift was not made.

Wally v. Allan, Wally gave Allan a guitar for use in his rock band. The court found that Allan accepted the gift. When a gift, such as the guitar, is beneficial to the donee, acceptance is presumed.

Lois v. Kate, Lois told Kate that she planned to give her a CD. Kate asked when she would give it to her. Lois said that she would leave the CD at the front desk of her record company. Lois left the CD at the desk and did not mention that Kate needed to leave any money to pay for the CD. Therefore, the court said that delivery of a gift occurred when Lois left the CD at the front desk. Although delivery generally occurs when a party hands the gift over to the other party. The above situation also amounts to delivery.

FACTS

CHAPTER OVERVIEW

This chapter explains the purpose of a facts statement and how to draft one. To do this, you need to learn how to determine which facts are legally significant. The chapter discusses the difference between a fact and a legal conclusion and demonstrates the different organizational structures for the facts section.

A. FACTS STATEMENT

The facts statement is a summary of the information that is relevant to the determination of whether a legal claim exists or whether a defense to such a claim can be made. It is also a summary of the status of a pending case.

A fact statement is an integral part of the office memorandum. Often, an attorney reads this statement to refresh his or her memory about the facts of the case before meeting with a client or a judge. The facts detailed in a memorandum also provide a reference point for your research and the framework for the application of the law.

1. Defining *Fact*

A fact may be a thing that is known with certainty. It can be an event. It can be an observation. The answer is not clear-cut. Some facts are pure facts, which means there is no dispute about them. For example, an individual's birth is a pure fact. Facts in a court document, such as a complaint or an answer, are asserted facts, which means the individual is claiming they occurred. Some information can be objectively tested. That is a fact. For the purpose of the facts statement, note all of this information as facts.

2. Legally Significant Facts

▼ What Facts Should Be Included in the Facts Statement?

All facts that might have an impact on the issues presented in a particular case must be included in the memo. These facts are called **legally significant facts.** A good rule is that if you plan to include a fact in your discussion of the law, it should be mentioned in the facts statement.

Legally significant facts are those facts that may affect how a court would decide a particular legal issue. To determine which facts are legally significant, you must understand the legal issue or issues presented in your case. A **legal claim** is composed of components called **elements** that must be proven before a claim is successful. Legally significant facts are those facts that might prove or disprove any of those elements.

For example, you are asked to research the factors a court will consider when it decides whether Sack and Shop Grocery Store was liable to Rebecca Harris, a patron, for a slip-and-fall accident that occurred in the store. Ms. Harris was injured when she slipped on a banana peel that a store employee failed to remove from the store floor for two days. Ms. Harris's shopping list included bananas, cherries, and strawberries. You determine that the action or legal claim is based on negligence. You learn that negligence is the breach of a duty of reasonable care that results in an injury to another person. The legal elements of negligence are as follows:

- existence of a duty
- breach of that duty
- injury caused by the breach of the duty

Legally significant facts are those facts that might prove or disprove any of those elements. In this case, the legally significant facts and the legal element that they might prove or disprove would include:

- The slip and fall occurred in the store. (injury, breach)
- Rebecca Harris slipped on a banana peel that a store employee left on the store floor for two days. (injury caused by the breach)
- Rebecca Harris suffered injuries as a result of the fall. (injury)
- Rebecca Harris shopped daily at the store. (duty)
- Rebecca Harris went to the store to make a purchase. (duty)

A fact that is not necessarily legally significant is:

- Rebecca Harris's shopping list included bananas, cherries, and strawberries.

This fact does not prove or disprove any of the elements.

Do not omit any legally significant facts even if you think that an attorney should remember them from client meetings. Attorneys are responsible for multiple cases, and these statements often are used to refresh their recollection. If a fact is not legally significant, you generally would exclude it. However, if the fact explains how a dispute or transaction arose or explains the relationship between the parties, then that fact should be noted. Such a **procedural fact** would assist the reader in understanding the status of a case.

Facts statements provide facts that are advantageous for your clients and those facts that are unfavorable to them. Remember that this is an objective memo. The facts should be presented in a neutral manner, devoid of emotion. Compare the following two examples.

EXAMPLE

Our client, Janice Kahn, seeks to sue Ronnie Randall for intentional infliction of emotional distress following a car accident in which Randall brutally struck Kahn's only child while the precious child was playing T-ball in the street with his friends. This brutal act was done in the presence of Ms. Kahn, a caring mother, who was gardening while watching her child play. As a result of the incident, Kahn was devastated and emotionally distraught.

EXAMPLE

Our client, Janice Kahn, seeks to sue Ronnie Randall for intentional infliction of emotional distress following a car accident in which Randall struck Kahn's child while the child was playing T-ball in the street with his friends. After Randall struck the child, he backed up and struck the boy again, running over his head with the rear tire. Ms. Kahn was gardening nearby while watching her child play.

The first example contains several adverbs and adjectives that slant the statement in favor of Kahn. The statement "Randall brutally struck Kahn's only child" characterizes the action as brutal. This is not a statement of fact. The adverb *brutally* should not be included in a facts statement. The second example is devoid of these **emotional adjectives or adverbs.** Instead of using the word *brutally*, the second example details the underlying acts that constitute a brutal strike:

> After Randall struck the child, he backed up and struck the boy again, running over his head with the rear tire.

The second example allows readers to draw their own conclusions. The facts statement should not be slanted. Facts such as that Kahn was "a caring mother" or that the child was "precious" should not be incorporated into a facts statement. You should mention only facts, not legal conclusions or definitions of the law.

3. Fact Versus a Legal Conclusion

A fact is a piece of information that might explain to the reader what occurred in a particular case. In contrast, a legal conclusion is an opinion about the legal significance of a fact. Read the following facts statement:

> Our client, Janice Kahn, seeks to sue Ronnie Randall for intentional infliction of emotional distress following a car accident in which Randall maliciously struck Kahn's only child while the child was playing T-ball in the street with his friends. This malicious and intentional act was done in the presence of Ms. Kahn, a caring mother, who was gardening while watching her child play.

The statements that the act was *malicious* and *intentional* are legal conclusions because the writer makes assumptions about the state of mind of the actor. The term *malicious* is a legal element of many claims; it describes a wicked state of mind. *Intentional* also describes a legal element. You should exclude such characterizations from your facts statements. Instead, describe the acts a person committed that could be considered malicious, or statements that could indicate that an act was intentional. For example:

> Randall struck Kahn's only child after he told a neighbor that he intended to hit the child with his car while the child was playing T-ball. Randall struck the child with his car while the car was traveling at 25 miles an hour.

The information about Randall's comments to the neighbor, coupled with the speed at which he struck the child, could indicate that Randall struck the child maliciously and intentionally. The proper place to discuss whether an act is either malicious or intentional is in the discussion section of the memo. A definition of the law also is not a statement of fact and should be noted only in the memo discussion.

4. Source of Information for a Facts Statement

Most often, information from a client interview is the basis for your facts statement. See the example in Illustration 9-7 later in this chapter. During a court dispute, information for the facts statement also can be found in witness statements, complaints, answers, or discovery materials, such as depositions and interrogatories. For these facts, note the source of the information. For transactions, information might be contained in various business records or contracts.

B. ORGANIZING THE FACTS STATEMENT

A facts statement can be organized in several ways: chronologically, by claim or defense, by party, or according to a combination of these three methods.

▼ What Are the Different Methods of Organizing a Facts Statement?

1. Chronological Organization

A chronological organization is based on the order of events. You start with the event that occurred first and end with the event that occurred last. You also can write the statement in reverse chronological order, beginning with the last event and ending with the first. For some claims, such as those stemming from an accident, a contract dispute, or a criminal case, chronological organization works well because these concerns often are ordered by time. See Illustration 9-1.

The statement in Illustration 9-1 first introduces the claim. In the succeeding paragraphs, the events are detailed in chronological order from start to finish. Illustration 9-2 starts with the last event and ends with the information about the beginning of the day.

ILLUSTRATION 9-1.   Chronological Organization

Dr. James Panhandle is suing our client, Hospitality Resorts International, Inc., for negligence stemming from injuries he sustained when he slipped and fell on January 28, 2012, at the Hospitality Resort of London. The doctor seeks $8 million in damages.

On the day of the accident, children were playing in the pool at 8:00 A.M. The children splashed water out of the pool and onto the marble floor near the pool. The floor had not been mopped at any time during the day.

At 8:00 P.M., Dr. Panhandle was walking slowly out of the hotel coffee shop that was adjacent to the pool. He slipped on the wet marble floor next to the pool.

The doctor hit his head on the marble floor, causing him to crack his skull and to bleed.

ILLUSTRATION 9-2.   Reverse Chronological Order

Dr. James Panhandle is suing our client, Hospitality Resorts International, Inc., for negligence stemming from injuries he sustained when he slipped and fell on January 28, 2012, at the Hospitality Resort of London. The doctor seeks $8 million in damages.

The doctor hit his head on the marble floor, causing him to crack his skull and to bleed.

At 8:00 P.M., Dr. Panhandle was walking slowly out of the hotel coffee shop that was adjacent to the pool. He slipped on the wet marble floor next to the pool.

On the day of the accident, children were playing in the pool at 8:00 A.M. The children splashed water out of the pool and onto the marble floor near the pool. The floor had not been mopped at any time during the day.

2. Organization by Claim or Defense

Facts statements also can be organized by claim or defense. In statements of this kind, legally significant facts that relate to a claim or a defense are grouped together. See Illustration 9-3. This method is useful when the issue does not concern events that can be organized by time sequence and the information involves individuals who are not parties to the action.

ILLUSTRATION 9-3.   Organization by Claim or Defense

Our clients, the Black Hawks, want to know whether the attorney-client privilege can be asserted by a former company president, Debbie Irl, and a current employee, Meredith Tildy, head of the cleaning staff. These questions arose while the plaintiff's attorney was deposing these individuals on July 8, 2012, as part of the discovery in a personal injury lawsuit stemming from a slip and fall at the stadium.

Irl, president of the Hawks at the time of the accident, left the organization in June 2012. During her tenure with the organization, she was a decision maker and she drafted the cleaning policy for the stadium. Irl had spoken with the Hawks' attorney, Ace Rudd, about the accident on July 10, 2012. Irl is not named as a party in the lawsuit and is merely a witness. During the deposition, the plaintiff's attorney asked Irl about her conversation with Rudd. Irl asserted the attorney-client privilege.

Meredith Tildy, the current head of the Hawks' cleaning staff, knew about the accident. Beer had been spilled the night before the accident. A patron told the staff to mop up the beer when it happened. Tildy knew that the cleaning staff had failed to clean up the beer. In her position, Tildy schedules the staff and decides whether the stadium should be cleaned completely each night. On July 10, 2012, Tildy spoke with Rudd, the company attorney, about the accident. The plaintiff's attorney asked Tildy about her conversation with Rudd. Based upon Rudd's advice, Tildy asserted the attorney-client privilege.

In Illustration 9-3's sample facts statement, the details are organized by claim. The first paragraph introduces the claims—the assertion of attorney-client privilege by Irl and Tildy. The next paragraph includes the facts that are legally significant to Irl's claim of attorney-client privilege. The final paragraph focuses on the facts that are legally significant to Tildy and Tildy's assertion of the attorney-client privilege. Because neither Irl nor Tildy is a party, this organization works well.

3. Organization by Party

Another way to organize the facts is to organize by party, grouping the facts according to the party the facts describe. This method is useful when multiple parties are involved in a dispute. See Illustration 9-4, which involves a dispute between three parties: a company and two individuals. The memo focuses on whether Whole In One is an employer under Title VII and whether two individuals are employees or independent contractors.

The first paragraph in Illustration 9-4 introduces the claim. The next paragraph describes one of the parties, Whole In One. The next paragraph describes another party, Walker. The final paragraph tells the reader about Radiant, the third party in the action.

ILLUSTRATION 9-4.   Organization by Party

Victoria Radiant and Karen Walker, two former Whole In One Enterprises workers, brought a federal sex discrimination lawsuit, based upon Title VII, against our client, Whole In One Enterprises, owned by Nancy and Craig Black. The lawsuit, filed in the U.S. District Court for the Northern District of Illinois, stems from the dismissal of the two women by the Blacks during 2011.

The Blacks own Whole In One Enterprises, which operates a miniature golf course and restaurant in Glenview, Illinois. During the 24-week, 2011 restaurant season, 10 people worked full-time and 14 people worked part-time for Whole In One. However, no more than 14 people worked on any one day. Of those 14 people, only 3 were full-time employees. The other full-time employees regularly took days off during the summer restaurant and golf season.

Among the full-time workers was Karen Walker, who worked as a public relations director for Whole In One. Walker responded to an ad that said that "an employer" sought an individual to perform public relations work. Whole In One hired Walker without a contract and told her she was prohibited from working for other firms. However, Walker worked from home and set her own hours. Whole In One required Walker to attend weekly staff meetings at the company offices, where Whole In One would review and revise Walker's work. The company supplied Walker with paper, pencils, stamps, and telephone service and paid for her life and health insurance. Whole In One did not withhold taxes from Walker's commissions.

Victoria Radiant, who had a two-year employment contract with the company, provided marketing services to Whole In One from October of 2009 until she was fired in 2011. Although Radiant worked in the company office, Whole In One management rarely supervised her work. The company paid for her continued education, provided her with bonuses, and deducted taxes from her weekly salary.

4. Combination of Chronological and Claim or Party Organization

Some facts statements do not lend themselves to one type of organization. Some facts should be arranged by the order of the events, and others do not fit neatly into this arrangement. Therefore, you might group facts in chronological order and by party or claim. See Illustration 9-5.

The facts statement in Illustration 9-5 concerns the question of whether Janice Kahn can successfully pursue a claim against Ronnie Randall for intentional infliction of emotional distress after Randall struck Kahn's 11-year-old son with Randall's car. The accident itself is best described in a chronological manner because the events can be explained in a sequential order. However, the witness statements and other "facts" that relate to whether Randall intentionally struck the child and whether Randall intended to cause emotional distress when he struck the child should be organized by issue or claim.

ILLUSTRATION 9-5. Chronological and Claim Organization

While driving a car, Ronnie Randall struck Janice Kahn's son at 5:00 P.M. on August 29, 2011. It was bright and clear. No skid marks appeared on the dry street following the accident. Janice Kahn was working in her garden about five feet from the accident scene at the time of the accident. Her son was playing a game in the street before Randall's car struck him. Kahn did not see the car strike her 11-year-old son. When she first looked up from her garden, she thought her son was dead. He was covered with blood and had several broken bones. However, Kahn's son was conscious after the accident.

Immediately after the accident, Randall, who had a blood alcohol level of .11, was cited for drunk driving and driving with a suspended driver's license. Police had charged him with drunk driving and suspended his license two weeks earlier after the car he was driving struck another child at the same spot. Randall has a history of alcohol abuse.

Following the accident, several witnesses said Randall was upset and wobbled as he walked. One witness said that Randall intentionally turned the steering wheel to hit Kahn's son. Kahn stated that Randall often swerved down her street to get her attention.

Rhonda Albert, Kahn's neighbor, said she heard Randall say he would get even with Kahn after Kahn broke off a ten-year relationship with him.

During Kahn and Randall's ten-year relationship, Randall was close to Kahn's son. He took him to ball games, including one in April, and attended the son's baseball games. Randall knew that Kahn's son was the most important person in her life.

Since the accident, Kahn vomits daily and suffers from anxiety and headaches. Dr. Susan Faigen, Kahn's internist, states that the vomiting, anxiety, and headaches are the result of the accident.

In some instances, your organization should be structured by the sequence of the events and by the parties. See Illustration 9-6.

In Illustration 9-6, the first paragraph introduces both parties, Bonnie Bill and Merriweather Halsey. The facts statement details most of the night's events in chronological order. However, the parties, Bill and Halsey, leave the fundraiser separately. At this point, the organization changes from chronological to one focusing on each party. First, facts that are legally significant to Bill's escapades are explained. These are noted in chronological order from start to finish. After the facts concerning Bill's adventure, the facts related to Halsey's acts at the bulb factory are detailed. These facts also are explained in chronological order. The final paragraph tells the reader the issues that will be considered in the memo.

ILLUSTRATION 9-6.   Chronological and Party Organization

Merriweather Halsey and Bonnie Bill were at the Masonic Temple for a fundraiser to fight AIDS. During the fundraiser Bill told a drunken Halsey that she intended to steal the $8,000 proceeds from the Masonic Temple and a pearl necklace from Alice McKinley after the fundraiser. Bill, who had helped organize the fundraiser, watched as the chairperson of the fundraiser opened the safe and placed the money in it. She memorized the combination and decided that she would use it later to steal the money.

After the fundraiser, Bill walked home to get a credit card and a crowbar to open the door if she needed it. Bill went to the Masonic Temple after the fundraiser, wearing a disguise, showed the guard her invitation, and told him that she had lost her mother's diamond brooch inside. Although the guard did not remember her, he allowed her to go into the temple. She wandered around the building for about an hour with the brooch inside her purse.

When the guard decided to eat his supper, Bill went to the safe. She opened it and took all of the money, except for $1,000.

Bill told the guard she had found the brooch and then left. She went to Alice McKinley's home, entered the house through an open ground-floor window, and took the pearl necklace she had seen Alice wearing earlier, and then left.

Merriweather Halsey considered borrowing money from a friend who worked at a local bulb factory. She wandered into the factory around 4:00 A.M., after the fundraiser. The guard had stepped away from the door for a break. She headed toward her friend's workstation, but she stumbled into an open office where the petty cash was kept. She fell over a secretary's desk. Her leg caught the desk and pulled open a drawer that contained $500. She thought about taking the money, but she passed out before she took it. She woke up about 6:00 A.M., when a secretary found her and summoned the security guard.

Halsey then fell into the security guard, causing him to crash his head into a planter. The guard cut his head and later required six stitches. Halsey thought the security guard was a robber, so she grabbed a letter opener from a nearby desk and told the security guard to back off. The security guard took the letter opener. Halsey's mind was still fuzzy from the alcohol, but she decided to pull a squirt gun out of her pocket to scare the robber.

The question is whether Bill or Halsey can be convicted of aggravated burglary under Houcktown County law.

C. WRITING THE FACTS STATEMENT

1. Prepare a List of Facts and Preliminary Statement

After you meet with an attorney to discuss your research assignment, make a list of the facts and draft a preliminary facts statement.

Illustration 9-7 shows an excerpt from a client interview. Following the interview is a list of the facts and a preliminary facts statement, Illustration 9-8, that includes all the facts provided in the interview.

ILLUSTRATION 9-7.   **Excerpt from a Client Interview**

Attorney: What can I do for you today, Mr. Grocer of Sack and Shop?

Grocer: Rebecca Harris, one of my regular customers, is suing me for $1 million.

Attorney: What happened?

Grocer: Ms. Harris came to the store to purchase cherries, strawberries, and bananas. When she was turning the corner in the produce section, she slipped on a banana peel.

Attorney: How long had the banana peel been on the floor?

Grocer: Two days.

Attorney: Did you or any of your employees know about the banana peel on the floor?

Grocer: Yes. One of the patrons told the head of the produce department to clean up the banana peel two days before Ms. Harris fell.

Attorney: Why wasn't it picked up?

Grocer: The produce department head was in a hurry to leave and forgot to do it. The next day, he was very busy and he kicked the banana peel into a corner. Apparently it was later knocked out of the corner and to the middle of the floor where Ms. Harris slipped on it.

Attorney: Were there any witnesses?

Grocer: I saw her slip.

Attorney: What was Ms. Harris doing when she slipped?

Grocer: She was walking to the green peppers.

Attorney: What day did the incident occur?

Grocer: July 8, 2012. The same day another accident occurred in the produce section that involved a piece of cut cantaloupe.

Attorney: Was Ms. Harris injured?

Grocer: She claims in the court papers that she hurt her head and broke her arm.

Attorney: Was anyone injured in the second accident?

Grocer: Yes. A man slipped on the cantaloupe and broke his finger.

2. Research the Issue

After you prepare your list and preliminary facts statement, the next step is to research the legal issue or issues and to determine the applicable law.

ILLUSTRATION 9-8.   Sample Preliminary Facts Statement Based on the Client Interview

BRIEF LIST OF FACTS:
Client: Sack and Shop Grocery Store
Plaintiff: Rebecca Harris

Slip and fall at grocery store on July 8, 2012.
Plaintiff slipped on a banana peel, which had been left on the store floor for two days.
Harris was walking to the green peppers.
Another accident happened in the same section when a man slipped on a cantaloupe and broke his finger.
A patron told the store employee to clean up the banana peel two days earlier.
The employee kicked it into a corner.
Somehow the peel got to the middle of the floor again.
Harris came to the store to purchase cherries, strawberries, and bananas.

Our client, Sack and Shop Grocery Store, is being sued for negligence by Rebecca Harris.

Harris went to the store to purchase cherries, strawberries, and bananas on July 8, 2012.

While Harris was in the produce section, she slipped on a banana peel that had been left on the floor by a grocery store employee. The employee dropped it on the floor two days earlier and had failed to clean it up after a patron asked him to do so. The employee had kicked the peel into the corner two days before the accident. Somehow the peel found its way to the middle of the floor on the date of the accident.

Harris sustained a broken arm and head injuries as a result of the slip and fall. Another man was injured in the produce department that same day when he slipped and fell on some cantaloupe.

3. Revise to Include Only Legally Significant Facts

Revise your list so that it includes only the legally significant facts, the facts that will have a bearing on the applicable law. See Illustration 9-9. To draft this list, you must determine the legal elements necessary to establish a claim. In the case of negligence, you would learn that negligence is the breach of a duty of reasonable care that results in injuries to another person. The elements then would be:

• duty of reasonable care
• breach of the duty
• a link between the breach of the duty and the resulting injuries
• injuries

ILLUSTRATION 9-9.   List of Legally Significant Facts

- The slip and fall occurred in the store on July 8, 2012. (breach and duty)
- Rebecca Harris slipped on a banana peel that had been left on the store floor for two days. (breach and duty)
- The store employee dropped the banana peel on the floor two days earlier. (breach and duty)
- A store employee knew about the banana peel on the floor two days before the accident. (breach and duty)
- The employee kicked the peel into the corner after a patron told him to clean it up. (breach and duty)
- Rebecca Harris suffered injuries as a result of the fall. (link and injuries)

You should review the facts and determine which facts may affect whether the plaintiff can establish one of these elements or whether the defendant would be able to disprove one of the elements—in other words, the legally significant facts. In this case, you should include all of the facts listed in Illustration 9-9. In that illustration, the element of the legal theory is noted in parentheses next to the legally significant fact. The fact that Harris was purchasing cherries, strawberries, and bananas is not legally significant. Similarly, the fact that another patron was injured in the produce section that day did not affect whether Harris was injured and therefore is not legally significant.

4. Organize the Facts

After you have made your list of facts, decide how to organize them. After you select your organizational method, group the legally significant facts together in the organizational style you have selected.

PRACTICE POINTER

Sometimes you will use multiple organization methods.

5. Rewrite the Facts Statement

The facts contained in Illustration 9-9 lend themselves to a chronological organization because they can be ordered by time. Illustration 9-10 is a rewritten facts statement that includes only the legally significant facts. Finally, remember to introduce the legal issue or issues presented in the facts statement, as shown in the first paragraph of Illustration 9-10.

ILLUSTRATION 9-10. Sample Facts Statement for Slip-and-Fall Case

Rebecca Harris, a store patron, is suing our client, Sack and Shop Grocery Store, for negligence.

While Harris was in the produce department on July 8, 2012, she slipped on a banana peel that had been left on the floor by a grocery store employee. The employee dropped it on the floor two days earlier and had failed to clean it up after a patron asked him to do so. When he was told to pick up the peel, the employee kicked the peel into the corner.

Harris sustained a broken arm and head injuries as a result of the slip and fall.

CHAPTER SUMMARY

A facts statement is designed to refresh an attorney's memory about a case or to educate a new attorney about the case. It is a statement of all facts that are legally significant (facts that might affect the outcome of a legal issue). Facts that are not legally significant should be omitted from a facts statement.

Facts statements can be organized in chronological or reverse chronological order, by claim or defense, by party, or any combination of these three.

To draft your statement, make a list of the facts, plan your organization, and then write the statement. Next, research the legal issue, then rewrite your facts statement because the legally significant facts may have changed based on your research.

In the next chapter, you will learn how to organize using the IRAC methodology.

KEY TERMS

asserted facts
chronological organization
elements
emotional adjectives
fact
facts statement
legal claim

legal conclusion
organization by claim or defense
organization by party
procedural fact
pure fact
reverse chronological order

EXERCISES

SHORT ANSWER
1. What is a facts statement?
2. What are legally significant facts?
3. What are pure facts?

4. What are asserted facts?
5. What are procedural facts?
6. What facts should be included in the facts statement?
7. What is the difference between a fact and a legal conclusion?
8. Where do you find the information to include in the facts statement?
9. List several methods for organizing a facts statement.
10. Explain two methods of organization.

DRAFTING A LIST OF RELEVANT FACTS

11. Review the following Uniform Commercial Code section and read the list of facts that follows. Make a list of the legally significant facts based on the statute. Next to each fact, list the relevant portion of the statute.

§2-315 Implied Warranty of Fitness for a Particular Purpose

Where the seller at the time of contracting has reason to know any particular purpose for which the goods are required and that buyer is relying on the seller's skill or judgment to select or furnish suitable goods, there is unless excluded or modified under the next section an implied warranty that the goods be fit for such purpose.

Facts

Your client is Sue A. Buyer. She lives at 3225 Wilmette Avenue, Glenview, Illinois. The defendants are Lee R. Merchant, owner of Mowers R Us, in Glenview, Illinois, and Manny U. Facture, the owner of a manufacturing concern that is not incorporated called Mowers, of Rosemont, Illinois. Ms. Buyer went to the defendant's store, Mowers R Us, to purchase a lawn mower for her new home. She was a first-time homeowner and was unfamiliar with lawn mowers. She had never operated a lawn mower because her brothers had always mowed the lawn when she was a child.

When she went to Mowers R Us, she asked to speak with the owner. She told Mr. Merchant: "I don't know anything about these mowers, and I need to talk with an expert." Mr. Merchant said, "I'm the owner, and you couldn't find a better expert anywhere in the Chicagoland area. I have been in the business of selling mowers for more than 40 years. I only sell mowers and the equipment to clean and repair them. Are you familiar with the type of lawn mower you would like?"

"No, I don't know anything about lawn mowers. I just know that I have to have a lawn mower that will mulch my grass clippings, because I cannot bag the clippings. The village of Glenview does not permit me to bag the clippings, so the clippings must remain on my lawn."

"You're absolutely correct. You must have a mulching mower," Mr. Merchant said. "That type of mower will grind the grass clippings, and you will not notice them on your grass. I have the perfect mower for you. It is a used model that will fit into your price range, only $200. It's a good brand, a Roro, and will mulch the grass as well as any of the new mowers. This one is true blue. You can purchase a separate mulching blade, which will easily attach to it for an additional $50," he added.

"Do you think that I need the mulching blade?" Ms. Buyer asked, "I've never used a lawn mower, so I don't know what to expect, and you appear to be the expert."

"I think that you could do without the mulching blade unless you want the grass ground up very fine."

"I think that I would like it ground up fine. I'll defer to your judgment. If you think a mulching blade is necessary, then I'll buy that with the mower. Do you think that this is the best mower for mulching, or should I go with a new one?"

"Absolutely the used one is best; I told you: it's a true value. It will mulch with the best of them."

"If you think it can do the job, I'll trust your judgment," said Ms. Buyer, "I'll take the mower and the mulching blade. Can you install the mulching blade? I don't know anything about the installation."

"Sure, we can install any blade for another $30."

Ms. Buyer purchased the mower and the blade. She used the mower after Mr. Merchant installed the new mulching blade. It barely cut the grass and certainly didn't mulch the clippings into fine pieces as Mr. Merchant had claimed.

She brought the mower back to Mr. Merchant. He said that he had made no warranties about the mower. He showed her the language on the receipt that said that he did not expressly warrant anything.

Ms. Buyer brought the mower to a Roro dealer. The owners of the Roro dealership, Abe Saul and Lou T. Wright, said that the mower Ms. Buyer had purchased from Mowers R Us was not a mulching mower. It was a mower built before mulching was popular. Therefore, it would not perform the mulching task. It was designed merely to cut the grass. "Any merchant who has been in business even for one year should have known that mowers built before 2000 were not designed for mulching," Mr. Wright said. He showed Ms. Buyer where the manufacturing date appeared on the mower. "Manufactured in August 1999," it said on the plate with the serial number. "Also, mulching blades cannot be placed on these old mowers. Any mower dealer should know that too," Mr. Wright added. "However, this mower isn't bad. It can cut the grass without mulching it."

Ms. Buyer brought an action against Mr. Merchant and Mr. Facture in the Cook County Circuit Court, Skokie, Illinois.

OBJECTIVE WRITING

12. Write three different discussions about your high school career. One discussion should present the experience in a negative manner. The second should attempt to persuade the reader that the experience was positive. Finally, write about your experience in a neutral manner, without any emotion. Compare the three discussions.

DRAFTING A FACTS STATEMENT

13. Draft a facts statement for our client, Ronnie Randall. Janice Kahn, the plaintiff, brought an action against Randall for intentional infliction of emotional distress. You should prepare your facts statement based on this excerpt from a deposition transcript, witness statements, and a police report. The facts statement will be included in a memo that discusses the issue of intentional infliction of emotional distress. For the purpose of this memo, intentional infliction of emotional distress is defined as follows:

> An act by a person that is extreme and outrageous conduct, done with intent to cause another to suffer severe emotional distress, and which results in distress and emotional injury to another. The emotional injury must manifest itself with a physical problem.

Below is a portion of Janice Kahn's deposition transcript.

Q. What were you doing when the accident occurred?
A. Working in my garden. I planted tomatoes, green peppers, carrots, and broccoli.
Q. Where is your garden located on your property?
A. In the front, near the street. It is next to a brick wall. I can't see the garden from my house.
Q. What direction were you facing in your garden?
A. North.
Q. Does that direction face the street?
A. No.
Q. What do you usually do in your garden when you work?
A. Weed it.
Q. What were you doing in your garden when the accident occurred?
A. Weeding it.
Q. Where is the street in relation to your garden?
A. About five feet.
Q. Where do the children generally play?
A. In the backyard.
Q. Where were the children playing on the day of the accident?
A. They were playing T-ball in the front yard.
Q. Were you watching the children at the time of the accident?
A. Yes I could see them.
Q. Did you see the accident occur?
A. Sort of.
Q. Did you or did you not see the accident?
A. I saw my son, who is 11 years old, on the ground covered with blood, and blood all over the front of the Cadillac.
Q. Did you actually see the driver strike your son?
A. No. But I know Ronnie hit him. I saw my son next to Ronnie's car. I heard him swerve.

Q. Did you know the driver?

A. Yes.

Q. How did you know him?

A. We met at a state fair. We dated for ten years. I broke up with him two weeks before the accident.

Q. Did he know your son?

A. He knew my son was the most important person to me, and he tried to kill him to pay me back for dumping him.

Q. Are you accusing the driver of intentionally striking your son?

A. Yes. He wanted to get back at me, so he hit my boy.

Q. What happened to your son on the day of the accident?

A. He sustained head injuries and several broken bones. He can't play T-ball for the rest of the season, and we had to cancel our vacation to the Dells because he's been hurting so much.

Q. Was he conscious when you first saw him after the accident?

A. He was awake, but I thought he was dead at first. He had blood everywhere. I knew the driver, Ronnie, was drunk when he hit him. He wasn't even looking where he was going. He always swerves down our street to get my attention.

Q. Did your son speak to you right after the accident?

A. Barely. I told him that Ronnie was speeding and trying to run him down on purpose. I was horrified to see the blood and the broken bones. I couldn't move and I was so angry at Ronnie because I knew he did this on purpose.

Q. Did you go to the doctor after this accident?

A. I went by ambulance with my son to the doctor. His doctor looked me over and said I was suffering from shock. Since then, I suffered from anxiety and headaches. I throw up every day.

Q. Have you seen a doctor for your complaints?

A. Yes. She said that they are related to the accident. I just keep thinking back to that day when the neighbor told me that Ronnie intentionally turned the wheel to hit my boy.

Q. Was your son able to move after the accident?

A. Slightly. He looked just like our neighbor's son did after Ronnie hit him with his car two weeks before at the same curve.

Police Report, State of Illinois

Ronnie Randall, the driver of a 2009 Cadillac, was cited for driving while under the influence of alcohol and/or drugs, reckless driving, and driving with a suspended license. I will ask the prosecutor to consider either reckless assault charges or vehicular homicide, depending upon the condition of the boy. I tested Randall for alcohol intoxication. His blood alcohol level was .11. Randall struck another boy, Tommy Albert, at the same site two weeks earlier. He was cited for reckless driving for that accident and drunk driving. As I arrested Randall, he said that he was daydreaming during the accident and that he did not mean to hit the child. There were no skid marks. The street was dry.

The boy's mother, Janice Kahn, was working in her garden about five feet from the accident scene at the time of the accident. Her son, Billy Kahn, was playing a game in the street.

Witness Statement

Two days before the accident, Rhonda Albert, a neighbor of Janice Kahn, heard Randall say that he planned to get even with Kahn after Kahn broke off her ten-year relationship with Randall. Albert saw the car strike Kahn's son. According to Albert, after the car struck the boy, Randall got out of his car and said, "Oh, my God. I didn't mean to hit him. Is he okay?" Albert could smell alcohol on Randall's breath.

Witness Statement

Rebecca Mark saw the driver, Ronnie Randall, turn the car toward Kahn's son.

REVIEW OF FACTS STATEMENTS

14. Now that you have reviewed the facts for the *Janice Kahn* case and have drafted a statement of your own, read the following statements of facts. Determine which facts statement is best. List any errors you find in any of the statements.

a. The plaintiff, a single mother, and the defendant, her ex-boyfriend, are involved in a lawsuit. The plaintiff alleges in her deposition that the defendant was driving recklessly and intentionally struck her son with his car. The defendant's motive was to pay her back for ending their relationship. He tried to kill her son for this reason. As a result of the accident, the plaintiff went into shock and suffers from anxiety, headaches, and vomiting.

b. The plaintiff was working in her tomato garden located in the front of the property about five feet from the street. She could see the children playing in the front yard. She did not see the driver, Ronnie Randall, hit her son with his Cadillac but did see blood on the front of the Cadillac and on her son, who was on the ground.

The plaintiff dated Randall for ten years and had just ended their relationship. She states that Ronnie hit her son to pay her back for ending their relationship. Two weeks before, Ronnie had hit a neighbor's son at the same curve.

The plaintiff states that her son was covered with blood, able to move slightly. He suffered head trauma and broken bones.

The plaintiff is suffering from shock after seeing her son. She remembers a neighbor telling her that Ronnie intentionally turned the wheel to hit her son.

The plaintiff suffers from anxiety and headaches and vomits daily.

c. Janice Kahn is bringing an action against Ronnie Randall for the intentional infliction of emotional distress. Her son was recently hit by Ronnie Randall's car on the street in front of the Kahn home. At the time of the injury, Kahn was working in the front yard near her son. Her son went into the street and Randall hit him. At the time of the accident, Randall was legally drunk and driving with a suspended license.

Randall had previously told Kahn's neighbor, a Ms. Albert, that he was going to get even with Ms. Kahn over the breakup of their ten-year relationship. He also told Ms. Albert that he knew that Ms. Kahn's son was very important to her.

Since the accident, Kahn vomits daily and suffers from anxiety and headaches. She has stated that Mr. Randall often drives by her home in an erratic fashion and on another occasion hit a neighbor's child. Kahn feels that Randall hit her son intentionally. Kahn did not see the injury take place but was at her son's side immediately after the injury. Kahn also says that Randall never slowed down until after he hit her son.

d. On August 12, 2011, Janice Kahn filed a lawsuit against Ronnie Randall for intentional infliction of emotional distress stemming from an accident involving Kahn's 11-year-old son.

On July 8, 2011, Janice Kahn was weeding her tomato garden while her children played T-ball a few feet away from her in the street. As she worked, Kahn heard a car swerve. She looked up to see her son, covered in blood, lying on the ground in front of a Cadillac, driven by Ronnie Randall.

Two neighbors witnessed the accident. Rebecca Mark saw the driver, Ronnie Randall, turn the car toward Kahn's son. Rhonda Albert also saw the car strike Kahn's son. According to Albert, after the car struck the boy, Randall got out of his car and said, "Oh, my God. I didn't mean to hit him. Is he okay?"

Albert could smell alcohol on Randall's breath. Police tested his blood alcohol level and found that it was. 11. Police cited Randall for drunk driving, speeding, and reckless driving.

After police arrived, an ambulance took Kahn and her son to the hospital, where he was treated for head injuries and broken bones. The doctor who treated Kahn's son told Kahn that she should be treated for shock. Since the accident, Kahn has suffered from anxiety and headaches and vomits daily. Her doctor said that the anxiety, headaches, and vomiting are the result of the accident.

The driver of the car involved in the accident was Kahn's former boyfriend. They had dated for ten years; however, Kahn broke off the relationship about two weeks before the accident. Kahn stated in her deposition that she believes Randall intentionally struck her son to pay her back for ending the relationship.

Also, two days before the accident Albert heard Randall say that he planned to get even with Kahn after Kahn broke off their ten-year relationship. However, the police report stated that Randall said that he was daydreaming during the accident and that he did not mean to hit the child. Since the breakup, Kahn has seen Randall often swerve down the street in front of her home. Two weeks before the accident, Randall hit Rhonda Albert's son with his Cadillac at the same curve.

15. Read the following statement. Make a list of the legally significant facts. Then prepare a facts statement for a memo which would explain the possible interests of all of the parties.

Also make a note about the organization. What type of organization did you use and why?

Nate Late, a business owner, has two partners in the operation of Loose Cannon Manufacturing in Gurnee Your state. He owns 33 1/3 parts of a $3 million company. Late is ill but is not dying. He is grooming a 26-year-old boy, Ivan T. All, to run the business. He tells his family he likes the boy and that he wants to teach him the business. The business owner, Nate Late, dies. The most current will leaves the estate of Late to his wife, Shirley Late, and his only son, Lou Sier. All tells Mrs. Late that Late intended to give All Late's one-third interest in the company and that Late told this to All in front of a banker on the day of his death. The conversation took place during a meeting and the agreement was never put into writing. Before this meeting, on the day of Late's death, other employees of Loose Cannon heard Late say that he intended for All "to get" the business. Family members knew that Late intended for All to run the business and for All to get something if the business was sold. None of the family believed that Late intended to give the business to this newcomer. Late's shares of stock were never given to All. The shares were in the safe deposit box shared by Late and his wife of 24 years.

Rob R. Baron also claims that Late promised to give him the shares in the future. Baron admits that Late did not physically give him the shares before he died, but Baron insists that Late said "I shall give you my shares in two years." Mrs. Late said that Mr. Late planned to give her the shares. He told her this when he opened the joint safety deposit box and gave her the key.

You work for a firm which has been retained by Mrs. Late. She would like to know if All can prove that Mr. Late gave All Mr. Late's interest in the company.

16. Rewrite this statement using a different type of organization. Does this organization make sense? If not, why not? If so, why?

Facts-Drafting Exercises

17. Make a list of the legally significant facts for the following problem. Then draft a facts statement.

You are a paralegal with the firm of Probing and Will. You must research whether Sarah Wakefield can renounce Adam Antwernts' will and collect a portion of the estate.

Your firm's client is Sarah Wakefield. She was married to Adam Antwernt. Antwernt died on February 1, 2012, in your state following a long illness. Wakefield was Antwernt's second wife. She had been married to him for more than 20 years and lived in their home in the Highlands of your state. Antwernt purchased the home with his first wife, Carry MacOver. MacOver died in 1988. When Antwernt married Wakefield he never changed the deed for the home to include Wakefield. Wakefield kept her maiden name. Antwernt adopted a son with MacOver in 1976. The son, who is 36 years old, is Grayson Antwernt.

Antwernt drafted his will in May of 2005. He and his wife were getting along fine. However, he excluded her from his will. He did not leave her any property. Instead, he left all of his property to Grayson. Antwernt's will was admitted to probate on July 8, 2012.

Wakefield wants to know whether Antwernt's will is valid and whether he can divest her of their marital property or whether she can renounce the will and collect a portion of the estate.

Grayson is out of town and his attorney told Wakefield that she will get her share of the estate once Grayson returns. He is scheduled to return on August 14, 2012.

THE IRAC METHOD

CHAPTER OVERVIEW

The IRAC chapter focuses on the writing style used for the discussion portion of the memo. IRAC is an acronym for Issue, Rule, Application, Conclusion. These are the building blocks of a memo's discussion. You will learn to identify issues and applicable legal authority. You will also learn how to extract the legally significant facts and apply them to the relevant law to draw substantiated conclusions. You will learn to identify effective IRAC use by dissecting discussions and labeling the IRAC components, and you will learn to draft IRAC sequences as well.

A. PURPOSES OF IRAC

▼ What Is IRAC?

IRAC stands for Issue, Rule, Application, Conclusion. IRAC is the architectural blueprint for the discussion portion of a legal memo. It gives legal writing continuity and clarity and organizes the contents of the discussion. IRAC provides legal support and analysis for the issues posed by the problem and guides the writer toward a well-supported conclusion.

IRAC benefits both the writer and the reader because the components are essentially a checklist designed to ensure that the discussion is analytically well thought-out and that it contains the necessary legal authority. IRAC is very important because it lets the reader see the particular legal point being addressed, the relevant legal rule, the application of the law to the facts, and the conclusion. It is formula writing in the same way that formula movie romances, westerns, and thrillers are. The predictability of the IRAC format enables the reader to obtain the information quickly.

NET NOTE

The CUNY Law School Writing Center Web site has handouts on using the IRAC format at www.law.cuny.edu/academics/WritingCenter/students/strategies-techniques/irac-crracc.html

---

B. IRAC COMPONENTS

Each IRAC sequence is composed of an issue, which is really a legal element or component; the **legal rule** or holding from a case or statutory authority; the application, which is a demonstration of how the legal authority applies to the problem that you are writing about; and the conclusion, the final assessment of how the rule applies to the facts of your problem.

▼ What Does an IRAC Paragraph Look Like?

This fact pattern forms the basis of the IRAC paragraph example.

> On August 7, 2011, Ms. Howard went to Rough & Tough Pawn Shop in Chicago to obtain a loan using a diamond ring as collateral. Rough & Tough loaned Ms. Howard $800, and she agreed to pay $75 per month for a total of 13-1/2 months. Ms. Howard knew that she would have to pay off the balance of $1,025 in 12 months because at that time

Rough & Tough would have the right to sell the ring. On September 11, 2011, Ms. Howard received a postcard from Rough & Tough stating that it was selling the shop and all of its assets to Able Pawn. Mr. Sam Able would assume the business of Rough & Tough, including all pawned items and outstanding loans. On the bottom of the postcard was a notice stating; "If you want your item, please pick it up by September 29, 2011, and pay off your note by September 29, 2011." Because Ms. Howard did not have the money to pay off the note, she decided to pay Able Pawn the $75 per month once the loan was transferred in the sale. In October 2011, Able Pawn was robbed and all the jewelry, including Ms. Howard's ring, was stolen. Able Pawn had a security alarm system and a guard dog to protect the property, but the robbers were able to circumvent these obstacles.

We will work through the following sample IRAC paragraph, based on the Howard fact pattern, and its components to illustrate how to draft an IRAC paragraph.

> **(I)** Whether a bailment for the mutual benefit of Rough & Tough and Howard existed. **(R)** A pawn is a form of bailment, made for the mutual benefit of bailee and bailor, arising when goods are delivered to another as a pawn for security to him on money borrowed by the bailor. *Jacobs v. Grossman*, 141 N.E. 714, 715 (Ill. App. Ct. 1923). In *Jacobs*, the court found that a bailment for mutual benefit arose because the plaintiff pawned a ring as collateral for a $70 loan given to him by the defendant. *Id.* **(A)** Similarly in our problem, Howard pawned her ring as collateral to secure an $800 loan given to her by Rough & Tough, the pawnbroker. **(C)** Therefore, Howard and Rough & Tough probably created a bailment for mutual benefit.

Note that the first sentence of the IRAC paragraph is a statement of the issue that will be examined in the paragraph. The issue is narrowly defined and focused on one of the analytical elements of the problem. The rule of law, the next component of the paragraph, provides the legal basis for the analysis of the issue. Then, it is appropriate to discuss some of the facts of the cited case if these facts help explain how the legal rule can be applied to your facts. Notice that everything that comes from an opinion is given citation credit.

The most important component of the IRAC paragraph is the application portion. The application is where you use the facts of your problem to demonstrate, but not to conclude, why the legal rule should apply to the issue posed. This is the legal analysis. (See Chapter 11 for more discussion.) The facts speak for themselves when you demonstrate how the legal rule applies to the scenario at hand by contrasting or paralleling the facts of the case and the problem. After laying out this relationship, you will then draw a conclusion. The conclusion answers the issue posed. The issue is the question being examined in the discussion, and the conclusion is the answer.

This example illustrates how the conclusion responds directly to the issue:

Issue: Whether a bailment for the mutual benefit of Rough & Tough and Howard existed.

Conclusion: Therefore, Howard and Rough & Tough probably created a bailment, for it was for their mutual benefit because a loan was given upon the receipt of valuable collateral.

1. Issues

The question presented is the overall legal **issue** that will be resolved in the memo. A **subissue** in the IRAC paragraph is a point or query that must be addressed to substantiate one legal element of the problem. When analyzing and writing about a legal problem objectively, it is often important to address subissues in the order that they must be resolved to support legal analysis. For example, the general rule for arson in Illinois is the malicious burning of the dwelling house of another. The question presented for a memo on arson would be:

Whether Mr. Smith committed arson by intentionally burning down his brother's factory.

The subissues addressed in the IRAC paragraphs would be:

Whether there was a malicious burning
Whether the factory is a dwelling house
Whether the factory of Mr. Smith's brother constitutes the property of another person

The subissues form the **topic sentences** of the IRAC paragraphs. They provide the analytical steps that you must take in your thought process and your legal reasoning to resolve the overall issue the problem poses; the overall question is the question presented for the entire memo. The topic sentences in the IRAC paragraph introduce the legal element in question that needs to be resolved to complete the steps necessary to thoroughly examine the problem and to determine a response to the question presented.

▼ What Is the Difference Between the Question Presented and the Issues in IRAC Paragraphs?

The question presented is the overall problem that must be resolved in the objective memo. The question presented for the Howard fact pattern is:

Whether Ms. Howard has a claim against Rough & Tough or against Able Pawn Shop for the value of her ring.

The subissues are determined by the legal elements or tests involved in the problem. The elements are discussed individually along with the relevant legal rule. There is a certain logical order when presenting the elements. Let the legal rules guide you in establishing the order of the subissues. Notice that each issue centers on a single step of the legal analysis necessary to fully examine the question presented.

The subissues that form the topic sentences of the IRAC paragraphs in a memo addressing Ms. Howard's problem would be as follows:

> The first issue is what type of relationship does a pawner and a pawnee have?
>
> What property rights do Ms. Howard and Rough & Tough Pawn have when they enter into a mutual bailment?
>
> Can Rough & Tough Pawn transfer its interest in Ms. Howard's property to Able Pawn?
>
> Did Rough & Tough Pawn receive the proper consent for the transfer of the ring from Ms. Howard?
>
> Is Rough & Tough liable for the loss of Ms. Howard's property after transferring its interest to Able Pawn?
>
> Is Able Pawn liable for the theft of Ms. Howard's property while it was in its possession?

All of these queries are really elements that must be addressed, step by step, to resolve the question presented.

Each of the subissues will be a topic sentence of the IRAC paragraph highlighting the analytical focus of the legal discussion in that paragraph. Each issue is a step in the thought process required to thoroughly prove all of the underlying elements necessary to address the question presented.

Notice how one issue statement logically leads into the next. A good test to see if your discussion is well organized is to write down all your issue statements from your IRAC paragraphs. If the issue statements flow logically, one to the next, then the organization of your discussion will be logical.

To analyze the problem thoroughly, a number of issues must be examined in the discussion. To make the analysis logical, the issues must be examined in a certain order.

2. Rules of Law

The **legal rule**, or synthesized compilation of the pertinent legal rules, follows the issue at the beginning of the IRAC paragraph. (For an in-depth discussion of the process of synthesizing authority, see Chapter 11)

A rule of law is the court's test, standard, or principle on the point. A rule also can be a statute and the legal elements laid out by the statute. A synthesis of a statute and a case applying or interpreting the statute also constitutes a rule.

In our IRAC example, note that the first sentence is the issue, and the second sentence is the legal rule.

Issue: Whether a bailment for the mutual benefit of Rough & Tough and Howard existed.

Rule, followed by pinpoint citation: A pawn is a form of bailment, made for the mutual benefit of the bailee and the bailor, arising when goods are delivered to another as a pawn for security to him on money borrowed by the bailor. *Jacobs v. Grossman*, 141 N.E. 714, 715 (Ill. App. Ct. 1923).

When organizing the discussion, first discern what issues are to be addressed, then find the pertinent mandatory authority that addresses the issues raised. Do not write the discussion around the authority but make the authority address the issues. To demonstrate clearly how the authority supports or addresses the issues raised, discuss the pertinent facts of the cited case after you state the case's holding or legal rule. This is particularly helpful when the holding is very broad. You must demonstrate that the cited case truly supports the premise discussed in the IRAC paragraph.

▼ Why Is Citation Important?

Citation is an essential component of the rule portion of the IRAC paragraph. (See Appendix B.) You must always give proper credit in *Bluebook* or *ALWD* format to any statement made that is not wholly your own. Any legal principle or authority must be attributed to its source. Proper attribution of authority tells the reader where you obtained the legal principle that supports the discussion. The cite allows the reader to find the source too. Most important, the cite tells the reader whether the authority is primary mandatory authority, primary persuasive, or secondary authority. A cite also provides information without including the information in the discussion's text. For example, you could write a rule as follows:

The state of Kimberly Supreme Court held in 1983 that individuals have a right to privacy. *Jones v. City of Moose*, 121 Kim. 12, 13 (1983).

A more effective version of the same rule, to include in the rule portion of the IRAC paragraph, is:

Individuals have a right to privacy. *Jones v. City of Moose*, 121 Kim. 12, 13 (1983).

The citation itself provides the information about the court, its jurisdiction and level, and the year. The text need not repeat this information. Citations are valuable sources of information about the legal authority presented in the rule component of the IRAC paragraph.

3. Application of the Law to the Problem's Facts

▼ How Do You Use the Legally Significant Facts?

Think of the legal rule as a test or a series of elements requiring certain facts to be used to support the outcome of the test. The facts used are **legally significant facts** because they bear legal significance as to the outcome of an issue. Our arson example mentioned at the beginning of the chapter illustrates this point.

THE ARSON HYPOTHETICAL

John Smith lived in Arkville. John Smith's brother, Richard Smith, lived in Barkville Estates. Richard Smith owned a factory in downtown Barkville. John Smith was consumed by a jealous rage over his brother Richard's success and intentionally and maliciously burned down the factory in Barkville. The question to be examined is whether John Smith committed arson by intentionally and maliciously burning down his brother's factory.

The general rule for arson is the malicious burning of a dwelling house of another. This general rule would be the legal authority used in the rule portion of the IRAC paragraph.

An IRAC paragraph on this topic would be as follows:

Issue: Whether John Smith committed arson when he burned down his brother's factory.

Rule: Arson is the malicious burning of a dwelling house of another. 9 Stat. §§21, 23 (2011).

Application: John Smith burned down the factory of his brother, Richard Smith. John Smith's actions were intentional and malicious. Richard resides in Barkville Estates.

Conclusion: John Smith did not commit arson because he burned down his brother's factory, not his brother's residence or dwelling house.

The **application** lays a factual foundation on which the conclusion can be based. The facts are selected because each fact illustrates a legal point related to your rule of law: the malicious act, the intentional burning down of a building, the use of the building—whether it serves as a residence or dwelling house or whether it serves another purpose. The rule indicates which facts you should examine. After you lay the factual foundation by using the problem's facts to illustrate how the law should apply, you can draw a conclusion.

4. Conclusion

The **conclusion** resolves the issue posed at the beginning of the IRAC sequence. The conclusion should reflect directly the issue posed. If you remove the rule and the application portions of the IRAC paragraph, the issue and the conclusion should read as if they are a question and an answer. The conclusion generally restates the issue and includes the basis for the answer. The arson example with John Smith illustrates the role of the conclusion.

Issues: Whether John Smith committed arson when he burned down his brother's factory.

Conclusion: John Smith did not commit arson because he burned down his brother's factory, not his residence or dwelling house.

Notice how the conclusion responds directly to the issue posed. The conclusion focuses directly on the question raised at the beginning of the IRAC sequence. Each element of the discussion is resolved before addressing the next element or issue.

PRACTICE POINTER

To test if your conclusion is focused on the issue raised, read the issue at the beginning of the IRAC sequence, then read the conclusion. If the issue and the conclusion read like a question and a reasoned answer that responds directly to the question raised, then you have stayed focused and adequately addressed the issue.

CHAPTER SUMMARY

IRAC—standing for Issue, Rule, Application, Conclusion—provides the structure for the legal discussion. The IRAC structure provides a checklist for you to make sure that you have included all the necessary components in the discussion and supported every premise with legal authority. Because it follows a predictable pattern, IRAC permits the reader to obtain information quickly. Mastering the IRAC format requires practice, which involves rereading and revising your work. Once you feel comfortable with the IRAC format, you should be confident that the discussion portions of your memos are logically ordered and analytically complete.

KEY TERMS

application	legal holding
citation	legal rule
conclusion	legally significant facts
IRAC	subissue
issue	topic sentence

EXERCISES

SHORT ANSWER
1. What does "IRAC" stand for? Define each component.
2. Why do we use the IRAC format?
3. What is a legally significant fact?

DIAGRAMMING IRAC COMPONENTS
4. Diagram the IRAC components of each paragraph in the discussion section. Note where the writing digresses from the IRAC format.

Discussion

To be successful in a claim against Rough & Tough or Able Pawn, Ms. Howard would have to prove that Rough & Tough was liable for the loss of her ring. First, for an action against Rough & Tough, she would have to show that the company had no right to transfer her pawned property without her written consent. Illinois Pawnbrokers Act, 205 Ill. Comp. Stat. 510/7 (2011). If pledged property was transferred without written consent of the property owner, the pawnbroker can be held responsible for loss or theft of pawned property because the property was in his safekeeping and was transferred illegally. *Jacobs v. Grossman*, 141 N.E. 714, 716 (Ill. App. Ct. 1923). Rough & Tough did not get a written consent for the transfer of Ms. Howard's property. In its defense the company could claim that written correspondence without the written consent would be enough to inform the pawner of the transfer of her property. Second, for an action against Able Pawn, Ms. Howard would have to show negligence in its care of her pawned ring. Illinois courts have ruled that in bailment for mutual benefit, the ordinary care or diligence that one would give to one's own property would be adequate to avoid negligence. *Id.* at 715; *Bielunski v. Tousignant*, 149 N.E.2d 801, 803 (Ill. App. Ct. 1958). Mrs. Howard would have to prove that a security system and a guard dog would not be ordinary care and diligence. In his defense Mr. Able could argue that these were sufficient to be considered ordinary care and diligence. For a claim against Village Jewelers to be successful, Ms. Howard would have to establish that she held good title to her property because a thief cannot convey good title to stolen property. *Hobson's Truck Sales v. Carroll Trucking*, 276 N.E. 89, 92 (Ill. App. Ct. 1971). Village Jewelers, which purchased the ring from the robbers, could not have good title to Ms. Howard's ring. Ms. Howard probably could have a successful claim against Rough & Tough and Village Jewelers. She probably would not be able to prove Able Pawn negligent in the care of her ring.

Does a pawnbroker have the right to transfer pawned property or interest in that property without written consent of the pawner? Pawned property cannot be transferred within a year from the pawner's default without written consent of the pawner. Illinois Pawnbrokers Act, 205 Ill. Comp. Stat. 510/7. One Illinois court ruled that a pawnbroker had no right to transfer the plaintiff's pledged diamond ring to another pawnbroker within a year of the plaintiff's default of her loan, without written consent of the pawner. *Jacobs*, 141 N.E. at 716. In our situation, Rough & Tough sold its shop and assets to Sam Able within two months of Ms. Howard's pawning her grandmother's engagement ring. Because the sale occurred within a year of Ms. Howard's transaction with

Rough & Tough, the company had a legal obligation under the Illinois statute to require a written consent for the transfer of her property. Also, the statute states that the time period for requirement of written consent for transfer of pledged property is established from the time of the pawner's default. 205 Ill. Comp. Stat. 510/7. Our client has not defaulted, and she deserves at least all the rights offered by the statute to a pawner who is in default. Rough & Tough did send Ms. Howard a postcard notifying her that it had sold all the pawned items and outstanding loans, including her ring, but it did not get her written consent for the sale of her property. Rough & Tough did not have the right to transfer Ms. Howard's ring without her written consent, and the sale of her property was probably not a legal sale.

Is a postcard sent to a pawner by a pawnbroker sufficient notice for the transfer of pawned property? Personal pawned property cannot be sold by a pawnee within one year from the time the pawner has defaulted in the interest payment unless the pawner has given written consent. Illinois Pawnbrokers Act, 205 Ill. Comp. Stat. 510/7. The statute uses a definite and clear term: "written consent." Ms. Howard did not default, and she would have at least all the rights of a pawner that did default. Therefore, the pawnbroker was required to receive her written consent before transferring her property. A postcard with written notice of a sale of pawned property is not a written consent by the pawner and would probably not be sufficient notice to constitute a legal sale.

5. Diagram the IRAC components of each paragraph in the discussion section. Note where the writing digresses from the IRAC format.

Facts

The Blacks came to us with the following problem and want to know what type of damages they are entitled to.

Mr. and Mrs. Black wanted to have a chair and a loveseat made to match the living room in their new home. The Blacks searched for weeks at various local furniture retailers for a furniture style and fabric that they liked but were unsuccessful. Finally, the Blacks went to a fabric sale at Fabric Retailers and found the upholstery fabric of their dreams. The Blacks purchased 50 yards of the fabric to make sure that they would have enough for any project. Mr. Black called all the furniture retailers in the area to inquire whether customers can have furniture covered in their own material. Finally, Comfy Furniture said that they permit customers to bring in their own material to cover upholstered furniture ordered from Comfy. The Blacks hurried over to Comfy with the 50 yards of fabric and placed an order for a chair and a loveseat using their own fabric. The price agreed on was the base price of $500 for the chair and $800 for the loveseat. Mr. Blaine, of Comfy Furniture, was their salesperson. Mr. Blaine said that the fabric was ideal for the styles selected because it required no matching. He added that there was plenty of yardage because 30 yards is adequate for jobs of this nature. The fabric was a small paisley print, with the right side having a lovely sheen and vibrant coloration. The Blacks placed the order on July 7, 2011, because they were planning a family reunion for Thanksgiving and felt that that date would give them plenty of time to completely decorate their living room. The new pieces would provide plenty of seating for the family reunion. The Blacks indicated to Mr. Blaine that they needed the furniture for the reunion. Mr. Blaine asserted that the furniture would be ready by September 15. The Blacks gave Comfy Furniture a deposit of $1,000. The loveseat and the chair were delivered to the Black home on September 10, but the furniture was upholstered with the fabric's reverse side showing. The Blacks were devastated.

Issues

Whether the Blacks are entitled to damages from Comfy Furniture for incorrectly upholstering their furniture.

Whether the Blacks are entitled to damages from Comfy Furniture for the expense of decorating their living room to match the furniture they did not receive in the agreed-on condition.

Discussion

Are the Blacks entitled to special damages from Comfy Furniture for the cost of the redecoration of their living room? An Illinois Appellate Court decided that the nonbreaching party should be put back in the position that it was in when the contract was formed. *Kalal v. Goldblatt Bros.*, 368 N.E.2d 671, 673 (Ill. App. Ct. 1977). The Blacks stated their intention at the beginning concerning the fabric, the redecoration of the living room, and the family reunion. This fact was a part of their original position. The living room was redecorated. The furniture was delivered; however, the fabric was incorrect. Therefore, the Blacks have a right to recover consequential damages for the cost of the redecoration of their living room because the end result was not achieved: correctly upholstered furniture, newly redecorated living room to match, and sufficient seating for the reunion. The conditions of the original contract were not met, and there was a breach of contract as embodied by the incorrectly upholstered furniture.

Under contract law, what damages are the Blacks entitled to pursue? Damages for breach of contract should place the plaintiff in a position he would have been in had the contract been performed. *Kalal*, 368 N.E.2d at 671. The plaintiffs in *Kalal* received a sofa that had been reupholstered in the wrong fabric after numerous delays, during which they had chosen three different fabrics in succession. *Id.* The court held that the defect could be remedied by the cost of reupholstering the sofa in the proper fabric. *Id.* at 674. The Blacks' sofa and loveseat were improperly upholstered. Comfy Furniture upholstered their furniture with the reverse side of the fabric showing. Therefore, they were entitled to damages equal to the cost of upholstering their furniture correctly. However, the Blacks' situation is distinguished from *Kalal* in that their furniture was delivered before the date set in the contract, and it can be argued by Comfy that there was time to remedy the defect before their target date of Thanksgiving.

Are the Blacks entitled to compensation for the loss of use of their furniture? The question of compensation for loss of use of the furniture was considered by both parties in *Kalal* to be appropriate since the plaintiffs in the case were without their furniture for several months while waiting for it to be reupholstered. *Id.* The Blacks have been similarly inconvenienced in that they, too, have been without the use of their new furniture. Thus, they are entitled to compensation for the loss of use of the furniture. However, it can be argued by Comfy Furniture that the furniture in the *Kalal* case was used and had been removed from the home for the purpose of reupholstering it. *Id.* In the present case, the furniture was new and had never been in the Blacks' home, and Comfy may argue that the Blacks did not actually suffer loss of use of the new furniture.

Are the Blacks entitled to damages for the expense of decorating their living room to match the furniture they did not receive in the agreed-on condition? The redecorating of the living room in *Kalal* was not in the contemplation of either party at the time the contract was executed. *Kalal,* 368 N.E.2d at 671. Subsequently, the court held that the only damages that were recoverable for breach of contract are limited to those that were reasonably foreseeable and were within the contemplation of the parties at the time the contract was executed. *Id.* at 674. By the express terms of the Uniform Commercial Code, the court cannot follow tort theories to award damages. The legislative history of the U.C.C. indicates that contractual disputes should apply to the findings of the court. *Moorman Mfg. Co. v. National Tank Co.,* 435 N.E.2d 443, 453 (Ill. 1982). The Blacks only told Mr. Blaine that they needed the furniture to be completed in time for a family reunion. Comfy knew that the Blacks were under a time constraint for the delivery, but apparently there was no communication regarding the redecorating of the living room. With regard to Comfy Furniture, the redecorating of the Blacks' living room was an unforeseeable event, and consequently they would not be held responsible for the expense. Because the fact that the redecorating of the living room was unforeseeable, it was not included within the terms of the contract. Therefore, Comfy only breached the express terms of the contract. The Blacks probably will not be awarded compensatory damages.

APPLICATION EXERCISES

6. Write an IRAC paragraph using the following information. You need not include all the information. The issue is whether the plaintiff can show that his attorney's failure to attend hearings was excusable neglect. A number of the text blocks below contain statements of rules. Other text blocks include legally significant facts. In some paragraphs, conclusions have been drawn for you. Combine the rules where necessary and form an IRAC paragraph for the issue.

> Fed. R. Civ. P. 60(b) provides for relief from judgment if plaintiffs can show that a mistake was made or that there was excusable neglect on the part of their attorney.
>
> Rule 60(b) is an extraordinary remedy, granted in only exceptional cases. *Harold Washington Party v. Cook City. Illinois Democratic Party,* 984 F.2d 875 (7th Cir. 1993).
>
> In this case, the plaintiff's attorney, Mark Adly, missed four court-set status hearings. He failed to appear. He failed to answer motions. Court status hearings are routinely held every three months.
>
> Adly claims he did not have any notice of the hearings. Adly knew status proceedings normally were held. He attended depositions in this

matter. Court records show that he was sent notices of the hearings to the address Adly says is correct.

"Excusable neglect may warrant relief under Rule 60(b)." *Zuelzke Tool & Eng'g v. Anderson Die Casting*, 925 F.2d 226 (7th Cir. 1991). In this case, the defendant relied on a third party who told them to refrain from further action because efforts were being made to have the defendant removed as defendant. *Id.* at 228. Anderson did not answer any complaints or file any pleadings. *Id.* The lack of response led the court to enter a default judgment against the company. *Id.* at 229. The district court refused the motion to vacate, saying that the defendant had voluntarily chosen not to control its fate in the litigation. *Id.*

7. Review the following paragraph. Note the issue, the rule, the application of law to facts, and the conclusion.

> An important factor in determining whether a funeral home is a nuisance is the suitability of its location. "Funeral homes are generally located on the edge of purely residential but not predominantly residential areas." Bauman v. Piser Undertakers Co., 34 Ill. App. 2d 145, 148, 180 N.E.2d 705, 708 (App. Ct. 1962). A carefully run funeral home may be located on a property zoned for business at the edge of a residential neighborhood. Id. The funeral home in this case is located in a predominantly rural area. It is outside the boundary lines of the Up and Coming Acres subdivision. It is a lawful business located on a parcel zoned for business. The funeral home is in a suitable location.

8. Read the following facts carefully.

> Mr. and Mrs. Mortimer reserved the party room at Harvey's Restaurant and gave Harvey's a $500 deposit. Their party was scheduled for November 3, 2011. Mrs. Mortimer sent the invitations out on October 1, 2011. The Mortimers agreed to the quoted price of $62.50 per person. The purpose of the event was for Mr. Mortimer to establish relationships with current and prospective legal clients.
>
> On October 20, 2011, Mrs. Mortimer called Harvey's to confirm party details. She was informed that the party room was under demolition and could not be used for the party. Mrs. Harvey offered to lower the price to $57.50 per person and reserve a portion of the dining room. Although she believed these arrangements were not suitable, Mrs. Mortimer agreed to use the dining room since the invitations were sent and many people accepted.
>
> Mrs. Mortimer ordered lump crab meat as an appetizer for the party. A waitress told Mrs. Mortimer that imitation crab meat was used when Mrs. Mortimer inquired about the crab's unusual crunchiness.
>
> The Mortimers want to sue Harvey's for breach of contract and believe that they relied to their detriment on this contract. They assert that Harvey's failed to notify them of the changes in a timely manner,

consequently preventing them from making other arrangements. Additionally, the Mortimers want to know if they have a cause of action for the substitution of imitation crab meat for genuine.

The following is a portion of a memo relating to one of the issues raised by the Mortimers. Read the paragraphs carefully and revise in IRAC format. Remember that each IRAC sequence can span more than one paragraph (for example, paragraph 1—issue and rule; paragraph 2—application and conclusion).

Did the Mortimers suffer a loss of business because of Harvey's Restaurant's promise of the entire party room? The Mortimers can argue that a false representation surrenders the restaurant's interest. "When parties enter into a contract for the performance of the same act in the future they impliedly promise that in the meantime neither will do anything to harm or prejudice the other inconsistent with the contractual relationship they have assumed. . . . If one party to the contract renounces it, the other may treat the renunciation as a breach and sue for damages at once." The restaurant can argue that the contract did not cover the entire performance but was modified; therefore, no harm was done to the contractual relationship. *Pappas v. Crist*, 233 N.C. 265, 25 S.E.2d 850 (1943).

The Mortimers can argue that "damages are not speculative merely because they cannot be computed with mathematical exactness, if, under evidence they are capable of reasonable approximation." *Hawkinson v. Johnston*, 122 F.2d 724 (8th Cir. 1941). The "rainmaking" potential was minimized because of the restaurant's failure to supply the room contracted for.

The restaurant would argue that the "period for which the damages can be reasonably forecast or soundly predicted in such a situation must depend on the circumstances and evidence of the particular case." *Id.* at 727. Therefore, the Mortimers can only quantify the number of RSVPs, not the number of rejects due to the smaller room.

9. This exercise will highlight organizational problems in the discussion and help you to write more logically.

Review the discussion section of a previously drafted memo. Label, in the margin, the issues, the rules, the application portions, and the conclusions. Examine each component to see where you digress from the IRAC format in the discussion. Revise the discussion to conform more closely with the IRAC format.

SYNTHESIZING CASES AND AUTHORITIES

CHAPTER OVERVIEW

You will learn about the methods of synthesis used when writing a memo. Synthesizing authority requires finding a common theme from two or more sources that ties together the legal rule. Cases are synthesized because it is hard to find a single decision that articulates the precise rule of law to support a point in a memo or brief. Often one case rule will expand another, so the two rules can be combined, or synthesized, to reflect an accurate statement of the law.

You will also become adept at synthesizing statutory authority as well as combining case law and statutes. Constitutions should be given the highest regard in the hierarchy of authority, then statutes. You will probably not use many constitutional provisions in your writing, but statutes play a very large role in legal research and writing. If you find case law that applies or interprets a statute, synthesize the statute and the rule from the case.

A. SYNTHESIS

Synthesis is the bringing together of various legal authorities into a unified cohesive statement of the law. The process of synthesizing authority requires finding a common theme or thread that relates to the various legal rules and tying the rules to that unified theme. Discussing related decisions and statutes separately in a memo makes your points sound more like a list than an integrated, well-thought-out whole. Synthesis adds analytical insight to your legal documents and makes reading them easier.

▼ What Is the Process of Synthesizing Legal Rules?

We synthesize cases and enacted law because memos and opinion letters are organized by legal issue and not by cited references. Frequently, more than one source of primary authority addresses a particular legal issue. The synthesis of related legal principles enables you to compare and to contrast the legal rules easily as well as to demonstrate how factual applications differ and to show how legal rules expand or contract. Often enacted law and case law are synthesized because the case law applies the statute or interprets the extent to which the statute can be applied. Sometimes the rules that are on point are derived from relevant statutes only. Enacted law that comes from more than one statute section also must be synthesized under a common legal principle to promote cohesiveness and to add your analytical viewpoint to the memo.

▼ Why Do We Synthesize Legal Authority?

The legal issues form the framework for the discussion. The synthesized authority groups the legal rules together to address the issues raised.

The following example demonstrates how one case defines an easement in gross and then another case explains how an easement in gross is retained. Both cases discuss easements in gross, yet one expands on the other. The facts on which the example is based are as follows:

> Robert and Jan Murray live in Evanston and are building an addition to their house on Ashland Avenue. There is eight feet between their house and their neighbor's, Mrs. Brown's, house. The properties are adjoining. A driveway does not separate the houses. Also, there is no alley that would provide access to either property. The Murrays' contractors and construction workers must enter Mrs. Brown's property to work on the addition. Mrs. Brown is not very pleased that workers are entering her property. The Murrays came to our office wondering whether they should purchase an easement from Mrs. Brown, their neighbor.

EXAMPLE

Should the Murrays purchase an easement in gross from Mrs. Brown? An easement in gross, sometimes called a personal easement, is a right in the land of another that is not permanently part of the title of the property. An easement in gross allows for use of the land of another for a limited purpose. *Willoughby v. Lawrence*, 4 N.E. 356 (Ill. 1886). It belongs to the easement holder independent of his ownership or possession of any tract of land and does not benefit the possessor of any tract of land in his use of it. *Schnabel v. County of DuPage*, 428 N.E.2d 671 (Ill. App. Ct. 1981). The Murrays are building an addition to their house. They want to have a right to use the adjoining land only to perform the construction of their addition. They do not need an easement that would be a permanent part of the property's title. The interest that the Murrays have in Mrs. Brown's land is personal and would not benefit either tract of land. Therefore, the Murrays can purchase an easement in gross from Mrs. Brown that would permit the workers to enter the Brown property for the limited purpose to complete the construction project.

B. TYPES OF SYNTHESIS

▼ What Are the Four Methods of Synthesizing Authority?

As we discussed previously, synthesizing primary authority requires finding a common theme that is used to unify all of the various rules related to the issue. The common legal theme can be developed by classifying the applicable precedent into categories. There are four basic ways to combine and to analyze legal rules to render a coherent distillation of the law:

1. **Primary authority** can be grouped by related rules of law found in the text of the decision or in the statute or constitution.
2. Synthesis can be focused around the **reasoning** that the judges use as the basis for the holdings
3. The various **facts** from different cases can form the foundation of the synthesis.
4. The **causes of action** are the last category of case synthesis.

To synthesize primary authority, you will group related legal rules. All the examples focus on this method of synthesis. Detailed instruction as to how to synthesize various sources of case law, case law combined with statutory authority, as well as two sources of statutory authority follow.

C. STEP-BY-STEP PROCESS TO SYNTHESIZING LEGAL RULES

The most effective synthesis of legal rules follows conscientious case briefing and careful reading of enacted law. Case briefing requires summarizing a decision in set categories: citation, procedure, issue, facts, holding, legal rule (the test or standard the court used to arrive at its decision), rationale (the court's reason for its holding), and disposition. (See Chapter 6.) The following steps take you through the synthesizing process.

1. *Summarize enacted law. Brief relevant decisions.* Once you have summarized enacted law, constitutional provisions, and statutes, after reading for their plain meaning, and carefully and meticulously briefed all the decisions that you plan to use in your memo, you can establish categories of legal rules to make comparing and contrasting authorities easier. It is far simpler to compare and to contrast seven rules from briefed decisions than to flip through printouts of authority.

2. *Outline the problem.* The next step is to formulate the analytical outline of your letter or memo and to pinpoint the issues and subissues that must be addressed to fully explore the memo topic.

3. *Relate research to legal issues raised.* To organize the primary authority, relate the research findings to the issues the problem raises. Remember: Legal writing is never organized around your sources of authority but around the issues the problem poses. After pinpointing the legal issues that will be explored, decide on the general rule relating to that point of law.

4. *Under each issue, organize your primary sources by hierarchy of authority.* Enacted law comes before common law, constitutions come before statutes, newer case decisions interpreting statutes come before common law cases, higher court holdings come before lower court holdings, and newer case holdings are more relevant than older holdings on the same point of law from the same court.

5. *Compare and contrast legal rules and statutes.* Using the case briefs that you prepared and the notes you made from the plain reading of the enacted law, compare and contrast the holdings and statutory texts.

6. *Formulate a statement of the law.* Your statement should incorporate all the primary sources that will be used under the subissue heading. Ask yourself: What are the similarities and differences between the various cases and statutes? In the cases, how do the legal rules or tests the court used differ from or expand on one another? How do the facts differ? What do the documents have in common?

7. *Correct citation.* Remember that you must attribute the authority for any legal statement, even if it is a clause, using the proper *Bluebook* or *ALWD* citation.

D. EXAMPLES OF CASE SYNTHESIS

This example demonstrates synthesizing the holdings from two legal decisions. A problem and two fictitious legal decisions are provided below on which case synthesis is performed.

EXAMPLES OF CASE SYNTHESIS

PROBLEM

Mr. and Mrs. Black wanted to have a chair and a loveseat made to match the living room in their new home. The Blacks searched for weeks at various local furniture retailers for a furniture style and fabric that they liked but were unsuccessful. Finally, the Blacks went to a fabric sale at Fabric Retailers and found the upholstery fabric of their dreams. The Blacks purchased 50 yards of the fabric of their dreams to make sure that they would have enough for any project. Mr. Black called all the furniture retailers in the area to inquire whether customers can have furniture covered in their own material. Finally, Comfy Furniture said that they permit customers to bring in their own material to cover upholstered furniture ordered from Comfy. The Blacks hurried over to Comfy with the 50 yards of fabric and placed an order for a chair and a loveseat using their own fabric. The price agreed on was the base price of $500 for the chair and $800 for the loveseat. Mr. Blaine, of Comfy Furniture, was their salesperson.

Mr. Blaine said that the fabric was ideal for the styles selected because it required no matching. He also offered that there was plenty of material, that 30 yards was adequate for a job of this nature. The fabric was a small paisley print, with the right side having a lovely sheen and vibrant coloration. The Blacks placed the order on July 7, 2012. They were planning a family reunion for Thanksgiving and felt that ordering in July would give them plenty of time to completely decorate their living room. The new pieces would provide plenty of seating for the family reunion. The Blacks indicated to Mr. Blaine that they needed the furniture for the reunion. Mr. Blaine asserted that the furniture would be ready by September 15. The Blacks gave Comfy Furniture a deposit of $1,000. The loveseat and the chair were delivered to the Black home on September 10, but the furniture was upholstered with the fabric's reverse side showing. The Blacks were devastated.

The legal issue is whether the Blacks are entitled to damages for the breach of the contract to upholster the furniture.

The legal principle surrounding this problem is the expectation interest in a contract. The expectation interest is the expectation of gain from the performance of the contract. The damages are assessed to give the nonbreaching party the measure of gain that he or she would have received if the contract was performed as agreed. Sometimes special or consequential damages are awarded in addition to the expectancy interest.

CASE A

The Cahill family ordered a sofa from the Acme Furniture Company in red tapestry, on June 1, 2011, due to be delivered in six weeks, on July 15, 2011. The Cahills paid $600 for the sofa at the time of the order. After 10 weeks, Acme delivered a gold sofa to the Cahill home. The Cahills called Acme to complain, and Acme picked up the sofa with the promise that it would be reupholstered in red. The sofa was delivered in green six weeks later. In the meanwhile, the Cahills decorated their living room to match the red sofa. After the sofa was delivered in green, 16 weeks after the initial order, the Cahills sued Acme for breach of contract and for damages resulting from the breach, which included the cost of redecorating their living room to match the red sofa. The legal rule is that the nonbreaching party can only collect damages to recoup the expected gain from the contract if performed as agreed. The nonbreaching party cannot receive damages for expenses incurred that were not in contemplation at the time the contract was formed. The Cahills are entitled to damages for the upholstering of the sofa in the incorrect color and are entitled to compensation for the loss of the use of their sofa for 16 weeks as well as the cost of a new red sofa.

CASE B

Jane Smith ordered a new car from Lunar Motors on June 1, 2011. The Lunar coupe in black was ordered, but the salesperson suggested that the gray floor model, which was used only for demo drives, would represent a $300 savings off the sticker price of the Lunar coupe. Ms. Smith agreed to purchase the floor model for $15,700 rather than pay $16,000 for the special-order car. The salesperson once again asserted that the floor model was new, was used only for demo drives, and had only 5 miles on the odometer. Ms. Smith returned to Lunar Motors on June 3, 2011, paid the $15,700 for the gray floor model Lunar coupe, and drove home. While driving home, Ms. Smith noticed that the car veered dramatically to the left. Ms. Smith took the car to her mechanic, who reported that the car was in an accident previously and had been repaired, but the frame was bent in such a manner as to distort the alignment. Ms. Smith contracted to and expected to receive a new, undamaged car with mileage and wear and tear due to demo drives. Ms. Smith did not contract to receive a damaged car. The salesperson asserted the car was like new. The holding of the court is that the nonbreaching party is entitled to the gain expected from the performance of the contract as agreed, and if the contract is not performed as agreed, the nonbreaching party is entitled to receive the benefit that she would have received if the contract had been performed as agreed. Ms. Smith is entitled to a complete refund of the $15,700 she paid for the car plus the daily cost of the loss of the use of the automobile to be tabulated by the fair market rental value per day of a Lunar coupe.

To synthesize the rule, or tests, from the fictitious cases, you would find a common theme that ties together the rules of law from both decisions. Basically, both cases state that the nonbreaching party in a contract is entitled to receive the benefit of the deal that would have been received if the contract had been performed as agreed. First, write a general statement of the law. Then, mention the legal rules from Case A and Case B as they pertain to the general statement of the law.

EXAMPLE

Are the Blacks entitled to damages compensating them for the breach of the contract to reupholster the loveseat and the chair?

Damages are assessed in a breach of contract action (to give the non-breaching party the measure of gain that he would have received if the contract had been performed as agreed) in a very specific manner. The nonbreaching party can collect damages to recoup the gain expected from the contract if the contract had been performed as agreed. Case A; Case B. If the contract is not performed as agreed, the nonbreaching party is entitled to the benefit he would have received if the contract had been performed as agreed. Case B. The nonbreaching party cannot be compensated for expenses incurred that were not in contemplation at the time the contract was formed. Case A. In the alternative, the nonbreaching party can be compensated for expenses incurred that were in contemplation at the time the contract was formed. Case A. In our problem, the Blacks contracted to have the chair and loveseat upholstered in paisley fabric with the correct side showing. The furniture was upholstered with the wrong side of the fabric showing. When ordering the furniture, the Blacks stipulated that they needed the pieces for a family reunion and that the pieces would provide the necessary seating. The Blacks were without their furniture because of Comfy Furniture's error. The Blacks communicated the need for the seating at the time of the contract formation. The Blacks should receive the gain they expected from the performance of the contract as agreed as well as compensation for the expense of providing alternative seating for the family reunion based on the rental cost of chairs.

An ineffective case synthesis based on our hypothetical problem would be as follows.

> Are the Blacks entitled to damages from Comfy Furniture for breach of contract? "The nonbreaching party is entitled to the gain expected from the performance of the contract as agreed and if the contract is not performed as agreed, the nonbreaching party is entitled to receive the benefit that she would have received if the contract had been performed as agreed." (Rule from) *Case B.* The Blacks were the nonbreaching party and anticipated a loveseat and a chair to be upholstered in paisley with the correct side showing. Therefore, the Blacks are entitled to be compensated by a damage award to put them in a position as if the contract had been performed as agreed. Are the Blacks entitled to be compensated for not having adequate seating for the family reunion? The nonbreaching party cannot receive damages for expenses incurred that were not in contemplation at the time the contract was formed. (Rule from) *Case A.* The Blacks alerted Mr. Blaine, the salesperson, that the couches were needed for a family reunion at Thanksgiving. The Blacks indicated that the additional seating provided by the chair and the loveseat would be necessary at the reunion when ordering the furniture. Since the need for the seating, that the furniture would provide, was in contemplation at the time the order was placed, the Blacks should be compensated for not having adequate seating at the time of the reunion. The damages should be measured by the cost of providing alternative seating.

This example, although clear and coherent, does not synthesize the decisions and unify the concepts articulated in the cases. Each rule is addressed separately, although one rule relates to the other. Also, the rules are presented in the form of holdings because they read as answers to the question before the court rather than as a test or principle. The authority is presented more as a list than as a cohesive unit.

When you have found a relevant statute for a problem, give it the highest regard, because statutes on point govern before case law. (See Chapters 1 and 2.) Generally, synthesize statutes separately from case law holdings. However, if you find cases that interpret and apply the relevant statutes, synthesize the statute text with the application found in case law. Always apply the plain meaning rule to statutes. The plain meaning of the statute text is derived from a reading of each word at its face value.

The problem below illustrates the synthesis of a statute and a case.

PROBLEM

FACT PATTERN

On August 7, 2012, our client, Jane Howard, obtained an $800 loan from Rough & Tough Pawn Shop, using her grandmother's engagement ring as collateral. Howard agreed to make monthly payments on the loan for a minimum of 13 months. After 12 months, Rough & Tough had the right to sell the ring and to refund Howard the difference between her outstanding debt and the price received for the ring.

On September 7, 2012, Howard received a postcard from Rough & Tough stating that its shop and its assets will be sold to Able Pawn. The postcard also stated that Able would assume the business of Rough & Tough, including the items pawned and the loans outstanding. The postcard alerted Howard to pick up the ring and to pay off her note by September 29, 2012, if Howard wanted to reclaim her property. Howard decided to continue to make her monthly payments to Able Pawn, where her loan would be transferred.

On October 1, 2012, Able Pawn was robbed and all the jewelry was stolen, including Howard's ring. The premises were protected by a security alarm system and a guard dog.

ISSUE

The issue to be examined is whether Rough & Tough had authority to sell its interest in Howard's ring.

STATUTORY AUTHORITY

The applicable statute is from the Pawnbrokers Regulation Act, 205 Ill. Comp. Stat. 510/10 (2012).

> *Sale of Property.* No personal property received on deposit or pledge or purchased by any such pawnbroker shall be sold or permitted to be redeemed or removed from the place of business of such pawnbroker

for the space of 48 hours after the delivery of the copy and statement required by Section 7 of this Act required to be delivered to the officer or officers named therein. If the pawner or pledger fails to repay the loan during the period specified on the pawn ticket, the pawnbroker shall automatically extend a grace period of 30 days from the default date on the loan during which the pawnbroker shall not dispose of or sell the property pledged. The parties may agree to extend or renew a loan upon the terms agreed upon by the parties. . . .

RELEVANT CASE LAW

This decision interprets and applies the relevant statute, so the statute and the decision should be synthesized.

JACOBS v. GROSSMAN
310 Ill. 247, 141 N.E.2d 714 (1923)

DUNCAN, J.

This case is brought to this court on a certificate of importance and appeal from a judgment of the Appellate Court for the First District, affirming a judgment of the municipal court of Chicago in favor of the appellee and against appellant in the sum of $330. Appellee, Minnie Jacobs, on April 8, 1921, began an action of replevin in the municipal court of Chicago against appellant, Harry Grossman, a licensed pawnbroker, to recover possession of a diamond ring delivered by herself to appellant to secure the payment of $70 borrowed from him. A replevin bond was given for $800, and a writ of replevin issued. It was returned April 12, 1921, served but no property found. Appellee then filed a count in trover, alleging possession of the ring of the value of $400 and the conversion of it by appellant. The case was heard before the court without a jury.

On June 3, 1919, appellee placed in pawn with appellant, a licensed pawnbroker doing business at 426 South Halsted Street, Chicago, the ring, and received thereon the sum of $70. Interest on the loan was paid to June 7, 1920. The pawn ticket issued to appellee contained this statement, "This office protected by the Chicago Electric Protective Company," and described the location and name of the pawnbroker as "Metropolitan Loan Bank, 426 South Halsted St." The ticket further described the goods pawned, the amount loaned, and the time of redemption. Between October 7 and 10, 1920, appellant sold all his interest in whatever pledges he had to Jacob Klein, another duly licensed pawnbroker at 502 South Halsted Street, for the sum of $16,000 or $17,000, which represented the principal sums loaned on said pledges with interest thereon. The pledges were sold by appellant to Klein upon the express understanding that the pledgors might redeem from Klein in the same manner as they could from appellant, had he not sold his interest in the pawns. It was admitted that Klein is a reputable business man, and it was also conceded by appellant that no notice was given by him, either expressly or impliedly, to the appellee of the transfer of her property. On January 8, 1921, the pawnshop of Klein was entered by four armed robbers. The robbers ordered the clerks employed there to hold up their hands, and they forcibly took from a safe a large number of articles, including the diamond ring in question of appellee, which has never been recovered.

There is an unimportant dispute in the record evidence as to whether appellee or her sister, after the sale of appellant's business to Klein, had called on Klein and secured an additional loan upon a diamond ring other than the one in question. The Appellate Court found that the evidence on this point showed that appellee's sister, and not appellee, was involved in that transaction. Appellant admits in his reply brief that he does not rely in any way on this testimony to show actual notice to appellee of the change in the possession of the pledge in question. As to the other material facts above set out, there is no dispute between the parties.

Counsel for appellant relies for a reversal of the judgment on two propositions: First, that a pawnbroker is bound only to use ordinary care for the safety of the pawner's property, and, if the property is lost or destroyed without the negligence of the pawnee, then he is not liable; second, that a pawnbroker has the right to assign or sell to another his interest in an article pledged to him.

A pawn is a species of bailment which arises when goods or chattels are delivered to another as a pawn for security to him on money borrowed of him by the bailor. It is the pignari acceptum of the civil law, according to which the possession of the pledge passes to the creditor, therein differing from a hypotheca. It is a class of bailment which is made for the mutual benefit of the bailor and bailee. All that is required by the common law on the part of a pawnee in the protection of the property thus entrusted to him is ordinary care and diligence. Consequently, unless a failure to exercise such care and diligence is shown, a pawnee is not answerable for the loss of the article pledged. 30 Cyc. 1169; *Standard Brewery v. Malting Co.*, 171 Ill. 602, 49 N.E. 507. This is an elementary principle, and there can be no question as to the accuracy and correctness of appellant's first proposition.

But the question arises as to whether or not appellant was guilty of negligence in transferring the interest of the pawner without giving her any notice of such transfer. Appellant's duty to her was to safely keep and protect the property pledged. It was a legal obligation on his part to appellee, from which he could not relieve himself by transferring the pledge to another without her consent. Appellee relied upon him to keep and protect her property where it would be reasonably safe, and he had in substance assured her by the language on the ticket that her property was insured or safeguarded. He violated this duty or obligation to her by transferring the possession of her property to another, to be kept at another place, which the evidence does not show to be protected by a protective company, and without giving her notice of such custody and transfer.

Whatever may be the right of the parties in a bailment for the mutual benefit of the bailor and the bailee, it is unquestionably the law that the parties may increase or diminish these rights by stipulations contained in the contract of bailment. 30 Cyc. 1167; *St. Losky v. Davidson,* 6 Cal. 643. The sum and substance of appellant's contract was that he would keep appellee's property at his office or shop described as aforesaid, and which was protected as aforesaid. The pawning of the ring by appellee under the circumstances imposed a personal trust upon appellant to personally keep the property at his shop and under the assurance of protection as aforesaid, and he could not at his will, without the consent of appellee, transfer the possession and custody thereof to another without such consent. The rule is stated in 3 R.C.L. 112, that any attempt on the part of the bailee in an ordinary simple bailment of a pawn to sell, lease, pledge, or otherwise part with the title or possession of the bailment, constitutes a conversion in every case where the bailment can be properly regarded as a personal trust in the bailee.

There is another controlling reason for holding that appellant is liable for the loss of the ring, and for holding that he could not transfer the possession of the article pawned to him to another and escape liability for a conversion. Section 10 of the Pawnbroker's Act (Smith-Hurd Rev. St. 1923, c. 107 1/2) provides, in part, as follows:

> No personal property pawned or pledged shall be sold or disposed by any such pawnbroker within one year from the time when the pawner or pledger shall make default in the payment of interest on the money so advanced by such pawnbroker, unless by the written consent of such pawner or pledger.

Appellant claims that the proper interpretation of this statute is that it prohibits the sale of an article, including the interest of the pledger or pawner as well as his own, and does not refer to a sale of only the interest of the pawnbroker or pledgee. The statute is not subject to such construction. It should be construed to mean what it says: That the property must not be sold or disposed of by the pawnbroker without the written consent of the pledgor. The statute does not confine itself to a sale, but also forbids any disposition of the same without consent as aforesaid. It cannot be seriously disputed that appellant did dispose of the property without the consent of appellee, within the meaning of the foregoing section of the statute.

The judgment of the Appellate Court is affirmed.

Judgment affirmed.

SAMPLE SYNTHESIS

Does Rough & Tough have the authority to sell its interest in Howard's ring? Unless the pawner and pawnbroker agree, pawned property may be sold or disposed of by any pawnbroker only after 30 days from the time the pawner defaults in the payment of interest on the money advanced by the pawnbroker. 205 Ill. Comp. Stat. 510/10 (2012). Where a pawnbroker neglected to give notice of the intent to sell his interest in a particular property and neglected to receive written consent for such sale, the pawnbroker lacked authority to transfer his interest in the property, the ring, to another. *Jacobs v. Grossman*, 141 N.E. 714, 715 (Ill. App. Ct. 1923). Although Rough & Tough gave Howard notice of its intent to sell the shop and its assets, R&T failed to obtain Howard's written consent to sell her ring. Additionally Jane Howard continued to make the payments on the loan so default is not an issue. Rough & Tough's transfer of the ring, the property, occurred during the term of the loan. Therefore, a court will probably find that Rough & Tough lacked the authority to sell its interest in Howard's ring to another pawnbroker.

The above example synthesizes the statute and the *Jacobs* case as they relate to the issue of a pawnbroker's authority to sell its interest in a pawned item without the consent of the pawner. Notice how the statute is mentioned first because its authority ranks higher than the case. The *Jacobs* case follows the statute because the rule is more detailed on the issue of a pawnbroker's duty to give notice before selling his interest in the pawner's property, a ring, and the facts are similar to Jane Howard's situation. Two sources of primary authority, a statute and a case, are used together in this sample synthesis because both sources relate to a single legal issue.

▼ How Do You Synthesize Two Sources of Statutory Authority?

Often you must use two or more sections of a statute in conjunction to explain the legal rule completely. Sometimes definitional provisions are located in one section and the applicable code section is located in another.

Facts: Mr. Thomas was arrested on charges of domestic battery. He punched his wife in the face three times and broke her nose. Mr. and Mrs. Thomas live in Illinois, but they are living apart.

Issue: Whether the Illinois domestic battery statute applies to an estranged husband and whether punching is considered battery.

This problem requires you to use two statutory provisions. One section defines the relevant terms, and the other section details actions that constitute domestic battery. The statutory definition of family and household members as pertaining to domestic battery follows.

725 Ill. Comp. Stat. 5/112A-3(3) (2012):

"Family or household members" include spouses, former spouses, parents, children, stepchildren and other persons related by blood or by present or prior marriage, persons who share or formerly shared a common dwelling, persons who have or allegedly have a child in common, persons who share or allegedly share a blood relationship through a child, persons who have or have had a dating or engagement relationship, persons with disabilities and their personal assistants, and caregivers. . . . For purposes of this paragraph, neither a casual acquaintanceship nor ordinary fraternization between 2 individuals in business or social contexts be deemed to constitute a dating relationship.

The domestic battery statute at 720 Ill. Comp. Stat. 5/12-3.2 (2012):

     (a) A person commits domestic battery if he intentionally or knowingly without legal justification by any means:
     (1) Causes bodily harm to any family or household member;
     (2) Makes physical contact of an insulting or provoking nature with any family or household member.

Sample synthesis using two statutory provisions:

We must determine whether the domestic battery statute, 720 Ill. Comp. Stat. 5/12-3.2 (2012), applies to married couples living apart and if so, whether Mr. Thomas, an estranged husband, committed domestic battery by punching his wife. The domestic battery statute applies to family members. "Family members" is defined to include "spouses formerly sharing a common dwelling." 725 Ill. Comp. Stat. 5/112A-3(3) (2012). "A person commits domestic battery if he intentionally or knowingly without legal justification by any means:

     (1) Causes bodily harm to any family or household member. . . ." 720 Ill. Comp. Stat. 5/12-3.2 (2012). Since Mr. Thomas is a spouse who formerly shared a common residence with his wife, he is a family or household member, and the domestic battery statute is applicable. Mr. Thomas punched his wife in the face three times, which caused her nose to break. The facts do not state that his mental capacity was altered by inebriation or severe mental illness, so his actions can be deduced to be intentional. The facts also do not indicate if Mr. Thomas was provoked to commit battery by extreme jealousy. It appears that there was no legal justification for the bodily harm inflicted on Mrs. Thomas by Mr. Thomas. Although Mr. Thomas is a spouse formerly sharing a common dwelling with Mrs. Thomas, he is a family member and is governed by the domestic battery statute. By punching his wife, breaking her nose, and causing her bodily harm, Mr. Thomas committed domestic battery.

CHECKLIST

1. Summarize the relevant statutes and brief the relevant cases.
2. Outline the problem.
3. Organize the primary authority.
4. Under each issue, organize your primary sources by hierarchy of authority.
5. Compare and contrast the case holdings and statutory text.
6. Formulate a statement of the law that incorporates all the primary sources that will be used under the subissue.
7. Attribute the authority for any legal statement by using the proper *Bluebook* or *ALWD* citation.

> *PRACTICE POINTER*
>
> When synthesizing authorities, always cite to every source that you use. Often the information gathered from the authority is not from the first page of the decision. You must use pinpoint cites to indicate from exactly where within the decision the information is obtained. Also, often you will use authorities more than once. This calls for subsequent citation format. Use *Bluebook* Rule 10.9 or *ALWD* Rule 12.20 for guidance on short citation when citing cases subsequently.

CHAPTER SUMMARY

Learning to synthesize authority is a mechanical process at first. Brief the cases and summarize the statutory authority. Insert the applicable authority in your outline by grouping together related statements of the law. Draft cohesive statements of the legal authority that you grouped together. Cite all authority accurately even if string citations are needed or if two separate clauses in a single sentence are each supported by a different authority.

As you become more adept at synthesis, you will see that your writing is smoother and less redundant. Synthesizing authority lets you write in one voice rather than awkwardly switching back and forth between your words and the words of the court.

KEY TERMS

causes of action	reasoning
facts	synthesis
primary authority	

EXERCISES

SHORT ANSWER
1. Why do we synthesize authority?
2. What are the four basic types of synthesis?
3. What are the steps required to synthesize legal rules?

APPLICATION
4. Read the following fact pattern and cases carefully. Draft a paragraph in which you synthesize the holdings of the cases. The issue that you will address is provided as well. Remember that proper synthesis requires

you to relate the authority to a common legal theme. The problem's issue will guide you in synthesizing the authority.

Facts

On November 29, 2011, Michael Jones purchased a used truck from Grimy's Auto and Truck Service. At the time of the purchase, Grimy's stated that the engine was completely overhauled and consisted of rebuilt and reconditioned parts, that all parts were guaranteed, and that invoices for all new parts would be provided. On December 13, 2012, after using the truck for over one year, Jones discovered that several engine parts were not rebuilt or reconditioned and that other engine parts were defective. These defects caused the truck to break down, resulting in lost wages and lost profits for Jones. Jones made repairs to the truck on December 13, 2012, December 16, 2012, and December 31, 2012. Jones did not attempt to return the truck and did not notify Grimy's that the truck was defective. The truck is currently disabled in Columbus, Ohio. Jones wants to sue Grimy's for damages for breach of contract.

Issue

Whether Jones continued to use the truck for more than a reasonable time after noticing the defects and failed to properly reject the truck and to notify Grimy's as to the defects.

Case A

A buyer of goods must alert the seller as soon as he discovers that the goods are not as agreed on. A buyer must rescind a sales contract as soon as he discovers the breach or after he has had a reasonable time for examination. The buyer waives the right to rescind a contract for the sale of goods by continuing to use allegedly defective goods for more than a reasonable time.

Case B

To meet the requirements of an effective rejection, the buyer must reject the goods within a reasonable time and reasonably notify the seller.

5. Read the following fact pattern and cases carefully. Draft a paragraph in which you synthesize the holdings of the cases. The issue that you will address is provided as well.

Facts

Robert and Jane Moore live in Evanston and have to repair the gutters on their house. There is eight feet between their house and their neighbor's. The properties are adjoining; the neighboring Kandler house is north of the Moore house. The Moore's contractors and carpenters must enter the Kandler property to work on the gutters on the north side of the house. Mrs. Kandler is not very pleased that workers are entering her property. The Moores came to our office to find out what they should do. The Moores specifically asked if they should obtain an easement to grant them a right of way on Mrs. Kandler's property to make the repairs.

Issue

What legal access would allow the contractors and carpenters, repairing the gutters on the Moore house, to enter the adjoining property belonging to Mrs. Kandler?

Statutory Authority

Ch. 12 §99: If the repair and maintenance of an existing single-family residence cannot reasonably be accomplished without entering onto the adjoining land, and if the owner of the adjoining land refuses to permit entry onto that adjoining land for the purpose of repair and maintenance of the single-family residence, then the owner of the single-family residence may bring an action in court to compel the owner of the adjoining land to permit entry for the purpose of repair and maintenance where entry will be granted solely for the purposes of repair and maintenance.

Case Y

The need to enter the land of an adjoining property for the purpose of making repairs to one's own property should not mandate that an easement be acquired. An easement grants a right of way, but only the landowner can create an easement. The adjoining landowner may view the repairs as a nuisance and would not grant the easement. Sometimes repairs must be performed on a single-family residence that require entering the adjoining land. Statute Ch. 12 §99 was created to avoid the need to obtain an easement to enter adjoining land when the sole reason for the right of way is to make repairs on a single-family residence.

REINFORCEMENT EXERCISE

6. Review a memo that you have recently completed. Examine the body of the discussion carefully. Highlight a paragraph that states the rule, its application, and conclusion. Examine a subsequent paragraph that expands on the initial rule by citing a separate opinion. Reformulate the rules statement to incorporate the initial rule and the subsequent rule to create a comprehensive statement of the law on that particular point.

CHAPTER 12

OUTLINING AND ORGANIZING A MEMORANDUM

CHAPTER OVERVIEW

In Chapters 7 through 11 you learned about the components of a legal memorandum as well as some drafting pointers. This chapter teaches you how to organize the discussion section of your memorandum. You are shown some outlining techniques. These are suggested techniques only. You may have a technique of your own that works well. Feel free to use it. In this chapter, you also learn how to draft thesis paragraphs for your discussion.

A. PURPOSE OF OUTLINING

The key to a well-organized memo is a well-drafted outline. Outlining allows you to organize your discussion easily so that it is smooth and cogent. An outline ensures that you cover all the legal rules and apply all the legally significant facts to those rules. An outline also simplifies your discussion drafting.

B. STEPS TO OUTLINING

The outline should be done in two stages, each of which consists of a number of steps. In the first stage, you compile a list of legal authorities, which includes the names of and the citations to authorities, a note about the legally significant facts presented in any case, and a statement that summarizes each authority's significance to the issues presented in your research problem. See Illustration 12-1. In the second stage, you arrange the discussion sections concerning each issue and, in some cases, arrange each paragraph. See Illustration 12-2.

1. Steps in Compiling a List of Legal Authorities

1. Draft the statement of the facts, the questions presented, and the conclusions.
2. Research your issues.
3. Read the cases.
4. Brief the authorities as discussed in Chapter 6. Once you have briefed the authorities, you will write a holding for each case. These holdings should be used in your list of authorities. These holdings will summarize the significance of the authorities. If the holdings are well written, they will incorporate important facts derived from the authorities.
5. Write a summary statement for each statute or other noncase authority you plan to cite.
6. Prepare a list of each of the relevant authorities. Note that not all authorities will be relevant. Include only those that help you to determine the law involved in your case. For your list, include the name of the authority. If the authority is a case, list the holding or summary statement of the significance of the authority. Note the complete citation. It is also helpful to list whether the authority is a primary binding, primary persuasive, or secondary authority.

Now review Illustration 12-1. Illustration 12-1 is a list of the significant authorities for the memo in Illustration 12-3.

ILLUSTRATION 12-1. List of Authorities

1. *Anderson v. St. Francis-St. George Hosp., Inc.,* 77 Ohio St. 3d 82, 671 N.E.2d 225 (1996): A civil battery occurs when one individual touches another individual without his or her consent and a physical injury occurs. (primary binding)

2. *Leichtman v. WLW Jacoc Communications, Inc.,* 92 Ohio App. 3d 232, 634 N.E.2d 697 (1994): A contact between a nonconsenting individual and a substance or an object such as cigar smoke is sufficient to be a touching within the context of the tort of civil battery because the substance or object would be an extension of the offender's body. (primary binding)

3. *Smith v. John Deere Co.,* 83 Ohio App. 3d 398, 614 N.E.2d 1148 (1993): A person intends his or her conduct when he or she undertakes an action with a knowing mind. (primary persuasive)

4. *Love v. Port Clinton,* 37 Ohio St. 3d 98, 524 N.E.2d 166 (1988): If a person consents to the touching, a battery has not occurred. (primary binding)

ILLUSTRATION 12-2. Outline of Battery Discussion

Element or Subissue 1
Issue: Did a touching occur?
Rule: Objects are extensions of body parts. Contact with a substance or an object can be touching (*Leichtman*)
Application of law to facts: Bucket contacted McMillan
Conclusion: A touching occurred
Element or Subissue 2
Issue: Did Mann intend to hit McMillan?
Rule: A person intends an act when it is done purposefully (*Smith*)
Application of law to facts: Mann purposefully threw the bucket at McMillan and said she intended to strike her
Conclusion: Mann had intent
Element or Subissue 3
Issue: Did McMillan consent to touching?
Rules: If a party consented to the touching, no battery occurred. (*Love*)
Application of law to facts: McMillan did not consent
Conclusion: A touching without consent as in this case can be a battery
Element or Subissue 4
Issue: Did McMillan suffer the requisite physical injuries as a result of the contact?
Rule: Physical injuries must result from contact for battery (*Anderson*)
Application of law to facts: McMillan sustained cuts and eye irritation from bucket and sand contact
Conclusion: McMillan had requisite physical injuries

ILLUSTRATION 12-3.   Memorandum: McMillan Battery Action

MEMORANDUM

To: William Mark
From: Ivy Courier
Date: November 7, 2011
Re: McMillan Battery Action

QUESTION PRESENTED
    Did an actionable battery occur when Mann intentionally struck McMillan with a bucket, without McMillan's consent, causing McMillan to suffer physical and monetary injuries?

CONCLUSION
    Mann's intentional striking of McMillan with a bucket and sand without McMillan's consent was a battery.

FACTS
    Our client, Mary McMillan, a 36-year-old bank teller, wants to bring an action for battery against Carol Mann, a 36-year-old mother, who threw a metal bucket filled with sand at McMillan at a local park. While McMillan sat on a park bench, she teased Mann's seven-year-old son. Mann did not like this teasing and threw a bucket filled with sand at McMillan. Sand landed in McMillan's eyes while she was wearing soft contact lenses. As a result, McMillan's contacts had to be replaced. The bucket also cut McMillan's eye and cheek. She required stitches in both places. McMillan asked Mann to pay for her doctor bills and for the new contacts. Mann refused and added, "I'm not sorry. I meant to hurt you."

DISCUSSION
    The issue presented is whether Mann's intentional touching of McMillan with a bucket rather than her person is a battery. A battery is the intentional touching of another without consent, which causes injury. *Anderson v. St. Francis-St. George Hosp., Inc.*, 77 Ohio St. 3d 82, 671 N.E.2d 225 (1996). A touching can occur when an object rather than an individual's body contacts another person. *Leichtman v. WLW Jacoc Communications, Inc.*, 92 Ohio App. 3d 232, 634 N.E.2d 697 (1994); *Smith v. John Deere Co.*, 83 Ohio App. 3d 398, 614 N.E.2d 1148 (1993). In this case, Mann intentionally struck McMillan with a bucket without McMillan's consent and that touching resulted in injuries. Therefore, a battery occurred.
    The threshold issue is whether a touching occurred when the bucket struck McMillan. A contact between a nonconsenting party and object rather than the actor's body can be a battery. *Leichtman v. WLW Jacoc Communications, Inc.*, 92 Ohio App. 3d 232, 634 N.E.2d 697 (1994); *Smith v. John Deere Co.*, 83 Ohio App. 3d at 398, 614 N.E.2d at

ILLUSTRATION 12-3. Continued

1148. In *Leichtman,* one person blew cigar smoke at another person, resulting in injuries. The court found that the cigar smoke was an extension of the person and that a contact between the smoke and the nonconsenting person met the requirement of a touching for civil battery. In this case, Mann threw the bucket at McMillan, and the bucket contacted her face. Following the reasoning in the *Leicht-man*case, the bucket would be an extension of Mann's body, and the contact between McMillan and the bucket would be considered a touching under the theory of civil battery.

Next, the question to consider is whether under the statute Mann intended to touch McMillan when she struck her with the bucket. A person intends his or her conduct when he or she undertakes an action with a knowing mind. *Smith v. John Deere Co.,* 83 Ohio App. 3d 398, 614 N.E.2d 1148 (1993). In *Smith,* a police officer handcuffed the plaintiff. The court found that the officer must have intended his actions because you could not accidentally handcuff a person. *Smith,* 83 Ohio App. 3d at 399, 614 N.E.2d at 1149. In McMillan's case, Mann aimed the bucket at McMillan purposefully trying to strike her, Mann later told McMillan that she deliberately threw the bucket at her. McMillan probably will be able to establish that Mann had intent.

The next factor to consider is whether McMillan consented to the contact. If a person consents to the touching, a battery has not occurred. *Love v. Port Clinton,* 37 Ohio St. 3d 98, 524 N.E.2d 166 (1988). In our case, McMillan did not consent to Mann's throwing of the bucket at her face. Therefore, McMillan did not consent to any contact. Finally, the question is whether McMillan suffered physical injuries. A battery occurs only if a plaintiff sustains physical injuries as a result of the touching. *Anderson v. St. Francis-St. George Hosp., Inc.,* 77 Ohio St. 3d 82, 671 N.E.2d 225 (1996). McMillan sustained cuts on her face and the sand flying out of the bucket into her eyes. McMillan will be able to show that she sustained physical injuries as a result of the contact with the bucket.

2. Organize Issues

After you have prepared a detailed list of authorities, you are ready to organize your issues and to determine each of the legal elements that your memo should address. Each legal theory is defined as several factors called elements. You can think of the elements as pieces of a puzzle. You must consider each element before you complete your discussion. You can think of your discussion of these elements as a discussion of the subissues of the questions presented. Your discussion of some of these subissues will be cursory; some elements can be discussed in a single sentence. Most subissues, however, will be discussed in one or more paragraphs, generally organized in the IRAC (Issues, Rules, Application, Conclusion) format discussed in Chapter 10.

▼ What Steps Should You Follow in Preparing Your
Outline of Each of the Issues?

The first step in organizing your outline is to write a **thesis paragraph.** This is the first paragraph of your discussion. It usually is a summary of the legal issue you plan to discuss. In the thesis paragraph you introduce the issue, define the applicable rule of law, introduce each legal element, apply the legally significant facts to the rule of law, and provide a short conclusion, usually one sentence long. When you have multiple issues, the thesis paragraph will introduce all the issues presented and give readers a roadmap of what will be discussed. Then, each issue will begin with a separate thesis paragraph.

3. Draft a Thesis Paragraph

The best and most typical format for the thesis paragraph is the IRAC format. (For a full discussion of this format, see Chapter 10.) The first sentence of a thesis paragraph introduces the overall issue presented in the memo. The second sentence explains the rule of law. The next sentence applies the rule of law to the facts of your case, and the final sentence states a conclusion. A general outline for a thesis paragraph, then, is:

1. Introduce the legal issue or question presented.
2. Summarize the legal rule for the question presented and each legal element to be discussed.
3. Apply the legally significant facts to the legal rule.
4. Conclude.

Review the thesis paragraph in Illustration 12-4. It is the first paragraph of the discussion section of the memo in Illustration 12-3. The first sentence introduces the issue: whether a battery occurred when Mann struck McMillan with the bucket. This sentence mirrors the question presented. See Illustration 12-3. The second sentence is the rule of law. In this sentence you introduce each of the legal elements or factors that will be discussed. In the *McMillan* case, the elements are touching, intent, lack of consent, and resulting physical injury. Each of these elements is discussed separately in the succeeding memo paragraphs. A thesis paragraph should introduce the reader to as many legal elements as possible in the thesis paragraph. The third sentence of this thesis paragraph is the application of the law to the facts. In this sentence, you explain to the reader the relationship between the relevant law and the facts of your case. In Illustration 12-4, the fact the Mann struck McMillan with the bucket without McMillan's consent was applied to the rule of law stated in the second sentence. The final sentence is a conclusion. This sentence explains to your readers your view of how the law and facts relate to each other. In the *McMillan* case, the writer concluded that a battery occurred.

OUTLINE OF THESIS PARAGRAPH FOR McMILLAN CASE

1. Introduce the battery issue or question presented.
2. Summarize the legal rule: battery is the intentional touching of another without consent that results in physical injury; touching can be done with an object.
3. Apply the legally significant facts to the legal rule: touching occurred when bucket struck McMillan.
4. Conclusion: battery occurred.

ILLUSTRATION 12-4. Thesis Paragraph

The issue presented is whether Mann's intentional touching of McMillan with a bucket rather than her person is a battery. A battery is the intentional touching of another without consent which causes injury. *Anderson v. St. Francis-St. George Hosp., Inc.*, 77 Ohio St. 3d 82, 671 N.E.2d 225 (1996). A touching can occur when an object rather than an individual's body contacts another person. *Leichtman v. WLW Jacor Communications, Inc.*, 92 Ohio App. 3d 232, 634 N.E.2d 697 (1994); *Smith v. John Deere Co.*, 83 Ohio App. 3d 398, 614 N.E.2d 1148 (1993). In this case, Mann intentionally struck McMillan with a bucket without McMillan's consent and that touching resulted in injuries. Therefore, a battery occurred.

4. Determine Which Element to Discuss First

The next step is to determine which element to discuss first. If a legal claim has a threshold issue or element, it should be discussed first. A threshold issue is an issue that, if decided one way, would eliminate any further consideration of the legal claim. For example, in a breach of contract case, you must decide first whether a contract was formed before determining whether a breach occurred. Because courts sometimes change current law or approach legal claims differently than expected or than the law provides, you should fully discuss all subissues or elements, even if your threshold issue would dispose of the legal claim. For the memo in Illustration 12-3, the touching is the threshold issue. If Mann did not touch McMillan, then McMillan could not bring an action for battery. Therefore, this issue must be considered first.

5. List Elements or Subissues

Next, make a list of the elements or subissues to discuss. In the *McMillan* case, the elements list might be as follows:

touching
intent
lack of consent
physical injury

6. Add Authority

Now add the authority or authorities that relate to each element:

> touching (*Leichtman, Smith*)
> intent (*Smith*)
> lack of consent (*Anderson*)
> physical injury (*Anderson*)

7. Refine Issues

You might refine the issues so that they include facts from your case or incorporate further questions that are raised by the issues. For example, the issue of touching involves a secondary question of whether contact with an object rather than a person is a touching sufficient to constitute a battery. Your new list might be as follows:

touching (*Leichtman, Smith*)
     object rather than person (*Leichtman*)
intent (*Smith*)
lack of consent (*Anderson, Love*)
physical injury (*Anderson*)

8. Arrange the Order of Elements

Now arrange the order of the elements. Touching is the threshold element or subissue, so you should discuss it first. The order of the other issues is a value judgment. If one or more elements can be easily discussed in a single sentence, often it is best to consider them after the threshold issue. If none of the elements is a threshold issue, then consider those elements that can be discussed easily first.

9. Organize into IRAC Paragraph

After you have determined the order of the elements, organize each element or subissue into an IRAC paragraph. Introduce the issue, present the rule, apply the law to the facts of your case, and conclude. For the *McMillan* memo, the discussion outline for each element might be as shown in Illustration 12-2. Review Illustration 12-2 and compare it to the text of the memo in Illustration 12-3. The discussion is derived entirely from the outline and follows it closely in IRAC format.

PRACTICE POINTER

If your outline is well drafted, your writing of the discussion will flow from it easily.

C. MULTI-ISSUE MEMORANDUM

If you have a multi-issue memorandum, you will use many of the same techniques discussed above.

▼ How Do You Organize a Multi-Issue Memorandum?

1. Determine how many issues you will discuss. Often an attorney will help you make this determination. Decide which issue should be discussed first. Again, consider whether there is a threshold issue. In the memo above, the first issue is whether Mann committed a battery. If a touching did not occur when the bucket struck McMillan, then the later issues do not need to be addressed. Therefore, this issue is the threshold issue and should be placed first. However, you should still discuss the later issues even if you determine that the first issue would be decided in a manner that would dispose of a case. Courts are unpredictable and might decide the issue differently than you did.
2. Determine the legal elements you will discuss and a logical order for this discussion.
3. Prepare a detailed outline of the discussion. For each issue, not each legal element you will address, the authority related to that element, and the legally significant facts applicable to that element.
4. Write a thesis paragraph. For a multi-issue memo, such as the one in Illustration 12-5, introduce the issues and explain the rules of law in the thesis paragraphs that introduce each issue. Your organization for a multi-issue memo might be as follows:

Thesis Paragraph
    Introduce all legal issues or questions presented
    Conclusions

Thesis Paragraph for Issue or Question Presented #1
    Introduce the legal issue or question presented
    Summarize the legal rule for the question presented #1 and each
        legal element to be discussed
    Apply the legally significant facts to the legal rule
    Conclusion

First Legal Element or Subissue
    Introduce the legal element
    Summarize the legal rule
    Apply the legally significant facts to the legal rule
    Conclusion

Second Legal Element or Subissue
    Introduce the legal element
    Summarize the legal rule

Apply the legally significant facts to the legal rule
Conclusion

Thesis Paragraph for Issue or Question Presented #2
Introduce the legal issue or question presented
Summarize the legal rule for the question presented #2 and each
legal element to be discussed
Apply the legally significant facts to the legal rule
Conclusion

First Legal Element or Subissue
Introduce the legal element
Summarize the legal rule
Apply the legally significant facts to the legal rule
Conclusion

Second Legal Element or Subissue
Introduce the legal element
Summarize the legal rule
Apply the legally significant facts to the legal rule
Conclusion

5. Use headings to introduce new issues. Use transitions to guide the
reader from one issue to another and one paragraph to another.

ILLUSTRATION 12-5.   Multi-Issue Memorandum: McMillan Battery Action

MEMORANDUM

To: William Mark
From: Ivy Courier
Date: November 7, 2011
Re: McMillan Battery Action

QUESTIONS PRESENTED
1. Did a battery occur when Carol Mann intentionally struck McMillan
with a bucket, without Mary McMillan's consent, causing McMillan to
suffer physical and monetary injuries?
2. Does eight-year-old Rachel McMillan have a valid claim for
intentional infliction of emotional distress against Carol Mann after
the child saw Mann throw a rusty metal bucket of sand at her mother's
face and head, causing physical injuries to the elder McMillan and
resulting in the child suffering from anxiety, headaches, and
vomiting?
3. Was Camp Cougar vicariously liable for the intentional torts of
Mann, a volunteer whom camp officials asked to supervise children in
the sandbox?

ILLUSTRATION 12-5.   Continued

CONCLUSIONS

1. When Mann intentionally struck McMillan on the head and in the face with a rusty, metal bucket and sand without McMillan's consent and McMillan was injured, a battery occurred.

2. Eight-year-old Rachel McMillan has a claim for intentional infliction of emotional distress against Carol Mann because the child can show that she suffered emotional distress as a result of Mann's extreme and outrageous act of intentionally throwing a rusty, metal bucket at the child's mother, causing the older McMillan to suffer physical injuries and the child to suffer from anxiety and post-traumatic stress syndrome—mental anguish no child should be expected to endure.

3. Camp Cougar will not be found vicariously liable for an intentional act of its agent, Mann, because it did not benefit from that act nor did the camp control Mann's actions.

FACTS

Our client, Mary McMillan, a 36-year-old bank teller, seeks to bring an action for battery against Carol Mann, a 36-year old mother, who threw a rusty, metal bucket filled with sand at her at a local camp. She also wants to bring an action against Camp Cougar for vicarious liability for the intentional torts of camp volunteer Carol Mann. Camp Cougar enlisted Carol Mann, a camper's parent, to act as volunteer supervisor of the sandbox during Parent Visitor Day at Camp Cougar. Camp Cougar officials told Mann to ensure that no one was injured while playing in the sandbox. Mann had handled this responsibility during Parent Visitor Day in the past. Mary McMillan came to see her eight-year-old daughter, Rachel, during Camp Cougar Parent Visitor Day. While McMillan sat on a camp bench, she teased Mann's seven-year-old son. Mann did not like this teasing and threw a rusty, metal bucket filled with sand at McMillan's head and face. Sand landed in McMillan's eyes while she was wearing soft contact lenses. As a result, McMillan's contacts had to be replaced. The bucket also cut McMillan's head, eye, and cheek. She lost a lot of blood from her head, requiring a transfusion of one pint of blood. She had stitches on her eyelid and cheek. After the bucket struck McMillan, Mann told McMillan in front of three witnesses, "I'm not sorry. I meant to hurt you."

Immediately after Rachel McMillan saw her mother bleeding, she began to cry and vomit. She told the camp counselors that her head hurt and she would not go with the camp director to the hospital. She said she was afraid the director would throw a bucket of sand at her if she didn't like what she said. The child missed the remainder of camp because she suffered from daily headaches and vomiting and she was afraid of the adults at the camp. A child psychologist examined the child and said she was suffering headaches, vomiting, and anxiety as

ILLUSTRATION 12-5.   Continued

a result of seeing a bucket thrown by an adult at her mother. He said she was experiencing post-traumatic stress syndrome.

DISCUSSION

This memo first will address whether Carol Mann can be held liable for battery when she intentionally struck McMillan with a rusty, metal bucket, without McMillan's consent, causing McMillan to suffer physical and monetary injuries. Next, the discussion will consider whether eight-year-old Rachel McMillan has a claim for intentional infliction of emotional distress against Mann after the child saw Mann throw a rusty, metal bucket of sand at her mother's head and face, resulting in injury to her mother and causing the young girl to suffer from anxiety, headaches, and vomiting. Finally, the memo will explore whether McMillan can establish that Camp Cougar was vicariously liable for the intentional actions of one of its volunteers, Carol Mann, that resulted in injury to McMillan.

I. Was Mann's Intentional Touching of McMillan with a Bucket Battery?

The issue presented is whether Mann's intentional touching of McMillan with a bucket rather than her person is a battery. A battery is the intentional touching of another without consent, which causes injury. *Anderson v. St. Francis-St. George Hosp., Inc.*, 77 Ohio St. 3d 82, 671 N.E.2d 225 (1996). A touching can occur when an object rather than an individual's body contacts another person. *Leichtman v. WLW Jacoc Communications, Inc.*, 92 Ohio App. 3d 232, 634 N.E.2d 697 (1994); *Smith v. John Deere Co.*, 83 Ohio App. 3d 398, 614 N.E.2d 1148 (1993). *Smith v. John Deere Co.*, 83 Ohio App. 3d 398, 614 N.E.2d 1148 (1993). A person intends his or her conduct when he or she undertakes an action with a knowing mind. If a person consents to the touching, a battery has not occurred. *Love v. Port Clinton*, 37 Ohio St. 3d 98, 524 N.E.2d 166 (1988). A battery occurs only if a plaintiff sustains physical injuries as a result of the touching. *Anderson v. St. Francis-St. George Hosp., Inc.*, 77 Ohio St. 3d 82, 671 N.E.2d 225 (1996). In this case, Mann intentionally struck McMillan with a bucket without McMillan's consent and that touching resulted in injuries. Therefore, a battery occurred.

The threshold issue is whether an intentional touching occurred when a bucket Mann threw struck McMillan. A touching can occur when an object rather than an individual's body contacts another person. *Leichtman v. WLW Jacoc Communications, Inc.*, 92 Ohio App. 3d 232, 634 N.E.2d 697 (1994); *Smith v. John Deere Co.*, 83 Ohio App. 3d at 398, 614 N.E.2d at 1148. In *Leichtman*, one person blew cigar smoke at another person, resulting in injuries. The court found that the cigar smoke was an extension of the person and that a contact between the smoke and the nonconsenting person met the requirement of a touching for civil battery. In this case, Mann threw the bucket

ILLUSTRATION 12-5.   Continued

at McMillan, and the bucket contacted her face and head. Following the reasoning in the *Leichtman* case, the bucket would be an extension of Mann's body, and the contact between McMillan and the bucket would be considered a touching under the theory of civil battery.

Next, the question to consider is whether under the statute Mann intended to touch McMillan when she struck her with the bucket. A person intends his or her conduct when he or she undertakes an action with a knowing mind. *Smith v. John Deere Co.*, 83 Ohio App. 3d 398, 614 N.E.2d 1148 (1993). In *Smith*, a police officer handcuffed the plaintiff. The court found that the officer must have intended his actions because you could not accidentally handcuff a person. *Smith*, 83 Ohio App. 3d at 399, 614 N.E.2d at 1149. In McMillan's case, Mann aimed the bucket at McMillan purposefully trying to strike her, Mann later told McMillan that she deliberately threw the bucket at her. McMillan probably will be able to establish that Mann had the statutory intent.

The next factor to consider is whether McMillan consented to the contact. If a person consents to the touching, a battery has not occurred. *Love v. Port Clinton*, 37 Ohio St. 3d 98, 524 N.E.2d 166 (1988). In our case, McMillan did not consent to Mann's throwing of the bucket at her face. Therefore, McMillan did not consent to any contact. Finally, the question is whether McMillan suffered physical injuries. A battery occurs only if a plaintiff sustains physical injuries as a result of the touching. *Anderson v. St. Francis-St. George Hosp., Inc.*, 77 Ohio St. 3d 82, 671 N.E.2d 225 (1996). McMillan sustained cuts on her face and the sand flying out of the bucket into her eyes. McMillan will be able to show that she sustained physical injuries as a result of the contact with the bucket.

II. Is Mann Liable for Intentional Infliction of Emotional Distress?

The next issue to consider is whether eight-year-old Rachel McMillan has a claim for intentional infliction of emotional distress against Carol Mann. To successfully prove intentional infliction of emotional distress, McMillan must show that Mann intentionally committed an extreme and outrageous that caused emotional distress that no reasonable person could be expected to endure. *Yeager v. Local Union 20*, 6 Ohio St. 3d 369, 453 N.E.2d 666 (1983). *Pyle v. Pyle*, 11 Ohio App. 3d 31, 34, 463 N.E.2d 98, 101 (1983). In the case, Rachel McMillan, a child, saw Mann, an adult, throw the rusty, metal bucket filled with sand at her mother's head and face, causing her mother to bleed. Seeing this act caused the child to suffer from anxiety, headaches, and vomiting daily. Several witnesses can testify that Mann said that she intended to harm McMillan. A child should not be expected to endure the pain of seeing her mother injured. Therefore, Rachel McMillan has a claim for intentional emotional distress.

The threshold issue is whether Mann's act of throwing a rusty, metal bucket at the head and face of another adult in front of children was an

ILLUSTRATION 12-5. Continued

extreme and outrageous act. An act is extreme and outrageous if it goes "beyond all possible bounds of decency," *Yeager,* 6 Ohio. St. 3d at 375, 453 N.E.2d at 672, and is regarded as "atrocious, and utterly intolerable in a civilized community." *Id.* In this case, Mann, an adult who was asked to supervise the sandbox and ensure the safety of others, threw a rusty, metal bucket filled with sand at another adult in front of young children, including her child and Rachel McMillan. The bucket struck the older McMillan causing her to bleed. That act went beyond all possible bounds of decency and was atrocious and utterly intolerable in a civilized community. This is especially true since Mann was charged with ensuring the safety of people in the sandbox area. Therefore, Mann's act would be found to be an extreme and outrageous act.

Next, the young McMillan must show that the act was done with intent. A person intends his or her conduct when he or she undertakes an action with a knowing mind. *Smith v. John Deere Co.,* 83 Ohio App. 3d 398, 614 N.E.2d 1148 (1993). If an actor knew or should have known that his or her actions would cause serious emotional distress, intent is established. *Phung v. Waste Mgt., Inc.,* 71 Ohio St. 3d 408, 410, 644 N.E.2d 286, 288 (1994). In this case, Mann not only knew or should have known that that throwing a rusty, metal bucket filled with sand at the head and face of another adult in front of the other adult's child resulting in the adult bleeding would cause an eight-year-old child to suffer serious emotional distress. For those reasons, the young McMillan should be able to show intent.

The third element McMillan must establish is that the extreme and outrageous act was the proximate cause of her emotional and physical distress. Proximate cause exists when an act precedes and produces an injury that is likely to have occurred as a result of the act or which might have been anticipated. *Jeffers v. Olexo,* 43 Ohio St. 3d 140, 143, 539 N.E.2d 614, 617 (1989). In this case, the young McMillan can show that a child likely would experience emotional distress when she saw her mother injured and bleeding. Therefore, the child will be able to establish that the extreme and outrageous act was the proximate cause of her emotional distress.

Finally, the child must show that she suffered from serious emotional distress. To establish serious emotional distress, the mental anguish she suffered must be serious and of a nature that "no reasonable man could be expected to endure it." *Id.* Serious emotional distress goes "beyond trifling mental disturbance, mere upset or hurt feelings" and "may be found where a reasonable person, normally constituted, would be unable to cope adequately with the mental distress engendered by the circumstances of the case." *Paugh v. Hanks,* 6 Ohio St. 3d 72, 78, 451 N.E.2d 759, 765 (1983). It is not necessary to prove any physical harm. *Pyle v. Pyle,* 11 Ohio App. 3d 31, 34, 463 N.E.2d 98, 101 (1983). Various neuroses, psychoses, and phobias are examples of serious emotional distress. *Paugh v. Hanks,* 6 Ohio St. 3d 72, 78,

ILLUSTRATION 12-5.   Continued

451 N.E.2d 759, 765 (1983). In this case, a psychologist examined the child and found that she suffered from post-traumatic stress syndrome, as well as physical symptoms such as headaches and vomiting after she saw an adult throw a bucket at her mother. Post-traumatic stress and anxiety coupled with these physical manifestations should be sufficient for young McMillan to establish serious emotion distress that is beyond mere upset or hurt feelings and which a reasonable person would be unable to cope.

III. Was Camp Cougar Vicariously Liable for Mann's Intentional Torts?

The final claim to consider is whether Camp Cougar will be vicariously liable to both McMillans for Mann's intentional torts. An entity can be held vicariously liable for the actions of its agent. *Byrd v. Faber*, 57 Ohio St. 3d 56, 58-59, 565 N.E.2d 584-586 (1991). A principal-agent relationship is established when one party exercises control over the actions of another and those actions are done for the benefit of the party exercising control. See *Hanson v. Kynast*, 24 Ohio St. 3d 171, 173, 494 N.E.2d 1091 (1986). However, a master only can be vicariously liable for its agent's intentional tort if the entity controlled the agent's conduct and the agent's acts benefited the entity. *Id.* In this case, Camp Cougar directed Mann to supervise a camp activity. Therefore, Mann may be found to be Camp Cougar's agent. However, Mann's actions did not benefit the camp and the camp did not exercise control over her actions. In fact, these actions may have harmed the camp. Therefore, it is unlikely that Camp Cougar would be found liable for Mann's torts.

The threshold issue is whether Mann is Camp Cougar's agent. A principal-agent relationship is established when one party exercises control over the actions of another and those actions are for the benefit of the party exercising control. See *Hanson v. Kynast*, 24 Ohio St. 3d 171, 173, 494 N.E.2d 1091 (1986). In this case, Camp Cougar directed Mann to act as the sandbox supervisor and specifically directed her to keep people safe. Therefore, Mann is likely to be found to be an agent of Camp Cougar.

The next issue to consider is whether a master can be vicariously liable for its agent's intentional torts. A master can be vicariously liable for its agent's intentional tort only if the master controlled the agent's conduct and the agent's acts benefited the master. See *Hanson v. Kynast*, 24 Ohio St. 3d 171, 173, 494 N.E.2d 1091 (1986). The camp did not direct Mann to injure McMillan and the camp did not benefit from Mann's actions. Therefore, Camp Cougar would not be vicariously liable for Mann's act of throwing the bucket of sand at McMillan or causing young McMillan's serious emotional distress because it did not control Mann's actions and the camp did not benefit from Mann's actions. Illustration 12-6 is an outline of the memo shown in Illustration 12-5.

Once you complete your outline, you are ready to begin writing your discussion. Follow your outline and use the applicable law and

ILLUSTRATION 12-5. Continued

the facts from cases when they are useful. Illustration 12-7 reprints a paragraph found in Illustration 12-5 and the original outline for that paragraph. Once you have completed your draft, compare the draft to the outline to ensure that you have incorporated all the components in your outline and that your text matches your outline organization.

ILLUSTRATION 12-6. Multi-Issue Outline

Thesis Paragraph
    Introduce issues
        Whether Carol Mann's touching of McMillan was battery?
        Whether Carol Mann committed the tort of intentional infliction of emotional distress?
        Whether Camp Cougar can be vicariously liable for Carol Mann's acts?

Heading: Issue 1 or Question Presented 1
    Introduce issue: Did Carol Mann commit the tort of battery?
    Rules: (1A) A battery is the intentional touching of another without the consent of the person touched that results in injury. (*Anderson*) (primary binding) (first element or subissue)
    (B) A contact between a nonconsenting party and object rather than the actor's body can be a battery (*Leichtman*) (primary binding) (first element subissue)
    Rule (2) A person intends his or her conduct when he or she undertakes an action with a knowing mind. (*Smith*) (primary binding) (second element or subissue)
    Rule (3) If a person consents to the touching, a battery has not occurred. *(Love)* (primary binding) (third element or subissue)
    Rule (4) A battery occurs only if a plaintiff sustains physical injuries as a result of the touching. (*Anderson*) (primary binding) (fourth element or subissue)
    Application of law to facts: In McMillan's case, Mann not only aimed the bucket at McMillan purposefully to strike her, she struck Mann with it and the sand. The bucket and the sand striking McMillan would be sufficient to establish that a "touching" occurred. Mann later told McMillan that she deliberately threw the bucket at her. McMillan's did not consent to being hit by the bucket and that touching resulted in injuries.
    Conclusion: The touching was a battery.

First Legal Element or Subissue 1
    Issue: Did a touching occur?
    Rule: Objects are extensions of body parts. Contact with a substance or an object can be touching (*Leichtman*)

ILLUSTRATION 12-6. Continued

Application of law to facts: Bucket contacted McMillan
Conclusion: A touching occurred

Second Legal Element or Subissue 2
    Issue: Did Mann intend to hit McMillan?
    Rule: A person intends an act when it is done purposefully (*Smith*)
    Application of law to facts: Mann purposefully threw the bucket at
      McMillan and said she intended to strike her
    Conclusion: Mann had intent

Third Legal Element or Subissue 3
    Issue: Did McMillan consent to touching?
    Rule: If a party consented to the touching, no battery occurred.
      (*Love*)
    Application of law to facts: McMillan did not consent
    Conclusion: A touching without consent as in this case can be a
      battery

Fourth Element or Subissue 4
    Issue: Did McMillan suffer the requisite physical injuries as a result
      of the contact?
    Rule: Physical injuries must result from contact for battery
      (*Anderson*)
    Application of law to facts: McMillan sustained cuts and eye irrita-
      tion from bucket and sand contact
    Conclusion: McMillan had requisite physical injuries

Thesis Paragraph to Introduce Issue 2
    Does eight-year-old Rachel McMillan have a claim for intentional
      infliction of emotional distress against Carol Mann?
    Rule: Intentional infliction of emotional distress occurs when an
      individual intentionally commits an extreme and outrageous
      that causes emotional distress that no reasonable person can
      be expected to endure. (*Yeager*) (primary binding)
    Application: Rachel McMillan, a child, saw Mann, an adult who was
      asked to supervise the sandbox and ensure the safety of others,
      throw the rusty, metal bucket filled with sand at her mother's
      head and face, causing her mother to bleed. Seeing this act that
      was "beyond all possible bounds of decency" and therefore
      extreme and outrageous caused the child to suffer from anxiety,
      headaches, and vomiting daily—symptoms no reasonable child
      should be expected to endure. Several witnesses can testify that
      Mann said that she intended to harm McMillan.
    Conclusion: Rachel McMillan has a claim for intentional emo-
      tional distress

Issue 2 First Element or Subissue 1
    Issue: Did Mann commit an extreme and outrageous act?

ILLUSTRATION 12-6.   Continued

Rule 1: An extreme and outrageous act is one that no reasonable person can be expected to endure. (*Yeager*) (primary binding) (*Pyle*) (primary persuasive)

Rule 2: An act is extreme and outrageous if it goes beyond all possible bounds of decency and is intolerable in a civilized community. (*Yeager*) (primary binding)

Application of law to facts: Mann, an adult who was asked to ensure safety in the sandbox, threw a rusty, metal bucket filled with sand at another adult in front of young children, including her child and Rachel McMillan, the injured party's daughter. That act goes beyond all possible bounds of decency and would be intolerable in a civilized community.

Conclusion: Mann's act would be found to be an extreme and outrageous act.

Issue 2 Second Element or Subissue 2

Issue: Was the extreme and outrageous act done with intent?

Rule 1: A person intends his or her conduct when he or she undertakes an action with a knowing mind. (*Smith*) (primary binding)

Rule 2: If an actor knew or should have known that his or her actions would cause serious emotional distress, intent is established. (*Phung*) (primary binding)

Application of law to facts: Mann said she intended to harm McMillan. In addition, Mann not only knew or should have known that that throwing a rusty, metal bucket filled with sand at the head and face of another adult in front of the other adult's child resulting in the adult bleeding would cause an eight-year-old child to suffer serious emotional distress.

Conclusion: The young McMillan should be able to show intent.

Issue 2 Third Element or Subissue

Issue: Was the extreme and outrageous act the proximate cause of McMillan's emotional and physical distress?

Rule: Proximate cause exists when an act precedes and produces an injury that is likely to have occurred as a result of the act or which might have been anticipated. (*Jeffers*) (primary binding)

Application of Law to Facts: A child would be expected or likely to experience emotional distress when she witnesses her mother injured and bleeding.

Conclusion: The young McMillan will be able to show that the act was the proximate cause of her emotional and physical distress.

Issue 2 Fourth Element or Subissue

Issue: Did the child suffered from serious emotional distress?

Rule 1 : To establish serious emotional distress, the mental anguish must be serious and of a nature that "no reasonable man could be expected to endure it." (*Paugh*) (primary binding) Serious

ILLUSTRATION 12-6. Continued

emotional distress goes beyond mere upset or hurt feelings, but exists when a reasonable person is unable to cope. *Id.*

Rule 2: Physical harm need not be shown. (*Pyle*)

Rule 3: Neurosis, psychosis and phobias can establish serious emotional distress. (*Paugh*) (primary binding)

Application of Law to Facts: A psychologist found that the child suffered from post-traumatic stress syndrome and suffered anxiety and physical symptoms such as headaches and vomiting. That should be sufficient to establish serious emotion distress that is beyond mere upset or hurt feelings and which a reasonable person would be unable to cope.

Conclusion: Young McMillan can show she suffered from serious emotional distress.

Introduce Issue 3.

Issue: Was Camp Cougar vicariously liable for Mann's intentional torts?

Rule 1: An entity can be held vicariously liable for the intentional actions of its agent if the entity controlled the agent's conduct and benefited from it. (*Blankenship*) (primary binding)

Application of Law to Facts: Mann may be found to be an agent for Camp Cougar. However, Mann's actions did not benefit the camp nor did the camp exercise control over her actions.

Conclusion: Even though Mann is likely to be found liable for these intentional torts and a master can be found liable for the intentional torts of its agent, it is unlikely in this case that Camp Cougar would be found liable for Mann's torts.

Issue 3 First Element or Subissue

Issue: Is Mann Camp Cougar's agent?

Rule: A principal-agent relationship is established when one party exercises the right of control over the actions of another and those actions are for the benefit of the party exercising control. (*Hanson*) (primary binding)

Application of Law to Facts: Camp Cougar directed Mann to act as the sandbox supervisor and specifically directed her to keep people safe exercising control over her actions and deriving benefit from her actions.

Conclusion: Mann is likely to be found to be an agent of Camp Cougar.

Issue 3 Element or Subissue 2

Is Camp Cougar, a master, vicariously liable for its agent's intentional torts?

Rule: A master can be vicariously liable for its agent's intentional tort only if the master controlled the agent's conduct and the agent's acts benefited the master. (*Hanson*) (primary binding)

ILLUSTRATION 12-6.   Continued

Application of Law to Fact: Camp Cougar did not direct Mann to throw the bucket and the camp did not benefit from Mann's conduct.

Conclusion: Camp Cougar would not be held liable for Mann's intentional acts.

ILLUSTRATION 12-7.   Writing from an Outline

Outline

First Legal Element or Subissue 1

Issue: Did a touching occur?

Rule: Objects are extensions of body parts. Contact with a substance even cigar smoke or an object can be a touching. (*Leichtman*)

Application of law to facts: Bucket touched McMillan when Mann threw it.

Conclusion: A touching occurred.

Paragraph Drafted from Outline

I. Did a battery occur when Mann struck McMillan with a bucket and sand?

Whether Mann committed the tort of battery turns on whether an intentional touching occurred when a bucket Mann threw struck McMillan. A touching can occur when an object rather than an individual's body contacts another person. *Leichtman v. WLW Jacoc Communications, Inc.*, 92 Ohio App. 3d 232, 634 N.E.2d 697 (1994); *Smith v. John Deere Co.*, 83 Ohio App. 3d at 398, 614 N.E.2d at 1148. In *Leichtman*, one person blew cigar smoke at another person, resulting in injuries. The court found that the cigar smoke was an extension of the person and that a contact between the smoke and the nonconsenting person met the requirement of a touching for civil battery. In this case, Mann threw the bucket at McMillan, and the bucket contacted her face and head. Following the reasoning in the *Leichtman* case, the bucket would be an extension of Mann's body, and the contact between McMillan and the bucket would be considered a touching under the theory of civil battery.

IN-CLASS EXERCISE

Review the following memo in Illustration 12-8. Prepare an outline of authorities and an outline based on this memo. (This is the reverse of the process you would normally use.) Then discuss your outline. Make a list of legally significant facts and note the legal standard.

ILLUSTRATION 12-8.   Sample Memorandum Slip and Fall Case

MEMORANDUM

To: Margaret Sterner
From: Marie Main
Date: January 28, 2012
Re: *Harris v. Sack and Shop*

QUESTION PRESENTED

Is Sack and Shop, a grocery store, liable for injuries sustained by Harris, a store patron who slipped on a banana peel that had been left on the grocery store floor for two days?

BRIEF ANSWER

Probably yes. Sack and Shop, a grocery store, probably will be liable based on negligence for injuries sustained by Harris, a store patron who slipped on a banana peel that had been left on the grocery store floor for two days.

FACTS

Our client, Sack and Shop Grocery Store, is being sued for negligence by Rebecca Harris.

Harris went to the store to purchase groceries on July 8, 2011. While she was in the produce section, she slipped on a banana that a grocery store employee left on the floor. The employee had dropped it on the floor two days earlier and had failed to clean it up after a patron asked him to do so.

Harris sustained a broken arm and head injuries as a result of the slip and fall.

DISCUSSION

The issue presented in this case is whether Sack and Shop Grocery Store was negligent when Rebecca Harris slipped in the store's produce section. A grocer will be found negligent if a store employee breached the store's duty of reasonable care to its patrons and, as a result of that breach, the patron was injured. *Ward v. K Mart Corp.*, 554 N.E.2d 223 (Ill. 1990). In *Ward*, the grocery store employee failed to clean up a banana for two days and that peel caused a patron to be injured. Similarly, in our case Sack and Shop failed to remove the banana peel for two days. Therefore, Sack and Shop is likely to be found liable for the injuries Harris sustained.

The first element to consider is whether Sack and Shop owed a duty of reasonable care to Harris. A grocery store owes a duty of care to any patron. *Ward*, 554 N.E.2d at 226. Harris was a customer in the store. Therefore, Sack and Shop owed her a duty of care.

The next question to consider is whether Sack and Shop breached its duty of reasonable care to Harris. A store will be found to have

ILLUSTRATION 12-8.   Continued

breached its duty of reasonable care to a patron if a store employee fails to properly and regularly clean the floor of the store. *Olinger v. Great Atl. & Pac. Tea Co.*, 173 N.E.2d 443 (Ill. 1961). In *Olinger,* the store was found liable because a store employee failed to clean the floor for one day and a patron slipped on a substance on the floor. 173 N.E.2d at 447. No one had told any store employee about the slippery substance. *Id.* at 447. Nonetheless, the Illinois Supreme Court found the store liable, saying that the store employees had sufficient time to notice the substance if they had used ordinary care. *Id.* In our case, Sack and Shop's employee had two days to clean the floor before Harris fell. In addition, a customer had placed the store employee on notice of the banana peel. Therefore, Sack and Shop breached its duty of care to Harris.

The plaintiff, however, still must establish proximate cause, that is, that the injury resulted as a natural consequence of Sack and Shop's breach of its duty. A store owner's failure to clear debris from a store floor, resulting in injury to a patron who slipped on the floor, was found to be the proximate cause of the patron's injuries. *Id.* at 449. In this case, Sack and Shop's failure to clean the peel from the floor was a breach of its duty of care to Harris. This breach resulted in injury to Harris. Sack and Shop's breach will be found to be the proximate cause of Harris's injuries.

The final element that must be established is that the plaintiff, Harris, suffered injuries. Harris sustained a broken arm and head injuries as a result of the slip and fall. Therefore, she will be able to show that she was injured.

CONCLUSION

Sack and Shop owed Harris a duty of reasonable care. The store is likely to be found to have breached that duty of reasonable care because an employee failed to remove a banana peel from the grocery store floor during the preceding two days. The injuries Harris sustained were directly caused by a slip on a banana peel. Therefore, Sack and Shop is likely to be found liable to Harris.

CHAPTER SUMMARY

Outlining is an important component of legal writing. It helps you organize the discussion section of your legal memorandum. To outline a legal memorandum, first draft a list of legal authorities. Second, arrange the discussion sections concerning each issue and, if necessary, arrange each paragraph of the memorandum.

The list of legal authorities should include the names and citations to the authorities, a note about the legally significant facts contained in the authority, if any, and a statement that summarizes the significance of the authority.

The legal issues of the discussion should be organized in the IRAC format discussed in Chapter 10. Each element of a legal issued should be addressed in this format.

Before you can begin writing your memorandum, you must organize your thesis paragraph. The thesis paragraph is the first paragraph of your discussion. It summarizes the legal issues you will discuss in the memorandum. This paragraph also should be organized in IRAC format, if possible.

You have been shown how to draft questions presented, issues, conclusions, brief answers, facts statements, and discussion sections. In addition, you have been taught how to synthesize authorities and how to use a legal writing convention called IRAC.

KEY TERMS

elements   thesis paragraph
list of legal authorities   threshold issue
outlining

EXERCISES

SHORT ANSWER
1. How do you organize a thesis paragraph?
2. How do you compile a list of legal authorities?
3. How do you determine which element to discuss first?
4. What format should each paragraph take?
5. Write the discussion section only for the memo below.

MEMORANDUM

To: Ruth Abbey
From: Gail Michael
Date: January 20, 2012
Re: *Kahn v. Randall,* Civ. 95 No. 988, File No. 8988977

QUESTION PRESENTED
Does Janice Kahn have a valid claim for intentional infliction of emotional distress against Ronnie Randall after Kahn saw Randall turn his car to strike Kahn's 11-year-old child in front of her, causing her to suffer from anxiety, headaches, and vomiting?

CONCLUSION
Janice Kahn probably has a valid claim for intentional infliction of emotional distress against Ronnie Randall. Kahn saw Randall turn his car to strike her 11-year-old child. Seeing this accident caused Kahn to suffer from anxiety, headaches, and vomiting daily. This act could be considered extreme and outrageous conduct if it was done with intent. Several witnesses can testify

that Randall said that he intended to harm Kahn and Kahn states that Randall turned the car to strike her son. Two factors, however, might show that Randall lacked intent: the statement that he made to the police that he did not intend to hit the child and the fact that his blood alcohol level was .11, possibly preventing him from formulating the needed intent.

FACTS

While driving a car Ronnie Randall struck Janice Kahn's son at 5 P.M. on August 29, 2011. It was bright and clear. No skid marks appeared on the dry street following the accident.

Janice Kahn was working in her garden about five feet from the accident scene at the time of the accident. Her son was playing a game in the street before Randall's car struck him. Kahn did not see the car strike her 11-year-old son. When she first looked up from her garden, she thought her son was dead. He was covered with blood and had several broken bones. However, Kahn's son was conscious after the accident.

Immediately after the accident, Randall, who had a blood alcohol level of .11, was cited for drunk driving and driving with a suspended driver's license. Police charged him with drunk driving and suspended his license two weeks earlier after the car he was driving struck another child at the same spot. Randall has a drinking history.

Following the accident, several witnesses said Randall was upset and wobbled as he walked. One witness said that Randall intentionally turned the steering wheel to hit Kahn's son. Kahn stated that Randall often swerved down her street to get her attention.

Rhonda Albert, Kahn's neighbor, said she heard Randall say he would get even with Kahn after Kahn broke off a ten-year relationship with him.

During Kahn and Randall's ten-year relationship, Randall was close to Kahn's son. He took him to ball games, including one in April, and attended the son's baseball games. Randall knew that Kahn's son was the most important person in her life.

Since the accident, Kahn vomits daily and suffers from anxiety and headaches. Dr. Susan Faigen, Kahn's internist, states that the anxiety, headaches, and vomiting are the result of the accident. The prevailing case is *George v. Jordan Marsh Co.*, 359 Mass. 244, 268 N.E.2d 915 (1971). In that case, the court held that one who without a privilege to do so by extreme and outrageous conduct intentionally causes severe emotional distress to another, with bodily harm resulting from such distress, is subject to liability for such emotional distress and bodily harm.

6. Write a thesis paragraph for this discussion section.

FACTS

Drake Industries has been leasing warehouse space at 2700 North Bosworth Avenue, in Chicago, Illinois, from the owner of the building, Michael Martin. Drake began leasing space from Martin beginning January 1, 2009 at $700 per month until the lease expired on December 31, 2009.

Martin offered a new lease to Drake on November 25, 2009, to be signed and returned by December 31, 2009. The new lease began January 1, 2010, and expired on June 30, 2010, and the rent increased to $850 per month, payable on the first of each month. Drake never signed or returned the new lease, but did pay the increased rent amount during the term of the unsigned lease ending June 30, 2010. Since then, Drake has continued paying $850 on the first day of each month. On August 15, 2010, Martin requested that Drake surrender the premises. Drake came to your firm to find out what type of tenancy he has and whether Martin gave Drake the proper notice to quit the premises.

DISCUSSION

Is Drake Industries a holdover tenant? A holdover tenancy is created when a landlord elects to treat a tenant, after the expiration of his or her lease, as a tenant for another term upon the same provisions contained in the original lease. *Bismarck Hotel Co. v. Sutherland*, 92 Ill. App. 3d 167, 415 N.E.2d 517 (1980). In *Bismarck*, defendant Sutherland's written lease expired. Bismarck presented her with a new lease that included a rent increase. She began to pay the increase but did not sign the new lease. Sutherland could not be a holdover tenant since the terms of the old lease were not extended to the terms of the new, unsigned lease. Drake Industries was offered a new lease in 2009 that included a rent increase. Since the terms were different from the original lease, Drake could not be considered a holdover tenant.

It is the intention of the landlord, not the tenant that determines whether the tenant is to be treated as a holdover. *Sheraton-Chicago Corp. v. Lewis*, 8 Ill. App. 3d 309, 290 N.E.2d 685 (1972). When a landlord creates a new lease and presents it to the tenant, it is clear that it was his intention that a new tenancy was created. *Holt v. Chicago Hair Goods Co.*, 328 Ill. App. 671, 66 N.E.2d 727 (1946). Martin presented Drake with a new lease to sign in November 2009, with new terms beginning January 1, 2010. It was never his intention to hold over the same lease from 2009. Therefore, Drake was not a holdover tenant and has never been one. 735 Ill. Comp. Stat. 5/9-202 (West 1993) could not apply to Drake. Martin could not demand double rental fees from Drake when it remained in possession of 2700 North Bosworth after the written lease expired on December 31, 2007.

Is Drake Industries a year-to-year tenant? When the payment of rent is annual, there arises a tenancy from year to year, even if the agreement provides for a payment of one-twelfth of the annual rental each month. *Seaver Amusement Co. v. Saxe et al.*, 210 Ill. App. 289 (1918). The terms of the 2009 written lease would have to have said "$8,400 a year rent, payable in monthly installments of $750" for it to have been considered a year-to-year lease. Since the terms of the 2009 lease only provided for monthly payments and not a yearly rental rate, Drake was not a year-to-year tenant. 735 Ill. Comp. Stat. 5/9-205 (West 1993) does not apply at all to Drake. Martin would not be required to tender 60 days' notice in writing to terminate the tenancy.

Is Drake Industries a month-to-month tenant? A month-to-month tenancy is created when a tenant remains in possession of the premises after a lease expires under different terms of tenancy. *Bismarck Hotel*, 92 Ill. App. 3d at 168,

415 N.E.2d at 517. By paying Bismarck's increased rental amount, different terms of the tenancy were established, so Sutherland's tenancy was considered month to month by the court. Drake remained at 2700 North Bosworth after its lease expired in 2009 but began paying the increased rent to Martin under the new terms of the unsigned lease. This established different terms of tenancy, so Drake has been a month-to-month tenant since 2010.

What type of notice is necessary to vacate the premises? Under 735 Ill. Comp. Stat 5/9/-207 (West 2008), notice to terminate a month-to-month tenancy must be given in writing 30 days before termination before any action for forcible entry and detainer can be maintained. Drake said that on August 15, 2010, Martin "requested" that Drake surrender the premises. An oral request may not be sufficient and Drake may maintain that proper notice has not been made and it need not surrender the premises by September 15, 2010. A forcible entry and detainer action could not be entered and maintained and Drake need not surrender the premises until proper notice has been given.

7. Review the discussion section in the multi-issue McMillan memo above and draft a list of authorities. Then draft an outline of the discussion section.
8. Review the discussion section below and draft a list of authorities. Then draft an outline of the discussion section.

Are the Blacks entitled to special damages from Comfy Furniture for the cost of redecorating their living room? An Illinois appellate court decided that the nonbreaching party should be put back in the position that it was in when the contract was formed. *Kalal v. Goldblatt Bros.*, 368 N.E.2d 671, 673 (Ill. App. Ct. 1977). The Blacks stated their intention at the beginning concerning the fabric, the redecoration of the living room, and the family reunion. This fact was a part of their original position. The living room was redecorated. The furniture was delivered; however, the fabric was incorrect. Therefore, the Blacks have a right to recover consequential damages for the cost of the redecoration of their living room because the end result was not achieved; correctly upholstered furniture, newly redecorated living room to match, and a new living room look for the reunion. The conditions of the original contract were not met, and there was a breach of contract as embodied by the incorrectly upholstered furniture.

Under contract law, what damages are the Blacks entitled to pursue? Damages for breach of contract should place the plaintiff in a position he would have been in had the contract been performed. *Kalal*, 368 N.E.2d at 671. The plaintiffs in *Kalal* received a sofa that had been reupholstered in the wrong fabric after numerous delays, during which they had chosen three different fabrics in succession. *Id.* The court held that the defect could be remedied by the cost of reupholstering the sofa in the proper fabric. *Id.* at 674. The Blacks' chair and loveseat were improperly upholstered. Comfy Furniture upholstered their furniture with the reverse side of the fabric showing. Therefore, they were entitled to damages equal to the cost of upholstering their furniture correctly. However, the Blacks' situation is distinguished from *Kalal* in that their furniture was delivered before the date set in the contract, and it can be argued by Comfy that there was time to remedy the defect before their target date of Thanksgiving.

Are the Blacks entitled to compensation for the loss of use of their furniture? The question of compensation for the loss of use of the furniture was considered by both parties in *Kalal* to be appropriate since the plaintiffs in the case were without their furniture for several months while waiting for it to be reupholstered. *Id.* The Blacks have been similarly inconvenienced in that they, too, have been without the use of their new furniture. Thus, they are entitled to compensation for the loss of use of the furniture. However, it can be argued by Comfy Furniture that the furniture in the *Kalal* case was used and had been removed from the home for the purpose of reupholstering it. *Id.* In the present case, the furniture was new and had never been in the Blacks' home, and Comfy may argue that the Blacks did not actually suffer loss of use of the new furniture.

Are the Blacks entitled to damages for the expense of decorating their living room to match the furniture they did not receive in the agreed-on condition? The redecorating of the living room in *Kalal* was not in the contemplation of either party at the time the contract was executed. *Kalal,* 368 N.E.2d at 671. Subsequently, the court held that the only damages that were recoverable for breach of contract are limited to those that were reasonably foreseeable and were within the contemplation of the parties at the time the contract was executed. *Id.* at 674. By the express terms of the Uniform Commercial Code, the court cannot follow tort theories to award damages. The legislative history of the U.C.C. indicates that contractual disputes should apply to the findings of the court. *Moorman Mfg. Co. v. National Tank Co.,* 435 N.E.2d 443, 453 (Ill. 1982). The Blacks only told Mr. Blaine that they needed the furniture to be completed in time for a family reunion. Comfy knew that the Blacks were under a time constraint for the delivery, but apparently there was no communication regarding the redecorating of the living room. With regard to Comfy Furniture, the redecorating of the Blacks' living room was an unforeseeable event and consequently they would not be held responsible for the expense. Because the fact that the redecorating of the living room was unforeseeable, it was not included within the terms of the contract. Therefore, Comfy only breached the express terms of the contract. The Blacks probably will not be awarded compensatory damages.

9. Finish the memorandum below. Write an outline and a discussion section based on this outline of authorities, facts, questions presented, and conclusions.

Outline of Authorities

1. *42 U.S.C. §2000e* **(1998):** The term "employer" means a person engaged in an industry affecting commerce who has fifteen or more employees for each working day in each of twenty or more calendar weeks in the current or preceding calendar year.

2. *Zimmerman v. North American Signal Co.,* **704 F.2d 347 (7th Cir. 1983):** Salaried workers or full-time workers counted as employees for every day of the week on the payroll whether they were present at work or not. Hourly paid workers are counted as employees only on the days when they are actually at work or days on paid leave. (primary binding)

   3. *Musser v. Mountain View Broadcasting*, **578 F. Supp. 229 (E.D. Tenn. 1984):** "Current calendar year" is the year of discrimination. (primary persuasive)

   4. *Wright v. Kosciusko Medical Clinic*, **791 F. Supp. 1327, 1333 (N.D. Ind. 1992):** "Each working day" is literal and must be a day on which an employer conducts normal, full operations. (primary persuasive)

   5. *Norman v. Levy*, **767 F. Supp. 144 (N.D. Ill. 1991):** Part-time workers counted only on the days that they actually work. (primary persuasive)

   6. *Knight v. United Farm Bureau Mut. Ins. Co.*, **950 F.2d 377 (7th Cir 1991):** The "economic realities" of the relationship between an employer and his or her worker must be weighted by applying five factors: (1) the amount of employer control and supervision over employee, (2) the responsibility for the operational costs, (3) the worker's occupation and the skills required, (4) the form of compensation and benefits, and (5) the length of the job commitment. *Knight*, 950 F.2d at 378. Control is the most important factor. *Id.* Knight is an insurance agent, is not permitted to sell insurance for any other companies, is required to attend weekly staff meetings in the office, and works a specified number of hours in the office (primary binding). *Knight*, 950 F.2d at 378. Company provided supplies and paid for business expenses. *Id.* Essential to company operation. *Id.* Paid commissions with no deductions. *Id.* Knight not an employee.

   7. *Mitchell v. Tenney*, **650 F. Supp. 703 (N.D. Ill. 1986):** The "economic realities" of the relationship between an employer and his or her worker must be weighed.

   8. *Vakharia v. Swedish Covenant Hosp.*, **765 F. Supp. 461 (N.D. Ill. 1991):** When an employee is economically dependent on an employer, the court is likely to find employment relationship. Plaintiff in *Vakharia* was a physician dependent on the hospital for business *Id.* at 463. (primary persuasive)

ILLUSTRATION 12-9.   Memorandum: Sex Discrimination Case

MEMORANDUM

To: Wallace Maine
From: Thomas Wall
Date: November 15, 2010
Re: Sex Discrimination Case against Whole In One No. C2008 CIV 190, G12399990

QUESTIONS PRESENTED

   1. Under Title VII, was Whole In One an employer when 14 people, including 3 full-time and 11 part-time workers, worked on any one day for 24 weeks and when 10 full-time employees were on the Whole In One payroll?

ILLUSTRATION 12-9. Continued

2. Under Title VII, was Walker an independent contractor rather than an employee when she worked exclusively for Whole In One, paid taxes quarterly rather than through deductions, and worked with limited company supervision?

3. Under Title VII, was Radiant an independent contractor rather than an employee when she worked with limited company supervision using company supplies and equipment and had taxes and medical deductions taken from her salary?

CONCLUSIONS

1. Whole In One was an employer. Under Title VII, an employer has at least 15 employees working for 20 or more weeks during the relevant year: Salaried employees are included in this number for each week they are on the payroll, while hourly workers are only counted on the days they actually work. In 2008, the year of the alleged discrimination, 14 workers, 3 full-time and 11 part-time people, worked for Whole In One on any day during the 24-week restaurant and golf season. However, 10 full-time workers were on the payroll. As these part-time workers are only counted on the days that they work, the number of part-time individuals included in the count of employees is 11 for each day of the 24-week season. Because full-time workers, however, are counted for each day of a week that they are on the payroll, all 10 of Whole In One's full-time workers would be included in the count of employees. In total, Whole In One had 11 part-time workers and 10 full-time workers "working" for 20 or more weeks during the relevant year, bringing the total count of employees to 21. Therefore, Whole In One was an employer under Title VII.

2. Walker was an employee. The Seventh Circuit will weigh five factors to determine whether she was an independent contractor or an employee for this Title VII lawsuit. The primary focus will be on the company's control of Walker. Although Walker worked from home, set her own hours, and had an impact in her commission pay, the company controlled her work by reviewing and revising it, restricting Walker's employment opportunities, and providing supplies for her. Therefore, the company exerted control over Walker and she would be considered an employee.

3. Radiant was probably an employee. To determine whether she was an employee or independent contractor for this Title VII lawsuit, the court will focus on five factors, primarily the amount of control the company exerted over Radiant's work. Whole In One provided Radiant with an office, supplies, a two-year contract, and additional training. Whole In One paid her regularly and deducted taxes from her salary. Although Whole In One did not actively supervise Radiant's work on a daily basis, she still worked in the company offices and was under the control of Whole In One. Therefore, the court probably will find that Radiant was an employee.

ILLUSTRATION 12-9.   Continued

FACTS

Victoria Radiant and Karen Walker, two former Whole In One Enterprises workers, brought a federal sex discrimination lawsuit based on Title VII against our client, Whole In One Enterprises, owned by Nancy and Craig Black. The lawsuit, filed in the U.S. District Court for the Northern District of Illinois, stems from the dismissal of the two women by the Blacks during 2008.

The Blacks own Whole In One Enterprises, which operates a miniature golf course and restaurant in Glenview, Illinois. During the 24-week 2008 restaurant season, 10 people worked full-time and 14 people worked part-time for Whole In One. However, no more than 14 people worked on any one day. Of those 14 people, only 3 were full-time employees. The other full-time employees regularly took days off during the summer restaurant and golf season.

Among the full-time workers was Karen Walker, who worked as a public relations director for Whole In One. Walker responded to an ad that said that "an employer" sought an individual to perform public relations work. Whole In One hired Walker without a contract and prohibited her from working for other firms. However, Walker worked from home and set her own hours. Whole In One required Walker to attend weekly staff meetings at the company offices, where Whole In One would review and revise Walker's work. The company supplied Walker with paper, pencils, stamps, and telephone service and paid for her life and health insurance. Whole In One did not withhold taxes from Walker's commissions.

Victoria Radiant, who had a two-year employment contract with the company, provided marketing services to Whole In One from October of 2006 until she was fired in 2008. Although Radiant worked in the company office, Whole In One management rarely supervised her work. The company paid for her continued education, provided her with bonuses, and deducted taxes from her weekly salary.

APPLICABLE STATUTE

The term "employer" means a person engaged in an industry affecting commerce who has fifteen or more employees for each working day in each of 20 or more calendar weeks in the current or preceding calendar year. 42 U.S.C. §2000e(b) (2008).

PERSUASIVE WRITING

CHAPTER OVERVIEW

Persuasive writing is used to convince a court, an opposing party, or an individual to adopt your client's assessment of the facts and interpretation of the applicable law. Persuasive writing eloquently articulates a position. This form of writing is used in many legal documents, the most common of which are litigation documents. Transaction documents such as contracts and leases are also persuasive forms of writing because they advocate a client's position or protect a client's rights.

Persuasive writing is used for litigation memos that are filed with the court. Litigation memos are persuasive documents detailing the legal and factual arguments to grant or deny a client's motion to dismiss and other procedural motions. As the word persuasive indicates, this style of writing is used to persuade. Persuasive writing is argumentative but the argument is based on the law, not just on whim or fury.

Just as with any other form of legal writing, the purpose and the audience determine the format and style of the document. Audience is especially important in persuasive writing. You want to make your point clearly and directly to a very busy reader. This requires drafting precise and succinct documents.

A. THE NATURE OF PERSUASIVE WRITING

▼ What Kinds of Documents Are Persuasive?

Persuasive writing is used in drafting advocacy memos in support of motions designed to convince a court to rule a certain way. Persuasive writing is also used in writing trial and appellate briefs. Trial briefs explain the leading legal issues anticipated to emerge in a trial while they emphasize the client's position. Trial briefs outline a case, offer the elements that will be proven, and include witnesses' names and pertinent facts and evidence. Trial briefs are submitted to the court in some but not all jurisdictions. Trial briefs are usually submitted in federal court. Regardless of whether an attorney files a trial brief with the court, he or she would use it to prepare for trial. Appellate briefs are formal documents submitted to the court in accordance with federal, state, or local court rules. Appellate briefs are filed in cases in which the parties are dissatisfied with a trial court judge's decision concerning a legal issue, evidentiary point, or finding of fact in a bench trial or a jury's verdict. By their nature, appellate briefs are designed to persuade the court that an error occurred in the trial. For example, an appellant may claim that the trial court erred when the jury was allowed to consider some evidence.

Litigation paralegals are often called upon to write persuasively. Also, at times transaction paralegals write persuasively, for example, in demand letters and default notices. Any time you write a document that asserts your client's position, you are writing persuasively. Initially, the complaint filed by the plaintiff is the first document that triggers the need to write persuasively. A complaint sets out the legal claim and issues combined with the specific facts. Additionally, advocacy memos are written persuasively. This chapter focuses on persuasive writing used in litigation documents.

▼ Which Aspects of Persuasive Writing Do Paralegals Perform?

Generally, in small firm practice, paralegals draft complaints, answers, and interrogatories. Infrequently, paralegals draft memoranda in support of motions filed with the court and trial briefs. Appellate briefs are rarely drafted by paralegals because this is a specialized practice area of the law reserved for attorneys who have developed this expertise. However, paralegals should be knowledgeable about all facets of persuasive writing. Often paralegals are requested to work on portions of a persuasive document or to extract the citations from a document to compile an authorities table. Paralegals are not authorized to sign court documents and pleadings. Only attorneys are licensed to practice law and to sign pleadings.

Frequently, paralegals check pinpoint citations to make sure that the cites are accurate. Firms do not want a brief rejected, by the court, due to incorrect citation format, so this is an important task. Additionally, paralegals check all facts against the record to make sure that the facts are accurate.

▼ What Is the Difference between Objective and Persuasive Writing?

Objective writing is neutral and seeks to inform the reader as to all the relevant law. In persuasive writing, the writer takes a position and attempts to convince the court and the reader that this position is correct. Persuasive writing seeks to solve a problem in favor of the client and conforms to the attorney's theory of the case. Law and facts that are harmful to the client's position are minimized and, if the jurisdiction permits, omitted. The goal in persuasive writing is for the reader to adopt your client's position. Your goal, as the writer, is to present the facts and the law in such a way that they guide the reader to adopt your client's position.

B. TECHNIQUES

▼ Is There a Formula for Persuasive Writing as There Is for Objective Writing?

Yes. As you learned, the formula for objective writing uses the IRAC structure in the discussion. See Chapter 10, The IRAC Method. The fundamental difference is that IRAC is the structure for crafting an objective discussion that poses a question and explores the answers neutrally; whereas in persuasive writing, the first "A" of the ARAC sequence is the writer's assertion (his or her position), followed by the Rule, the Application, and the Conclusion (the rest of the ARAC sequence proves the writer's assertion). To write persuasively, use the ARAC or CRAC structure (ARAC and CRAC being virtually synonymous; ARAC is the acronym for Assertion, Rule, Application, Conclusion, and CRAC is the acronym for Conclusion, Rule, Application, Conclusion).

The ARAC formula sounds quite similar to IRAC, yet there is an important difference. Instead of posing a question or viewing an issue objectively, you make an assertion based on the theory of your case and then support it with the relevant legal rule, the factual foundation, and legal analysis—that is, you explain why that rule of law relates to your assertion and then you draw a conclusion. Notice that there are important similarities between ARAC and IRAC—the Rule, the Application, and the Conclusion are essential components of both formats. The Rule provides the legal basis of the argument, the Application relates the legal rule to the instant problem or case, and the Conclusion demonstrates the nexus between the rule and the facts and provides a resolution. Just as in objective writing, the application segment is most important and should never be skipped, for it tells the reader why the rule of law applies to this factual and legal scenario.

The following is an example of a paragraph from an objective memo written in IRAC format:

> (ISSUE) Did Jones indicate acceptance of the truck and waive his right to seek damages by repairing and continuing to use the truck for more than a reasonable time? (RULE) A buyer must rescind a sales contract as soon as he discovers the breach, or after he has had reasonable time for examination. He waives this right to rescind by continuing to use the goods for more than a reasonable time. *Olson Rug Co. v. Smarto*, 204 N.E.2d 838, 841 (Ill. App. Ct.1965). In *Olson*, the court found that the Smartos indicated acceptance and waived their right to rescind the contract by continuing to use the carpeting for more than one year after the defects were discovered. *Id.* (APPLICATION) Our problem differs from *Olson* because Jones did not discover that the truck was defective until he made the first repair on December 13, 2012, over one year after he purchased the truck. However, one year is more than reasonable time for examination. (CONCLUSION) Therefore, Jones indicates acceptance of the truck, waiving his right to recover damages, by repairing and continuing to use the truck after more than a reasonable time for inspection passed.

For purposes of comparison, an ARAC paragraph follows. Notice how it is written in a persuasive tone, beginning with the writer's assertion.

> (ASSERTION) The plaintiff failed to give notice of defects within a reasonable time. The plaintiff did not put the defendant on notice, as to the truck's defects, until over one year after the defects were discovered. (RULE) "A buyer must notify a seller of defects within a reasonable time thereof notwithstanding acceptance." *Stamm v. Wilder Travel Travelers*, 358 N.E.2d 382, 385 (Ill. App. Ct. 1976). Furthermore, if a buyer fails to reject a good within a reasonable time, acceptance takes place. *Vitromar Piece Dye Works v. Lawrence of London, Ltd.*, 256 N.E.2d 135, 137 (Ill. App. Ct. 1969). (APPLICATION) Here, the plaintiff made various repairs and replaced components over a one year period. The truck was purchased in November 2011, and repairs were made between December 2012

and March 2013. The plaintiff failed to notify Grimy's of any defects until over one year after the purchase date. (CONCLUSION) Since the plaintiff did not notify Grimy's as to the defects within a reasonable time, he has accepted the truck.

The IRAC paragraph begins with a question and the answer is reached by using a neutral exploration of the law and by applying the facts. The ARAC sequence begins with a premise, an Assertion of what the party considers to be true, and the Rule, Application, and Conclusion that follow support the Assertion. A close examination of various sentences in the IRAC and the ARAC paragraphs further underscores the differences between persuasive and objective writing. Aside from beginning the sequence with an assertion, persuasive writing uses strong adjectives and conjures emotional reactions. The Application portion of the objectively written paragraph is as follows:

> Our problem differs from Olson because Jones did not discover that the truck was defective until he made the first repair on December 13, 2012, over one year after he purchased the truck. However, one year is more than reasonable time for examination.

▼ What Are Some Techniques Used in Persuasive Writing?

Comparing objective and persuasive writing emphasizes the techniques used to craft an argument. Look at how the objective application segment differs from the persuasive application: Here, the plaintiff made various repairs and replaced components over a one year period. The truck was purchased in November 2011, and repairs were made between December 2012 and March 2013. The plaintiff failed to notify Grimy's of any defects until almost two years after the purchase date.

First, persuasive writing tries to depersonalize the opposing party. Notice how Grimy's is referred to by name whereas Jones is referred to as "the plaintiff." Another hallmark of persuasive writing is using language to arouse emotion or form an opinion. An example of this technique is used in the persuasive sentence "The plaintiff failed to notify Grimy's of any defects until almost two years after the purchase date." Labeling behavior and using adjectives are persuasive writing techniques.

▼ Are There Any Other Tools That Are Helpful for Persuasive Writing?

In persuasive writing, an attorney cannot ignore relevant law or facts but can make an effort to enhance or emphasize facts and law favorable to his or her client's position and minimize facts and law that are unfavorable. The goal is to write the rule statement accurately and yet in the best light for your client. The facts are presented so that favorable information is highlighted and harmful information is minimized. Beneficial facts are stated in short, direct sentences, whereas harmful facts are obscured in longer sentences, with several clauses. A frequently used method is to write the facts that are favorable to your client in the active voice and to write the facts that are harmful in the passive voice. Passive voice deemphasizes the actor. Therefore, if you want to deemphasize your client's actions, use passive voice, as in the Grimy example above. The body of the brief is generally written in the CRAC or ARAC format.

A portion of a facts statement from an objective memo follows:

> On November 29, 2011, Mr. Jones paid $15,225 to Grimy's Auto and Truck Repair Service, Inc., of Stream Grove, Illinois, as payment in full for the purchase of a 2005 Kenworth truck. As part of the purchase agreement, Grimy's represented to Jones that it had completely overhauled the engine, using newly rebuilt parts for which Grimy's would provide invoices. Grimy's represented that the parts were guaranteed. Also, Grimy's stated that the tractor/trailer was in as-good-as-new condition and was ready for standard interstate trucking. Because of an equipment failure, on December 13, 2012, Mr. Jones received an invoice totaling $3,604.18 from a repair shop for replacement of the nos. 5 and 6 cylinders.

Notice how both parties are referred to by name. The facts are reiterated in chronological order. Emotional adjectives are not included.

A facts statement from a persuasive document follows for comparison:

> Grimy's Auto and Truck Repair Service, Inc., of Stream Grove, Illinois, sold the plaintiff a 2005 Kenworth truck on November 29, 2011, which was represented as being completely overhauled. At the time of purchase, the truck was in as-good-as-new condition and was ready for standard interstate trucking. One year after the purchase, on December 13, 2012, the plaintiff received an invoice for $3,604.18, from a repair shop, for the replacement of the nos. 5 and 6 cylinders.

The passage of time between the purchase and the repair is emphasized, whereas the representations made by Grimy's are deemphasized. The party being represented is referred to by name and the opposition is depersonalized.

▼ Are There Any General Rules for Writing Persuasively?

First, persuasive writing begins at the level of word choice, sentence structure, and paragraph formation. When you receive an assignment requiring persuasive writing, follow the prewriting techniques outlined in Chapter 3, Getting Ready to Write. When you receive your assignment, ask yourself: What is the purpose? The purpose of the document determines its form. Is the document for a trial court or an appellate court? If so, it is either a trial or an appellate brief. Is the document a letter demanding an individual to perform in a specific manner? Then the document is a demand letter. The purpose determines the rhetorical stance. If the document is a letter, you know that it does not have to be drafted in ARAC format but must be persuasive. If the document is a memo to be used to prepare for trial or to convince a judge to rule on behalf of your firm's client, then it must be written following the ARAC format. Next, you must assess the intended audience. Reader awareness is important. Who will read the document? What type of education does he or she have? How should the document sound? It is at this level that the persuasive tone of the document is determined. Select powerful, emotional words and you will sway the reader toward your side if you can substantiate your position with law and facts. Generally, short sentences are used for beneficial information, and long, clause-ridden sentences are used to obscure detrimental facts.

▼ When Does the Need to Write Persuasively Arise?

Paralegals write persuasive documents, including memos, under the direction and supervision of the attorney assigning the project. Most frequently, paralegals draft demand letters. Demand letters are persuasive correspondence requesting that the recipient perform a certain act or produce a certain document. Additionally, paralegals work on aspects of court filings. Often, a paralegal will verify authorities and citation formats. Also, a paralegal must be aware of the different types of persuasive documents. However, remember that paralegals are not authorized to sign court documents and pleadings. Only attorneys are licensed to practice law and to sign court documents and pleadings.

ETHICS ALERT

File all pleadings on time. Ethical sanctions occur because of late filings.

C. TYPES OF PERSUASIVE WRITING

1. Complaints

▼ What Is a Complaint?

A complaint is the document filed with the trial court that initiates the proceedings. A complaint is a short statement of the facts of the case, and a statement of why the plaintiff is entitled to win. The jurisdiction determines the contents of the complaint. Some jurisdictions, such as federal court, require a statement of the basis for jurisdiction. Some jurisdictions require fact pleading that identifies all facts alleging a valid cause of action. Notice, required in some jurisdictions, is a short statement of the case's basis, or grounds, and why the plaintiff is entitled to win.

The parties must be clearly identified. Note whether a party is a corporation or a partnership, and its state of residence and address. In some federal complaints, a diversity statement is included to indicate the basis for the case being heard in federal court. An example of a diversity statement is: "The plaintiff is a citizen of Illinois. The defendant is a corporation doing business in the state of Ohio. The matter in controversy, exclusive of interests and costs, exceeds $75,000."

Paragraphs are numbered in a complaint. State all claims the plaintiff has and use separate counts for different claims. At the end of the complaint, ask the court for specific remedies. This request is called the prayer for relief.

▼ How Do You Know What to Include in a Complaint?

Interview your client. Determine the facts of the case. Do some preliminary research to determine what facts are necessary to support each element of a legal claim the plaintiff might have. You must plead each element of a claim. If you fail to do so, a defendant will file a motion to dismiss the complaint for failure to state a claim. Often, statutes and court cases establish the elements of the cause of action, the "magic language" that should be included in a claim. Generally, the elements of the legal rule provide the elements. As a writer, follow the order and format of the rule's elements, if available, because this will present a familiar order for the reader. Review relevant statutes and court cases before drafting the complaint. However, you do not cite to a statute or court case in a claim, except when required in the jurisdictional statement. Outline all the information, legal and factual, to support allegations in the complaint.

When you have gathered the information, use a form book or ask to see examples of complaints created by members of your firm or legal department. Form books are excellent resources because they include all the necessary elements to include when drafting a complaint. Remember that the forms must always be tailored to your client's situation because the facts are unique to each case. Another excellent source is *American Jurisprudence Proof of Facts* 2 *d* published by Thomson Reuters. *Proof of Facts* has a checklist of necessary facts and legal rules that you should include to build a case.

Each paragraph should contain one simple, thorough thought. Do not incorporate multiple ideas into one numbered paragraph. By keeping the statement simple, you will know what a defendant is admitting or denying.

Your complaint should allow the reader to understand the plaintiff's story and to see it in his or her mind.

The damages and the relief sought should always be included in the complaint.

Illustration 13-1 is an example of a complaint:

ILLUSTRATION 13-1.   Sample Complaint

IN THE CIRCUIT COURT OF MILL COUNTY, ILLINOIS
COUNTY DEPARTMENT, LAW DIVISION

MICHAEL JONES,	)	
	)	
Plaintiff	)	No. 95L 27901
	)	
v.	)	
	)	
GRIMY'S AUTO AND TRUCK SERVICE,	)	
INC., an Illinois Corporation	)	
	)	
Defendant	)	

COMPLAINT AT LAW

This is an action brought in the Circuit Court of Mill County, Illinois, to recover for the breach of warranty of merchantability arising out of the sale of a defective truck that was said to have been completely overhauled and consisting of newly rebuilt, reconditioned parts. The defendant was aware that Michael Jones purchased the truck for the purpose of using the vehicle for interstate trucking. Plaintiff seeks money damages for lost wages and profits and for the expense of servicing the truck. Plaintiff demands a trial by jury.

PARTIES

The Plaintiff is a citizen of Illinois and engages in the business of interstate trucking. Defendant, Grimy's Auto and Truck Service, Inc., is a corporation organized under the laws of Illinois with its principal place of business in that state.

BREACH OF WARRANTY OF MERCHANTABILITY

1. On or about November 29, 2011, and for some time before that, Defendant Grimy's Auto and Truck Service, Inc., was in the business of buying, reconditioning, and then selling used trucks. The business is located at 2300 Stream Road, village of Stream Grove, county of Cook, and state of Illinois.

2. On November 29, 2011, Plaintiff, Michael Jones, purchased from Defendant, Grimy's Auto and Truck Repair Service, a 2005 Kenworth

ILLUSTRATION 13-1. Continued

C/D Serial Number 239999L with Title Number AB1234 and paid the agreed purchase price of Fifteen Thousand Two Hundred Twenty Five ($15,225.00) Dollars, in full (a copy of said sales documents attached as Exhibit "A"), the price normally charged for reconditioned, rebuilt trucks intended for interstate trucking.

3. The price agreed upon between the Plaintiff and the Defendant for the purchase of the truck was a price for a truck with a recently overhauled engine with all new or rebuilt parts, and one ready for road use in interstate trucking.

4. Jones agreed to purchase the truck, after Defendant was informed that the truck would be used in interstate trucking, and after Defendant made the following representations:

   a. the engine of the truck was completely overhauled and consisted of newly rebuilt, reconditioned parts;
   b. all parts in the rebuilt engine would be guaranteed and Plaintiff would be supplied with invoices for parts purchased to overhaul the engine; and
   c. the tractor/trailer was "like brand new" and ready for use of the type and extent generally involved in the interstate trucking industry.

5. The truck was not as represented by agents and/or employees of Defendant Grimy's Auto and Truck Service because the heads were old and had not been reconditioned, and other parts, including at least two pistons, two rods, two sleeves, and injectors, were not new, were defective, and had not been reconditioned.

6. As a consequence of the failure of the truck to be as agreed on, the truck broke down, Plaintiff could not perform his services as a trucker, and the Plaintiff was thus without work for an extended period of time resulting in lost wages and profits.

7. As a consequence of the failure of the truck to be as represented, Plaintiff was required to expend the following additional sums in repair of the vehicle:

   a. $3,604.18 for replacement of nos. 5 and 6 cylinders, which took place on December 13, 2012;
   b. $40.88 for repair of the shut-down solenoid on December 16, 2009;
   c. $99.88 for repair of rear lights on December 16, 2012;
   d. $312.49 for replacement of broken path tube in no. 6 cylinder on December 16, 2012;
   e. $120.00 for tow of vehicle on February 2, 2013;
   f. $247.00 for tow of vehicle to Grimy's Auto and Truck Service on March 13, 2013; and
   g. Estimated repair costs of $9000.00 to repair vehicle, which is currently disabled in Columbus, Ohio.

ILLUSTRATION 13-1.   **Continued**

Therefore, the Plaintiff, Michael Jones, demands judgment against Defendant, Grimy's Auto and Truck Service, Inc., in the following amounts:

a. $6000.00 in lost profits;
b. $8000.00 in lost wages;
c. $4424.43 in expenditures in repair of the vehicle;
d. $15,225.00 for loss of use of said vehicle; and
e. Such other damages occurring as a consequence of the breach of said contract, plus the costs of this action.

_____

Attorney for Plaintiff

Ted Kane, Esq.
Wall & Smith, P.C.
123 West Monroe Street
Mill, Illinois 60666
(999) 888-8888

Read the complaint carefully. Notice how the complaint tells the story of the plaintiff's grievance while listing the factual elements necessary to support a cause of action. The form books will help you draft the complaint by listing the elements that you must prove to substantiate the facts. Always ask the assigning attorney to tell you the relevant jurisdiction for the pleading. The jurisdiction may control the timing for the filing and the type of form. Also check the local court rules for filing criteria.

2. Answer

After the complaint is filed, the defendant responds to, or answers, the complaint. One option is that the defense may file a motion to dismiss either the entire action or at least one of the counts, to narrow the issues for trial. This is often called claim consolidation. If the plaintiff files a five count complaint and the defendant is successful in dismissing two counts then the defense only has to contend with three counts at trial. The rules of civil procedure for the appropriate jurisdiction provide the basis for dismissal of a complaint. For actions in state court, you look to the relevant state's code of civil procedure. Always ask the assigning attorney about the jurisdiction. In federal court you would look to the Federal Rules of Civil Procedure. The defendant must file an answer to any counts for which the defendant does not seek a motion to dismiss.

▼ What Is an Answer and What Is Its Purpose?

The answer is designed to address each of the points the plaintiff states in the complaint. It is called a pleading because it is a statement of the defendant's position concerning the case. Some of the plaintiff's allegations will be admitted by the defendant; many more, however, will be denied; in some cases, a defendant will state that he or she has insufficient information to admit or deny an allegation. The answer also is the time to plead any affirmative defenses. Affirmative defenses are claims a defendant may present that would bar the plaintiff's recovery. In some jurisdictions, verified answers must be filed to verified complaints. These complaints and answers are signed by the parties, and can be used in court as evidence.

▼ When Is an Answer Filed?

An answer is usually filed within a time period stated in the court rules. Many jurisdictions provide for a 20-day period between the service date and the filing of an answer. In some cases, the defendant will file a motion to dismiss an action rather than answer the complaint within the same time frame. Such a motion is filed when the complaint fails to state a claim or the court lacks jurisdiction or authority to hear a claim. Sometimes complaints will contain multiple claims for legal relief. Defendants can answer those claims while simultaneously filing a motion to dismiss other claims. See Illustration 13-2 for an example of an answer to one count of a complaint, and Illustration 13-3 for an example of a motion to dismiss other counts of the same complaint.

PRACTICE POINTER

Always check local court rules for filing requirements for all pleadings. The *ALWD Citation Manual*, in Appendix 2, has all of the local court rules for citations.

ILLUSTRATION 13-2.   Sample Answer

IN THE CIRCUIT COURT OF MILL COUNTY, ILLINOIS
COUNTY DEPARTMENT, LAW DIVISION

MICHAEL JONES,	)	
	)	
Plaintiff	)	No. 95L 27901
	)	
v.	)	
	)	
GRIMY'S AUTO AND TRUCK SERVICE,	)	
INC., an Illinois Corporation	)	
	)	
Defendant	)	

ILLUSTRATION 13-2.   Continued

ANSWER OF DEFENDANT
GRIMY'S AUTO AND
TRUCK SERVICE

Defendant, Grimy's Auto and Truck Service, for its answer to the Plaintiff's Complaint, states that it is a corporation organized under the laws of Illinois with its principal place of business in that state and the defendant further states as follows:

1. The defendant admits the allegations contained in paragraph 1.

2. The defendant admits that on November 29, 2011, Michael Jones purchased from Grimy's Auto and Truck Repair Service a 2005 Kenworth C/D Serial Number 239999L with Title Number AB1234 and paid Fifteen Thousand Two Hundred Twenty Five ($15,225.00) Dollars. The defendant further states that it lacks sufficient knowledge to admit or deny the remaining allegation of paragraph 2.

3. The defendant denies the allegations contained in paragraph 3 of the complaint.

4. The defendant denies the allegations contained in paragraph 4 of the complaint.

5. The defendant denies the allegations contained in paragraph 5 of the complaint.

6. The defendant states that it lacks sufficient knowledge to admit or deny that Plaintiff was without work for an extended period of time resulting in lost wages and profits. The defendant denies the remaining allegations contained in paragraph 6 of the complaint.

7. The defendant denies the allegations contained in paragraph 7 of the complaint.

Defendant, Grimy's Auto and Truck Repair Service, denies that plaintiff is entitled to judgment in any sum whatsoever and further prays for judgment in its favor and against the plaintiff together with the costs incurred in the defense of this suit.

Respectfully submitted,

By ————————————————
One of the Attorneys for Defendant
Grimy's Auto and Truck Service

Maggie Bourn
Coolar, Bourn, Lopez & Post
20 N. Wacker Drive, Suite 1910
Chicago, Illinois 60606-1229
(312-111-1111)
I.D. #11122

▼ What Are the Components of an Answer?

The top of the answer is the caption. It indicates the name of the court in which the case is filed, the case docket number, the name of the case, and the word "answer." Each document filed with the court should have a title, such as the word "answer," that identifies the type of pleading or motion being filed. Next comes the body of the answer. And finally, a signature line appears for the attorney. Each document filed with the court must be signed by the attorney, unless the jurisdiction in which the complaint was filed and answered permits otherwise. Paralegals should never sign the answer. Verified complaints or answers must be signed by the party involved in the lawsuit who is filing the document. Most states require that you include a statement called a certificate of service, which certifies that copies of the document have been sent to the other parties who are of record in the action, and is generally signed by an attorney and contains the date and the name of the document being sent.

▼ How Do You Draft the Body of an Answer to a Complaint?

First, ask the assigning attorney whether a sample answer is available for you to review. Check form books for the appropriate jurisdiction and review your firm's bank of pleadings, if available. Next, read the complaint. Discuss the allegations, both factual and legal, with the assigning attorney. Outlining is important here. Make a list of allegations your client knows are true, a list of the allegations that are to be denied, as well as a list of the allegations for which your client does not know enough information either to admit or to deny the statement. Next, consider any affirmative defenses (you might need to consult the assigning attorney), Finally, begin drafting your answer according to examples from your firm's files or from a form book. For each statement in the answer, you should note the corresponding paragraph in the complaint. For example, to admit an allegation, you would state, "the defendant admits the allegation contained in paragraph 3 of the complaint." This allegation would correspond to the statement in the complaint.

The denial can simply be the word "denied," although some attorneys prefer a full statement. Lawyers sometimes use the words "averment" or "avers" in the complaint or answer. To aver is to declare or allege; an averment is an allegation or declaration. These are old-fashioned terms, although some attorneys still use them.

3. Motions

▼ What Is a Motion?

A motion is a vehicle by which an attorney asks a court to act. A motion to dismiss the claim is a defense motion. The defense may assert that the complaint fails to state a cause of action and is therefore substantially insufficient in law. Another motion that the defense may make is that the complaint should be dismissed if it appears beyond a doubt that the plaintiff can prove no set of facts in support of his claim that would entitle him to relief. The language of the motion is based on the statute, either on the state or federal level, depending on the jurisdiction, and is usually derived from a form book. The motion itself should contain only a brief statement of the relief sought and a synopsis of the reasons supporting the motion. The format of the motion can be obtained from a form book. The actual motion should be written in direct, simple language. Motions are usually quickly ruled on by the judge prior to the trial and are used to narrow the number of counts in the complaint that must be decided at trial. If you move to dismiss counts four and five of a five-count complaint, and the judge rules in your favor, then you only have to deal with counts one through three at trial. Consult a text on litigation for a more detailed explanation of pre-trial procedure. For an example of a Motion to Dismiss, see Illustration 13-3.

ILLUSTRATION 13-3.   Sample Motion to Dismiss

IN THE CIRCUIT COURT OF MILL COUNTY, ILLINOIS
COUNTY DEPARTMENT, LAW DIVISION

MICHAEL JONES,	)	
	)	
Plaintiff	)	No. 95L 27901
	)	
v.	)	
	)	
GRIMY'S AUTO AND TRUCK SERVICE,	)	
INC., an Illinois Corporation	)	
	)	
Defendant	)	

MOTION TO DISMISS

The Defendant, Grimy's Auto and Truck Service, Inc., who moves to strike and dismiss the Complaint of Plaintiff, pursuant to §2-615 of the Illinois Code of Civil Procedure, 735 Ill. Comp. Stat. 5/2-615 (2012), and in support states as follows:

1. The complaint is substantially insufficient in law as to state a cause of action because plaintiff exercised ownership over the truck

ILLUSTRATION 13-3. Continued

and indicated acceptance of the vehicle by making repairs and replacing parts over a two-year period, and plaintiff failed to reject the truck in a timely manner because Grimy's was not alerted to the defects until two years after plaintiff was first aware of them.

5 September 2013

By Harry H. Harrison, Esq.

1515 Byrd Street
Mill, Illinois
(999) 888-1234
Attorney for Grimy's

▼ What Is a Memo in Support of Motions or an Advocacy Memo?

Another document that is written persuasively is the Memorandum in Support of a Motion. This is commonly called a litigation memo in support of, or against, a motion. The motion to dismiss is based on the applicable state or federal statute and the language is generally gleaned from a form book or an in-house form where the applicable information is inserted in the blanks. When a motion to dismiss is filed in response to a complaint, a memo is attached articulating the legal and factual argument, the support, as to why the judge should rule in favor of the motion. This memo is called an advocacy memo. A frequent use for this type of memo is to support or oppose a motion to dismiss for failure to state a claim, for insufficient facts, or to request a judgment on the pleadings. This technique is used to hasten the resolution of the litigation process and to narrow the issues that are involved in the case. Sometimes a judge will rule on one issue, leaving only two issues outstanding to be resolved at trial. Sometimes a judge will rule on the entire matter and dismiss all of the counts.

Memoranda are submitted to the court to support the requested relief, articulated in the motion, especially when there is a disputed issue of importance. The memorandum in support of a motion (also called an advocacy memo) should contain the complete argument. Ask the attorney assigning the project for examples of memos in support of motions that have been drafted at your office. Follow the format in the examples. See Illustration 13-4 for an example of a memorandum in support of a motion to dismiss. The components of an advocacy memo are:

1. *Introduction:* identifies the party filing the motion, states the purpose, describes the issues it addresses and states the relief requested.
2. *Statement of facts (or other basis for the argument):* what the case is about. Here you provide the necessary factual information to indicate why the motion should be granted. Carefully outline the beneficial and detrimental facts. You want to emphasize any facts that support your client's position and detract from information that can hinder your client's case. Use the active voice and short, succinct sentences to state beneficial facts, and use the passive voice in long, clause-ridden sentences to obscure detrimental information. State beneficial facts at the beginning and the end of the Facts section. Keep the facts short. Your audience is a busy, overburdened judge. Select words that are simple and express the facts succinctly. It is not necessary to go into elaborate detail.
3. *Argument:* combines facts and law to show that the motion should be granted. This section of the memo requires time devoted to the pre-writing process. You should carefully assess the purpose of the memo in support of the motion to dismiss. Basically, either you want the entire matter dismissed or you are using the memo to narrow the issues that will arise at trial. Because you can often successfully dismiss one or two counts in a five-count complaint (leaving only three or four counts to contend with at trial) examine your goals carefully. Next, assess the audience. Who is the judge? Has anyone at your firm or legal department ever appeared before him or her? Is it a municipal court, appellate court, or supreme court? Is it a state court or a federal court? How busy is the court? Is the docket overloaded? Select your language, voice, and the length of the document accordingly.

   After performing research and gathering the facts, it is time to outline. This is the most important stage of the prewriting process. Outline the assertions that you want to make, and prove with the relevant law and facts. Assertions are statements regarding the client's position that you are alleging to be true. The argument is written in ARAC format. ARAC is the acronym for Assertion, Rule, Application, and Conclusion.

   Sometimes a judge focuses most carefully on the beginning of the argument and gets distracted before finishing the memo. Therefore, list your assertions in the following order: The strongest and broadest assertion always comes first, especially if it is supported by case law from the highest court and is on point. The narrowest and weakest assertion is addressed in the middle. End with your second strongest point. Your reader's attention is strongest at the beginning and the end of each section.

   Your argument is strengthened when your memo includes at least one authority that you know your opponent will rely on. Distinguish this authority to show how it is not beneficial, and you will disarm the opponent. Usually, you do not start with or end with a case that you are distinguishing but rather include it in the middle of your argument.

4. *Conclusion:* summarizes the conclusions you reached, based on the law as applied to your facts, that you explored in greater in the body of your argument and states the relief you seek.

ILLUSTRATION 13-4. Memorandum in Support of a Motion to Dismiss

IN THE CIRCUIT COURT OF MILL COUNTY, ILLINOIS
COUNTY DEPARTMENT, LAW DIVISION

MICHAEL JONES,	)	
	)	
Plaintiff	)	No. 95L 27901
	)	
v.	)	
	)	
GRIMY'S AUTO AND TRUCK SERVICE,	)	
INC., an Illinois Corporation	)	
	)	
Defendant	)	

DEFENDANT'S MEMORANDUM IN SUPPORT OF
DEFENDANT'S MOTION TO DISMISS

STATEMENT OF FACTS

On November 29, 2011, the defendant, Grimy's Auto and Truck Service, sold a 2005 used truck to Michael Jones for the agreed purchase price of $15,225. Grimy's is in the business of buying, reconditioning, and then selling used trucks. **The purchase agreement was based on defendant's representation that the engine of the truck was completely overhauled and consisted of newly reconditioned parts; that all the parts in the rebuilt engine would be guaranteed and plaintiff would be supplied with invoices for parts purchased to overhaul the engine; that the tractor/trailer was "like brand new" and ready for road use in interstate trucking.** While in possession of the truck, the plaintiff repaired the vehicle on his own and replaced various components, altering the original motor. Furthermore, the plaintiff failed to notify the defendant of the defects until two years after they had been discovered. The plaintiff, Michael Jones, alleges that the truck was not in the agreed condition as represented by Grimy's. Jones further alleges that the heads in the truck were old and had not been reconditioned and other parts, including at least two pistons, two rods, two sleeves, and

ILLUSTRATION 13-4.   Continued

injectors were not new, were defective, and had not been reconditioned. The defendant has moved for an order dismissing the complaint pursuant to §2-615 of the Illinois Code of Civil Procedure because the plaintiff has failed to state a cause of action.

[Read the sentence, above, that is in bold type. This sentence is a good example of how long, complex sentences are used to obscure facts that are not beneficial to your client. The sentence is also written in passive voice to obscure facts.]

THE DEFENDANT'S MOTION TO DISMISS SHOULD BE GRANTED BECAUSE

PLAINTIFF WAIVED HIS CLAIM FOR BREACH OF WARRANTY OF

MERCHANTABILITY BY ACCEPTING THE TRUCK THROUGH HIS CONDUCT AND

BY FAILING TO NOTIFY DEFENDANT OF THE DEFECTS IN A TIMELY MANNER

[The caption, above, states the defendant's overall assertion. This is a terse statement of what the defendant is trying to prove. The caption also presents an opportunity for the writer to assert her point. All headings serve as opportunities to persuade the reader.]

Section 2-615 of the Illinois Code of Civil Procedure provides for dismissal of a complaint if it is insufficient in law. 735 Ill. Comp. Stat.5/2-615 (2012). Defendant's motion to dismiss, pursuant to §2-615, alleges that the complaint was insufficient in law because the plaintiff waived his claim for breach of contract.

PLAINTIFF'S CONDUCT CONSTITUTES ACCEPTANCE

[This caption is one component of the caption at the beginning of the argument, and guides the judge through the argument.]

The Uniform Commercial Code states that acceptance of goods occurs when the buyer:

1. after a reasonable opportunity to inspect the goods signifies to the seller that the goods are conforming or that he will take or retain them in spite of their non-conformity; or
2. fails to make an effective rejection, but such acceptance does not occur until the buyer has had reasonable opportunity to inspect them; or
3. does any act inconsistent with the seller's ownership; but if such act is wrongful as against the seller it is an acceptance only if ratified by him.

810 Ill. Comp. Stat. 5/2-60 (2012).
The plaintiff repaired and altered the original engine, indicating that he accepted the truck. If a buyer repairs, alters, or modifies a good he has indicated that he intends to accept the good as his own. *Brule C.*

ILLUSTRATION 13-4. Continued

E. & E., Inc. v. Pronto Foods Corp., 3 Ill. App. 3d 135, 139, 278 N.E.2d 477, 480 (1971). When a buyer rejects a good, yet continues to use it, his actions are inconsistent. The buyer's continued use amounts to a waiver of the right to reject the good and instead signifies acceptance.

This type of conduct satisfies the three elements for acceptance as set forth in the Uniform Commercial Code. *Id.* In the instant case, Jones replaced two cylinders and a broken path tube and repaired the shutdown solenoid and the rear lights. The plaintiff has significantly altered the original engine that Grimy's installed in the truck. The plaintiff's act of rejecting the truck after making repeated repairs and changing the original motor is inconsistent. Since Jones altered the truck engine and continued to use the vehicle, he waived his right to reject the truck and instead indicated, by his behavior, his acceptance.

Jones exercised ownership over the truck by making repairs. When a buyer acts in a way in which he would have no right to act unless he was the owner, he has accepted the goods. *Pirie v. Carroll*, 28 Ill. App. 2d 181, 185, 171 N.E.2d 99, 102 (1960). By repairing the engine himself and replacing some of the parts without alerting Grimy's as to the defects, Jones exercised ownership over the truck.

PLAINTIFF FAILED TO GIVE NOTICE OF DEFECT WITHIN A REASONABLE TIME

The plaintiff did not put Grimy's on notice as to the truck's defects until two years after the first mechanical problem was discovered. "A buyer must notify a seller of defects within a reasonable time thereof notwithstanding acceptance." *Stamm v. Wilder Travel Travelers*, 44 Ill. App. 3d 530, 535, 358 N.E.2d 382, 385 (1976). Furthermore, if a buyer fails to reject a good within a reasonable time, acceptance takes place. *Vitromar Piece Dye Works v. Lawrence of London*, 119 Ill. App. 2d 301, 306, 256 N.E.2d 135, 137 (1969). Here, the plaintiff made various repairs and replaced components over a two-year period. The truck was purchased in November 2011 and repairs were made between December 2012 and March 2013. The plaintiff failed to notify Grimy's of any defects until two years after the purchase date. Since plaintiff did not notify Grimy's of defects within a reasonable time he accepted the truck.

PLAINTIFF WAIVED HIS CLAIM FOR BREACH OF WARRANTY OF MERCHANTABILITY

Plaintiff waived his claim for breach of contract because his conduct was inconsistent with his intent to enforce that claim. An individual may waive a known existing right "either expressly or by conduct inconsistent with an intent to enforce that right." *Whalen v. K-Mart Corp.*, 166 Ill. App. 3d 339, 342, 519 N.E.2d 991, 994 (1988). An individual may not seek judicial enforcement after a known right has been relinquished. *Id.* Jones accepted the truck through his actions. Replacing parts on his own and altering the original motor are acts inconsistent with his intent to reject

ILLUSTRATION 13-4.   Continued

the truck. Since Jones's conduct is inconsistent with his intention to reject the truck, he has waived his right to claim a breach of contract.

CONCLUSION

For these reasons, the defendant respectfully requests that this court issue an order dismissing this complaint for failure to state a cause of action.

Respectfully submitted,

_____

Harry H. Harrison, Esq.
Attorney for the Defendant

▼ How Do You Organize an Argument?

1. Rely on the prewriting skills addressed in Chapter 3, Getting Ready to Write. Discern the purpose and audience.
2. Talk with the supervising attorney to determine the client's allegations or assertions. What is the client's assessment of the facts? The attorney assigning the project will provide guidance for the client's legal argument. You should ask the attorney about the arguments that he or she will make on the client's behalf. Once you establish the client's stance (an example of this is the large heading at the beginning of the argument in the memo in support of the motion of dismiss), break this down into components, or elements. The elements are illustrated in the captions in the preceding memo illustration.
3. Research to find relevant and timely legal support for all your assertions. Remember that the most recent cases from the highest court in the appropriate jurisdiction are at the top of the hierarchy of authority. Also, when you find cases that support the opposing party's argument, think of ways to minimize them and distinguish them. You can say that the case that may be contrary to your argument can only be applied in a very limited way or only under a limited set of facts. This will help refute your opponent's legal support.
4. Outline. Use the ARAC format to apply the law to the facts and draw a conclusion that supports the assertion made.

An outline of the persuasive argument used in the memo in support of the motion to dismiss follows:

Heading: Plaintiff waived his claim for breach of contract by accepting the truck through his conduct and by failing to notify defendants of defects in a timely manner.

Assertion 1—Jones's actions of repairing the truck's engine demonstrated his acceptance of the vehicle.

Rule or Rules of law.

Application: This demonstrates why the rule or rules of law support your assertion in the instant case. Discuss all repairs made with specificity. Use the facts of the cited case and the facts of your client's situation to show parallels before drawing your conclusion.

Conclusion: A succinct restatement of your assertion. Always conclude what you assert.

Assertion 2—Jones indicated his acceptance by acting in a manner that was inconsistent with Grimy's ownership of the truck.

Rule or Rules of law.

Application: Discuss all engine and vehicle parts replaced by Jones.

Conclusion: Restate the assertion with some additional information to show why you are concluding in this manner.

Assertion 3—Jones failed to give proper notice as to the truck's defects within a reasonable time.

Rule or Rules of law as to what is a reasonable period of time.

Application: Discuss the actions Jones took, and the dates on which they occurred, and when he actually alerted Grimy's as to the truck's defects. Do not draw conclusions but let the facts illustrate the untimely notice. This is the factual foundation where you state the legally significant facts.

Conclusion: Conclude what you asserted but with more precision. Your conclusion that the notice was not timely will flow logically because your application laid the factual foundation.

Assertion 4—Failure to give timely notice caused Jones to waive his claim for breach of contract.

Rule or Rules of law: Cases and/or statutes supporting your assertion.

Application: Lay the factual foundation indicating the length of time between knowledge of the first flaw or defect and when notice to Grimy's was actually given.

Conclusion: Conclude what you assert but with more precision.

Outlining carefully in the prewriting stage is an efficient allocation of your time. Writing is much easier once you have carefully outlined the argument. Preparing an after-the-fact outline, that is, outlining an argument that you already wrote, is a good way to revise and to check organization.

4. Trial Briefs

▼ What Is a Trial Brief?

This term is used in two ways. Attorneys file trial briefs to support motions that ask the court to take a particular action. These are essentially memoranda in support of motions. Often, however, attorneys want to explain the reasons why a court should take the requested action. In such cases, attorneys file trial briefs that provide an argument as to why the judge should grant the request. A trial brief is also a document that is provided to a court just before trial. Some briefs are filed with the court. Others are used merely for an attorney's trial preparation, helping attorneys to refine their arguments. These briefs may include witness lists, motions to limit evidence (called motion in limine), and stipulations (that is, evidence attorneys are willing to accept as true without proof).

▼ How Do You Draft a Trial Brief or Memorandum in Support of a Motion?

First, research the legal issues. After you have your authorities and the facts of your case, you are ready to outline your brief. Ask the supervising attorney for the legal arguments that she plans to address. Prepare a list of the relevant facts. Decide upon an order for your legal arguments. Next, draft the brief or memorandum.

When you begin drafting your briefs, concisely state the purpose of the brief or memorandum and the motion it supports. Next, explain the relevant facts. Summarize the legal arguments that support your request for action. Explain each argument in detail. Be sure to apply the supporting legal authorities to the facts of your case. Next, summarize your arguments. And finally, repeat your request for relief.

The procedure for drafting a trial brief that is filed just before trial will vary by local court rule.

5. Summary Judgment Motions

▼ What Is a Summary Judgment Motion?

A summary judgment motion asks a trial court to rule in favor of party without a trial. Such a motion is made when the facts are not disputed and the only issue to be decided is a question of law. Summary judgment is often used to eliminate one or more claims so that the trial will focus on fewer issues. State and federal courts provide for summary judgment motions. However, some states may combine the motion to dismiss with the summary judgment motion calling it a summary disposition motion.

ETHICS ALERT

The decision about which motion to file is a legal decision to be made only by a licensed attorney.

▼ What Should Be Included in a Motion for Summary Judgment and How Do You Draft One?

A motion for summary judgment should include a brief statement of the purpose of the motion. Next, state the relevant facts. Provide any supporting evidence that is not controverted. For example, if your firm represents the defendant and the plaintiff makes a statement in a deposition that is favorable to your case and there is no evidence to counter that statement, it is uncontroverted. Deposition pages, and often the entire deposition, should be included with the motion, and the deposition pages should be cited in the motion. Check your local court rules to determine if you are permitted to use pages rather than the entire document. Other evidence such as affidavits often are filed with motions for summary judgment. Once you have stated the facts and told the court that the facts are not disputed, you should begin to explain why the motion should be granted. Explain the legal issues and provide legal authorities that support your argument. Finally, repeat your request that the court grant your motion for summary judgment.

PRACTICE POINTER

Always check your firm's memo and brief file for examples and research.

---

6. Appellate Briefs

Briefs, for trial court and appellate court, are other vehicles for persuasive writing. Appellate court briefs follow detailed local court rules as to format, structure, and copies required by the particular court. Please check the rules of the particular appellate court where you are filing the brief to find out the requirements. The rules are in the particular jurisdiction's code as well as in many lawyers' desk books.

The parts of the sample brief, shown in Illustration 13-5, are labeled for your reference. Appellate briefs are very specialized documents written to appeal an error of law made by the trial court. Judges and counsel read these briefs. Many of the same persuasive writing techniques used in drafting memos in support of motions to dismiss are used in drafting appellate briefs. Both documents are persuasive in nature and are formal documents designed to sway a court to rule in your party's favor. Again, the determination to file an appellate brief is a legal decision to be made only by a licensed attorney because the attorney must decide if an error was made at the trial level. Appellate practice is a very specialized area that few attorneys engage in.

ILLUSTRATION 13-5. Sample Appellate Brief

No. 88 L 2377

IN THE APPELLATE COURT OF ILLINOIS
FIRST JUDICIAL DISTRICT

	)
Michael Martin	)
	)
	) On Appeal from the Circuit
	) Court of Cook County,
	) Illinois County Department,
	) Law Division
v.	)
	)
	) Honorable Sam Smith,
Drake Industries	) Judge Presiding

> This is the cover sheet, which has the docket number, the parties the court hearing the appeal, request for oral argument, and counsel's name.

Brief of Appellant

John Johnson, Esq.
12 South Erie
Chicago, Illinois 60000
Attorney for Appellant

Oral Argument Requested

POINTS AND AUTHORITIES*

> *This is a table of contents listing the captions and headings as well as the cases, statutes, and other authorities falling under the headings, Paralegals often work on this section.

ILLUSTRATION 13-5. Continued

No. 88 L 2377

> This repeats the information on the cover sheet.

IN THE APPELLATE COURT OF ILLINOIS
FIRST JUDICIAL DISTRICT

Michael Martin	)	
	)	
	)	On Appeal from the Circuit
	)	Court of Cook County,
	)	Illinois County Department,
	)	Law Division
v.	)	
	)	
	)	Honorable Sam Smith,
Drake Industries	)	Judge Presiding

Brief of Appellant

INTRODUCTION

> This is an appeal from an order deciding that Drake Industries had a month-to-month tenancy.

ISSUE PRESENTED FOR REVIEW

> This is the question before the court.

Whether by following all the terms of the unsigned lease, did the tenant create a valid lease that upon expiration makes a tenant a holdover tenant or a tenant at sufferance.

ILLUSTRATION 13-5.   **Continued**

STATEMENT OF FACT

> **These are the facts, written from the appellant's perspective.**

Michael Martin appeals from the Circuit Court of Cook County's holding that Drake Industries had a tenancy from month to month. The holding requires that Michael Martin give thirty days' notice to Drake Industries to vacate the premises. Michael Martin appeals from that order.

Michael Martin is the owner of record of the real property and structure located at 2700 North Bosworth, Chicago, Cook County, Illinois. Drake Industries, an Illinois corporation, entered into a lease for Martin's property on January 1, 1993. Terms of the lease called for seven hundred dollars ($700) per month rent until expiration of the lease on December 31, 2004.

In November of 2004, Martin gave a new lease to Drake Industries to be signed and returned by December 31, 2004. The lease specified new terms calling for an increase in the rent to eight hundred and fifty dollars ($850) per month, to be paid on the first day of every month. The lease term was from January 1, 2005, through June 30, 2012. The lease was unsigned and was never returned to Martin. Drake Industries, however, continued its tenancy without interruption, and followed the terms of the new lease, by paying the increased rent on the first day of each month, including July 1, 2012.

Martin made a written demand of the tenant to deliver up and surrender possession of the premises on July 15, 2012. Martin filed an action for forcible entry and detainer against Drake Industries on August 16, 2012, based on their refusal to leave the premises. Martin contended that Drake Industries entered into a valid oral lease that expired on June 30, 2012, and that Drake Industries is now a holdover tenant and a tenant at sufferance.

The trial was held on September 1, 2012, with Drake Industries still in possession of the premises. The trial court determined that a month-to-month tenancy existed between the parties. Martin now appeals from that order.

ARGUMENT

> **This is the persuasive discussion, or argument. It is written in ARAC format. The heading and captions guide.**

DRAKE INDUSTRIES IS BOUND BY THE LEASE BECAUSE DRAKE ACCEPTED THE LEASE. DRAKE INDUSTRIES IS A WILLFUL HOLDOVER TENANT AND A TENANT AT SUFFERANCE.

ILLUSTRATION 13-5.   Continued

This court should reverse the trial court's decision finding that Drake Industries has a month-to-month tenancy. Drake Industries demonstrated acceptance of the unsigned lease and willfully held over after the lease term expired.

A. Drake Industries Demonstrated Acceptance of the Lease Making It Valid and Binding, Even Though Lease Was Never Signed

Drake Industries accepted the lease and all its terms. A tenant is bound by the terms of a lease, whether or not the lease is signed, if the tenant accepted the lease. *McFarlane v. Williams*, 107 Ill. 33, 43 (1883); *Housing Authority of the County of Franklin v. Moore*, 5 Ill. App. 3d 883, 890, 284 N.E.2d 456 (1972). A tenant's occupancy and use of the premises demonstrated an acceptance of the terms of the lease, whether or not the lease was signed. *Cuthbert v. Stemin*, 78 Ill. App. 3d 562, 570, 396 N.E.2d 1197, 1203 (1979); *Housing Authority*, 5 Ill. App. 3d at 890, 284 N.E.2d at 461; *Baragiano v. Villani*, 117 Ill. App. 372, 375 (1904). "By accepting the lease and thus acting upon it, it became valid and binding, and the lessor and lessee were bound by its covenants, although it was not signed by lessee." *Henderson v. Virden Coal Co.*, 78 Ill. App. 437, 442 (1897).

Herein, defendant demonstrated acceptance of the lease by the actions taken, even though the lease was never signed. The lease was tendered to defendant on November 25, 2004, specifying that the term would begin on January 1, 2005, and terminate on June 30, 2012. The lease also specified a rent of $850 per month to be paid on the first day of every month. The lease was never returned to Martin with a signature upon it, but defendant continued occupancy of the premises and complied with the terms of the lease by paying $850 rent on the first day of every month. By following the terms of the lease along with the continued occupancy and use of the premises defendant accepted the lease and all its terms, making a signature unnecessary.

Defendant also acted upon the lease by paying the rent on the first day of each month. Since defendant accepted and acted upon the lease, the lease became valid and binding and defendant was bound by all the covenants within the lease, even though defendant never signed the lease.

B. No Notice Was Necessary to Demand Possession of the Property from Defendant

No notice to quit or a demand of possession is necessary when the lease term has expired. Martin was not required to give notice and defendants had a duty to surrender possession of the property. When a tenancy is for a certain term, and the term has expired, the tenant is then bound to surrender possession and no notice to quit is necessary. 735 ILCS §5/9-213 (2012). It is the tenant's duty to

ILLUSTRATION 13-5.   Continued

surrender possession upon expiration of the lease. *Poppers v. Meager*, 148 Ill. 192, 202, 35 N.E. 805, 808 (1894).

Since the defendant accepted the lease and the lease was valid, no notice to quit or demand of possession was necessary upon expiration of the lease. Defendant had a duty to surrender possession of the premises to Martin on June 30, 2012, so no notice was necessary.

C. Defendant, by Willfully Remaining in Possession of the Property after Expiration of the Lease, Became a Tenant at Sufferance

Defendant became a tenant at sufferance after remaining in possession of the premises after the lease term expired. Defendant's possession can be terminated whenever Martin wished. "A tenant who remains in possession after his lease expires becomes a tenant at sufferance whose possession can be put to an end whenever the landlord wishes." *General Parking Corp. v. Kimmel*, 79 Ill. App. 3d 883, 886, 398 N.E.2d 1104, 1107 (1979). The lease expired on June 30, 2012, and defendant refused to give up possession of the property when Martin demanded possession on July 15, 2012. The tenant, defendant, became a tenant at sufferance at the expiration of the lease; the defendant's possession can be ended at any time the landlord, Martin, desires.

D. By Holding over Possession of the Property, Defendant Could Be Treated as a Holdover Tenant or as a Trespasser

Defendant, by not surrendering possession of the premises and by willfully holding over, after the expiration of the lease, could be treated as either a holdover tenant or as a trespasser. Martin, as the landlord, can elect to treat defendant as either a holdover tenant or as a trespasser. If a tenant holds over after the expiration of the lease, the landlord can exercise his exclusive right to treat the tenant as a trespasser or permit the original terms of the lease to still be in effect. *Sheraton v. Lewis*, 8 Ill. App. 3d 309, 310 290 N.E.2d 685, 686 (1972). Herein, defendant held over possession of the premises by remaining in possession after July 31, 2012, even though the lease expired on June 30, 2012. Martin, as landlord, had the option to treat the defendant either as a holdover tenant under the same terms of the previous lease or as a trespasser. Martin elected to treat defendant as a trespasser so defendant is required to relinquish possession of the premises.

CONCLUSION

For these reasons, Michael Martin respectfully requests that this court reverse the trial court's order that the defendant had a tenancy from month to month.

ILLUSTRATION 13-5. Continued

Respectfully submitted,

James Michaels
Attorney for Michael Martin

James Michaels, Esq.
330 Jamestown Avenue
Chicago, Illinois 60001

▼ Are There Any General Tips for Writing an Appellate Brief?

1. Draft the facts using the active voice for beneficial facts, and the passive voice for harmful facts. You have an ethical duty to disclose all facts, but you can present the facts in the best light for your client. Rely on short, succinct sentences for emphasis, and long, convoluted sentences to obscure information.

2. Start with the broadest and strongest assertion.

3. Use your strongest case or statute first. Rely on the hierarchy of authority to determine the strength of the source. The newest case from the highest court in the appropriate jurisdiction is stronger than an older case from a lower court. Ask the supervising attorney for guidance here.

4. Rely on the ARAC format when crafting the argument. ARAC stands for Assertion, Rule, Application, Conclusion.

5. Always revise your writing. Do an after-the-fact outline to determine if the organization, logic, and flow of the argument is effective. Remember that your reader is a very busy judge so you want your writing to be clear and easy to follow.

6. Check the local court rules for the form of the appellate brief for the particular court where you intend to file.

7. Ask to see samples of briefs drafted by members of your firm or legal department.

8. Before filing the brief, always update the validity of your authority by Shepardizing, either in print or on Lexis, or by using Westlaw's KeyCite.

NET NOTE

The Web site http://www.tsulaw.edu/centers/faculty/tip/tipno20.pdf has tips for appellate writing.

---

7. Other Forms of Persuasive Writing

▼ Are There Any Instances When Persuasive Writing
Is Used in a Transaction?

Contracts and leases that favor one side are persuasive documents. Letters articulating a client's position are persuasive documents. This is particularly the case with demand letters. Default notices and eviction notices are also persuasive documents.

Illustration 13-6 is an example of persuasive writing, in letter format, stating a client's demands. This type of letter, because it may change a party's legal position and makes legal representations, must be signed by an attorney but often paralegals participate in the drafting process.

ILLUSTRATION 13-6. Sample of Persuasive Writing, Letter Format

---

1 DuPage National Center
New York, NY 10010

December 19, 2012

Mr. Hal Smith
Cloth & Cloth
33 City Center
New York, New York 10021

Re: Bobbin & Thread Company
     Request for Contract Termination and final payment

Dear Mr. Smith:

We represent Bobbin & Thread Co. Our client has referred to us the now terminated contract between Cloth & Cloth and Bobbin & Thread Company for the supply of 3000 cones of thread per month. We demand that the contract be terminated immediately due to the failure of Cloth & Cloth to pay the invoices for August 2012, September 2012, October 2012, and November 2012.

Cloth & Cloth is obligated to Bobbin & Thread for the amount of $1500 per month for the 3000 cones of thread shipped to Cloth & Cloth's New York factory.

We demand that Cloth & Cloth pay Bobbin & Thread $6000 immediately for the past due invoices. Additionally, the contract is now terminated due to the failure of Cloth & Cloth to pay for the thread in a timely manner.

ILLUSTRATION 13-6.   Continued

I would be happy to discuss this matter with you at your convenience.

Very truly yours,

_____

Farrell Henry, Esq.

CHAPTER SUMMARY

In this chapter you learned about the nature of persuasive writing and its role in litigation and in transactions. The ARAC formula for drafting a persuasive document was explored and examples of persuasive documents were included. Your goal in using persuasive writing is to make a clear, direct assertion and to support this assertion with the relevant authority (cases, statutes, and constitutional provisions if applicable) and the client's facts so that the reader will adopt your conclusion. Paralegals are becoming more and more involved in writing persuasive documents. Consider this chapter a starting point for developing persuasive writing techniques that will become refined with experience.

KEY TERMS

answer	litigation memo
appellate brief	motion to dismiss
ARAC	persuasive writing
argument	summary judgment
brief	trial brief
complaint	

EXERCISES

1. Take the discussion portion of an objective memo and reformulate it into persuasive format. Take a position and rewrite the issues and make them assertions.
2. Use the persuasive material that you created in the first exercise, and extract the points and authorities from the document that you drafted. Write the headings and captions to indicate the assertions that you are making, and organize the headings, captions, and authorities into a table of points and authorities like the table included in our appellate brief sample.

3. Draft a letter that articulates a position so that it has a persuasive tone. The following fact pattern will guide you through the process.

> Dr. Jones owns an orthopedic clinic. Ms. Smith received treatment from the clinic following a car accident. Ms. Smith was diagnosed as having whiplash. Ms. Smith has not paid for services she received that were rendered by the clinic. Dr. Jones sent three bills requesting payment. Ms. Smith's response to the final bill is that she should not pay because the accident was not her fault and Mr. Driver should pay because he was at fault. At this point, Dr. Jones retained your firm to help collect the amount owed. Ms. Partner assigned the project of drafting the letter requesting payment from Ms. Smith to you.

4. Find a form for a complaint in your jurisdiction.
5. Where do you find the rules for filing an appellate brief for your jurisdiction?

CHAPTER 14

IN-HOUSE AND OBJECTIVE CLIENT DOCUMENTS

CHAPTER OVERVIEW

You learned about an objective memorandum in the previous chapters. This chapter discusses other objective documents you may write as paralegals. Paralegals often are asked to write objective summaries of client interviews, meetings, a case's progress, or a deposition. The format for each document will vary. Every attorney and firm has a style it prefers for each document. This chapter provides some examples of such documents and a few tips for drafting them. Each document should be outlined, drafted, and rewritten before it is submitted to an attorney or placed in a file.

A. CLIENT OR WITNESS INTERVIEW SUMMARY

▼ What Is a Client or Witness Interview Summary?

A client or **witness summary** is a written record of an interview you conduct with a client or witness. It also might be a summary of an interview an attorney conducts and you attend. It should contain client or witness statements, information about documents an individual brought to the interview, or information about any other tangible evidence that may be relevant to a legal claim, such as photographs, written contracts, receipts, and the like that you learn about during the interview. Your impressions of the client or witness should be noted in a separate document to avoid potential disclosure during the discovery process. A witness statement might be discoverable, but your impressions are likely to be protected from disclosure by the **attorney-client privilege.**

The summary of the client or witness statements, documents, or evidence should be objective; your impressions could be subjective.

▼ What Questions Should You Ask Yourself Before
You Begin to Write?

Before you begin to write your statement, ask yourself: Who, What, Where, When, and Why (the five journalistic "W"s).

1. Client's Statements

For the client statement, consider the following questions:

- Who does the legal question involve?
- What are the circumstances?
- What happened?
- Who witnessed or participated in what happened?
- What is the essence of the legal problem?
- What does the client hope to get as a result of speaking with the lawyer or paralegal?
- Where did the problem arise? (Be specific. Note the state, the county, and the municipality, if any. Note any location, such as a home, a store, or the like.)
- When did the problem arise?
- Is the problem a continuing issue?
- Why is the client seeking legal advice?

If you are summarizing a discussion with an established client, these questions may vary. But this list will provide you with a starting point to guide you in your interview and your summary of any interviews with a client.

Note the client's statements in the summary. If the statements are important, use direct quotations. Quotations will provide an attorney with better sense of the client's statements. However, only use direct quotations that add value to the summary. If a client's quotations are not easily understood, it is better to paraphrase the statements.

2. Witness Statements

For witness statements, consider the following questions and comments:

- What is the witness's name, address, phone number, date of birth, social security number, and employment record? What was the witness's address and place of employment at the time of the event witnessed?
- What does the witness know about the incident? What did the witness see? Try to picture the event. If you cannot clearly see what happened during the event, ask the witness to explain it. What did the witness hear? If relevant, what did the witness smell if anything? What other observations did he or she make?
- Ask the witness to describe any documents or evidence such as photographs, clothing, or products in detail. Ask where each item is located and its condition and note that in the statement.
- Finally, provide your impressions of the client or the witness. Does the individual speak clearly? Is the person articulate? Does the person present himself or herself well? Is the individual well dressed and well kept? What is the person's demeanor? Note these comments in a separate document so that they can be protected by attorney-client privilege and cannot be obtained in the discovery process.

▼ How Do You Draft a Client or Witness Summary?

Next, you will draft the statement and file it or provide a copy to the assigning attorney. To draft the statement, first make a list of the relevant facts. Next, outline the statement. Often these statements flow best when they are written in chronological order. However, some claims may be presented in topical order. A chronological organization is based upon the order of events. Start with the first event and end with the last. Another method is to write the statement in reverse chronological order, beginning with the last event and ending with the first. For statements related to an accident, a contract dispute, or a criminal case, chronological organization works well. Write the statement clearly and concisely. Only list relevant facts that the witness observed. Use the witness's words and tone. Only use direct quotations if they are clear and succinct.

Illustration 14-1 is a brief statement of a phone conversation.

ILLUSTRATION 14-1.   Summary of a Phone Conversation

SUMMARY OF A PHONE CONVERSATION WITH WITNESS KAREN BURNS, ON MARCH 30, 2012, CONCERNING HER INTERACTIONS WITH PLAINTIFF'S ATTORNEY

Michael Porer, the Plaintiff's attorney in Cartoon v. Welcome Matt International 12CIV88 sent Karen Burns his transcription of a conversation between Porer and Burns at her home on February 14, 2012. In addition, Porer sent Burns an affidavit.. Burns told Porer that she would not sign the affidavit for several reasons. She said the transcription was inaccurate and contained many grammatical errors. She also is upset with Porer because he misled her as to his relationship with Drew Cartoon. Porer threatened Burns. He told her that she perjured herself. He also said that she would be subpoenaed for a deposition. He told her that she had been influenced by Welcome Matt's lawyers and they had told her what to say. Burns said Porer was very irritated that Ms. Burns would not sign the affidavit.

The summary is concise. It communicates the problems the witness had with the opposing attorney and a statement she made to that attorney. This statement simply conveys the witness statements to the attorney.

Below is an example of a witness interview. Headings are used to guide the reader in this example contained in Illustration 14-2.

ILLUSTRATION 14-2.   Summary of Witness Interview

MEMORANDUM

To: The File
From: Cara Marcus
Date: March 28, 2012
Re: Summary of Interview with Witness Wanda Weber, on March 28, 2012, in the matter of Cartoon v. Welcome Matt International

BACKGROUND

Wanda Weber, 1001 Arlington Road, Wilmot, IL, is a newspaper reporter for the *Arlington Herald*. She has held that position for five years. On December 20, 2011, she was a patron at the Welcome Matts Hotel in Cancun, Mexico.

DESCRIPTION OF THE ACCIDENT

On December 20, 2011, at about 10 A.M., Weber saw Drew Cartoon, an old man, reading the newspaper and drinking a cup of coffee as he walked toward the pool area. Cartoon was looking at the newspaper rather than where he was walking. He then slipped on the marble floor next to the pool. Weber saw Cartoon hit his head on the floor. Then she saw that Cartoon's head was bleeding. He was conscious after he hit his head and he called for help. The hotel staff held fresh-looking napkins

ILLUSTRATION 14-2. Continued

from the serving carts against Cartoon's head. The staff called paramedics. The paramedics arrived and took Cartoon away while he was still conscious.

DESCRIPTION OF THE POOL AREA

Signs were posted at various locations near the pool asking patrons to walk carefully because the floor was wet. The signs also asked patrons to use the long mat placed between the coffee shop and the pool. The mat, the signs said, was to ensure the patrons' safe passage from the shop to the pool. The signs were written both in English and in Spanish. Cartoon did not use the mat. Instead, he crossed from the coffee shop to the pool on a diagonal and traveled on the wet marble floor.

OTHER WARNINGS

When Weber checked in, the hotel staff member told her to walk carefully near the pool and to use the matted walkway rather than walk on the marble floor as it is often wet. Weber heard the staff tell this warning to other individuals in the check-in area.

CAM:jc

B. MEETING SUMMARIES

As paralegals, you will attend many meetings. If you work in the litigation arena, some meetings may include only the defense attorneys, the clients, and you. Other meetings will include co-counsel. If you work in other practice areas, you may attend a client board meeting. An attorney may ask you to take notes during the meeting and then draft an objective summary of the meeting.

▼ What Should Be Included in a Meeting Summary?

A meeting summary should explain the primary purpose of the meeting, any issues discussed, and any matters that were mentioned but that will be explored fully at a later date. The summary should note the meeting participants, the venue (if it is significant), and who did not attend. You should include the date of the meeting and the date of any future meetings that were set. If your client or your opponent's client said anything that was extremely important, you might want to quote directly what was said.

▼ How Do You Draft a Meeting Summary?

First, take copious notes during the meeting. Note each topic discussed as well as who supported and who rejected an issue discussed. Write quotations for any statement you think might be significant to your case or transaction. Second, review your notes. Third, draft an outline of your summary. List the important topics to be included. Next to the topics include any important statements and note the individuals who supported or rejected those topics. Fourth, draft the summary in sentence format from your detailed outline. Finally, review your summary. Edit it and rewrite it.

Summary Drafting Checklist

1. Take notes.
2. Review your notes.
3. Write a detailed outline.
4. Draft your summary.
5. Review and revise your summary.

Assume that an attorney asked you to attend an Illinois Department of Transportation hearing concerning the widening of an Illinois road. The firm's clients are considering litigation to block the road widening. Illustration 14-3 is an example of such a meeting summary.

ILLUSTRATION 14-3.   Meeting Summary

MEMORANDUM

To: Barry Michaels
From: Cara Marcus
Date: January 21, 2012
Re: Meeting Concerning the Widening of Willow Road, January 20, 2012

This meeting was one of two informational sessions the Illinois Department of Transportation (IDOT) recently held to solicit comments concerning the $55 million project to widen Willow Road between Milwaukee Avenue and the Edens Expressway and to explain the project to the community.

IDOT will review the comments and compile a list by the fall of 2012. Following that, public hearings will be held in the fall or winter of next year. A final decision concerning the project is scheduled for spring of 2013. The department will spend two years developing the final plans and acquiring property. The construction would begin in 2016.

IDOT representatives said that the proposed plan calls for the widening of Willow Road between Milwaukee Avenue and the Eden's

ILLUSTRATION 14-3. **Continued**

Expressway. One through lane is slated to be added to each side of the street. In addition, left and right turn lanes and median strips will be built. At Pfingsten and Willow Roads, the proposal suggests that right turn lanes be added at all four corners of Willow Road.

No changes in the turn lanes are expected at Greenwood and Willow Roads. Only additional lanes will be added.

Left turn lanes are proposed for Shermer Avenue on both sides of Willow Road. No change will be made to Willow Road at Shermer.

In Northfield, Willow Road may be widened to five lanes. Overpasses or pedestrian-controlled stop lights may be installed to accommodate the children who cross Willow on their way to school.

The project plans include a median strip the entire length of Willow Road. Villages will be asked where openings should be placed. This median will limit the left turn access into the shopping areas and some streets.

The speed limit is expected to remain the same. However, the speed limit along Willow Road near Sanders may be decreased.

To date, $16 million has been approved, but not appropriated by the state legislature. As soon as a final project plan is devised, the $16 million will be appropriated. The legislature then will determine whether to allocate the remaining money needed for the project.

Planners say that the widening of Willow Road is necessary to accommodate the tremendous increase in traffic. When IDOT studied the traffic in 2011, it projected a 15 to 20 percent increase in traffic by the year 2018. Recent IDOT studies show that that figure has been exceeded and planners expect traffic to increase by another 15 to 20 percent.

The first paragraph describes the purpose of the meeting and when it was held. The next paragraph explains the status of the project. The remaining paragraphs provide details concerning the plans that were disclosed during the meeting.

C. STATUS MEMOS

▼ What Is a Status Memo, and Who Reads It?

A **status memo** is a summary of the progress of a case or transaction. See Illustration 14-4. This document is placed in a file, sent to attorneys or other legal team members, or sent to a client. Some clients require status memos. A status memo is especially useful to an attorney or paralegal who may be added to a transaction or case team after a case has started. Such a memo will provide them with information about the background of a case and a history of the action that already has occurred or is about to occur.

▼ How Often Should a Status Memo Be Prepared?

It will vary. Some clients require a status memo each time you appear in court or at a deposition. Some clients require such memos monthly. Attorneys also have varied expectations. Always ask the assigning attorney how often to post such a memo for attorney and client review. You, however, should make a notation in your file each time you work on a case. Such a status memo can be short and simple, such as "Drafted interrogatories to be served on the defendant." If, however, you meet with a client or attend a hearing or deposition, your summary should be more detailed.

▼ What Should the Detailed Summary Include?

The items included will vary depending upon the timing of your draft. For example, your first draft should note what happened and who was involved in the client's matter. Include where and when the case or transaction arose and why your firm is handling it.

ILLUSTRATION 14-4. Example of a Status Memo for the File

MEMORANDUM

To: File
From: Randall Arthur
Date: November 7, 2011
Re: Status of the Case

BACKGROUND
    This is an action for breach of contract and quantum meruit. At one point, the plaintiff, Nut Services, Inc., sought to collect damages for promissory estoppel. After the defendant's two successful motions to dismiss, plaintiff decided not to refile that claim.

RELATIONSHIP OF THE PARTIES
    The action stems from a series of informal transactions between Rock Tube and Conduit Corporation and Nut Services, Inc., in 2011. At one time, Nut Services acted as an "outside cutter" for Rock Tube and Conduit. At some point, Rock personnel gave cutting business to other cutting houses and to its own in-house operation. Nut had relied solely on the business from Rock. Without that business, Nut went out of business on April 1, 2011.
    When Ken Kiser, the president and owner of Nut, decided to go out of business, he offered to sell Rock some of his operation's equipment and tools. For several reasons, Rock agreed to some trades.

TED SIMONS'S RECOLLECTION OF THE TRADES
    Ted Simons, a former Rock employee, who now works in Rockville, MD, made the deals with Nut's Kiser. Simons stated that Rock wanted the used equipment because it could get it without any lead time. Also,

ILLUSTRATION 14-4. Continued

most of the equipment was in good shape. Finally, the agreement called for Rock to give Kiser material instead of cash. That material cost Rock much less than the cash value. Simon said the material was useless to Rock.

Complaint Count I

Rock offered and paid $20,000 in cash and $15,000 in materials for the saw and all accessories. The requisition for the check asked for $35,000. Kiser signed the purchase order saying $20,000 cash paid, $15,000 in materials owing.

Complaint Count II

Mort Williams, a Rock worker, received many of these agreed upon items. The plaintiff took his deposition on July 26, 2011. A summary is in the file as is the abstract and a copy of the transcript. Rock received a forklift, four saws, screw drivers, a cart, a drill, and a press.

Rock agreed to trade $10,000 in cash plus steel worth $18,000 to the plaintiff for this equipment. The steel was useless to Rock, but Kiser had a buyer for it. Eventually Rock paid $12,000 because Kiser would not accept the tender of materials. Both Mark Carter and Sidney White say that the materials were tendered. The $12,000 was to settle the equipment purchase.

Complaint Count III

Simons says he never agreed to purchase these items separate from the other equipment. He says that they were part of the earlier materials trade. There is some duplication of items between the lists attached to the complaint.

IMPRESSIONS OF SIMONS

I think that he is telling the truth. He has no reason to lie. He does not want to hurt Kiser because of his long-standing relationship with Kiser.

PLEADINGS

Plaintiff recently filed a third amended complaint. We have filed an answer. To date, we have filed motions to dismiss the previous complaints. The judge dismissed Count II earlier because plaintiff had not sufficiently pled delivery, but he incorporated the deposition into his pleadings this past round and we decided to answer the complaint.

DISCOVERY

Based upon conversations with Mark Carter, Sidney White, and Simons, I prepared the discovery answers. After attorney Cara Marcus reviewed them, they were sent to the client for review and signature. They should be filed soon. I have also prepared our discovery. Cara Marcus has that for review.

The plaintiff has taken one deposition. Discovery will close in January.

ILLUSTRATION 14-4.   Continued

SETTLEMENT
   Ms. Marcus has tried to settle this case several times. First, she offered $10,000 to the plaintiff on behalf of our clients before the lawsuit was filed. Plaintiff formally demanded $30,000. She next offered $7,000. She later increased the offer to $9,000. Plaintiff then wanted $20,000. Ms. Marcus has settlement authority for $20,000, but the client wants the settlement to be closer to $10,000. The attorneys met with the judge though plaintiff's counsel would not settle. However, the judge indicated that trial could be up to two years away. Ms. Marcus recommended that settlement negotiations be stalled because a delay will force the plaintiff to settle.

D. DEPOSITION SUMMARIES

▼ What Is a Deposition Summary?

A deposition summary is a variation of a meeting summary. See Illustration 14-5. It explains what happened during a specialized meeting called a deposition. For a deposition, an individual is placed under oath and questioned by one or more attorneys. The purpose of the session is to elicit information from the individual that is relevant to the pending court action. The deposition information, called deposition testimony, is transcribed by a court reporter. This transcript may be used during trial instead of a live witness in some cases, or it might be used to contradict statements a witness later may make during trial. The individual being questioned is called the deponent. The deposition summary tells the reader what a deponent said, as well as any serious objections that were raised to the testimony. Evidentiary exhibits also might be noted.

▼ When and Why Do You Draft a Deposition Summary, and Who Will Read It?

If you attend a deposition, you may be asked to write a summary of the proceedings. This summary will be read by the assigning attorney. Often it will also be read by other litigation team members and your client. Some insurance companies routinely require defense attorneys to draft a deposition summary after each deposition. The summary is designed to be a quick overview of a deposition.

▼ How Do You Draft a Deposition Summary?

The process for drafting a deposition summary is similar to that of writing a meeting summary. First, take copious notes during the deposition. This is a summary of the deponent's statements. You should not list any independent facts in the notes. In your notes, be certain to write carefully the name of the deponent, his or her age, any addresses the person provides, and any business or organizational affiliation mentioned. Note if the individual is related to any of the parties involved in the action. Note each topic. Second, review your notes. Third, draft an outline of your summary. List the important topics to be included. Next to the topics, include any important statements. Fourth, draft the summary in sentence format from your detailed outline. You need not include every statement made. You might find the use of headings will help organize your summary and will assist your reader in locating topics. Finally, review your summary. Edit your summary and rewrite it.

Summary Drafting Checklist

1. Take notes.
2. Review your notes.
3. Write a detailed outline.
4. Draft your summary.
5. Edit your Summary and rewrite it.

ILLUSTRATION 14-5. Example of a Deposition Summary

MEMORANDUM

To: File
From: Mary Bourn
Date: July 8, 2012

SUMMARY OF DEPOSITION OF MORT WILLIAMS, JULY 8, 2012
Personal Information and Employment

Mort Williams, 65, lives at Rural Route 1, Box 216, Crystal Lake, Illinois. He is currently a supervisor at Rock Wire and Tubing. He has worked for the corporation for 25 years. He supervises shipping, receiving, maintenance, and packaging at the Wauconda plant, at 166 South Western Avenue. He has been at the Wauconda plant about eight months.

During 2011 and 2012, Mr. Williams was a shop superintendent at the Lake Forest plant.

During that time, Williams could sign requisitions for equipment, but Ted Simons was the individual who could purchase items.

In 2011, Williams traveled to Nut Services' Niles plant three to five times to inspect some saws Rock was considering purchasing. Williams confirmed that Rock bought some saws from Nut. He said he did not know the details of the purchase, such as the price or value of the equipment. Simons was the only Rock person involved in these details.

ILLUSTRATION 14-5.   Continued

Rock received four cold saws, some hand tools, a tool box, blades, a drill, a press, and a forklift from Nut.

Next, Williams reviewed Exhibit 5 which is the document attached to the Second Amended Complaint. He did not recognize the signature of Ted S. as the signature of Ted Simons. He noted that some items listed in Exhibit 2 duplicated items listed in Exhibit 5.

The court reporter was Mary Kramer of Weston Roads Associates of Lake Forest, IL. Her phone number is 847-888-2800. Ms. Crane did not order a transcript at this time as plaintiff's counsel did not order a transcript. If the plaintiff's counsel orders a transcript, Ms. Crane will order a transcript at that time.

E. DEPOSITION ABSTRACTS

▼ What Is the Difference Between a Deposition Summary and a Deposition Abstract?

A deposition summary is a brief explanation of the deposition proceedings. In contrast, the **deposition abstract** details each relevant statement and notes the specific page of the transcript that contains the statement. See Illustration 14-6. Some people will refer to deposition abstracts as deposition summaries. However, one is narrative, while the other normally is not.

▼ Who Will Read the Deposition Abstract?

The assigning attorney will read the deposition abstract. Often other litigation team members, new team members, clients, and expert witnesses will review the abstract.

▼ What Is the Purpose of a Deposition Abstract, and When Is It Drafted?

The primary function of the abstract is to assist an attorney in preparing for trial. Some abstracts are prepared immediately after the deposition transcript arrives in an attorney's office. Others, however, are drafted just before trial. Deposition transcripts can be unwieldy. The abstracts provide attorneys with a quick reference to specific topics or statements addressed. This reference facilitates an attorney's trial preparation, especially the development of direct or cross-examination of the deponent. In addition, abstracts help in preparing discovery requests, noting additional facts that must be determined before trial. They also are used to find evidence to submit with a summary judgment motion.

▼ What Format Is Used for a Deposition Abstract?

The format will vary by attorney. Ask the assigning attorney if he or she has a preference. Many attorneys ask you to place a short statement following page references. Do not include every item mentioned at a deposition. Routine introductory questions can be omitted. Include the name and address of the deponent, the date of the deposition, the names of the attorneys, and a list of all exhibits. Also mention any questions the deponent did not answer based on advice of counsel as well as any questions that have been certified.

ILLUSTRATION 14-6. Example of a Deposition Abstract

Nut Services v. Rock Tube and Conduit
Abstract of the deposition of Mort Williams,
taken July 8, 2012, pp. 1-62

Page(s)	Exhibit(s)	Summary to Testimony
6-7		Rock cut tubing between 2011 and 2012.
11-13		Williams was shop superintendent at the Lake Forest warehouse until it closed. Then he went to Wauconda as a superintendent.
21		When Williams was the Lake Forest superintendent, he had authority to requisition items for Rock, but could not buy items.
22		Ted Simons was Williams's immediate supervisor. He could approve purchases.
23		Williams first met Ken Kiser at Kiser's business (called Nut) in Palatine in 2000 or 2001.
27-29		Williams went to Nut three or four times to see equipment.
32		Williams did not know the reason Nut and Mr. Kiser were selling cutters. He did not know if Nut was going out of business.
32		Rock bought four saws, which, in 2011, were still used eight hours a day.
35-36		After Nut went out of business, Rock decided to purchase some of Nut's saws and other equipment. It was Ted Simons's decision.
37		Williams did not discuss the purchase price of that equipment with Ted, nor was he involved at any time during this first trip to Nut's plant, or anytime thereafter, in negotiating the purchase price of any of these things.

ILLUSTRATION 14-6.   Continued

Page(s)	Exhibit(s)	Summary to Testimony
40		Rock received some hand tools and some big equipment.
41		Williams could not remember everything about the transaction, and he has no list of everything that was agreed to.
42		Mr. Kiser delivered some items and Rock picked up others.
45		Williams and Ted picked up hand tools and a tool box. Williams could not remember all the tools that they picked up.
46		Williams signed some receipts.
48		Williams does not know what the cost of anything was.
50-52	2	Rock received the items on Exhibit No. 2 attached to the Plaintiff's Complaint.
50-52		Williams does not know the purchase price or value of the items listed on Exhibit 2.
50-52	5	Williams did not recognize the handwriting or signature in the upper right-hand corner of Plaintiff's Exhibit No. 5 for identification that is attached to Plaintiff's Complaint as Addendum A.
53-54		Rock received the forklift.
58-61		Rock also received 40 saw blades, carts, a drill, and a press.
62	2, 5	There may be some duplication between the items of Exhibit No. 2 and those on Exhibit No. 5.

Some attorneys prefer a chronological format designed to explain the information contained in the deposition based on the timing of the events. Others prefer a topical organization. Some prefer a summary that is done in the same order as the deposition transcript. Such a summary is merely a condensed version of the deposition with the page numbers highlighted. This type of summary works well if any attorney has organized the deposition questions and the deposition has followed the organization. You might follow such a summary with a short index by topic followed by a page number reference. Focus on the responses and not the questions.

▼ How Do You Draft an Abstract?

First, discuss the case with the assigning attorney if you do not know the important case issues. You need to understand the facts and issues of a case before you begin to abstract the deposition. Ask the attorney how detailed the abstract should be. At some large firms, an associate may take a deposition. However, the partner may be the person who will try the case. The partner may need a more detailed deposition because he or she did not question the deponent during the deposition.

When you begin, focus on the issues and facts that are relevant to the case. The deposition abstract should be concise. To be useful, it should not be as lengthy as the original transcript. Paraphrase statements if possible. Be careful to do so accurately and to reflect the comments the deponent made. However, if a statement is made that you deem to be significant, quote it.

Some individuals obtain a copy of the transcript and highlight the sections for abstracting. They then dictate the summaries. Others receive the deposition on disk and edit it for their abstract. This can be a very efficient method.

F. TRANSACTION SUMMARY

Another specialized document paralegals occasionally draft is a transaction summary. It outlines a transaction and provides the salient details of the deal. The items included in the summary will vary depending upon the type and complexity of the transaction. For example, such a document drafted for a simple real estate transaction may include the purchase price, the down payment, a mortgage amount, the mortgage principal and interest payment per month, closing costs, a list of any expenses prepaid by the seller such as taxes or condominium assessments, fixtures included in the sale, closing costs, and the total costs owed at closing. But for a complex sale of assets and a business, the document may state the assets sold to the buyer and any excluded assets as well as a statement of assets and liabilities.

To draft a summary of the transaction, review the underlying contract first. Next review any amendments made to the contract. Finally, review correspondence between the parties. For the purchase of a home, the purchase price, down payment, and fixtures included in the sale should be noted on the contract or any contract amendments. The mortgage amount and principal and interest would be found in a letter from the lender if a mortgage was a contingency noted in the contract. Prepaid expenses such as taxes and any association dues that should be paid for the property the deal involves often will appear on the title work provided by a title company. The associations, if any, provide a statement before closing that dues have been paid outside of a closing. Therefore, you must review all this correspondence before drafting the document. Next, review any title company charges such as recording fees and the cost of title insurance. These are considered part of the closing costs. Once you have reviewed all the relevant documents, you are ready to prepare your transaction summary. Review Illustration 14-7, the transaction summary for the $1.8 million purchase of a home in Glenview, Illinois. The purchasers, Sarah and Bill Hope, have secured a mortgage in the amount of $1,440,000. The down payment for the property was $360,000. The prepaid taxes are $6,442. The total closing costs are $1,518. The principal and interest is $4,168.54.

ILLUSTRATION 14-7. Transaction Summary

Sarah and Bill Hope agreed to purchase 1816 Drury Lane in Glenview, IL, 60025, from Randall and Eve Benjamin on November 15, 2012. The sale includes the following fixtures: a Kitchen-Aid electric/convection double oven, a Maytag dishwasher, a DCM cook top, a Kitchen-Aid refrigerator, a Maytag refrigerator, a U-line refrigerator, a U-line wine cooler, a U-line beverage center, a Panasonic microwave, two Rheem hot water heaters, two Trane furnaces and air conditioning units, built-in bookshelves in the library, fireplace tools, an alarm system, three garage door opener remotes and a garage door opener, all ceiling fans and electrical fixtures throughout the building, and all storm windows and screens. The closing is December 1, 2012.

Purchase Price: The purchase price for the property is $1.8 million. It includes all the fixtures specified above as well as the structure and the one and one-half acres of land.

Purchase Option: Based on the agreement, the purchasers have the right, after closing, to purchase from the seller an additional quarter acre of land adjacent to the property. The purchase price for such property would be the then fair market value of the property. This option must be exercised within ten years of the closing anniversary.

Down Payment: The purchasers provided a down payment of $360,000.00 to the broker, Koenig & Strey, in Northbrook, IL. The money is being held in an escrow account.

Mortgage Amount: The purchasers have secured a 30-year fixed rate mortgage from BankOne in the amount of $1,440,000.00. The monthly principal and interest is $4168.54.

Closing Costs: The closing costs due from the seller are $978 for the title policy and $252 for the document preparation and closing room. The purchasers owe $318 for recording fees, release fees, and other closing costs.

Accrued Expenses: The seller owes $6,442 for the taxes accrued up to the date of closing. As taxes are paid in the arrears, the amount due for taxes is 110 percent of the most recent taxes billed. This amount is based on the contract provisions.

Total Amount Due at Settlement: The purchaser will owe one month's principal and interest of $4168.54 plus $318 for closing costs for a total of $4,486.54. The seller will owe $6,442 in taxes, $252 for document preparation, and $978 for the title policy, for a total of $7,672.00.

ETHICS ALERT

Be sure to have an attorney review any documents sent to clients. Be careful not to provide clients with any legal advice. That is the attorney's job.

CHAPTER SUMMARY

In this chapter you learned the purpose and some suggested inclusions of information for a variety of objective documents you will draft as paralegals, including summaries of client and witness statements, meetings, depositions, and summaries of a case's progress. In addition, you learned what a deposition abstract is and how to draft one.

KEY TERMS

attorney-client privilege   deposition summary
client summary   meeting summary
deponent   objective
deposition   status memo
deposition abstract   witness summary

EXERCISES

1. Draft a summary of the following exchange with the client. C is the client and A is the attorney.

A: Hello. What can I do for you today?
C: Hi. I am Arthur Lehman. I am here to find out whether I have a case against my neighbor.
A: What happened?
C: My neighbor and I have been fighting for years. His willow tree droops into my backyard and the leaves go into my pool. He doesn't like me because I won't let him swim in my pool. This weekend, I had a pool party. My neighbor decided to cut down the willow tree and let the branches fall into my backyard. One of the big branches hit me on the head. I just got out of the hospital.
A: When did this happen?
C: 7:00 P.M. on Saturday.
A: How did the neighbor cut the tree?
C: With a chain saw.
A: Did the neighbor know you were there?
C: He could hear the party music. He asked me to keep the noise down, and asked how long I was going to have people at the party. I told him I would keep the noise down and that people would be there until midnight. So he knew someone might be under the tree.
A: What time did this conversation take place?
C: 6:30 P.M., when the party was beginning.

A: Did anyone else hear the conversation?

C: Yes, my other neighbor, who was watering her garden. I then asked her to join the party.

A: What is your neighbor's name?

C: Marc Enrico.

A: What about the female neighbor who heard the conversation?

C: Karen Tate.

A: What happened when Mr. Enrico cut the tree?

C: He was in the tree. He was looking at me, then he cut the big branch. It landed on my head. The guests also saw it.

A: What guests?

C: Cindy Wood, Janice Christopher, and Ivan Jones.

A: What happened to you?

C: My guests called an ambulance. The ambulance took me to the hospital. I passed out. They said I had a head injury so they had to keep me overnight. I needed 16 stitches to my face because the branch cut me.

A: How big was the branch?

C: About six feet long and six inches in diameter.

A: What would you like me to do?

C: Sue the creep.

A: We will review your case this week and determine what if any claims we can make. We will also discuss the matter with your witnesses. Then we will call you about it. Our fee . . .

2. Draft a summary of the witness statement. P is the paralegal and W is the witness, Karen Tate. You spoke with her October 1, 2011.

W: I could hear the party music. I was watering my garden. Then Arthur asked me to join the party.

P: Did you hear Mr. Enrico say anything to Mr. Lehman?

W: Yes. He asked him to keep the noise down, and he asked how long people would be at the party. He was nasty; he told me a minute earlier that he was angry at Arthur because he didn't ask him to join the party.

A: Did he say anything else to you about Mr. Lehman?

W: Yes. He said he would get him to take notice of him and he would get back at him. He said he felt like punching Arthur.

A: What time did this conversation take place?

W: 6:30 P.M., when the party was beginning.

A: Did you see Mr. Enrico cut the tree branch?

W: Yes.

A: What happened when Mr. Enrico cut the tree?

W: He was in the tree. He was looking at Arthur and the other guests and shaking his fists. He yelled, "I'm going to get you Lehman," then he cut the big branch. It landed on Arthur's head.

3. The attorney has determined that there is a claim. You have interviewed the other witnesses. You also have drafted and filed a complaint after you spoke with Mr. Lehman. The attorney signed the complaint. He then asked you to draft interrogatories and to investigate the defendant. Draft a memo to the file concerning these events.

4. Draft a meeting summary for a meeting you attended concerning the rezoning of a residential parcel of land as industrial-class land. The residents oppose the proposal because the land is between two residential developments. The rezoning would allow for an industrial plant to manufacture rubber tires. The subdivisions are old and the neighborhood is not wealthy. The board did not take any action, but plans to on April 2, 2012. The meeting was January 20, 2012. About 200 residents appeared. Another developer has a plan for a strip mall that would benefit the neighborhood.

5. Draft a deposition summary of the following deposition testimony.

STATE OF ILLINOIS	)	SS	Page 1
COUNTY OF COOK	)		

IN THE CIRCUIT COURT OF COOK COUNTY
COUNTY DEPARTMENT–LAW DIVISION

JANICE KAHN,	)	
	)	
Plaintiff	)	No. 96L 219
	)	
v.	)	
	)	
	)	
RONNIE RANDALL,	)	
	)	
Defendant	)	

The deposition of Janice Kahn, called by the defendant for examination, pursuant to notice and pursuant to the provisions of the Illinois Code of Civil Procedure and the Rule of the Supreme Court of the State of Illinois, for the purpose of discovery, taken before Christina M. Marks, CSR and Notary Public in and for the County of Cook and the State of Illinois, at Suite 2900, One University Center, Chicago, Illinois, on May 16, 2012, at 10:00 A.M.

Present:

Robert Marcus and Associates
By Carol Pinkus
2 North Wabash St., Suite 7890
Chicago, Illinois 60602
    appeared on behalf of the plaintiff

McQuade, Foley and Viner
By Sarah Lillian
8 North LaSalle St. Suite 1650
Chicago, Illinois 60602
    appeared on behalf of the defendant

Witness   Page 2
  Janice Kahn
Examined by Sarah Lillian

No exhibits were marked

1.	JANICE KAHN,	Page 3

2.   having been first duly sworn, was examined and testified as
3.   follows:

4.   EXAMINATION
5.   by MS. LILLIAN

6.   Q. Let the record reflect that this is the discovery deposition of
7.   Janice Kahn, K-A-H-N, taken pursuant to the Rules of Civil Pro-
8.   cedure of the State of Illinois and the Country of Cook. Mrs.
9.   Kahn, my name is Sarah Lillian, and I represent Mr. Ronnie Ran-
10.   dall. I am going to be asking you a series of questions today
11.   about the facts underlying the lawsuit that you have brought
12.   against Mr. Randall. I would like to give you some instructions
13.   before we start. Because the court reporter has to take down
14.   your answers, she has to be able to hear what you're saying.
15.   So a shake or a nod won't do it. You have to answer out loud,
16.   okay?
17.   A. Okay.
18.   Q. If you would like to stop at any time, please let me know and I will
19.   be happy to accommodate you if you need to take a break. If there
20.   is anything that you don't understand, I would like you to say so
21.   and ask me to rephrase the question or just tell me that you do
22.   not understand. If you do not say so, I am going to have to assume
23.   that you understood the question that I'm asking and that you're
24.   answering, okay?
25.   A. Okay.
26.   Q. What is your full name?
27.   A. Janice Lori Kahn.
28.   Q. Are you married?
29.   A. No.

1.	*Q.* Have you ever been married?	Page 4
2.	*A.* Yes, to Albert Kahn before he died.	
3.	*Q.* When did he die?	
4.	*A.* 2001.	
5.	*Q.* Before your marriage to Mr. Kahn, what was your name?	
6.	*A.* Janice Lori Winer.	
7.	*Q.* What is your address?	
8.	*A.* 113 Tinkerway, Northbrook, Illinois.	
9.	*Q.* How long have you lived there?	
10.	*A.* Twelve years.	
11.	*Q.* Do you own your home?	
12.	*A.* Yes.	
13.	*Q.* Is it a single family residence?	
14.	*A.* Yes.	
15.	*Q.* Do you have any children?	
16.	*A.* Yes. I have a son.	
17.	*Q.* What is your son's name?	
18.	*A.* Billy Kahn.	
19.	*Q.* Is Billy short for something else?	
20.	*A.* Yes. William.	
21.	*Q.* When was your son born?	
22.	*A.* Twelve years ago. April 1, 2000.	

1.	*Q.* Do you have any other children?	Page 5
2.	*A.* No.	
3.	*Q.* Are you employed?	
4.	*A.* Yes.	
5.	*Q.* Where are you employed and what do you do?	
6.	*A.* Middleton High School in Crystal Lake, Illinois, as a teacher.	
7.	*Q.* How long have you worked there?	
8.	*A.* Fifteen years.	
9.	*Q.* Were you employed before you began working at Middleton?	
10.	*A.* No.	
11.	*Q.* Have you ever been involved in another lawsuit?	
12.	*A.* No.	
13.	*Q.* Not even as a witness?	
14.	*A.* No.	
15.	*Q.* Do you recall August 29, 2011?	
16.	*A.* Yes.	
17.	*Q.* What happened on that day?	
18.	*A.* Ronnie Randall struck my son with his car.	
19.	*Q.* What were you doing when the accident occurred?	
20.	*A.* Working in my garden. I planted tomatoes, green peppers,	
21.	carrots, and broccoli.	

22.	*Q.* Where is your garden located on your property?	
23.	*A.* In the front near the street. It is next to a brick wall.	
24.	I can't see the garden from my house.	

1.	*Q.* What direction were you facing in your garden?	Page 6
2.	*A.* North.	
3.	*Q.* Does that direction face the street?	
4.	*A.* No.	
5.	*Q.* What do you usually do in your garden?	
6.	*A.* Weed it.	
7.	*Q.* What were you doing in your garden when the accident	
8.	occurred?	
9.	*A.* Weeding it.	
10.	*Q.* Where is the street in relation to your garden?	
11.	*A.* About five feet.	
12.	*Q.* Where does your son generally play?	
13.	*A.* In the backyard.	
14.	*Q.* Where was he playing on the day of the accident?	
15.	*A.* He was playing t-ball in the front yard.	
16.	*Q.* Were you watching him at the time of the accident?	
17.	*A.* Yes. I could see him.	
18.	*Q.* Did you see the accident occur?	
19.	*A.* Sort of.	
20.	*Q.* Did you or did you not see the accident?	
21.	*A.* I saw my son, who was 11 years old, on the ground covered with	
22.	blood and blood all over the front of the Cadillac.	
23.	*Q.* Did you actually see the driver strike your son?	
24.	*A.* No. But I know Ronnie hit him. I saw my son next to Ronnie's	
25.	car. I heard him swerve.	

1.	*Q.* Did you know the driver?	Page 7
2.	*A.* Yes.	
3.	*Q.* Who was the driver?	
4.	*A.* Ronnie Randall.	
5.	*Q.* How did you know him?	
6.	*A.* We met at a state fair. We dated for ten years. I broke up with him	
7.	two weeks before the accident.	
8.	*Q.* Did he know your son?	
9.	*A.* He knew my son was the most important person to me and he	
10.	tried to kill him to pay me back for dumping him.	
11.	*Q.* Are you accusing the driver of intentionally striking your son?	
12.	*A.* Yes. He wanted to get back at me so he hit my boy.	
13.	*Q.* What happened to your son on the day of the accident?	

14.   *A.* He sustained head injuries and several broken bones. He can't
15.   play baseball for the rest of the season and we had to cancel our
16.   vacation to the Dells because he's been hurting so much.
17.   *Q.* Was he conscious when you first saw him after the accident?
18.   *A.* He was awake but I thought he was dead at first. He had blood
19.   everywhere. I knew the driver, Ronnie, was drunk when he hit
20.   him. He wasn't even looking where he was going. He always
21.   swerves down our street to get my attention.
22.   *Q.* Did your son speak to you right after the accident?
23.   *A.* Barely. I told him that Ronnie was speeding and trying to run him
24.   down on purpose, I was horrified to see the blood and the broken
25.   bones. I couldn't move and I was so angry at Ronnie because I
26.   knew he did this on purpose.
27.   *Q.* Did you go the doctor after this accident?

---

1.   *A.* I went by ambulance with my son to the doctor.   Page 8
2.   His doctor looked me over and said I was suffering from shock.
3.   Since then, I've had headaches and felt anxious. I throw up
4.   every day.
5.   *Q.* Have you seen a doctor for your complaints?
6.   *A.* Yes. She said that they are related to the accident. I just keep
7.   thinking back to that day when the neighbor told me that
8.   Ronnie intentionally turned the wheel to hit my boy.
9.   *Q.* Was your son able to move after the accident?
10.   *A.* Slightly. He looked just like our neighbors' son did after
11.   Ronnie hit him with his car two weeks ago at the same
12.   curve.
13.   *Q.* That is all the questions I have. Do you have any questions?
14.   Ms. Pinkus: No.

---

6. Draft a deposition abstract for the above testimony.

LETTER WRITING

CHAPTER OVERVIEW

This chapter explains letter-writing basics, such as format and types of letters. It provides examples of a variety of letters you might use in practice.

Letter writing is one of the basic tasks you will perform as paralegals. Most letter-writing conventions apply to legal correspondence in much the same way as they do to other business communications. Paralegals should be aware of the components of basic letters as well as some special rules for legal communications.

A. BASICS OF LETTER WRITING

The mechanics of letter writing is similar to any other legal writing project. You plan it, draft it, and revise it. In planning your communication, you must determine your audience and outline what you plan to say to your reader. When revising the letter, use proper grammar and consider any revisions that would make the letter clearer. Proofread your letter.

▼ What Formats Are Used?

Letters may be drafted using a variety of formats. Letters may be sent via post, facsimile, e-mail, or in a text message. Regardless of the mode of transmission, professional formatting is still required. Often the firm letterhead is set in the template for any e-mail correspondence. When in doubt as to style, always ask the supervising attorney, but it is best to always err on the side of formality. Look through the firm's correspondence file to get an idea of the format you should use. Firm style or personal taste generally determines the format of your letters. The formats are **full block, block, modified block**, and **personal style.**

In a full block letter, you do not indent the paragraphs. The paragraphs, the complimentary close, and the dateline are flush left. See Illustration 15-1. For block format, all paragraphs and notations are flush left, except for the date, the reference line, the complimentary close, and the signature lines, which are just right of the center of the page. See Illustration 15-3. In a modified block style letter, the first line of each paragraph is indented about five characters. See Illustration 15-6. In a personal style letter, often written to friends, the inside address is placed below the signature at the left margin.

B. COMPONENTS OF A LETTER

1. Letterhead and Headers

A letter is divided into several sections: the date, the name and the address of the addressee called the inside address, a reference line, a greeting to the addressee, the body of the letter, and the complimentary closing.

You should draft the first page of a letter on firm letterhead. The **letterhead** is the portion of the firm's stationery that identifies the firm, generally the attorneys, and sometimes the firm's paralegals. It usually includes the firm's address and its telephone and facsimile numbers. Additional pages should not carry the firm letterhead but should be placed on matching paper with a **header** on each page. The header identifies the letter and is generally placed on the top right side of the page. A header includes the name of the addressee, the date, and the number of the page:

> Cheryl Victor
> November 15, 2012
> Page Two

ILLUSTRATION 15-1. Full Block Letter

[1]Fuzzwell, Cubbon and Landefelt
888 Toledo Road
Ottawa Hills, Ohio 43606
(419) 535-7738

[2]November 7, 2012

[3]Via Federal Express
Mr. Stuart Shulman
Navarre Industries
708 Anthony Wayne Trail
Maumee, Ohio 45860

[4]Re: Settlement of Kramer v. Shulman

[5]Dear Mr. Shulman:

[6]I have enclosed a copy of the settlement agreement that we drafted and that has been signed by Mr. Kramer. Please sign the agreement and forward it to me at the above address by November 30, 2012.

If you have any questions, please feel free to call me at 535-7738.

[7]Sincerely,

Mara Cubbon
Legal Assistant

[8]cc: Randall Fuzzwell
[9]Enc.
[10]MAC/wlk

ILLUSTRATION 15-1. **Continued**

1. Letterhead
2. Date
3. Recipient's address and method of service
4. Reference line
5. Greeting
6. Body of the letter
7. Closing
8. Carbon copy notation
9. Enclosure of notation
10. Initials of drafter/typist

ETHICS ALERT

Check your state law as to whether your name may appear on the letterhead.

2. Date

The **date** should be placed at the top of the letter just below the firm's letterhead. The date is one of the key components of a letter concerning any legal matters. Date the letter with the same date as the date of mailing. This date can be crucial in determining a time line in a legal proceeding. Timing in sending documents and correspondence is often important in legal transactions and litigation matters. Therefore, be careful to include the date of mailing rather than the date of writing the letter. For example, if you prepare a letter on July 4 after the last mail pickup, you should date the letter July 5 because that is the date it would actually be mailed. This may seem like a purely technical distinction if you put the letter in the mail on July 4. However, some court cases and negotiations turn on the date of mailing. With e-mail, the date is easily discerned, but the recipient will consider the date of receipt the next business day.

3. Method of Transmission

If the letter is being sent by a method other than U.S. mail, it should be indicated on the top of the address and then underlined as follows:

Via Email and U.S. Mail
Cheryl Victor
Vice President
Arizona Money Makers
1000 Tempe Road
Phoenix, Arizona 85038

This notation should start at least two lines below the date. See Illustration 15-1.

4. Inside Address

The next part of the letter, the **inside address**, should contain the name of the person to whom the letter is addressed, the individual's title if he or she has one, the name of the business if the letter is for a business, and the address.

5. Reference Line

The **reference line** is a brief statement regarding the topic of the letter. For example, if the letter concerns a contract for the sale of a particular property, your reference line would say:

Re: Sale of commercial property—2714 Barrington Road, Toledo, Ohio

Some firms and corporations ask that the reference line contain a client number, claim number, or case number, so investigate your firm's style.

PRACTICE POINTER

If possible, review letters in a file written by the assigning attorney. Note the attorney's style for the reference line and follow it.

---

6. Greeting

In general, your **greeting** depends on how familiar you are with an individual. An individual whom you do not know should be addressed as "Dear Ms. White." If you know an individual well, you may address, formally, such that person by first name. If you are uncertain whether to address the individual by first name, use a title and the individual's last name. If you are addressing a letter to a particular person, such as the custodian of records, but you do not know the person's name, try to determine the person's name. If necessary, call a company or agency to determine the appropriate recipient for the letter. Your letter is more likely to be answered quickly if it is addressed to the appropriate person rather than "To whom it may concern." In addition, it may provide you with an opportunity to establish a rapport with the individual to whom the letter is addressed.

7. Body of Letter

The **body** of the letter follows the greeting and should begin with an opening sentence and paragraph that summarizes the purpose of the letter. Draft the body of the letter carefully. Outline the letter before writing it to be sure that you address all the necessary points. List each point you want to cover. For Illustration 15-1, your outline might read as follows:

1. enclose settlement agreement
2. ask for signature and return date
3. ask addressee to call if he has questions

Consider your audience. If you are writing to a layperson who is unfamiliar with the law, explain any legal terms you use often using definitions provided in a dictionary, or use simple language. However, do not provide any legal opinions. If you are addressing your letter to an individual who is familiar with the law, such as a judge, a paralegal, an in-house counsel, or an attorney, you do not need to explain such terms. To do so might be considered condescending.

ETHICS ALERT

Do not offer any legal advice or opinions in the letter. If an attorney is not signing the letter, do not request the recipient to take any action that would change her legal position or require her to make a legal decision.

---

8. Closing

End your letter with a **closing** in which you invite a response, such as "Please do not hesitate to call if you have any questions," or thank the addressee for assistance, such as "Thank you in advance for your cooperation." Finally, end the letter with a complimentary closing such as "Sincerely," "Very truly yours," or "Best regards" placed two lines below the final line of the body of the letter. Place your name four lines below the closing to allow for a signature. Include your title, that is, paralegal or legal assistant.

ETHICS ALERT

Be sure that your reader knows that you are a paralegal rather than an attorney. The easiest way to do this is to add your title after your name in the closing. If the letter is to be written for the attorney's signature, present the letter to the attorney for review and for her signature prior to sending.

Do not provide legal advice in your letter or represent yourself as an attorney. Ethical codes and state laws prohibit paralegals who are not licensed to practice law from providing legal opinions or from representing themselves as attorneys. To avoid any confusion or possible misrepresentation, include your title after your name when you write a letter.

9. Copies to Others and Enclosures

If you are copying a third party on the letter and want the original addressee to know this, note it with a "cc" at the bottom left margin of the letter following the closing. The cc indicates **carbon copy** sent to the person listed. (Although photocopies have replaced carbon copies, cc is still used.) Indicate to whom a copy of the letter was sent as "cc: Mike Sterner." See Illustration 15-2. If you do not want the original addressee to know that you copied a letter to another person, note on the draft or file copy "bcc," which means **blind carbon copy.** That notation should only appear on the draft or file copy of the letter and not on the recipient's letter.

ILLUSTRATION 15-2.   Letter Confirming Deposition

Law Offices of Sam Farrell
2714 Barrington Road
Findlay, Ohio 45840
(419) 267-0000

January 28, 2013

Ms. Karen Dolgin
2903 W. Main Cross Street
Findlay, Ohio 45840

Re: Deposition of Robert Harrold
    Harrold v. Sofer

Dear Ms. Dolgin:

This letter is to confirm our conversation today in which you stated that you will present the plaintiff, Robert Harrold, for a deposition at the law office of Sam Farrell, 2714 Barrington Road, in Findlay, on March 18, 2013, at 2 p.m. This deposition is being rescheduled at your request because the plaintiff had a family commitment set for February 15, 2013, the date originally set for the deposition.

ILLUSTRATION 15-2.   Continued

If you have any questions or additional problems, please feel free to call me at (419) 267-0000, extension 608.

Best regards,

Craig Black
Paralegal

cc: Sam Farrell
    Wally Sofer
CMB/klm

The next notation is for **enclosures**, such as court orders, contracts, or releases. Place the abbreviation **Enc.** or **Encs.** at the bottom left margin of the letter. See Illustration 15-1.

Finally, the letter should note your initials in all capital letters as the author of the letter and then the initials in lowercase letters of the person who typed the letter. If your initials are RAS and the typist's are HVS, then the notation under the enclosure or cc notation would read RAS/hvs.

C. TYPES OF LETTERS

Paralegals write letters to clients to confirm deposition dates, meeting dates, hearing dates, or agreements. These letters are called confirming letters. Other letters provide a status report of a case or summarize a transaction. Some letters accompany documents, such as those for document productions, contracts, or settlement releases. These are called transmittal letters. Other letters may request information. Some letters explain the litigation process to clients. See Illustration 15-3.

1. Confirming Letters

Confirming letters reaffirm information already agreed to by you and the recipient. It is a good practice to follow up any conversation with a client or an opposing attorney or paralegal with a confirming letter that summarizes the conversation, any agreements made, or any future acts to be accomplished. See Illustration 15-2. For example, after you discuss a document production with a client and set a meeting date to review the records, send a letter summarizing the conversation. Such confirming letters provide you with a reminder of the conversation and allow anyone who reviews the file later to know what you and the client discussed should you be unavailable. Often to expedite this process,

ILLUSTRATION 15-3.   Letter Concerning Deposition Schedule

Law Offices of Sam Farrell
2714 Barrington Road
Findlay, Ohio 45840
(419) 267-0000

January 28, 2013

Wally Sofer
Chief Executive Officer
1000 Hollywood Way
Houcktown, Ohio 44060

      Re: Deposition of Wally Sofer
        <u>Harrold v. Sofer</u>

Dear Mr. Sofer:

This letter is to advise you that you are required to submit to a deposition by the plaintiff's attorney at 10 a.m. on March 1, 2013, at the law office of Karen Dolgin, 2903 W. Main Cross Street in downtown Findlay. During this deposition, the plaintiff's attorney will ask you questions related to the above-referenced court case, and you will provide answers while under oath and in the presence of a court reporter. Mr. Farrell also will be present to represent you during the deposition.

Mr. Farrell and I would like to meet with you at least once before the deposition to discuss your case and this important part of your case.

I will call you Wednesday to schedule an appointment next week to prepare for your deposition.

Please bring any accident reports, citations, or other documents that relate to the accident if you have not already provided them to our office.

I look forward to speaking with you this week.

                        Sincerely,

                        Craig Black
                        Paralegal

cc: Sam Farrell
CMB/klm

confirming letters are sent via e-mail and the billing partner and supervising attorney are copied on the correspondence.

If opposing counsel has agreed to produce documents or provide a witness for a deposition at a particular time, write a confirming letter to the opposing counsel summarizing these facts and asking to be contacted if there are discrepancies. This can be sent via e-mail with the supervising attorney's permission. Whenever a deposition is rescheduled or continued, it is imperative that a confirming letter be sent via e-mail and post to avoid future discovery disputes. Whenever your client is deposed, send him or her a copy of the deposition for review. A sample of such a letter is found in Illustration 15-4.

2. Status Letters and Transaction Summary Letters

Often you will be asked to provide a **status report** of a case, especially to insurance companies and other clients. See Illustration 15-5. These letters provide clients with an overview of the current activities in a court case, transaction, or other legal matter.

Transaction summary letters often follow a business transaction such as a real estate closing. In these letters, you summarize a transaction.

ILLUSTRATION 15-4.   Letter Enclosing Deposition Transcript

Law Offices of Sam Farrell
2714 Barrington Road
Findlay, Ohio 45840
(419) 267-0000

July 11, 2012

Mr. William Gary
709 Franklin Street
Findlay, Ohio 45840

Re: Deposition on July 8, 2012

Dear Mr. Gary:

Enclosed is a copy of the transcript of your July 8, 2012, deposition. Please review the transcript carefully and note any statements that were incorrectly transcribed. You may not rewrite your testimony, but you should note any inaccurate transcriptions. You may correct the spelling of names and places. If you find any serious mistakes, please call me to discuss these problems.

When you review the deposition, please do not mark the original transcript. Instead, note any discrepancies on a separate sheet of paper. Please note the page and line of any discrepancies. I will have my

ILLUSTRATION 15-4.   Continued

secretary type a list of the discrepancies, and we will discuss these changes before we send them to the court reporter. These changes must be received by the court reporter within 30 days; therefore, I would appreciate your prompt review of the transcript and would like to review your changes by July 30, 2012. If we fail to provide the changes to the court reporter within 30 days, we will forfeit your right to correct the transcript and any inaccuracies will be part of the record.

If you have any questions, please do not hesitate to call me.

Thank you for your cooperation in advance.

Best regards,

Benjamin Farrell
Paralegal

Enc.
BSF/jas

ILLUSTRATION 15-5.   Status Report Letter

Cosher, Cosher and Smith
960 Wyus Boulevard
Madison, Wisconsin 53606

June 12, 2012

Mr. Cal L. Medeep
Pockets Insurance Company
10 Wausau Way
Wausau, Wisconsin 54401

Re: <u>Kelsey v. Cocoa</u>
   Your claim number: C100090888

Dear Mr. Medeep:

This letter is to provide you with a status report concerning the progress of the above-referenced matter. To date, we have requested that the plaintiff answer interrogatories and requests for admissions. I sent a copy of these requests to you about a week ago. The plaintiff is required to answer these requests within 30 days. We will send you a copy of the plaintiff's answers as soon as we receive them. We are scheduled to depose the plaintiff on September 1, 2012.

ILLUSTRATION 15-5. Continued

The plaintiff's attorney is scheduled to depose a representative of Oleo Company on October 13, 2012.

At this time, the court has not scheduled a settlement conference, but is likely to do so before the end of the year.

Please feel free to call if you have any questions.

Sincerely,

Alicia R. Samuel
Legal Assistant

ARS/yml

In other letters, you will **request information**, often from the custodian of records. See Illustration 15-6.

Often you will be responsible for coordinating document productions. Illustration 15-7 shows a sample **transmittal letter** to a client concerning a request to produce documents.

Many letters will be written to accompany documents, releases, and checks. See Illustrations 15-8 and 15-9.

ILLUSTRATION 15-6. Request for Information

Cosher, Cosher and Oleo
960 Wyus Boulevard
Madison, Wisconsin 53606

August 12, 2012

Sarah Rachel
Custodian of Records
Federal Deposit Insurance Corp.
9100 Bryn Mawr Road
Rosemont, Illinois 60018

Re: Freedom of Information Act Request

Dear Ms. Rachel:

Based on the Freedom of Information Act, 5 U.S.C. §552 et seq., I am requesting that your agency provide copies of the following:

Each and every document that relates to or refers to the sale of the property located at 2714 Barrington Road, Glenview, Illinois, 60025.

ILLUSTRATION 15-6. Continued

The documents should be located in your Rosemont, Illinois office.

Under the act, these documents should be available to us within ten days. If any portion of this request is denied, please provide a detailed statement of the reasons for the denial and an index or similar statement concerning the nature of the documents withheld. As required by the act, Cosher, Cosher and Oleo agrees to pay reasonable charges for copying of the documents upon the presentation of a bill and the finished copies.

Thank you in advance for your cooperation in this matter.

Sincerely,

Lillian Eve Farrell
Paralegal

LEF/dag

3. Demand Letter

A **demand letter** is a letter that states your client's demands to another party. A common letter paralegals write is a demand letter. Often the demand letter seeks to collect debts. Such a letter may need to comply with the requirements of your state's fair-debt collection laws. See Illustration 15-10.

ILLUSTRATION 15-7. Request to Produce Documents

Carthage, Katz and Kramer
1001 B Line Highway
Darlington, Wisconsin 53840

February 28, 2013

Ms. Karen Taylor
Carolton Corp.
1864 Merrimac Road
Sylvania, Ohio 43560

Re: Carolton v. Franklin

Dear Ms. Taylor:

Enclosed please find a request from the defendants asking you to produce documents. The date scheduled for the production of these

ILLUSTRATION 15-7.   Continued

documents is April 1, 2013. Some documents may be protected from disclosure because they may contain confidential trade secret information, and others may be protected because they are communications between you and your attorney or the result of your attorney's work. We must respond in writing by March 25, 2012, in order to raise any of these claims.

As we must review the documents to determine whether any documents are protected, we should compile the documents no later than March 15, 2012. This will allow us time to review, to index, and to number each document.

I will be available to assist you in gathering documents to respond to this request. I will call you this week to schedule an appointment.

If you have any questions, please feel free to call.

Sincerely,

Eileen Waters
Paralegal

Encs.
EDW/jnn

In a demand letter, you should state that your firm represents the creditor or other client, as well as the client's desire for full payment of the claim. Specify the amount demanded or state the action sought, and ask the debtor either to make payment or to contact your office within a certain number of days. Then state the action that the firm will take if the demand is not met within the specified time period.

ILLUSTRATION 15-8.   Letter Accompanying Document

Janis, Max, & Jordan
1600 Bradley Street
Wilmette, Illinois 60091

March 4, 2013

Eve Lillian
Lake County Recorder of Deeds
18 N. County Street
Waukegan, Illinois 60085

Re: 1785 Central Street
    Deerfield, Illinois 60015

ILLUSTRATION 15-8. Continued

Dear Mrs. Lillian:

Enclosed please find two original quit claim deeds, one dated December 30, 2003, and one dated January 2, 2013, relating to the above-referenced property. Both deeds have been marked "exempt" from state and county transfer tax. A check for $50.00 to cover the recording fees ($25 each) is enclosed. Please record these deeds at once and return the originals to Jacki Farrell at the 1785 Central Street address.

Thank you for your assistance.

Sincerely,

Jennifer Lauren
Legal Assistant

Encs.
cc: Jacki Farrell
JML/jch

4. Opinion Letters

Opinion and advice letters advise clients about the legal rules that apply to their situation. Most law firms will not have paralegals draft even a preliminary opinion letter. If your firm asks you to draft a preliminary letter, be sure not to sign the letter with your name. Always have the supervising attorney review the opinion letter carefully before it is sent to another attorney for signing. An **opinion letter** must be signed by an attorney because, as its name suggests, the letter states a legal opinion. Many firms require that opinion letters are signed only by partners, as the letter makes the firm responsible for the opinion offered.

ILLUSTRATION 15-9. Letter Accompanying Check

Howard & Farrell
Central and Carriage Way
Evanston, Illinois 60202

April 22, 2013

William German
Chicago Bar Association
124 Plymouth Court
Chicago, Illinois 60611

ILLUSTRATION 15-9. Continued

Re: Commercial Real Estate Contract Prepared by the Real Property Law Committee

Dear Mr. German:

Enclosed please find a check for $30.00 to cover the mailing fees and the cost of a copy of the Real Estate Contract referenced above. Please send me a copy of the contract at your earliest convenience.

Thank you for your cooperation.

Sincerely,

M. Seth Jordan
Paralegal

Enc.
cc: Rachel Jacob
MSJ/ear

ETHICS ALERT

If you sign an opinion letter, this could be construed as the unauthorized practice of law. If you sign the attorney's name, without her consent, that is tantamount to practicing law.

ILLUSTRATION 15-10. Demand Letter

Law Office of Randall William
145 Franklin Street
Madison, Wisconsin 53606

April 1, 2013

Michelle Hirsh
889 Barrington Road
Middleton, Wisconsin 53608

Re: Furniture Crafters Account 4155

Dear Ms. Hirsh:

Our office represents Furniture Crafters in the collection of the $468.00 debt due on the above-referenced account. Furniture Crafters requests that you pay the full amount of the debt, $468.00, immediately.

ILLUSTRATION 15-10. Continued

You must pay this amount in full or contact our firm at the above telephone number or address within seven days. If we do not hear from you within seven days, we will proceed to court in this matter.

Sincerely,

Randall William
Paralegal

RAW/bgh

If you must draft a preliminary version of an opinion letter, the process is similar to writing an IRAC paragraph. Start with a statement of the legal issue. Your next sentence, however, should answer the issue. In the paragraph following the answer to the issue, state the law and apply the legally significant facts to the law. Provide information about any legal issues that present problems and incorporate the legally significant facts into that discussion.

The final paragraph should state your opinion as to the conclusion or answer to the issue presented and provide your prediction of the outcome for the legal situation. Clients often request opinion letters prior to entering a business transaction or to request the tax consequences of a proposed business transaction.

Discuss this letter with the attorney who will be signing it and be sure that it is the attorney's opinion rather than your own that is conveyed to the client. Be sure that the attorney reviews the letter before signing it. If the attorney does not initiate a discussion with you about the letter, you should do so to ensure that the attorney reviewed it. Although you may draft the letter for the attorney to review, be sure that the attorney signs the letter before it is sent to the recipient. Even under direction by an attorney, a paralegal can never give legal advice, suggest a change in a legal position, or reach a legal conclusion. Opinion letters provide legal advice, suggest that a client change his legal position, and also reach a legal conclusion; this is why it is imperative that the letter is signed by the attorney supervising the matter.

5. E-mail

E-mail notes have become very common. Many of the same rules apply in the same way to an e-mail note as they would to any other letters. Maintain professionalism in e-mails even though the format is considered casual. Consider your audience and outline what you plan to say. Use proper grammar. Proofread your e-mail. If you would address a letter using a title such as Mr. or Mrs., do so in the e-mail. Include your mailing address and your telephone number so that the party can contact you using methods other than e-mail. If you are sending an **attachment** such as a document to be reviewed, be sure you notify the party in advance so that the person doesn't mistakenly delete the attachment, believing it may contain a virus.

PRACTICE POINTER

Check with your firm concerning whether to draft any e-mails that include client confidences. E-mails can be intercepted and may not be secure. Some firms, however, have security measures in place to facilitate such communications. Most firms have a confidentiality warning as part of the firm's e-mail template. However, e-mails can still be forwarded and intercepted. If a matter is very sensitive, consider alternative transmission formats such as printed letters sent via post.

When sending e-mails, remember that e-mails can be forwarded to other recipients. Most firms now include confidentiality information in the e-mail template stating that the e-mail should be viewed only by the intended recipient. Whenever writing an e-mail in any context, always make sure that it is professional, truthful, and accurate before hitting send.

PRACTICE POINTER

Some e-mail programs allow you to request a return receipt that lets you know that the reader opened the e-mail. For critical e-mail it is a good idea to request such a receipt. If something is time critical and you must ensure that the party received the document, consider sending the letter by messenger.

NET NOTE

Do not use all capital letters in an e-mail. That is considered screaming.

---

6. Social Media

Social media, such as Facebook, LinkedIn, and Twitter, are now frequently used by many legal professionals. Law firms and corporations rely on social media for marketing and networking. Client and professional correspondence have not yet adopted social media as a form of communication in the law firm environment. Most firms are adopting social media policies. Before using social media at work to communicate to clients and other parties, ask your supervising attorney if it is appropriate. Although Twitter would seem like the ideal method to quickly communicate concise information with a large group, it is still considered too informal for professional correspondence. Many senior legal professionals have not adopted social media. Twitter has a unique characteristic in that each "tweet" is limited to 140 characters. Also, with Twitter, the sender can not control where the "tweet" goes and who reads it, so many client confidentiality issues are raised.

Facebook and LinkedIn require the user to subscribe, and not everyone subscribes to such services. Always ask the supervising attorney if social media is the appropriate format for communication prior to corresponding. Always be professional in all of your communication, regardless of format.

PRACTICE POINTER

Before using any form of social media in the work environment, check if the firm or company has a social media policy in place. Remember that social media has not been adopted by everyone and that it is considered very informal for professional correspondence. Additionally, be aware of client confidentiality when using social media for professional communication.

CLASS DISCUSSION

Please read over the following letter and find the flaws.

Law Office
Attorneys at Law
1818 Main Street
Ossining, New Jersey 07555

Mr. Ronald Tolbert
1501 South Street
Morris City, New Jersey 07345

Dear Mr. Tolbert:

Thank you for your correspondence recently. We will see where we can get this week and then write again next week. I do think we should try to get this done in the next few weeks and then put this matter to bed. As previously indicated, I do have a substantial problem with time this week but lets see where we can get.

I don't have time now to respond to all your points and I don't know that we necessarily agree or for that matter disagree with any of the various issues, legal or other that you raise. I can respond more fully as to our position on thise various items as we go forward. I don't know that we need to get into those issues now anyway. I would like to comment on our need to receive a copy of the settlement letter.

I know that the settlement letter is important for our client. Please send the settlement letter as soon as you are able. In any event, if I am missing something, please let me know.

Sincerely,
Diane Russell
Paralegal

CHECKLIST

1. "Never give legal advice" is the first rule of letter writing for paralegals.
2. Be informative.
3. Consider your audience. If you are addressing a client, do so courteously and write at a level that the client will understand. If you were asked to answer a client's questions, be sure that you do. You should always be respectful to the addressee.
4. Choose your words carefully. You want to make certain that your words express what you intend.
5. Write succinctly and directly. Your reader is busy so you want to communicate clearly and in as few words as possible. Avoid unnecessary details.
6. Always be professional even if e-mail is the selected transmission format.

CHAPTER SUMMARY

Letter writing is an essential part of your daily routine as a paralegal. Most letter-writing conventions that apply to business communication apply to legal correspondence. However, paralegals should be careful about dating letters concerning legal matters. Letters should be dated with the date of mailing, which may or may not be the date of drafting.

A letter should contain a date, the name and address of the addressee, a reference line, a greeting to the addressee, the body of the letter, and the complimentary closing.

Confirming letters reaffirm information already agreed to between you and the recipient. Status letters provide an up-to-date review of the process of a pending matter. Transaction summary letters explain particular transactions. Letters also are written to accompany documents, such as releases and checks, or to state your client's demands to a third party, such as for payment.

As with any written document, letters should be outlined, written, and then rewritten if necessary.

It is important to avoid the unauthorized practice of law when writing letters. Do not give any legal advice in a letter that you sign. A letter must be signed by an attorney when it contains legal advice, suggests that a client change her legal position, or states a legal conclusion. Last, in any professional communication, regardless of the format or the medium, professionalism and client confidentiality are of paramount importance.

KEY TERMS

attachment	header
blind carbon copy (bcc)	inside address
block letter	letterhead
body	modified block letter
carbon copy (cc)	opinion letter
closing	personal style letter
confirming letter	reference line
date	request information
demand letter	social media
e-mail	status report
enclosure line	transaction summary letter
full block letter	transmittal letter
greeting	

EXERCISES

SHORT ANSWER

1. What are the basic components of a letter?
2. What is a reference line?
3. How do you indicate that you are sending a copy of a letter to another person?
4. How do you indicate that you want someone to receive a copy, but you don't want the addressee to know that the other person received a copy of the letter?
5. What are confirming letters?
6. What is a status report letter?

7. What are transmittal letters?
8. What are demand letters?
9. Should you provide a legal opinion in a letter?

LETTER WRITING

Prepare the following letters as if you were a paralegal with the law firm of Oleo, Hackett and Blank, 1000 Madison Way, Madison, Wisconsin 53606. Addressee names are identified for you, but you may supply each one's address yourself.

10. Write a letter to Madison Insurance Corporation explaining that your law firm will be representing Carol White for a lawsuit against its insured, Harold Watson, stemming from an automobile accident that occurred on September 1. The Madison claims adjuster is Howie Mark. Harold Watson's insurance policy number is 1280. You once had a difficult time dealing with Mr. Mark and Madison Insurance in the past, so you send your letter by certified mail. Enclose a copy of the police report. Send a blind copy to your client. You write it at 5 P.M. on December 24. You realize that December 25 is a holiday and that mail will not go out until the next day.

11. Your firm represents a client, Karen Taylor, who sustained a neck injury during an automobile accident between Carter McLaughlin and Robert Carroll. Write a letter to Dr. Nancy Martin asking for a detailed report concerning the present and future medical problems of that client. Dr. Martin is an orthopedic surgeon. Indicate that you have a signed release from the client to enclose.

12. Your firm represents Margaret Weston in a divorce case. Write a short letter to her informing her of the final hearing date in her divorce case. The date is June 16, in Lucas County Domestic Relations Court, 900 W. Adams Street, Toledo, Ohio 43602.

13. Your client needs to give testimony at a deposition on November 15, at 10 A.M. at your offices. Please draft a letter asking William Hesse to be at the deposition. Explain to him that you will meet with him in advance to discuss his testimony.

14. Your firm has just settled a case involving Karen Douglas and your client, the Wentworth Industries, in Morristown, New Jersey. The case was settled for $88,000. The Wentworth corporation paid Douglas for injuries she sustained when she fell at a Mexican hotel. You do not want to admit any liability in your letter or admit any ownership interest in the Mexican hotel, the CanCan. You merely want to tender the check to Douglas in full satisfaction of any claims she or her husband have against Wentworth. You also have the signed settlement agreement to send her and the court dismissal of the action.

15. You are assigned the preparation of a letter that explains the status of a pending insurance defense litigation matter. The matter is set for trial on November 15 of this year. Two depositions have been taken—the plaintiff's and the defendant's. Interrogatories have been answered by both sides and a settlement conference is scheduled with the judge in the

case on October 31. The judge is Eve G. Halsey of Ohio Common Pleas Court in Columbus, Ohio. You expect that a representative of the restaurant where the incident took place will attend the settlement conference and that an insurance company representative also will attend as required by the local court rules. Your firm will be calling several witnesses from the restaurant to testify at the trial and you and the partner on the case, Wally Taylor, will be preparing these witnesses to testify beginning in October. Send this letter to your client, Schroeder Insurance Enterprise, 250 W. Wilson Street, Wilmette, IL 60091. The person you deal with at the insurance company is Thomas Kennedy, a claims manager. You are sending this letter via Express Mail. The letter is being typed by Taylor's secretary Jan Marie Maggio. She will send a blind copy of the letter to an associate on the case, Janis Farrell. She also will send a carbon copy of the letter to Mr. Taylor.

16. The following letter was written and signed by a paralegal. Please list three problems that could arise from this letter.

January 1, 20_____

Sent by Mail and Fax to:

Re: Contract to purchase real estate dated December 15, 20_____

Dear Mr. Smith:

Per your request the Seller hereby agrees to extend the attorney approval contingency until 5:00 P.M., January 15, 20__.

I specifically note to you that I am in receipt of your first amendment and its Exhibits A, B, and C.

As to paragraph 3 of your first amendment, I note to you that I am posting in the mail to you a proposed limited warranty and a Waiver and Disclaimer of Implied Warranty of Habitability. I request that you review the same after I have advised you that my client has reviewed the same. I am also posting it in the mail to them. It is specifically noted that what will be provided will be a limited warranty and that we will expect the parties to sign a waiver and disclaimer and I further note that I want to end this thing and accordingly, I provide for a date of January 15, 20__.

I expressed to you that I was unhappy with the contingencies in paragraph 5 of the contract. In fairness, I request that if it does not appear that your client will be able to meet the contingencies, namely, either sell her home or secure financing, that she will notify us at the earliest date and to then voluntarily agree to a termination of the contract.

Looking forward to a closing with you soon.

Very truly yours,

Mary Walton
Paralegal

CITATION

The *Bluebook* is the guide to citation form for all legal documents, whether office memos or Supreme Court briefs. The *Bluebook*, formally known as the *Uniform System of Citation*, 19th Edition, governs because of convention and tradition rather than by the mandate of the state legislature. The *ALWD Citation Manual*, 4th Edition, by Darby Dickerson offers easily comprehended citations. Also, the *ALWD* guide contains "Fast Formats" for every category of citation. These provide terrific examples of formats for all legal resources. New forms of citation are emerging due to the advent of nonproprietary cases, called public domain citations, in which the case is not attributed to a publisher. Generally, the *Bluebook* is the bible for citation format for all legal personnel. This appendix is designed to give you a start in your citation process. If ever in doubt as to citation format, rely on the *Bluebook*.

▼ What Is a Citation?

A citation is really an address indicating where the cited material can be found so that anyone reading your document can find the material if he or she wants to.

The abbreviations must be consistent so that everyone knows what they mean. We rely on a similar convention with street addresses and postal abbreviations. The abbreviation for avenue is Ave.; the postal abbreviation for New York is NY.

▼ What Documents Are Cited?

Any source of authority that you discuss in any legal document is cited. Any concept or idea that is not your own must be cited; this is called attributing authority to your ideas. Citing credits the source from which the idea or legal rule came. It also tells the reader where he or she can find the original source. Citations are used for all authority, whether it is primary authority such as a case or a statute, or secondary authority such as a treatise or a law review article. Also cited are looseleaf services, practitioners' materials, and newspaper articles.

The *Bluebook* has two citation formats, one for briefs and memos and the other for law review articles. *ALWD* has one format. Paralegals rely on the brief and memo format for citation.

▼ What Are the Components of a Citation?

Generally, the components of a cite are the name of the particular document, the volume or title where the document is located, the name of the publication that contains the document, and the specific page, section, or paragraph where the document is found. Also included is the year that a case was decided or the publication date of a book or volume of statutes. For example:

Jacobs v. Grossman, 310 Ill. 247, 141 N.E. 714 (1923)

The name of the document is the case name, *Jacobs v. Grossman.* Parallel citations are given in the example so that you can find the case in both reporters; the official reporter is always mentioned first and the unofficial reporter mentioned second. Each state has its own rules regarding the necessity of including parallel citation information for documents submitted to its court. Some states do not have state reporters and rely on the regional reporters so parallel citation is not an issue. Always check the local court rules. The first number preceding the reporter abbreviation is the volume number of the reporter. Next is the reporter abbreviation and then the page number where the case begins in the reporter. The year that the case was decided is included in parentheses. *Bluebook* **Table T.1** lists reporter abbreviations, as does *ALWD* Appendix 1.

Using the *Bluebook* takes practice. The *Bluebook* is organized by rules. Each rule details the citation format for each type of document. The index is very helpful in finding specific references to the citation format for an individual document such as a statute, an administrative regulation, or a law review article. For additional examples, use the Fast Formats in the *ALWD Citation Manual.* The Fast Formats are easily located in the index of the *ALWD Citation Manual.*

The following portion of the appendix provides examples of the materials and sample cite formats. These examples will help you navigate your way. If the illustration here does not provide adequate information, you can turn to the *Bluebook* or *ALWD* rule mentioned to obtain more detailed treatment.

NET NOTE

Check the ALWD Web site for the latest updates and citation details at www.alwd.org/publications/fourth_edition_resources.html.

▼ How Are Pending and Unreported Decisions Cited?

You should provide the docket number, the court, and the full date of the most recent disposition of the case, as well as the full case name.

slip opinion cite: Gillespie v. Willard City Bd. of Educ., No. C87-7043 (N.D. Ohio Sept. 28, 1987)—*Bluebook* format, Rule 10.8.1; *ALWD* format, Rule 12.18

with page cite: Gillespie v. Willard City Bd. of Educ., No. C87-7043, slip op. at 3 (N.D. Ohio Sept. 28, 1987)

According to the *ALWD Citation Manual,* always check the local court rules to see if unpublished cases can be cited. See *ALWD* Sidebar 12.7.

▼ How Do You Cite a State Case?

Bluebook **Rule 10** and *ALWD* **Rule 12.4** discuss citation formats for state cases. Also check *Bluebook* Jurisdiction-Specific Citation Rules and Style Guides at BT2 for local court citation rules. The first example below shows the citation for an Illinois case with parallel authority included. The second example shows the same case cited in a brief to an Illinois court or to the United States District Court for the Northern District of Illinois.

With parallel cites: Thompson v. Economy Super Marts, 221 Ill. App. 3d 263, 581 N.E.2d 885, 163 Ill. Dec. 731 (App. Ct. 1991)—*Bluebook* format

Thompson v. Economy Super Marts, 221 Ill. App. 3d 263, 163 Ill. Dec. 731, 581 N.E.2d 885 (1991)—*ALWD* format

In a brief: Thompson v. Economy Super Marts, 581 N.E.2d 885 (Ill. App. Ct. 1991)—*Bluebook* and *ALWD* formats

Check the jurisdiction's citation rules and the firm's requirements when you use a state decision in a memorandum or a brief. See *Bluebook* **Table T.1** and *ALWD* Appendix 2. If you are citing a state case to a state court in which the case was decided, provide both the official citation, if one exists, and the regional citation, as the first example on page 541 shows, if court rules or the assigning partner requires it. Always list the official citation first. When you cite a state case in a memorandum addressed to a federal court or to a court of a state different from the state that decided the case, include only the regional citation as the second example on page 541 shows. If you are using only the regional citation, remember to place the abbreviation for the deciding court in parentheses. See *Bluebook* **Rule 10.4** and *ALWD* **Rule 12.6.** Additionally, follow the local court rules references in *Bluebook* blue pages BT2, *ALWD* Appendix 2, and *ALWD* **Rule 12.4**. However, if parallel citations are required, see *ALWD* **Rule 12.4** and *Bluebook* **Rule 10.3.1.**

Every state has its own rules regarding the reporter designated as "official" and whether the state has adopted public domain citations. Always check with the supervising attorney and the court rules. *Bluebook* **Table T.1** lists Web sites for each state, and ALWD Appendix 2 excerpts the local court citation rules. Some states, like Oklahoma, use the regional reporter as their official reporter. Increasingly, states have adopted public domain citations as their official cites that should be cited in accordance with *Bluebook* **Rule 10.3.3** and *ALWD* **Rule 12.16** (also called neutral citations). These cites are designed to allow readers to find the case in a computerized system that does not rely on commercial publishers. Cites to commercial reporters such as West's may be used to augment public domain citations.

The public domain format is as follows: case name, followed by the year of the decision, the deciding court, and the sequential number of the decision. In some jurisdictions, the sequential number of the decision is the docket number. To cite to a specific portion of the decision, you may add a reference to the paragraph.

Public domain citation: State v. Kienast, 1996 S.D. 111 ¶ 2—*Bluebook* and *ALWD* formats

Use neutral, or public domain, citations when local court rules permit according to *ALWD* **Rule 12.16.**

▼ How Do You Cite Decisions Found in the *Federal Reporter* or the *Federal Supplement?*

Bluebook Rules **10.1-10.6** and **Table T.1** and *ALWD Citation Manual* **Rule 12.6** and Appendices 1 and 4 provide detailed coverage of the citation format for cases from the *Federal Reporter* and the *Federal Supplement*. The case name is placed first and underlined. Next, place the volume number. The reporter abbreviation is next. For the *Federal Reporter,* the abbreviation is "F." The number of the series, second or third, should be placed next to the "F." For the Federal Supplement, the reporter is abbreviated "F. Supp." The page number follows the abbreviation for the reporter. Next, place an abbreviation denoting the appropriate court and the date of the decision. Be certain to include a geographic designation for the district courts.

Federal Reporter case: Zimmerman v. North Am. Signal Co., 704 F.2d 347 (7th Cir. 1983)—*Bluebook* and *ALWD* formats
Federal Supplement case: Musser v. Mountain View Broad., 578 F. Supp. 229 (E.D. Tenn. 1984)—*Bluebook* and *ALWD* formats

▼ How Do You Cite a Decision Contained in the *Federal Rules Decisions* Reporter?

The abbreviation for the *Federal Rules Decisions* is F.R.D. A case would be cited according to *Bluebook* **Table T.1** and *ALWD* Appendix 1, as follows:

Barrett Indus. Trucks v. Old Republic Ins. Co., 129 F.R.D. 515 (N.D. Ill. 1989)

PRACTICE POINTER

When starting an in-house memo assignment, ask the attorney about his citation preferences and look at examples in the firm's memo and brief bank. Sometimes the attorney's preferences will differ from the local court rules.

▼ How Do You Cite a U.S. Supreme Court Case?

According to the *Bluebook,* once a U.S. Supreme Court case is published in an advance sheet of the *U.S. Reports,* the *U.S. Reports* citation, and only the *U.S. Reports* citation, is the proper citation, without any parallel citations. See **Rule 10, T1.1** and *ALWD* **Rule 12.4(c)** generally. The cite format is diagramed on page 87 of the *Bluebook.*

Erie R.R. v. Tompkins, 304 U.S. 64 (1938)—*Bluebook* and *ALWD* formats

Erie R.R. v. Tompkins, 304 U.S. 64, 58 S. Ct. 817, 82 L. Ed. 1188 (1938)— *ALWD* format permissible when an attorney requests it.—*ALWD* **Rule 12.4(c).**

However, if a Supreme Court opinion has been published in the *West Supreme Court Reporter* but not yet in the *U.S. Reports,* the *Supreme Court Reporter* citation should be used. See *Bluebook* **Table T1.1.**

If a Supreme Court opinion has not yet been published in *U.S. Reports, Supreme Court Reporter,* or *U.S. Reports, Lawyers' Edition,* then you should cite to *United States Law Week.* See *Bluebook* **Table T1.1.** The court designation, U.S., should be placed in parentheses with the full date. See *Bluebook* **Rule 10.4(a).** The citation would read as follows:

UAW v. Johnson Controls, 59 U.S.L.W. 4209 (U.S. Mar. 20, 1991)

The *ALWD Citation Manual* in **Rule 12.4(c)(2)** states to include only one source of U.S. Supreme Court opinions, in the illustrated order of preference. However, parallel citation of Supreme Court cases is permitted if attorneys request it.

▼ How Do You Use Short Citation Forms?

Short citation forms and subsequent cite formats are explained in *Bluebook* B4.2, and Rule 10.9. Also see *ALWD* **Rule 12.20**.

Full citation: Seymour v. Armstrong, 64 P. 612, 613 (Kan. 1901).

Subsequent citation when there is an intervening cite: *Seymour v. Armstrong*, 64 P. at 613. *Bluebook* Rule 10.9.

Seymour, 64 P. 613. *Bluebook* and *ALWD* Rule 12.20(b) if using only the first party will not cause confusion.

A subsequent citation without an intervening cite requires the use of *Id.*: *Id.* at 613. *Bluebook* page 14 and *ALWD* Rule 11.3.

Use of *Id.* with parallel citations (note: follow local court rules to determine requirements for parallel citation):

Full cite *Thompson v. Economy Super Marts*, 221 Ill. App. 3d 263, 581 N.E.2d 885, 163 Ill. Dec. 731 (App. Ct. 1991).

Short cite without intervening citations *Id.* at 263, 581 N.E.2d at 887, 163 Ill. Dec. at 733—*ALWD* Rule 12.20(f) and *Bluebook* B4.

▼ How Do You Cite a Decision Reported on Westlaw?

Bluebook **Rule 18.3.1** and *ALWD* **Rule 12.12** explain how an unpublished decision found only on either Westlaw or LEXIS should be cited. For Westlaw, first provide the name of the case and underline it. The next part of the citation is the docket number. In the example that follows, that number is No. 82-C4585. The next part of the citation is the year that the decision was issued. Next, indicate "WL" for Westlaw and finally the Westlaw number assigned to the case. Place the date in the parentheses.

WESTLAW example: Clark Equip. Co. v. Lift Parts Mfg. Co., No. 82-C4585, 1985 WL 2917, (N.D. Ill. Oct. 1, 1985)—*Bluebook* format

Clark Equip. Co. v. Lift Parts Mfg. Co., 1985 WL 2917 (N.D. Ill. Oct. 1, 1985)—*ALWD* format, Rule 12.12(a)

▼ How Do You Cite a Decision Reported on LEXIS?

For LEXIS citations, first state the name of the case, the docket number, the year of the decision, the name of the LEXIS file that contains the case, and the name LEXIS to indicate that the case is found on LEXIS. Next place the date in parentheses.

LEXIS example: Barrett Indus. Trucks v. Old Republic Ins. Co., No. 87-C9429, 1990 U.S. Dist. LEXIS 142 (N.D. Ill. Jan. 9, 1990)—*Bluebook* format

Barrett Indus. Trucks v. Old Republic Ins. Co., 1990 U.S. Dist. LEXIS 142 (N.D. Ill. Jan. 9, 1990)—*ALWD* format

If a decision is published in a hard-copy reporter, you should not use the Westlaw or LEXIS citation. This is stipulated in *Bluebook* **Rule 18.1** and *ALWD* **Rule 12.12(a).**

▼ How Do You Indicate a Page or Screen Number for the Case?

An asterisk should precede any screen or page numbers. See *Bluebook* **Rule 18.3.1** and *ALWD* **12.12(b).**

WESTLAW screen no.:   Clark Equip. Co. v. Lift Parts Mfg. Co., No. 82-C4585, 1985 WL 2917, at *1 (N.D. Ill. Oct. 1, 1985)—*Bluebook* format

LEXIS screen no.:   Barrett Indus. Trucks v. Old Republic Ins. Co., 1990 U.S. Dist. LEXIS 142, at *1 (N.D. Ill. Jan. 9, 1990)—*ALWD* format

▼ How Do You Cite Internet Resources?

Bluebook **Rule 18** covers Internet materials. *ALWD* **Rule 23.1(i)** covers electronic journals. *ALWD* rules 38 and 40 cover electronic citation formats and Internet sites. Only rely on Internet resources if there is no other way to obtain the material, because the Internet format is transient in nature. However, if you can obtain the resource in a PDF file, then it is a reliable version. *Bluebook* Rule 18.2.1 states that you can use sources on the Internet in lieu of the hard-copy source when the online format is the official resource for the publication or the document. This is occurring more frequently with federal, state, and municipal resources. You can use Internet sites as an additional cite when the identical information can be obtained in hard copy as well as on the Internet but the Internet resource is more accessible.

Karin Mitra, *Information v. Commercialization: The Internet and Unsolicited Electronic Mail,* 4 Rich. J.L. & Tech. 6 (Spring 1998), *available at* http://www.richmond.edu/jolt/v4i3/mitra.html—*Bluebook* Rule **18.2.2**

Karin Mitra, *Information v. Commercialization: The Internet and Unsolicited Electronic Mail,* 4 Rich. J.L. & Tech. 6 (Spring 1998) (http://www.richmond.edu/jolt/v4i3/mitra.html)—*ALWD* format

▼ How Do You Cite Documents Retrieved in PDF Files?

Documents are widely available for retrieval in Portable Document Format, "PDF." LEXIS and Westlaw now permit most resources to be saved and printed in PDF. Documents in PDF maintain the pagination from the hard-copy source and do not permit end-user manipulation.

    Bluebook Rules 18.1 and 18.2 and *ALWD* Rule 40.1(C)(3) address citing to PDF documents.

PRACTICE POINTER

It is both cost- and time-efficient to attach PDF versions of cases and statutes to e-mailed memos rather than printing or photocopying the resources.

▼ How Do You Cite Federal Statutes?

Always cite to the official statutory compilation. The first entry in the citation is the title number, then the abbreviation for the statutory compilation, and then the section or paragraph number. *Bluebook* **Rule 12** and *ALWD* **Rule 14** detail all the various rules pertaining to citing statutes and codes, state or federal. Always cite to the year of the code's compilation, not the year that the particular statute section was enacted. For example:

    12 U.S.C. §211 (2006)—*Bluebook* and *ALWD* formats

If a code section is well known by a popular name, then include the name in the citation. For example:

    Strikebreaker Act, 18 U.S.C. §1231 (2006)—*Bluebook* and *ALWD* formats

You may rely on an unofficial version for updating purposes. All the following are citations to the identical statute.

    26 U.S.C. §61 (2006)—*Bluebook* and *ALWD* formats
    26 U.S.C.A. §61 (West 2011 & Supp. 2012)—*Bluebook* and *ALWD* formats
    26 U.S.C.S. §61 (LexisNexis 2010)—*Bluebook* format
    26 U.S.C.S. §61 (Lexis 2010)—*ALWD* format

As with the U.S.C., the year included in the citation is the year that the code volume was published, not the year that the statute was enacted. In the U.S.C.A. example above, the first year mentioned, 2011, is the year that the particular volume of the code was published; the second date, 2012, is the year of the pocket part supplement that updates the code volume. For the unofficial codes, the publication date is printed either on the title page of the bound volume or on the back of the title page.

▼ How Do You Cite a Section of a Constitution, Federal or State?

Bluebook **Rule 11** and *ALWD* **Rule 13** outline the citation format. The United States Constitution citation refers to the particular article, section, and clause being used. For example:

U.S. Const. art II, §2, cl. 1—*Bluebook* and *ALWD* formats

This cite is used when you are referring to the body of the Constitution. A special citation format is required when you are referring to an amendment currently in force. For example:

U.S. Const. amend. II

State constitutions are indicated by the name of the state in the *Bluebook* abbreviated format. *Bluebook* **Table T.1** and *ALWD* **Appendix 1** indicate the accepted state name abbreviation; this is not necessarily the postal abbreviation. For example, the state of Washington's postal abbreviation is WA, but the *Bluebook* abbreviation is Wash. A section of the Washington state constitution would be cited as follows:

Wash. Const. art I, §2—*Bluebook* and *ALWD* formats

Years or dates are not included in citations to constitutions, state or federal, that are current. Parenthetical notations after the citation indicate the year a constitutional provision was repealed or amended. An example is the Eighteenth Amendment to the U.S. Constitution prohibiting the sale of liquor. The Twenty-First Amendment later repealed this. *Bluebook* **Rule 11** and *ALWD* **Rule 13.3** cover this:

U.S. Const. amend. XVIII (repealed 1933)—*Bluebook* format
U.S. Const. amend. XVIII (repealed 1933 by U.S. Const. amend XXI)—*ALWD* format

▼ How Do You Cite to a Legislative History of a Statute?

Bluebook **Rule 13** and *ALWD* **Rule 15** detail the citation format for all the components of the legislative process: the bill, the committee report, the debates, and transcripts of the hearings.

▼ How Are the *Code of Federal Regulations* and the *Federal Register* Cited?

Rule 14 of the *Bluebook* and *ALWD* **Rule 19** provide the citation format for administrative and executive materials, which include the *Code of Federal Regulations* and the *Federal Register*. See also *Bluebook* **T.1** for each jurisdiction's administrative material. Title 21 of the C.F.R.§101.62 from 2011 is cited as:

21 C.F.R. §101.62 (2011)—*Bluebook* and *ALWD* formats

A *Federal Register* entry from volume 73 beginning on page 26200, from May 8, 2008, would be cited as:

> 73 Fed. Reg. 26200 (May 8, 2008)—*Bluebook* and *ALWD* formats

▼ How Do You Cite to a Legal Dictionary?

The information for the correct citation format for dictionaries is found in **Rule 15.8** of the *Bluebook* and **Rule 25.1** of *ALWD*.

> Black's Law Dictionary 712 (9th ed. 2009)—*Bluebook* format
> *Black's Law Dictionary* 712 (9th ed., West 2009)—*ALWD* format

▼ How Are Legal Encyclopedias Cited?

ALWD **Rule 26** and *Bluebook* **Rule 15.8** discuss legal encyclopedias. A citation to the discussion of easements would be as follows:

> 25 Am. Jr. 2d *Easements and Licenses* §90 (2004 and Supp. 2011)—*Bluebook* and *ALWD* formats
> 28A C.J.S. *Easements* §18 (2008 & Supp. 2011)—*Bluebook* and *ALWD* formats

▼ How Do You Cite to *American Law Reports?*

This is found in **Rule 16.7.6** of the *Bluebook* and **Rule 24** of *ALWD*.

> William B. Johnson, Annotation, *Locating Easement of Way Created by Necessity,* 36 A.L.R.4th 769 (1985)—*ALWD* and *Bluebook* formats

▼ How Do You Cite to a Law Review or Law Journal?

Bluebook **Rule 16** and *ALWD* **Rule 23** indicate the citation form for a law review article, as follows:

> Mitchell N. Berman, *Justification and Excuse, Law and Morality,* 53 Duke L.J. 1 (2003)—*Bluebook* and *ALWD* formats

Abbreviations for the journal names are found in **Table 13** of the *Bluebook* and *ALWD* Appendix 5. A legal newspaper is cited according to *Bluebook* **Rules 16.5** and **16.6**:

> Wayne Smith, <u>Remote Access: Striking a Balance</u>, Law Tech. News, Jan. 2005, at 11—*Bluebook* and *ALWD* formats

ALWD **23.1(d)(3)** states if place of publication can't be discerned from title, include it in parentheses.

▼ How Do You Cite the Restatements?

Bluebook **Rule 12.9.5** and *ALWD* **Rule 27.1** indicate that the Restatements are cited as follows:

> Restatement (Second) of Contracts §235 (1979)—*Bluebook* and *ALWD* formats

Note that for *Bluebook* format the year is the year that the Restatement section was adopted. This information is given on the title page of every volume of the Restatements. When you are citing to a comment that follows the Restatement section, **Rule 3.4** of the *Bluebook* applies. For example:

> Restatement (Second) of Contracts §235 cmt. a (1979)—*Bluebook* format (date adopted)
>
> *Restatement (Second) of Contracts* §235 (1981)—*ALWD* format
>
> *Restatement (Second) of Contracts* §235 cmt. a (1981)—*ALWD* format

Note that *ALWD* format for the *Restatements* requires that the year is the date of volume publication—*ALWD* format, **Rule 27.1.**

▼ How Do You Cite an Ethics Rule Found in the *ABA Model Code of Professional Responsibility?*

The rules for citation of ethics codes are found in *Bluebook* **Rule 12.9.6** and *ALWD* **Rule 17.** Rule 1.10 of the *ABA Model Code* would be cited as follows:

> Model Code of Professional Responsibility Rule 1.10 (1992)

▼ How Do You Cite an ABA Ethics Opinion?

The rules for citation of ethics opinions are contained in *Bluebook* **Rule 12.9.5** and **12.9.6** and *ALWD* **Rule 17.4.** For example:

> ABA Comm. on Professional Ethics and Grievances, Informal Op. 88-1526 (1988)—*Bluebook* format
> Model Code of Professional Responsibility Rule 1.10 (ABA 1992)—*ALWD* format

▼ How Do You Cite the Various Federal Rules?

Cite the federal rules in accordance with *Bluebook* **Rule 12.9.3** and *ALWD* **Rule 17** as follows:

> Fed. R. Civ. P. 56
>
> Fed. R. Crim. P. 1
>
> Fed. R. App. P. 26
>
> Fed. R. Evid. 803

Only include the year when the rule is no longer in force by providing the most recent year that it appeared and the year repealed. For example:

Fed. R. Civ. P. 9 (2006) (repealed 2008)—*Bluebook* 12.9.3

Fed. R. Civ. P. 9 (repealed 2008)—*ALWD* 17.2

NET NOTE

Go to www.law.cornell.edu/citation for "An Introduction to Basic Legal Citation" by Peter Martin. Click on the relevant topic in the sidebar.

CITATION EXERCISES

For the following citations, assume that these cases are being used in a brief for the U.S. District Court for the Northern District of Ohio. Correct the citation, if possible. If not, specify what is wrong. If an item is missing, note it and tell where it belongs.

1. How would you cite the following slip opinion?

Michele Greear, et. al., plaintiffs, vs. C.E. Electronics, Inc., et. al., defendants, decided in the United States District Court for the Northern District of Ohio Western Division, docket number C 87-7749, decided by Judge Richard B. McQuade, Jr. on September 12, 1989.

2. When responding to a motion for summary judgment, the plaintiff must submit proof of each and every element of his claims so that a reasonable jury would find in his favor.

Anderson v. Liberty Lobby, Inc., 477 U.S. 242, 105 S.Ct. 989, 10 L.Ed. 2d 1111 (1986).

3. When the relationship of the parties is so clear as to be undisputed, it can be decided as a matter of law that no apparent or actual relationship existed.

Mateyka v. Schroeder, 504 N.E.2d 1289 (1987).

4. In a diversity action, a court must apply the conflict of law principles of the forum state. Dr. Franklin Perkins School v. Freeman, 741 F.2d 1503, 1515, n.19 (1984); Pittway Corp. v. Lockheed Aircraft Corp., 641 F.2d 524, 526 (7th Cir.); Klaxon Co. v. Stentor Electric Mfg. Co., 313 US 487, 496 (1941).

5. Gizzi v. Texaco, 437 F.2d 308 (3rd).

6. Zimmerman v. North American, 704 F.2d 347 (1983).

7. E.E.O.C. v. Dowd, 736 F.2d 1177.

8. Musser v. Mountain View Broadcasting, 578 F. Supp. 229 (1984).

9. United States v. Upjohn, 449 U.S. 383.
10. Indicate what, if anything, is missing from this citation: Consolidation Coal Co. v. Buryus-Erie Co., 89 Ill. App. 2d 103 (1982).

CITATION PRACTICE

Provide the correct citation form for the following; use case name abbreviations found in either the *Bluebook* or the *ALWD Citation Manual.*

1. Trzcinski v. American Casualty Company
   901 Federal Reporter Second Series 1429
   Seventh Circuit Court of Appeals
   1990
2. Wade v. Singer Company
   130 Federal Rules Decisions 89
   Northern District Court of Illinois 1990
3. Pryor v. Cajda
   662 Federal Supplement 1114
   Northern District Court of Illinois 1987
4. Longman v. Jasiek
   91 Illinois Appellate Court Reports Third Series 83
   46 Illinois Decisions 636
   414 North Eastern Second Series 520
   Third District Court of Appeals 1986
5. Gulf Oil Corporation v. Gilbert
   91 Lawyers Edition 1055
   330 United States Reports 501
   67 Supreme Court Reporter 839
   1947
6. Wyness v. Armstrong World Industries Incorporated
   131 Illinois Reports Second Series 403
   546 North Eastern Reporter Second Series 568
   Supreme Court of Illinois 1989
7. Title 28 of the United States Code, section 1404(a) from the year 2006.
8. Title 42 of the Code of Federal Regulations, part 400.200 from the year 2011.

SHORT CITATION

Write the following information in short citation format.

1. Smith v. Jones, 96 N.E.2d 17 (Ill. App. Ct. 1965).
   You are using text from p.18 of the N.E.2d.
   How would you cite this the first time?
   How would you short cite it to page 18 if it is cited in full in the immediately preceding citation?
2. Cranshaw v. Marge, 321 F.2d 97 (5th Cir. 1935).
   You need to short cite this case to reflect attributing authority to page 99 of the decision.

CITATION FOR RESOURCES OTHER THAN CASES

1. How would you cite to a federal statute that appeared in the 2012 pocket part of Title 42 of the United States Code Annotated at section 1201 that was in a volume published in 2004?
2. How would you cite a law review article that appeared in volume 78 of the Columbia University Law Review in 1985? The article is entitled Tax Aspects of Marital Dissolution, and begins on page 1587. The author is John Reese.
3. How would you cite Megan's Law found in Title 42 of the United States Code at section 14071(e) in the 2006 Code?
4. How would you cite volume 63 of the Federal Register at page 59,231 from October 1, 1991?
5. How would you cite the Procter & Gamble 2003 annual report accessed on June 5, 2004, at pg.com/investors? Choose the "Financial Results and Events" tab, and then click the "Annual Reports" link. Click "2003 Annual Report."

CITATIONS FOR ONLINE RESOURCES

1. How would you cite an unreported opinion available on LEXIS where you are relying on a statement from page 3 of that opinion? The opinion is from 2005 and was found in the US Dist Ct file. The LEXIS case number is 15976. The date of the decision is April 13, 2005. The case name is *Panera Bread Store v. Baguette Company.* The docket number is No. 05-1721.
2. You have found a new C.F.R. provision on Westlaw and you know it was printed in hard copy in the 2011 C.F.R. The provision is in Title 5 at section 12.
3. You retrieved a recent final regulation in the *Federal Register,* volume 76 at page 9080. It will be codified in the C.F.R. at 27 C.F.R. part 1. The material was accessed at www.gpoaccess.gov/fr. Please provide the citation according to the *Bluebook* or the *ALWD.*
4. You have found an article in the Yale Law Journal. You know that the journal is available in hard copy at the law school library across town and the identical article is available in full text on the Web. You want to cite to both sources to improve access. What rule do you follow in the *Bluebook?*

    The article is from volume 114, number 7, May 2005. The article is titled: "The Sarbanes-Oxley Act and the Making of Quack Corporate Governance" by Roberta Romana. The article begins on page 1521. The Yale Law Journal Internet site is www.yale.edu/yalelj.

B

WRITING STRATEGIES

Strategies for Tackling A Writing Assignment

1. When you receive the assignment
    A. Clarify the Purpose of the assignment
        i. To Inform and evaluate—Objective—Memo and possibly Letter/email
        ii. To Persuade—Persuasive—Brief
        iii. To Summarize—Factual—Chronological account—Interview summary
    B. Determine Audience—Reader Expectation
    Generally, write succinctly, precisely and directly. Assume that the reader is very busy yet unfamiliar with the facts and the authorities.
        i. Attorney
        ii. Judge
        iii. Attorney and/or client
    C. Clarify the issue and the assignment task—what are you writing about?
        i. Refine the precise question or questions you are to examine
2. Create an outline
    A. List the points you are to address or the parts of the issue you are to examine
    B. Perform research
    C. Summarize research under each relevant point

        i. Make sure that your citations are completely accurate so that the reader can find the information in the source.

       ii. Write the information, derived from the source, in your own voice.

     iii. Summarize the authority accurately.

     iv. Reserve quoted language for emphasis or for when the source states the point in a manner that is unique.

3. Write a rough draft.
4. Print out the draft in hard copy.
5. After the fact Outline
   A. Examine each paragraph.
      i. Note the point of each paragraph in left margin.
      ii. Note how each paragraph advances the analysis, if applicable, in the right margin.
   B. Is the authority accurately summarized and cited?
   C. Does the authority clearly support each point?
   D. Is the connection between the authority and point supported clearly for the unfamiliar reader? Context for analysis?
   E. Do you provide adequate factual/legal context for the discussion?
   F. Is the factual basis for the discussion apparent?
   G. Do you support the analysis with the relevant facts from the instant case and draw parallel facts from the cited cases?
6. Revising
   A. Examine the after the fact outline—Write the point of each paragraph in order and insert how each paragraph advances the analysis.
      i. Do the points of each paragraph present a logically ordered discussion?
      ii. Does each paragraph advance the analysis and draw the reader to the next point?
      iii. Use this information to draft clear thesis statements.
      iv. If it is a persuasive document, do you reach a clear landing on each element?
   B. Check the authority used.
   C. Are the rules and the facts from the cases clear for the unfamiliar reader?
   D. Writing Mechanics
      i. Sentence Fragments
      ii. Modifiers—do modifiers appropriately modify the subject of the sentence? Is this clear?
      iii. Clauses—main clauses and subordinate clauses
      iv. Diction—word choice

SAMPLE MEMORANDA

ILLUSTRATION C-1.   Sample Memorandum

MEMORANDUM

To: Benjamin Joyce
From: William Randall
Date: January 28, 2012
Re: *Harris v. Sack and Shop*

QUESTION PRESENTED

Is Sack and Shop, a grocery store, liable for injuries sustained by Harris, a store patron who slipped on a banana peel that had been left on the grocery store floor for two days?

BRIEF ANSWER

Probably yes. Sack and Shop, a grocery store, probably will be liable based on negligence for injuries sustained by Harris, a store patron who slipped on a banana peel that had been on the grocery store floor for two days.

FACTS

Our client, Sack and Shop Grocery Store, is being sued for negligence by Rebecca Harris.

Harris went to the store to purchase groceries on July 8, 2011. While she was in the produce section, she slipped on a banana peel that a grocery store employee left on the floor. The employee had dropped it

ILLUSTRATION C-1. Continued

on the floor two days earlier and had failed to clean it up after a patron asked him to do so.

Harris sustained a broken arm and head injuries as a result of the slip and fall.

DISCUSSION

The issue presented in this case is whether Sack and Shop Grocery Store was negligent when Rebecca Harris slipped in the store's produce section. A grocer will be found negligent if a store employee breached the store's duty of reasonable care to its patrons and, as a result of that breach, the patron was injured. *Ward v. K Mart Corp.*, 554 N.E.2d. 223 (Ill. 1990). In *Ward*, the grocery store employee failed to clean up a banana peel for two days and that peel caused a patron to be injured. Similarly in our case Sack and Shop failed to remove the banana peel for two days. Therefore, Sack and Shop is likely to be found liable for the injuries Harris sustained.

The first element to consider is whether Sack and Shop owed a duty of reasonable care to Harris. A grocery store owes a duty of care to any patron. *Ward*, 554 N.E.2d at 226. Harris was a customer in the store. Therefore, Sack and Shop owed her a duty of care.

The next question to consider is whether Sack and Shop breached its duty of reasonable care to Harris. A store will be found to have breached its duty of reasonable care to a patron if a store employee fails to properly and regularly clean the floor of the store. *Olinger v. Great Atl. & Pac. Tea Co.*, 173 N.E.2d 443 (Ill. 1961). In *Olinger*, the store was found liable because a store employee failed to clean the floor for one day and a patron slipped on a substance on the floor. 173 N.E.2d at 447. No one had told any store employee about the slippery substance. *Id.* at 447. Nonetheless, the Illinois Supreme Court found the store liable, saying that the store employees had sufficient time to notice the substance if they had used ordinary care. *Id.* In our case, Sack and Shop's employee had two days to clean the floor before Harris fell. In addition, a customer had placed the store employee on notice of the banana. Therefore, Sack and Shop breached its duty of care to Harris.

The plaintiff, however, still must establish proximate cause, that is, that the injury resulted as a natural consequence of Sack and Shop's breach of its duty. A store owner's failure to clear debris from a store floor, resulting in injury to a patron who slipped on the floor, was found to be the proximate cause of the patron's injuries. *Id.* at 449. In this case, Sack and Shop's failure to clean the peel from the floor was a breach of its duty of care to Harris. This breach resulted in injury to Harris. Sack and Shop's breach will be found to be the proximate cause of Harris's injuries.

ILLUSTRATION C-1.   Continued

The final element that must be established is that the plaintiff, Harris, suffered injuries. Harris sustained a broken arm and head injuries as a result of the slip and fall. Therefore, she will be able to show that she was injured.

CONCLUSION

Sack and Shop owed Harris a duty of reasonable care. The store is likely to be found to have breached that duty of reasonable care because an employee failed to remove a banana peel from the grocery store floor during the preceding two days. The injuries Harris sustained were directly caused by a slip on a banana peel. Therefore, Sack and Shop is likely to be found liable to Harris.

ILLUSTRATION C-2.   Sample Memorandum: McMillan Battery Action

MEMORANDUM

To: William Houck
From: Ivy Courier
Date: November 7, 2011
Re: McMillan Battery Action

QUESTION PRESENTED

Did an actionable battery occur when Mann intentionally struck McMillan with a bucket, without McMillan's consent, causing McMillan to suffer physical and monetary injuries?

CONCLUSION

Mann's intentional striking of McMillan with a bucket and sand was an actionable battery.

FACTS

Our client, Mary McMillan, a 36-year-old bank teller, wants to bring an action for battery against Carol Mann, a 36-year-old mother, who threw a metal bucket filled with sand at McMillan at a local park. While McMillan sat on a park bench, she teased Mann's seven-year-old son. Mann did not like this teasing and threw a bucket filled with sand at McMillan. Sand landed in McMillan's eyes while she was wearing soft contact lenses. As a result, McMillan's contacts had to be replaced. The bucket also cut McMillan's eye and cheek. She had stitches in both places. McMillan asked Mann to pay for her doctor bills and for the new contacts. Mann refused and added, "I'm not sorry. I meant to hurt you."

ILLUSTRATION C-2. Continued

DISCUSSION

The issue presented is whether Mann's intentional touching of McMillan with a bucket rather than her person is an actionable battery. A battery is the intentional touching of another without consent, which causes injury. *Anderson v. St. Francis-St. George Hosp., Inc.*, 77 Ohio St. 3d 82, 671 N.E.2d 225 (1996). A touching can occur when an object rather than an individual's body contacts the other party. *Leichtman v. WLW Jacoc Communications, Inc.*, 92 Ohio App. 3d 232, 634 N.E.2d 697 (1994); *Smith v. John Deere Co.*, 83 Ohio App. 3d 398, 614 N.E.2d 1148 (1993). In this case, Mann intentionally struck McMillan with a bucket without McMillan's consent and that touching resulted in injuries. Therefore, a battery occurred.

The threshold issue is whether a touching occurred when the bucket struck McMillan. A contact between a nonconsenting party and object rather than the actor's body can be a battery. *Leichtman v. WLW Jacoc Communications, Inc.*, 92 Ohio App. 3d 232, 634 N.E.2d 697 (1994); *Smith v. John Deere Co.*, 83 Ohio App. 3d at 398, 614 N.E.2d at 1148. In *Leichtman*, one person blew cigar smoke at another person, resulting in injuries. The court found that the cigar smoke was an extension of the person and that a contact between the smoke and the nonconsenting person met the requirement of a touching for civil battery. In this case, Mann threw the bucket at McMillan, and the bucket contacted her face. Following the reasoning in the *Leichtman* case, the bucket would be an extension of Mann's body, and the contact between McMillan and the bucket would be considered a touching under the theory of civil battery.

Next, the question to consider is whether under the statute Mann intended to touch McMillan when she struck her with the bucket. A person intends his or her conduct when he or she undertakes an action with a knowing mind. *Smith v. John Deere Co.*, 83 Ohio App. 3d 398, 614 N.E.2d 1148 (1993). In *Smith*, a police officer handcuffed the plaintiff. The court found that the officer must have intended his actions because you could not accidentally handcuff a person. *Smith*, 83 Ohio App. 3d at 399, 614 N.E.2d at 1149. In McMillan's case, Mann aimed the bucket at McMillan, purposefully trying to strike her, Mann later told McMillan that she deliberately threw the bucket at her. McMillan probably will be able to establish that Mann had the statutory intent.

The next factor to consider is whether McMillan consented to the contact. If a person consents to the touching, a battery has not occurred. *Love v. Port Clinton*, 37 Ohio St. 3d 98, 524 N.E.2d 166 (1988). In our case, McMillan did not consent to Mann's throwing of the bucket at her face. Therefore, McMillan did not consent to any contact. Finally, the question is whether McMillan suffered physical injuries. A battery occurs only if a plaintiff sustains physical injuries as a result of the touching. *Anderson v. St. Francis-St. George Hosp., Inc.*, 77 Ohio St. 3d 82, 671 N.E.2d 225 (1996). McMillan sustained cuts on her face and the sand flying out of the bucket into her eyes. McMillan will be able to show that she sustained physical injuries as a result of the contact with the bucket.

ILLUSTRATION C-3.   Multi-Issue Memorandum: McMillan Battery Action

MEMORANDUM

To: William Mark
From: Ivy Courier
Date: November 7, 2011
Re: McMillan Battery Action

QUESTIONS PRESENTED

1. Did a battery occur when Carol Mann intentionally struck McMillan with a bucket, without Mary McMillan's consent, causing McMillan to suffer physical and monetary injuries?

2. Does eight-year-old Rachel McMillan have a valid claim for intentional infliction of emotional distress against Carol Mann after the child saw Mann throw a rusty metal bucket of sand at her mother's face and head, causing physical injuries to the elder McMillan and resulting in the child suffering from anxiety, headaches, and vomiting?

3. Was Camp Cougar vicariously liable for the intentional torts of Mann, a volunteer whom camp officials asked to supervise children in the sandbox?

CONCLUSIONS

1. When Mann intentionally struck McMillan on the head and in the face with a rusty, metal bucket and sand without McMillan's consent and McMillan was injured, a battery occurred.

2. Eight-year-old Rachel McMillan has a claim for intentional infliction of emotional distress against Carol Mann because the child can show that she suffered emotional distress as a result of Mann's extreme and outrageous act of intentionally throwing a rusty, metal bucket at the child's mother, causing the older McMillan to suffer physical injuries and the child to suffer from anxiety and post-traumatic stress syndrome—mental anguish no child should be expected to endure.

3. Camp Cougar will not be found vicariously liable for an intentional act of its agent, Mann, because it did not benefit from that act nor did the camp control Mann's actions.

FACTS

Our client, Mary McMillan, a 36-year-old bank teller, seeks to bring an action for battery against Carol Mann, a 36-year-old mother, who threw a rusty, metal bucket filled with sand at her at a local camp. She also wants to bring an action against Camp Cougar for vicarious liability for the intentional torts of camp volunteer Carol Mann. Camp Cougar enlisted Carol Mann, a camper's parent, to act as volunteer supervisor of the sandbox during Parent Visitor day at Camp Cougar. Camp Cougar officials told Mann to ensure that no one was injured while playing in the sandbox. Mann had handled this responsibility during Parent Visitor day in the past. Mary McMillan came to see her eight-year-old

ILLUSTRATION C-3.   Continued

daughter, Rachel, during Camp Cougar Parent Visitor day. While McMillan sat on a camp bench, she teased Mann's seven-year-old son. Mann did not like this teasing and threw a rusty, metal bucket filled with sand at McMillan's head and face. Sand landed in McMillan's eyes while she was wearing soft contact lenses. As a result, McMillan's contacts had to be replaced. The bucket also cut McMillan's head, eye and cheek. She lost a lot of blood from her head, requiring a transfusion of one pint of blood. She had stitches on her eye lid and cheek. After the bucket struck McMillan, Mann told McMillan in front of three witnesses, "I'm not sorry. I meant to hurt you."

Immediately after Rachel McMillan saw her mother bleeding, she began to cry and vomit. She told the camp counselors that her head hurt and she would not go with the camp director to the hospital. She said she was afraid the director would throw a bucket of sand at her if she didn't like what she said. The child missed the remainder of camp because she suffered from daily headaches and vomiting and she was afraid of the adults at the camp. A child psychologist examined the child and said she was suffering headaches, vomiting, and anxiety as a result of seeing a bucket thrown by an adult at her mother. He said she was experiencing post-traumatic stress syndrome.

DISCUSSION

This memo first will address whether Carol Mann can be held liable for battery when she intentionally struck McMillan with a rusty, metal bucket, without McMillan's consent, causing McMillan to suffer physical and monetary injuries. Next, the discussion will consider whether eight-year-old Rachel McMillan has a claim for intentional infliction of emotional distress against Mann after the child saw Mann throw a rusty, metal bucket of sand at her mother's head and face, resulting in injury to her mother and causing the young girl to suffer from anxiety, headaches, and vomiting. Finally, the memo will explore whether McMillan can establish that Camp Cougar was vicariously liable for the intentional actions of one of its volunteers, Carol Mann, that resulted in injury to McMillan.

1. Was Mann's Intentional Touching of Mcmillan With A Bucket Battery?

The issue presented is whether Mann's intentional touching of McMillan with a bucket rather than her person is a battery. A battery is the intentional touching of another without consent, which causes injury. *Anderson v. St. Francis-St. George Hosp., Inc.*, 77 Ohio St. 3d 82, 671 N.E.2d 225 (1996). A touching can occur when an object rather than an individual's body contacts another person. *Leichtman v. WLW Jacoc Communications, Inc.*, 92 Ohio App. 3d 232, 634 N.E.2d 697 (1994); *Smith v. John Deere Co.*, 83 Ohio App. 3d 398, 614 N.E.2d 1148 (1993). A person

ILLUSTRATION C-3.   Continued

intends his or her conduct when he or she undertakes an action with a knowing mind. If a person consents to the touching, a battery has not occurred. *Love v. Port Clinton,* 37 Ohio St. 3d 98, 524 N.E.2d 166 (1988). A battery occurs only if a plaintiff sustains physical injuries as a result of the touching. *Anderson v. St. Francis-St. George Hosp., Inc.,* 77 Ohio St. 3d 82, 671 N.E.2d 225 (1996). In this case, Mann intentionally struck McMillan with a bucket without McMillan's consent and that touching resulted in injuries. Therefore, a battery occurred.

The threshold issue is whether an intentional touching occurred when a bucket Mann threw struck McMillan. A touching can occur when an object rather than an individual's body contacts another person. *Leichtman v. WLW Jacoc Communications, Inc.,* 92 Ohio App. 3d 232, 634 N.E.2d 697 (1994); *Smith v. John Deere Co.,* 83 Ohio App. 3d at 398, 614 N.E.2d at 1148. In *Leichtman,* one person blew cigar smoke at another person, resulting in injuries. The court found that the cigar smoke was an extension of the person and that a contact between the smoke and the nonconsenting person met the requirement of a touching for civil battery. In this case, Mann threw the bucket at McMillan, and the bucket contacted her face and head. Following the reasoning in the *Leichtman* case, the bucket would be an extension of Mann's body, and the contact between McMillan and the bucket would be considered a touching under the theory of civil battery.

Next, the question to consider is whether under the statute Mann intended to touch McMillan when she struck her with the bucket. A person intends his or her conduct when he or she undertakes an action with a knowing mind. *Smith v. John Deere Co.,* 83 Ohio App. 3d 398, 614 N.E.2d 1148 (1993). In *Smith,* a police officer handcuffed the plaintiff. The court found that the officer must have intended his actions because you could not accidentally handcuff a person. *Smith,* 83 Ohio App. 3d at 399, 614 N.E.2d at 1149. In McMillan's case, Mann aimed the bucket at McMillan, purposefully trying to strike her, Mann later told McMillan that she deliberately threw the bucket at her. McMillan probably will be able to establish that Mann had the statutory intent.

The next factor to consider is whether McMillan consented to the contact. If a person consents to the touching, a battery has not occurred. *Love v. Port Clinton,* 37 Ohio St. 3d 98, 524 N.E.2d 166 (1988). In our case, McMillan did not consent to Mann's throwing of the bucket at her face. Therefore, McMillan did not consent to any contact. Finally, the question is whether McMillan suffered physical injuries. A battery occurs only if a plaintiff sustains physical injuries as a result of the touching. *Anderson v. St. Francis-St. George Hosp., Inc.,* 77 Ohio St. 3d 82, 671 N.E.2d 225 (1996). McMillan sustained cuts on her face and the sand flying out of the bucket into her eyes. McMillan will be able to show that she sustained physical injuries as a result of the contact with the bucket.

ILLUSTRATION C-3. Continued

2. Is Mann Liable For Intentional Infliction of Emotional Distress?

The next issue to consider is whether eight-year-old Rachel McMillan has a claim for intentional infliction of emotional distress against Carol Mann. To successfully prove intentional infliction of emotional distress, McMillan must show that Mann intentionally committed an extreme and outrageous that caused emotional distress that no reasonable person could be expected to endure. *Yeager v. Local Union 20*, 6 Ohio St.3d 369, 453 N.E.2d 666 (1983). *Pyle v. Pyle*, 11 Ohio App.3d 31, 34, 463 N.E.2d 98, 101 (1983). In the case, *Rachel McMillan*, a child, saw Mann, an adult, throw the rusty, metal bucket filled with sand at her mother's head and face, causing her mother to bleed. Seeing this act caused the child to suffer from anxiety, headaches, and vomiting daily. Several witnesses can testify that Mann said that she intended to harm McMillan. A child should not be expected to endure the pain of seeing her mother injured. Therefore, Rachel McMillan has a claim for intentional emotional distress.

The threshold issue is whether Mann's act of throwing a rusty, metal bucket at the head and face of another adult in front of children was an extreme and outrageous act. An act is extreme and outrageous if it goes "beyond all possible bounds of decency," *Yeager*, 6 Ohio. St. 3d at 375, 453 N.E.2d at 672, and is regarded as "atrocious, and utterly intolerable in a civilized community." *Id.* In this case, Mann, an adult who was asked to supervise the sandbox and ensure the safety of others, threw a rusty, metal bucket filled with sand at another adult in front of young children, including her child and Rachel McMillan. The bucket struck the older McMillan causing her to bleed. That act went beyond all possible bounds of decency and was atrocious and utterly intolerable in a civilized community. This is especially true since Mann was charged with ensuring the safety of people in the sand box area. Therefore, Mann's act would be found to be an extreme and outrageous act.

Next, the young McMillan must show that the act was done with intent. A person intends his or her conduct when he or she undertakes an action with a knowing mind. *Smith v. John Deere Co.*, 83 Ohio App. 3d 398, 614 N.E.2d 1148 (1993). If an actor knew or should have known that his or her actions would cause serious emotional distress, intent is established. *Phung v. Waste Mgt., Inc.*, 71 Ohio St. 3d 408, 410, 644 N.E.2d 286, 288 (1994). In this case, Mann not only knew or should have known that that throwing a rusty, metal bucket filled with sand at the head and face of another adult in front of the other adult's child resulting in the adult bleeding would cause an eight-year-old child to suffer serious emotional distress. For those reasons, the young McMillan should be able to show intent.

The third element McMillan must establish is that the extreme and outrageous act was the proximate cause of her emotional and physical

ILLUSTRATION C-3. Continued

distress. Proximate cause exists when an act precedes and produces an injury that is likely to have occurred as a result of the act or which might have been anticipated. *Jeffers v. Olexo*, 43 Ohio St. 3d 140, 143, 539 N.E.2d 614, 617 (1989). In this case, the young McMillan can show that a child likely would experience emotional distress when she saw her mother injured and bleeding. Therefore, the child will be able to establish that the extreme and outrageous act was the proximate cause of her emotional distress.

Finally, the child must show that she suffered from serious emotional distress. To establish serious emotional distress, the mental anguish she suffered must be serious and of a nature that "no reasonable man could be expected to endure it." *Id.* Serious emotional distress goes "beyond trifling mental disturbance, mere upset or hurt feelings" and "may be found where a reasonable person, normally constituted, would be unable to cope adequately with the mental distress engendered by the circumstances of the case." *Paugh v. Hanks*, 6 Ohio St. 3d 72, 78, 451 N.E.2d 759, 765 (1983). It is not necessary to prove any physical harm. *Pyle v. Pyle*, 11 Ohio App.3d 31, 34, 463 N.E.2d 98, 101 (1983). Various neurosis, psychosis and phobias are examples of serious emotional distress. *Paugh v. Hanks*, 6 Ohio St. 3d 72, 78, 451 N.E.2d 759, 765 (1983). In this case, a psychologist examined the child and found that she suffered from post-traumatic stress syndrome and as well as physical symptoms such as headaches and vomiting after she saw an adult throw a bucket at her mother. Post-traumatic stress and anxiety coupled with these physical manifestations should be sufficient for young McMillan to establish serious emotion distress that is beyond mere upset or hurt feelings and that a reasonable person would be unable to cope.

3. Was Camp Cougar Vicariously Liable For Mann'S Intentional Torts?

The final claim to consider is whether Camp Cougar will be vicariously liable to both McMillans for Mann's intentional torts. An entity can be held vicariously liable for the actions of its agent. *Byrd v. Faber*, 57 Ohio St. 3d 56, 58-59, 565 N.E2d 584-586 (1991). A principal-agent relationship is established when one party exercises control over the actions of another and those actions are done for the benefit of the party exercising control. See Hanson v. Kynast, 24 Ohio St.3d 171, 173, 494 N.E.2d 1091 (1986). However, a master only can be vicariously liable for its agent's intentional tort if the entity controlled the agent's conduct and the agent's acts benefited the entity. *Id.* In this case, Camp Cougar directed Mann to supervise a camp activity. Therefore, Mann may be found to be Camp Cougar's agent. However, Mann's actions did not benefit the camp nor did the camp exercise control over her actions. In fact, these actions may have harmed the camp. Therefore, it is unlikely that Camp Cougar would be found liable for Mann's torts.

ILLUSTRATION C-3.   Continued

The threshold issue is whether Mann is Camp Cougar's agent. A principal-agent relationship is established when one party exercises control over the actions of another and those actions are for the benefit of the party exercising control. See *Hanson v. Kynast*, 24 Ohio St. 3d 171, 173, 494 N.E.2d 1091 (1986). In this case, Camp Cougar directed Mann to act as the sandbox supervisor and specifically directed her to keep people safe. Therefore, Mann is likely to be found to be an agent of Camp Cougar.

The next issue to consider is whether a master can be vicariously liable for its agent's intentional torts. A master can be vicariously liable for its agent's intentional tort only if the master controlled the agent's conduct and the agent's acts benefited the master. See *Hanson v. Kynast*, 24 Ohio St. 3d 171, 173, 494 N.E.2d 1091 (1986). The camp did not direct Mann to injure McMillan, nor did the camp benefit from Mann's actions. Therefore, Camp Cougar would not be vicariously liable for Mann's act of throwing the bucket of sand at McMillan or causing young McMillan's serious emotional distress because it did not control Mann's actions nor did the camp benefit from Mann's actions.

INDEX